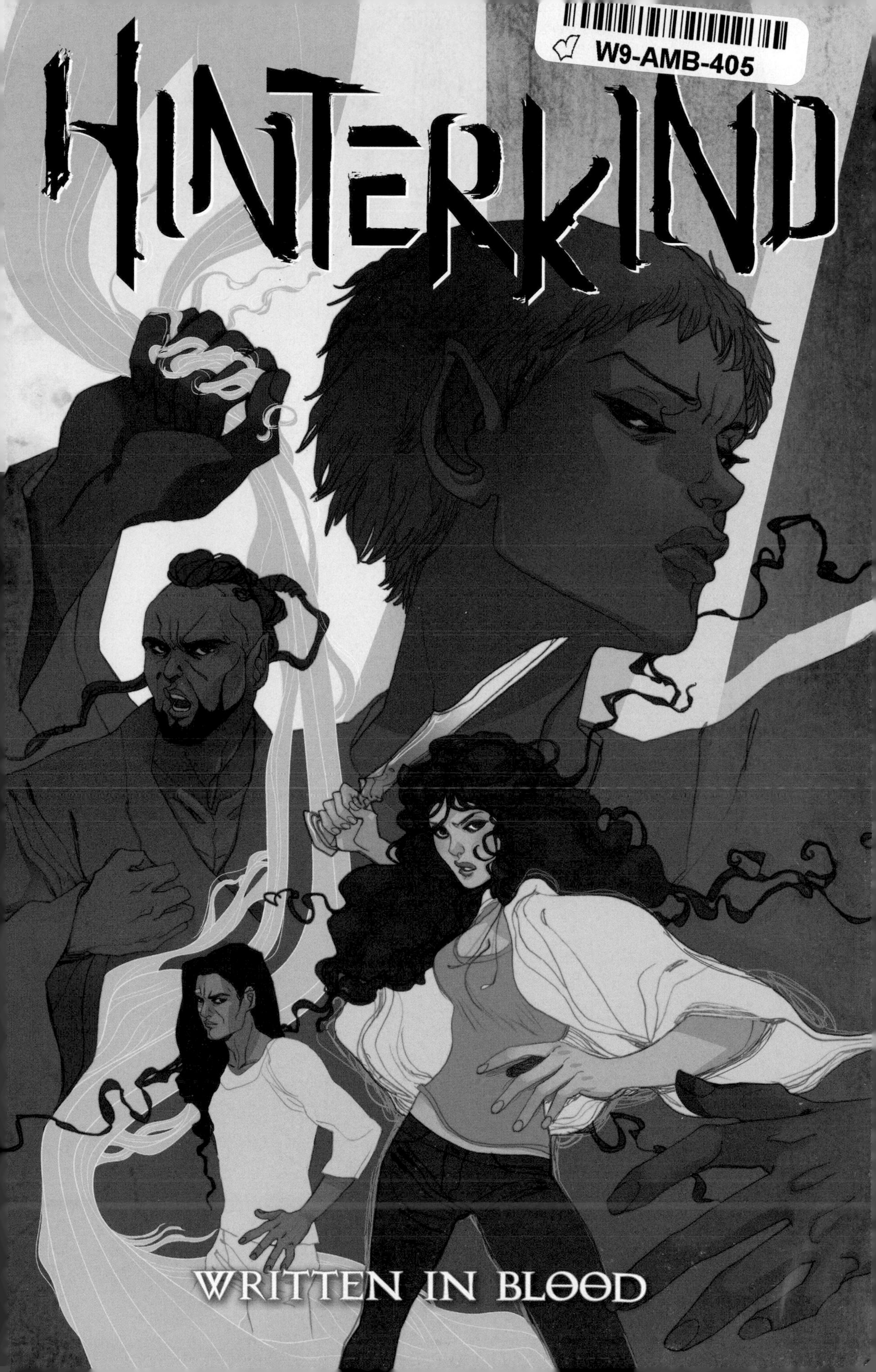
HINTERKIND
WRITTEN IN BLOOD

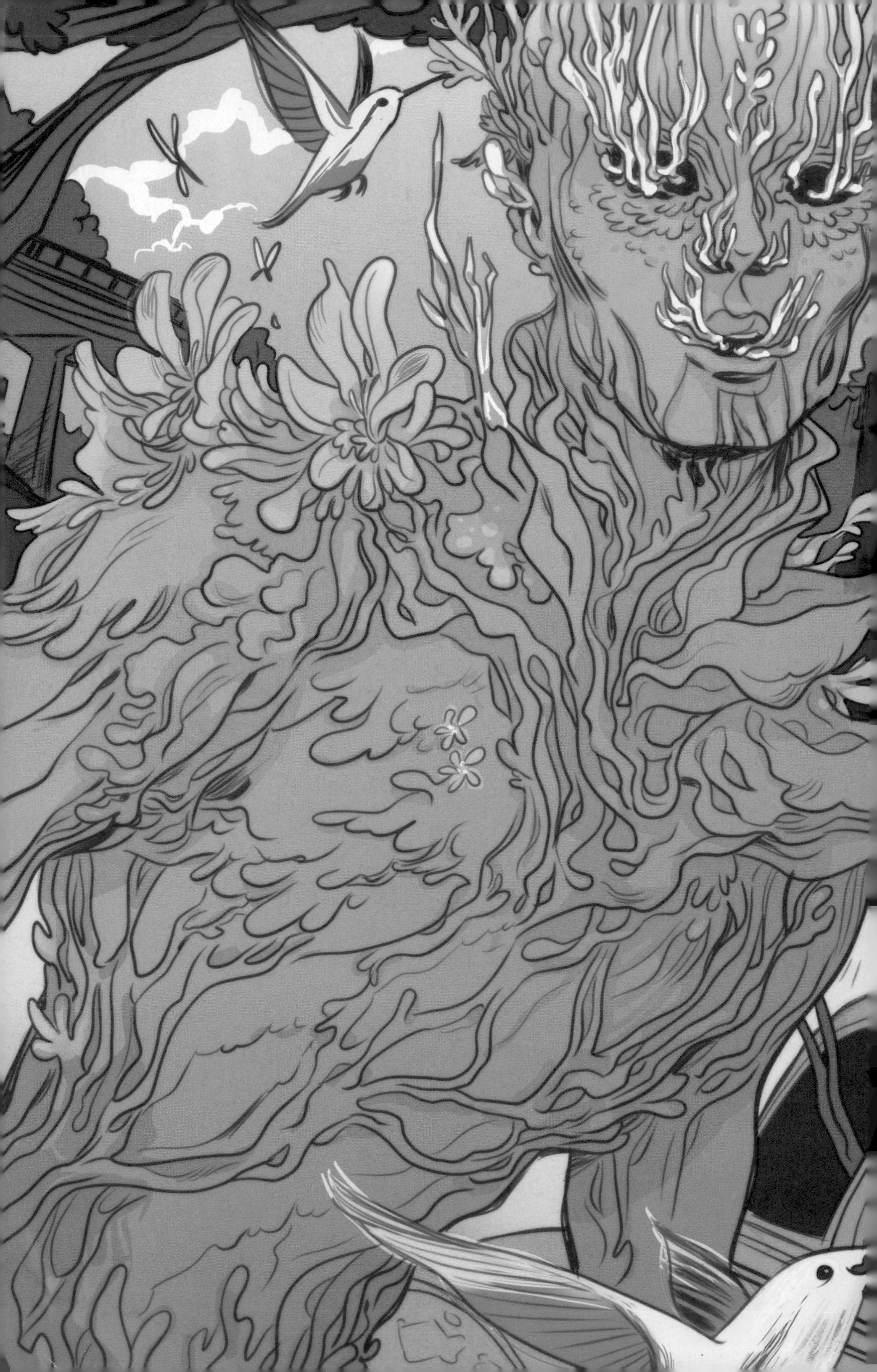

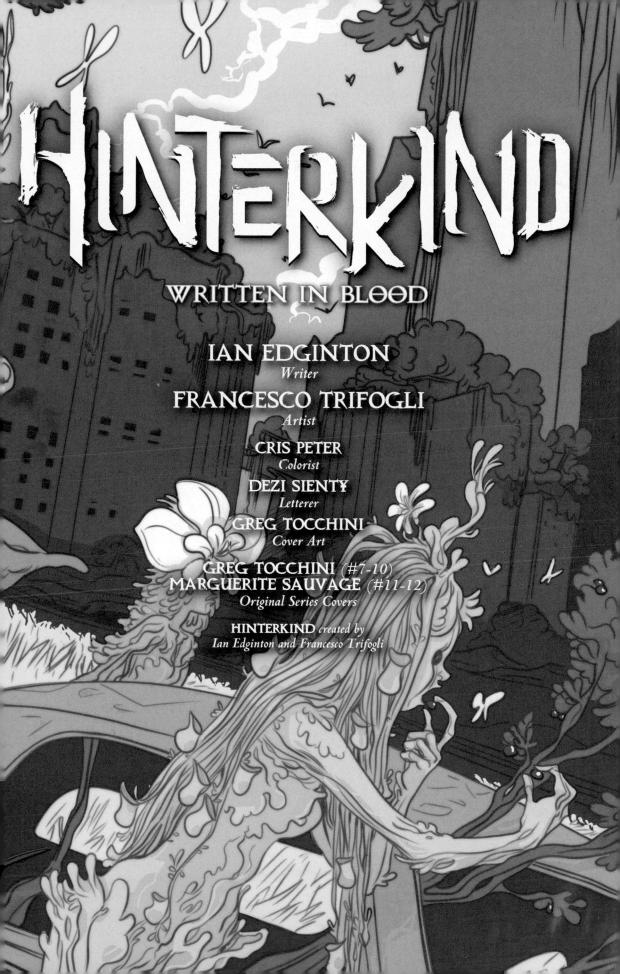

HINTERKIND

WRITTEN IN BLOOD

IAN EDGINTON
Writer

FRANCESCO TRIFOGLI
Artist

CRIS PETER
Colorist

DEZI SIENTY
Letterer

GREG TOCCHINI
Cover Art

GREG TOCCHINI *(#7-10)*
MARGUERITE SAUVAGE *(#11-12)*
Original Series Covers

HINTERKIND *created by*
Ian Edginton and Francesco Trifogli

WILL DENNIS Editor – Original Series
GREGORY LOCKARD Associate Editor – Original Series
SCOTT NYBAKKEN Editor
ROBBIN BROSTERMAN Design Director – Books
CURTIS KING JR. Publication Design

SHELLY BOND Executive Editor – Vertigo
HANK KANALZ Senior VP – Vertigo and Integrated Publishing

DIANE NELSON President
DAN DIDIO AND JIM LEE Co-Publishers
GEOFF JOHNS Chief Creative Officer
AMIT DESAI Senior VP – Marketing and Franchise Management
AMY GENKINS Senior VP – Business and Legal Affairs
NAIRI GARDINER Senior VP – Finance
JEFF BOISON VP – Publishing Planning
MARK CHIARELLO VP – Art Direction and Design
JOHN CUNNINGHAM VP – Marketing
TERRI CUNNINGHAM VP – Editorial Administration
LARRY GANEM VP – Talent Relations and Services
ALISON GILL Senior VP – Manufacturing and Operations
JAY KOGAN VP – Business and Legal Affairs, Publishing
JACK MAHAN VP – Business Affairs, Talent
NICK NAPOLITANO VP – Manufacturing Administration
SUE POHJA VP – Book Sales
FRED RUIZ VP – Manufacturing Operations
COURTNEY SIMMONS Senior VP – Publicity
BOB WAYNE Senior VP – Sales

Library of Congress Cataloging-in-Publication Data

Edginton, Ian, author.
  Hinterkind. Written in blood / Ian Edginton, writer ; Francesco Trifogli, artist.
    pages cm
  ISBN 978-1-4012-5070-6 (paperback)
  1. Graphic novels. I. Trifogli, Francesco, illustrator. II. Title.

PN6737.E34H57 2014
741.5'942—dc23

2014027352

SUSTAINABLE
FORESTRY
INITIATIVE

Certified Chain of Custody
20% Certified Forest Content,
80% Certified Sourcing
www.sfiprogram.org
SFI-01042
APPLIES TO TEXT STOCK ONLY

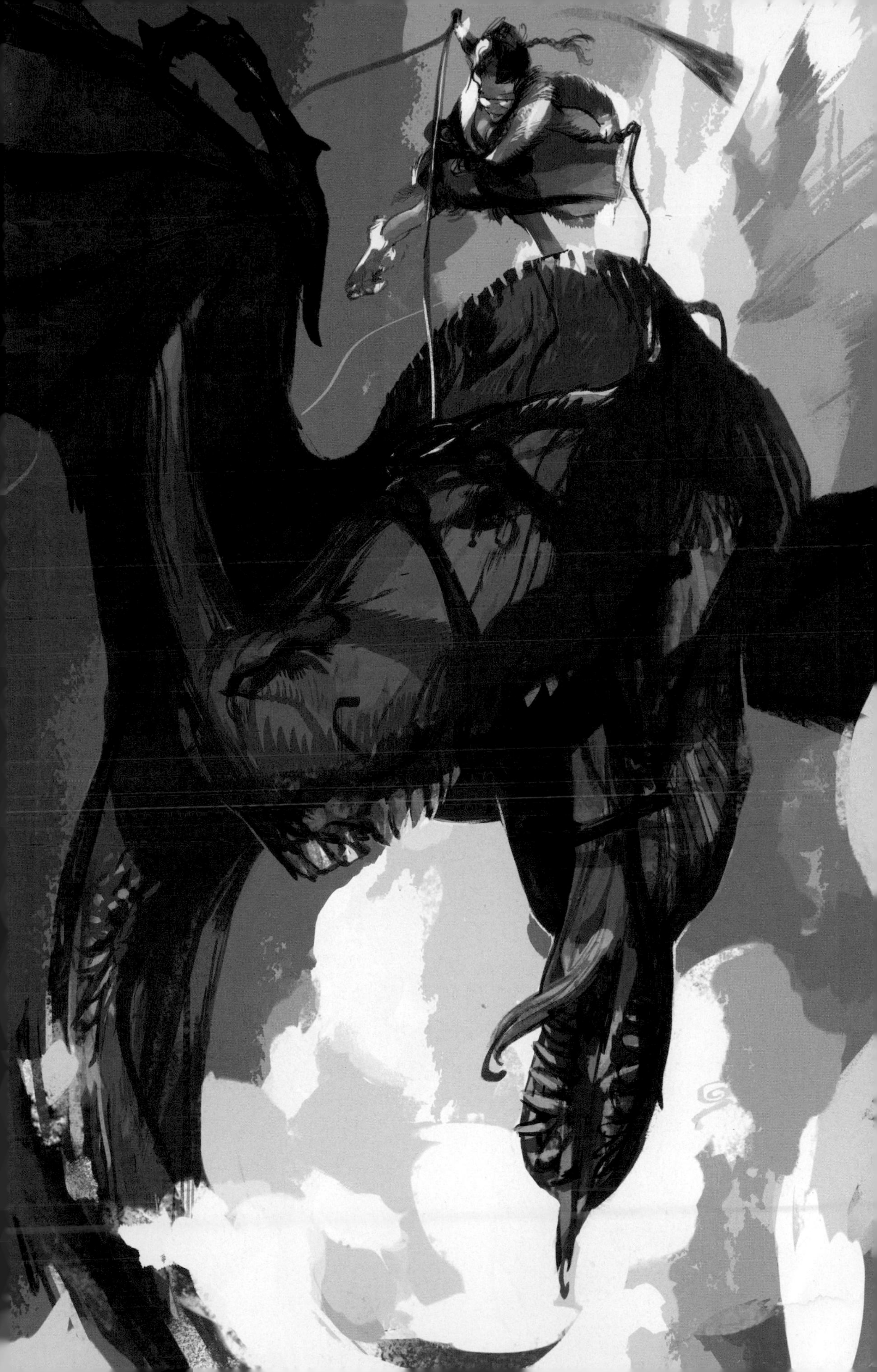

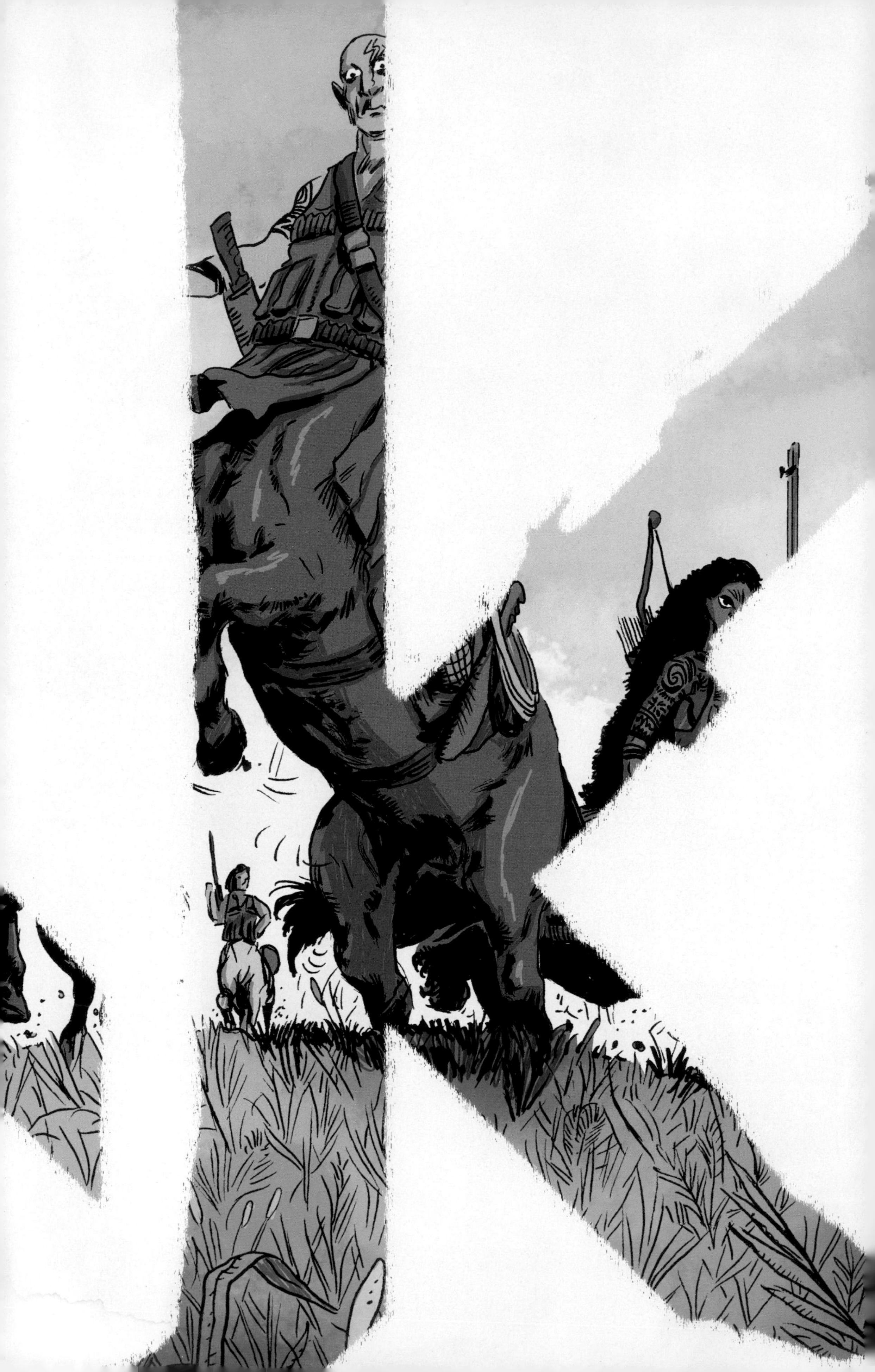

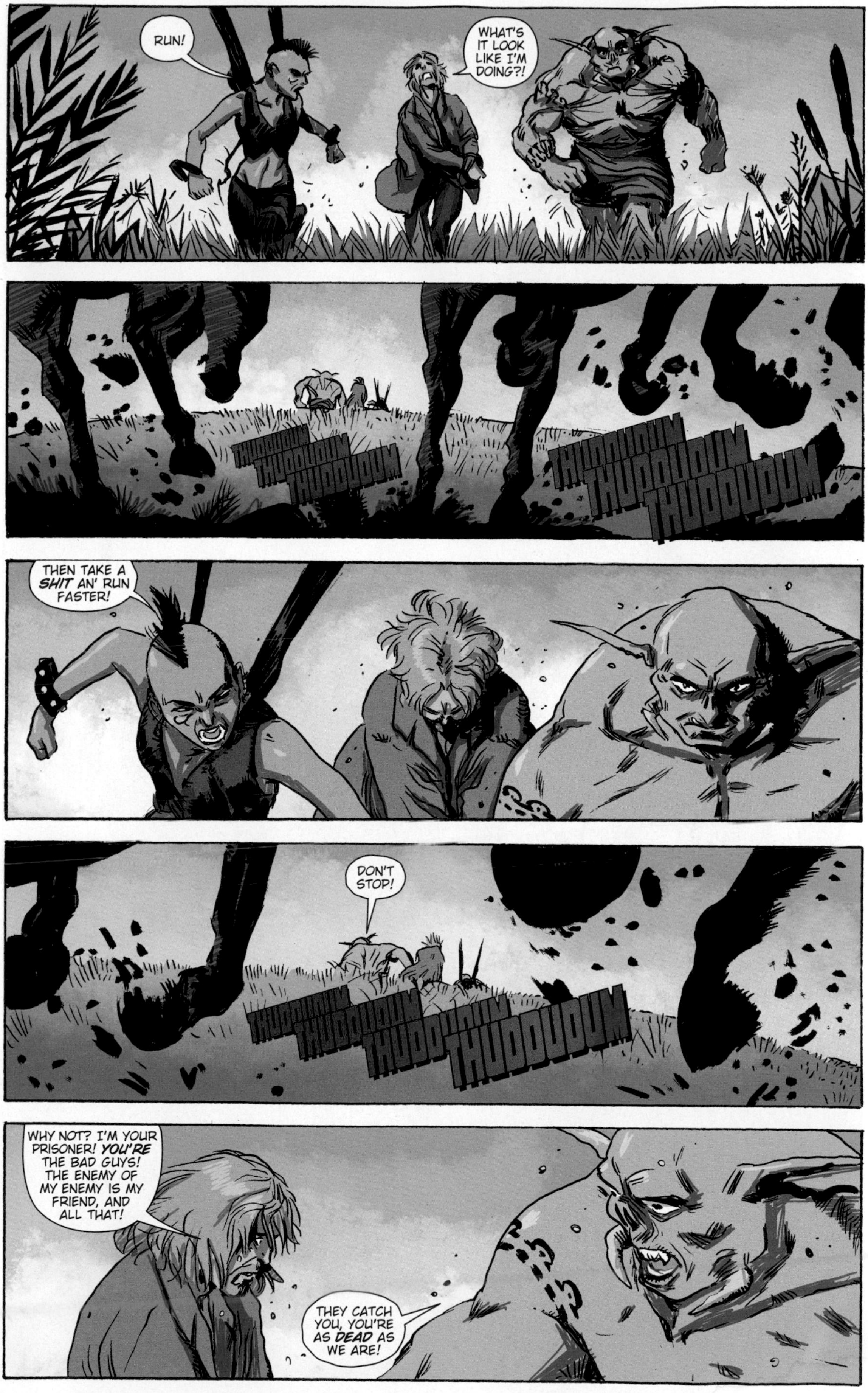
RUN!
WHAT'S IT LOOK LIKE I'M DOING?!
THUDDUDUM THUDDUDUM THUDDUDUM
THUDDUDUM THUDDUDUM THUDDUDUM
THEN TAKE A SHIT AN' RUN FASTER!
DON'T STOP!
THUDDUDUM THUDDUDUM THUDDUDUM THUDDUDUM
WHY NOT? I'M YOUR PRISONER! YOU'RE THE BAD GUYS! THE ENEMY OF MY ENEMY IS MY FRIEND, AND ALL THAT!
THEY CATCH YOU, YOU'RE AS DEAD AS WE ARE!

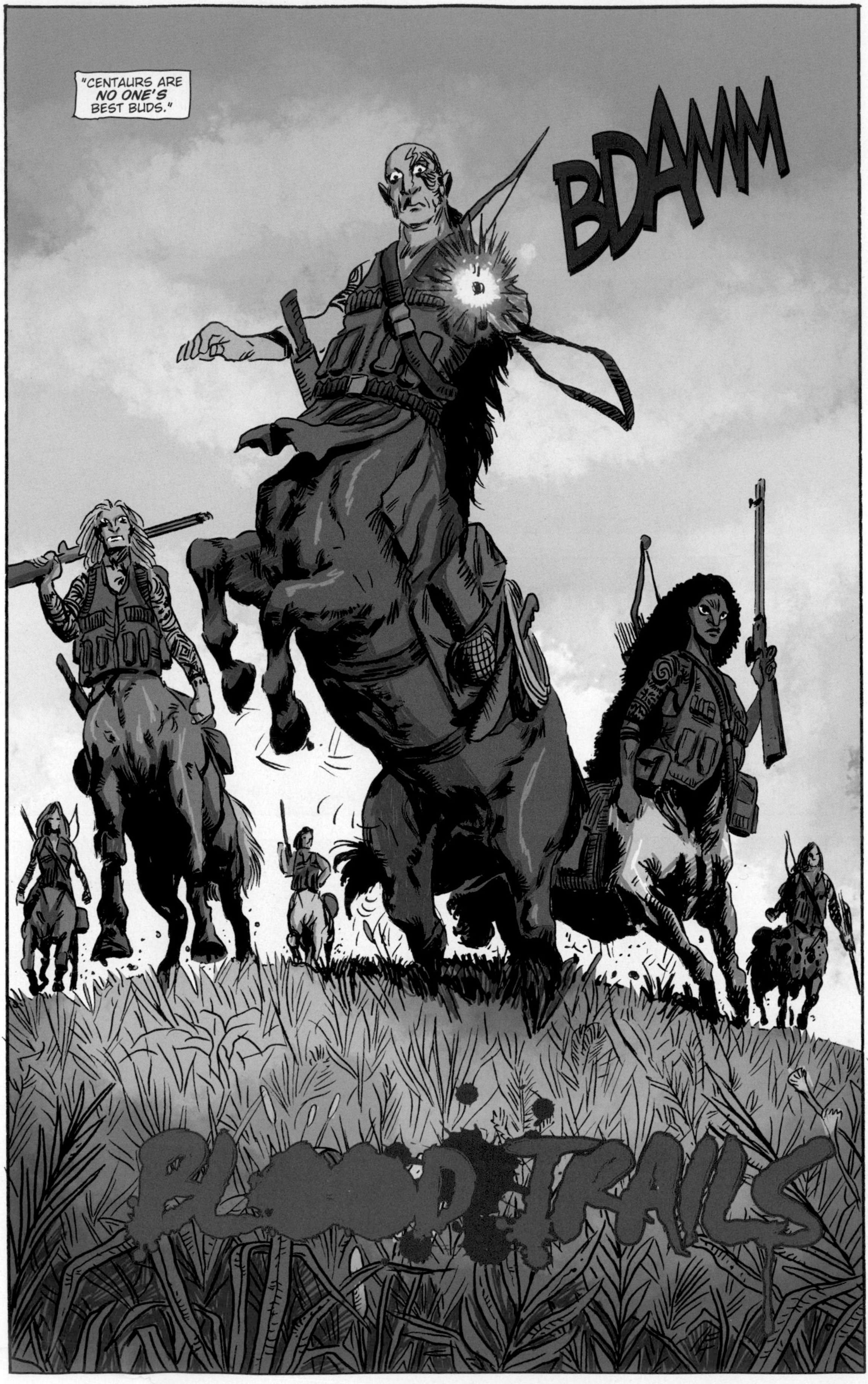
"CENTAURS ARE NO ONE'S BEST BUDS."
BDAMM
BLOOD TRAILS

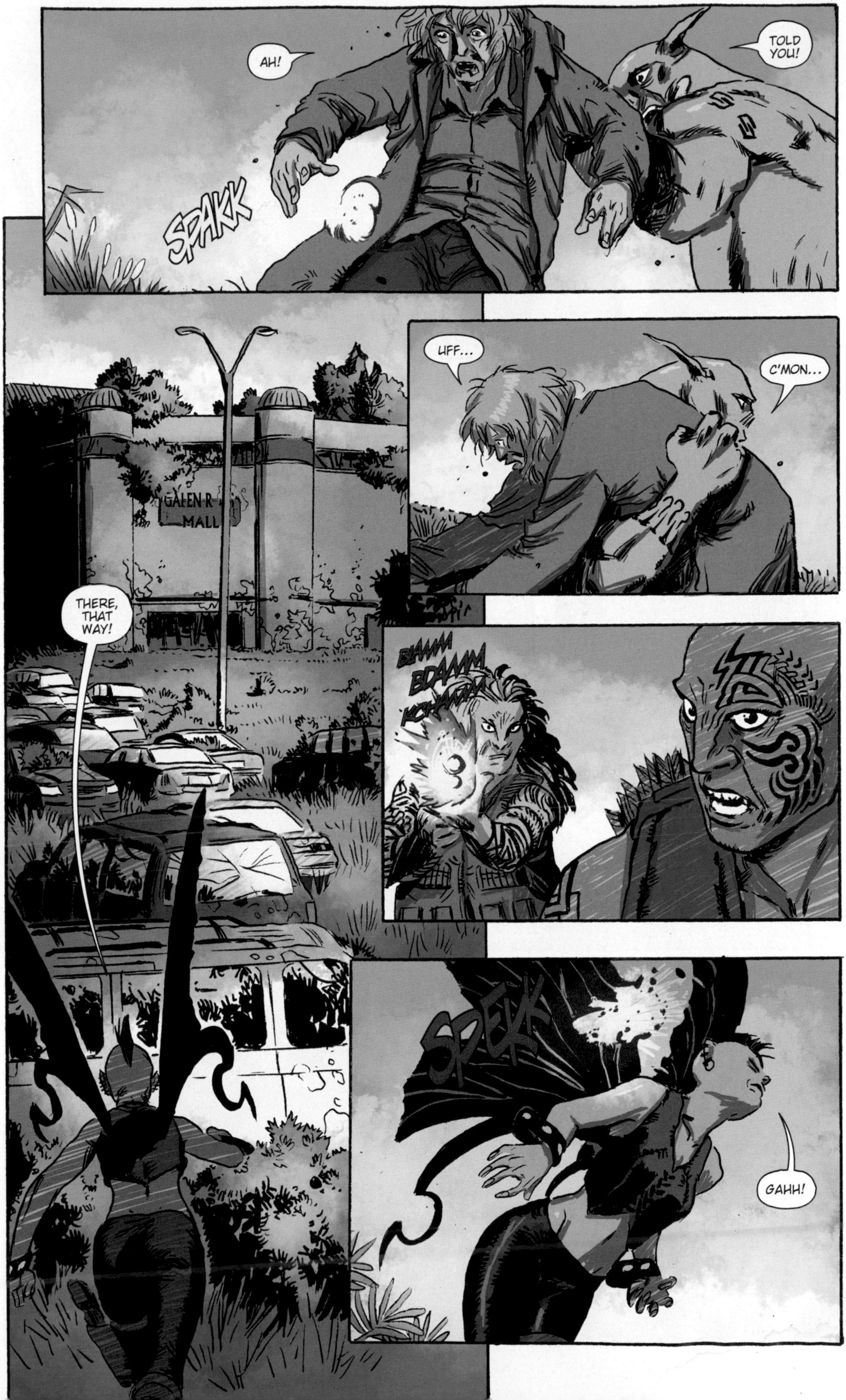
AH!
TOLD YOU!
SPAKK
UFF...
C'MON...
GALEN R MALL
THERE, THAT WAY!
BDAAAM
KCHAAAM
SPEKK
GAHH!

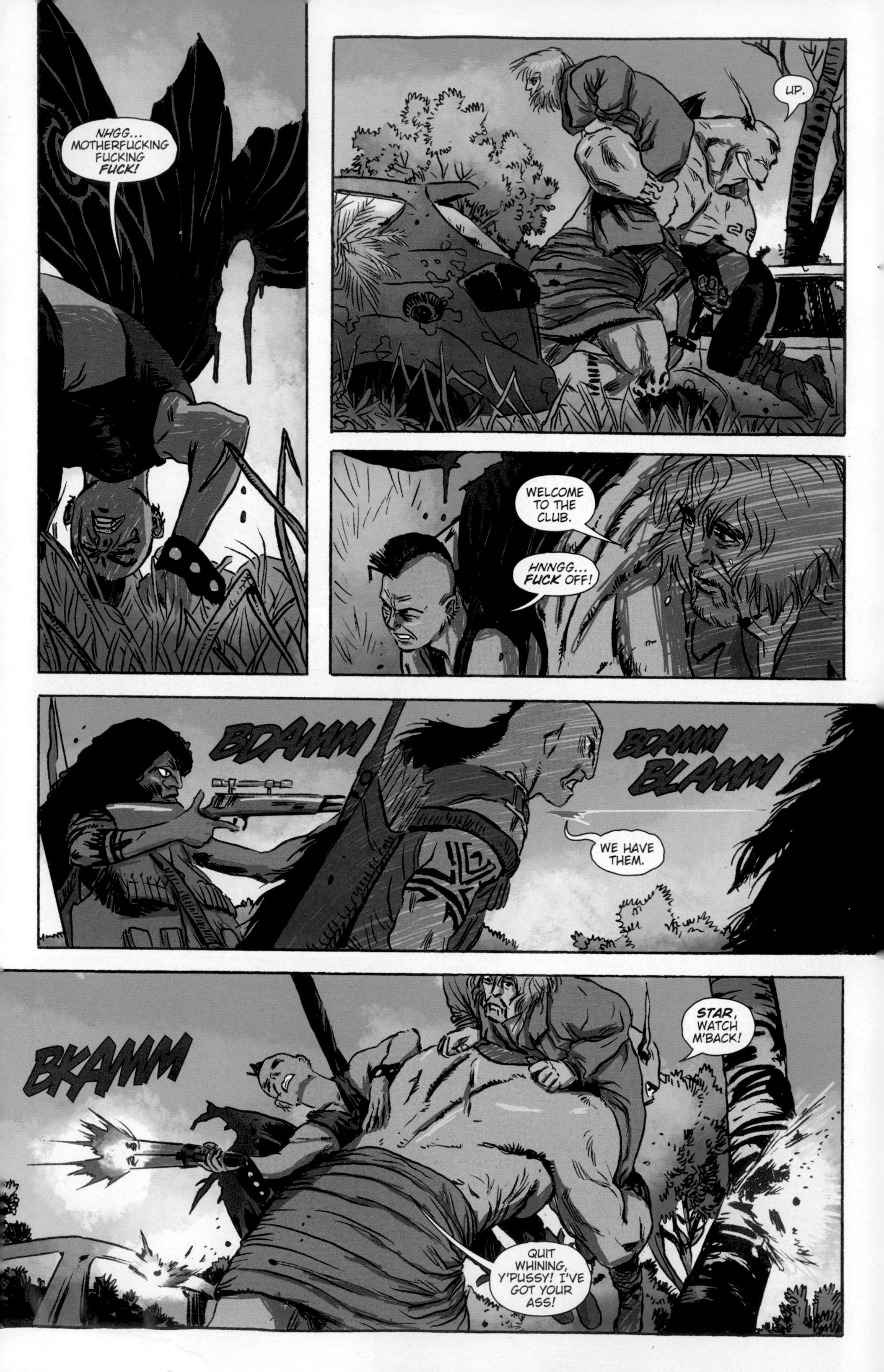
NHGG... MOTHERFUCKING FUCKING *FUCK!*
UP.
WELCOME TO THE CLUB.
HNNGG... *FUCK* OFF!
BDAMM
BDAMM
BLAMM
WE HAVE THEM.
BKAMM
STAR, WATCH M'BACK!
QUIT WHINING, Y'PUSSY! I'VE GOT YOUR ASS!

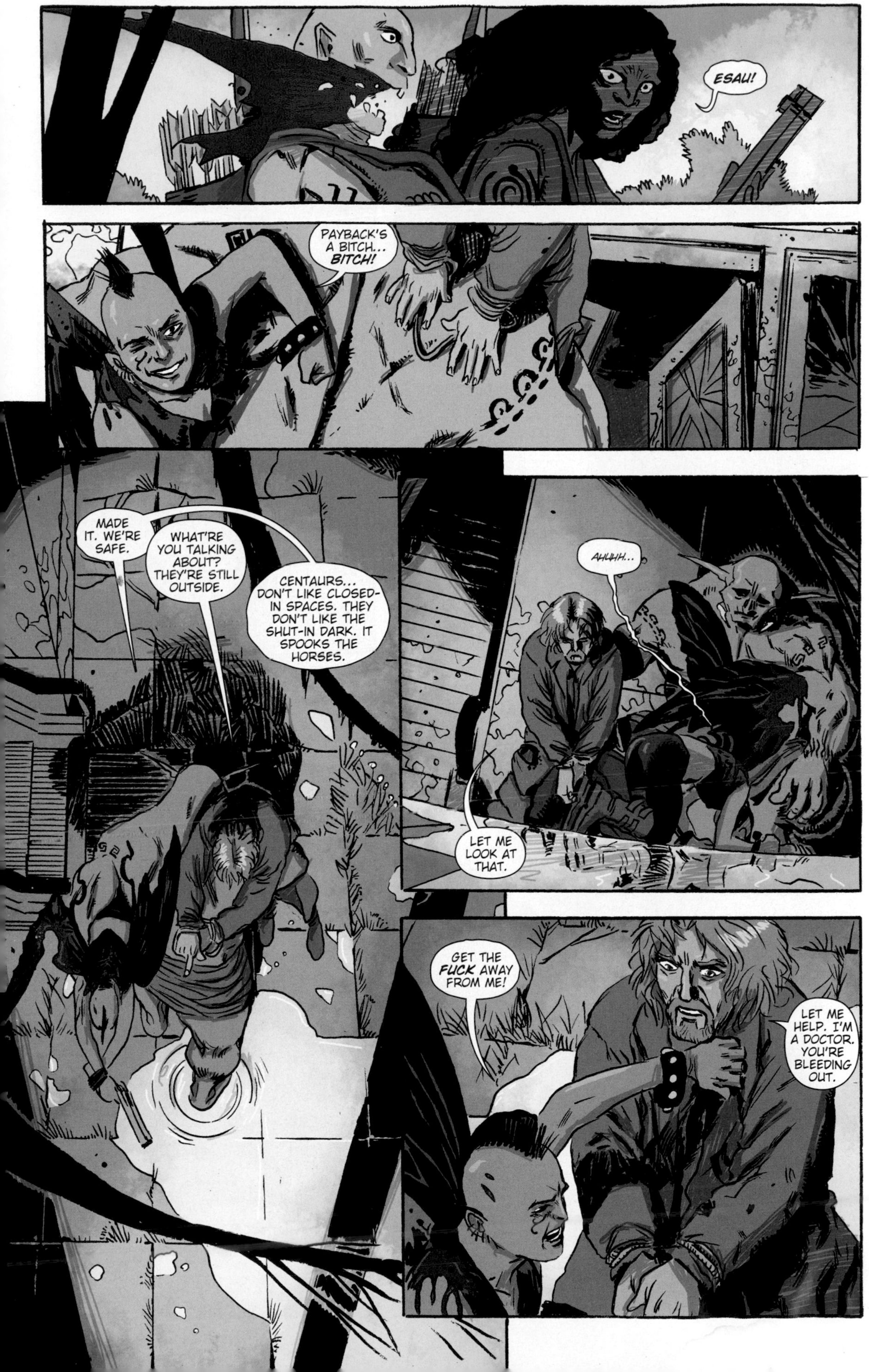
ESAU!
PAYBACK'S A BITCH... BITCH!
MADE IT. WE'RE SAFE.
WHAT'RE YOU TALKING ABOUT? THEY'RE STILL OUTSIDE.
CENTAURS... DON'T LIKE CLOSED-IN SPACES. THEY DON'T LIKE THE SHUT-IN DARK. IT SPOOKS THE HORSES.
AHHHH...
LET ME LOOK AT THAT.
GET THE FUCK AWAY FROM ME!
LET ME HELP. I'M A DOCTOR. YOU'RE BLEEDING OUT.

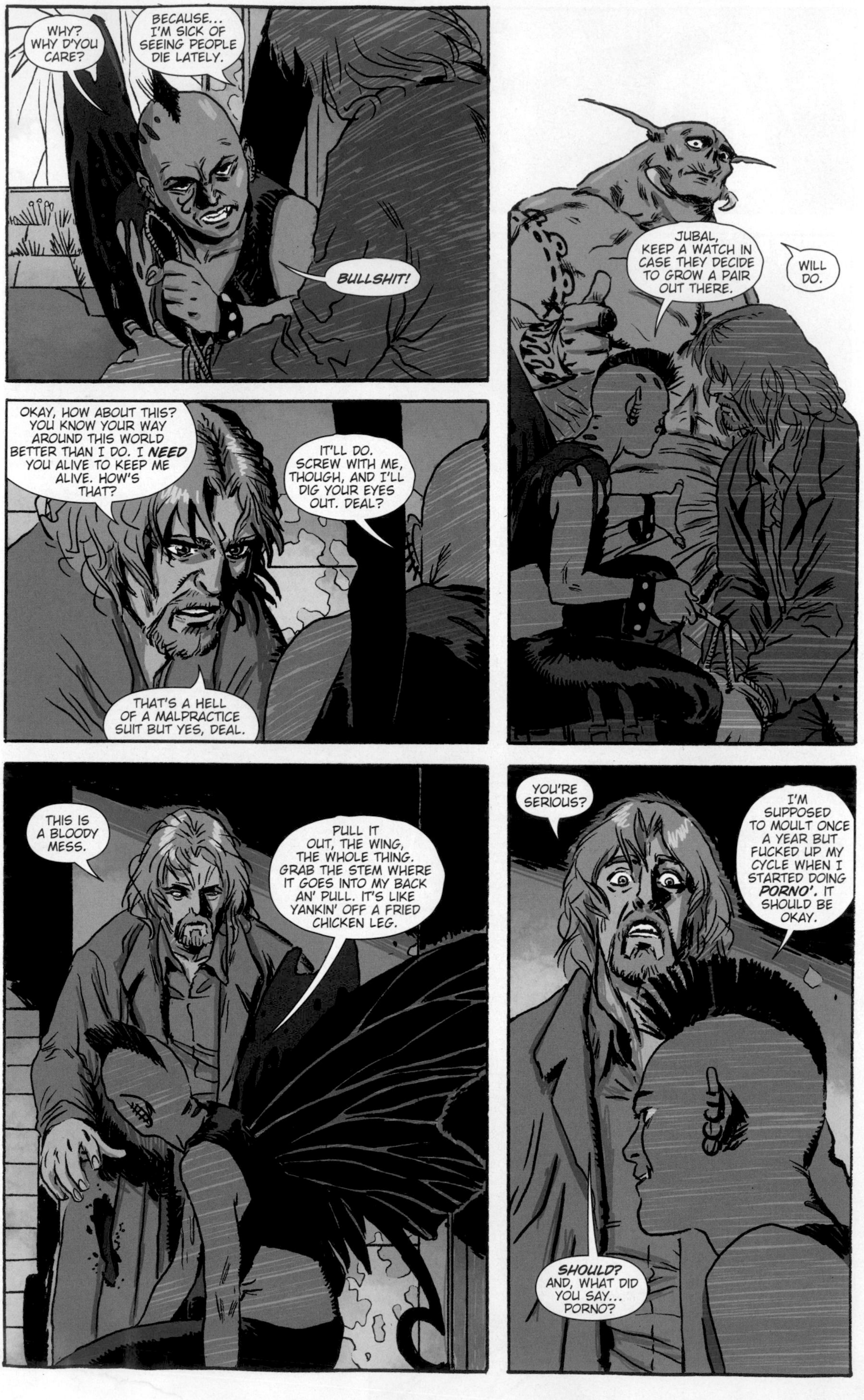
WHY? WHY D'YOU CARE?
BECAUSE... I'M SICK OF SEEING PEOPLE DIE LATELY.
BULLSHIT!
JUBAL, KEEP A WATCH IN CASE THEY DECIDE TO GROW A PAIR OUT THERE.
WILL DO.
OKAY, HOW ABOUT THIS? YOU KNOW YOUR WAY AROUND THIS WORLD BETTER THAN I DO. I NEED YOU ALIVE TO KEEP ME ALIVE. HOW'S THAT?
IT'LL DO. SCREW WITH ME, THOUGH, AND I'LL DIG YOUR EYES OUT. DEAL?
THAT'S A HELL OF A MALPRACTICE SUIT BUT YES, DEAL.
THIS IS A BLOODY MESS.
PULL IT OUT, THE WING, THE WHOLE THING. GRAB THE STEM WHERE IT GOES INTO MY BACK AN' PULL. IT'S LIKE YANKIN' OFF A FRIED CHICKEN LEG.
YOU'RE SERIOUS?
I'M SUPPOSED TO MOULT ONCE A YEAR BUT FUCKED UP MY CYCLE WHEN I STARTED DOING PORNO'. IT SHOULD BE OKAY.
SHOULD? AND, WHAT DID YOU SAY... PORNO?

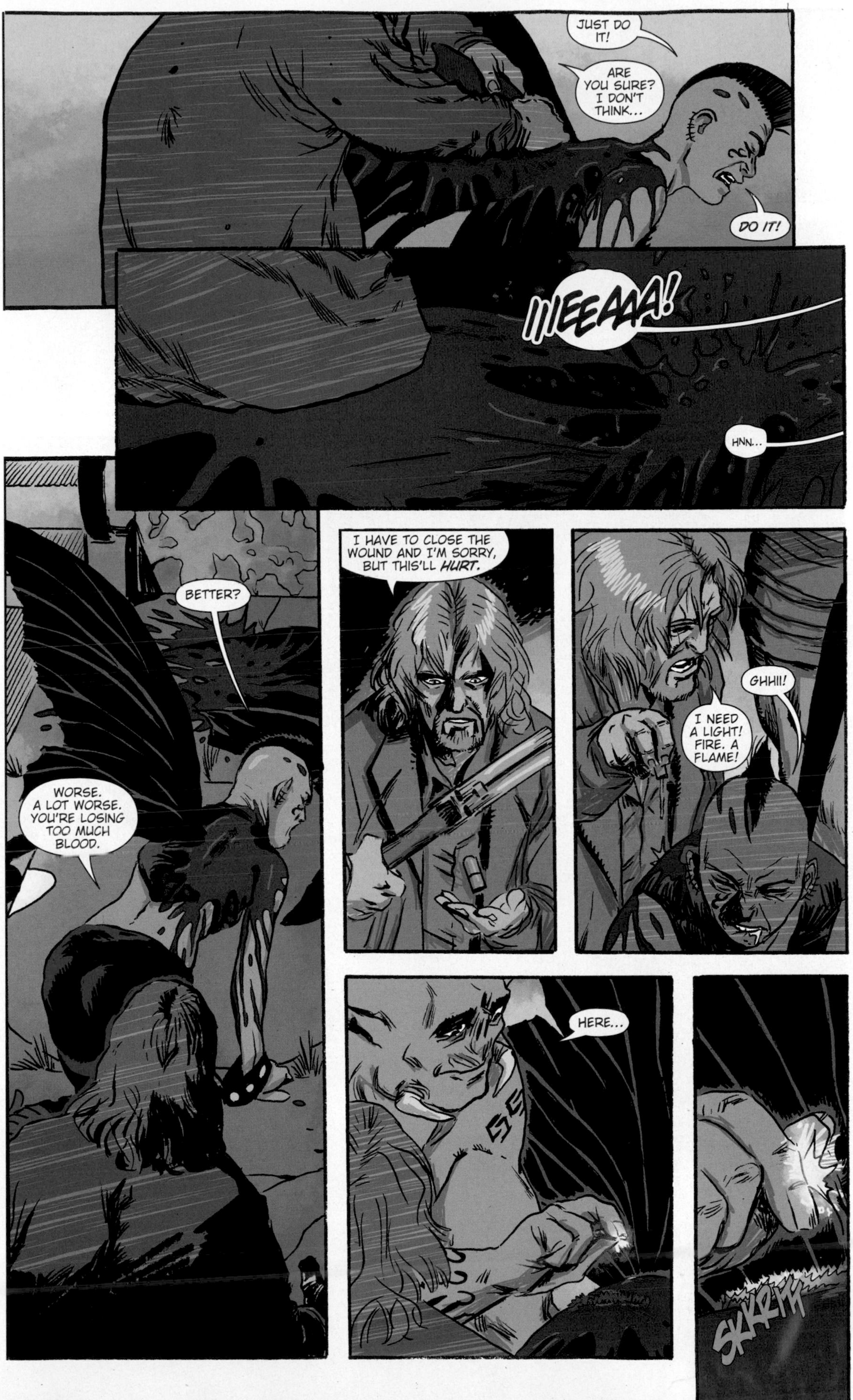

JUST DO IT!
ARE YOU SURE? I DON'T THINK...
DO IT!
IIIEEAAA!
HNN...
BETTER?
WORSE. A LOT WORSE. YOU'RE LOSING TOO MUCH BLOOD.
I HAVE TO CLOSE THE WOUND AND I'M SORRY, BUT THIS'LL HURT.
GHHII!
I NEED A LIGHT! FIRE. A FLAME!
HERE...
SKRKK

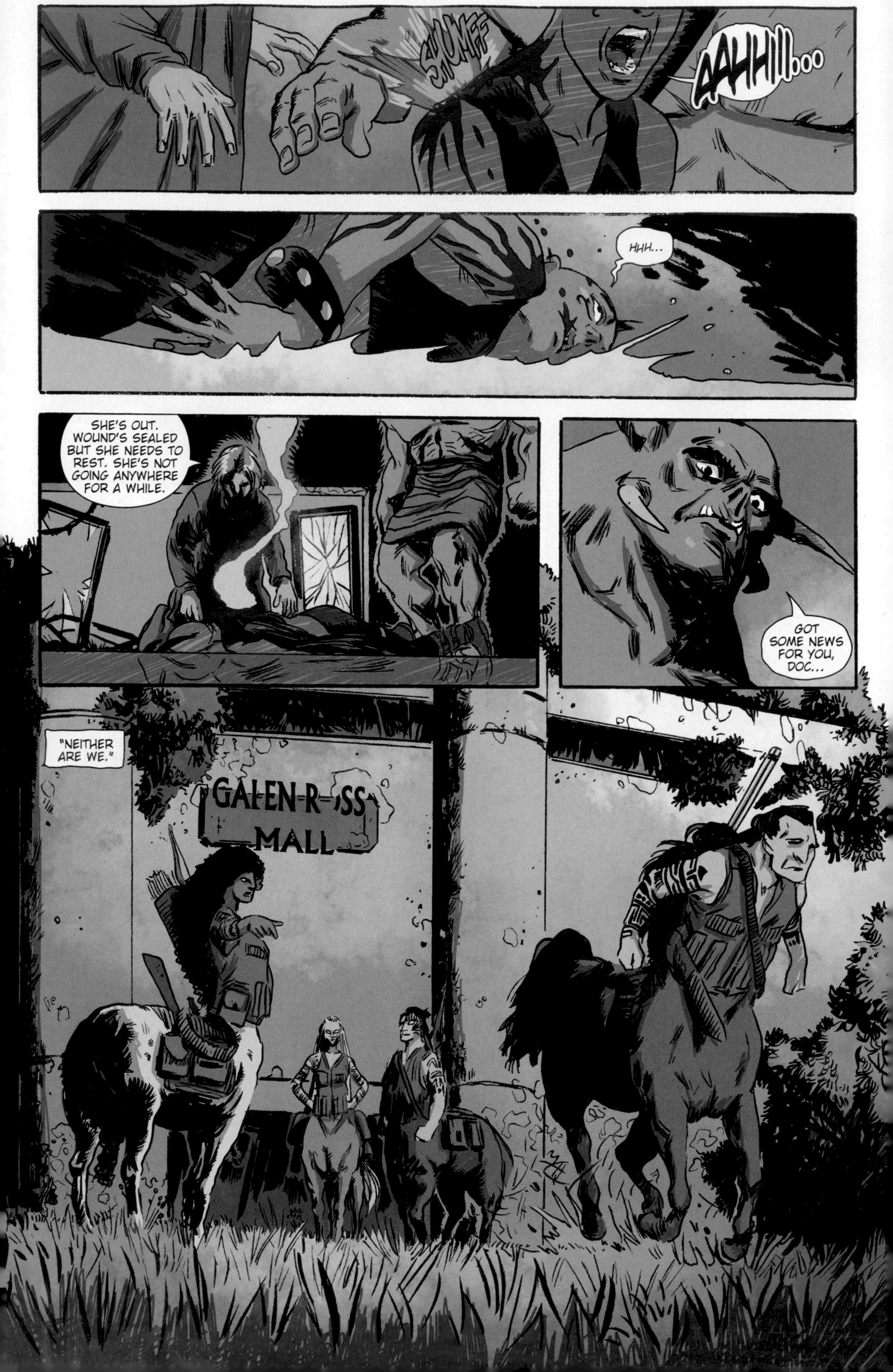
SHUNFF
AAHHIII...
HHH...
SHE'S OUT. WOUND'S SEALED BUT SHE NEEDS TO REST. SHE'S NOT GOING ANYWHERE FOR A WHILE.
GOT SOME NEWS FOR YOU, DOC...
"NEITHER ARE WE."
GALEN-R-SS MALL

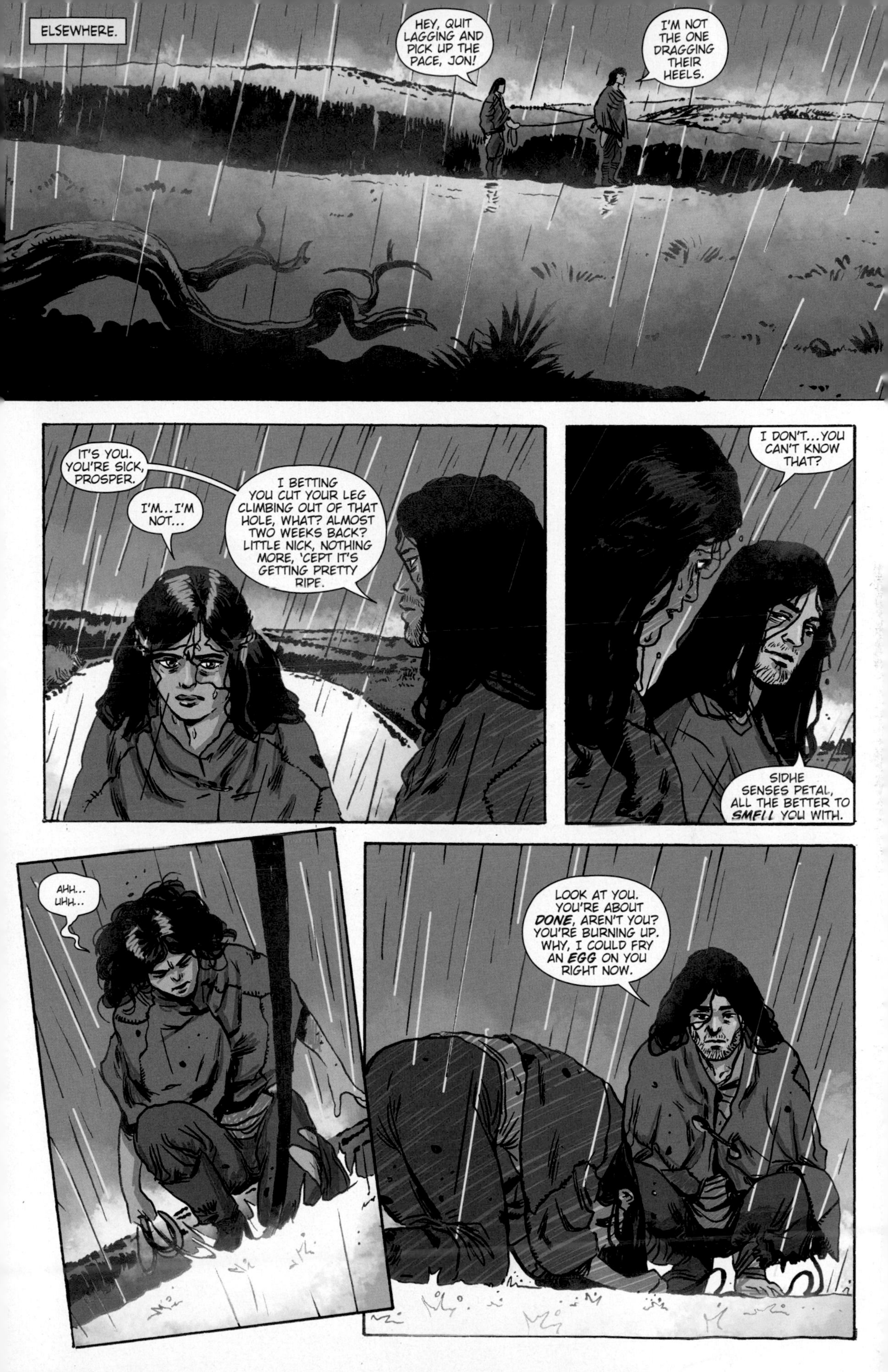
ELSEWHERE.
HEY, QUIT LAGGING AND PICK UP THE PACE, JON!
I'M NOT THE ONE DRAGGING THEIR HEELS.
IT'S YOU. YOU'RE SICK, PROSPER.
I'M...I'M NOT...
I BETTING YOU CUT YOUR LEG CLIMBING OUT OF THAT HOLE, WHAT? ALMOST TWO WEEKS BACK? LITTLE NICK, NOTHING MORE, 'CEPT IT'S GETTING PRETTY RIPE.
I DON'T...YOU CAN'T KNOW THAT?
SIDHE SENSES PETAL, ALL THE BETTER TO SMELL YOU WITH.
AHH... UHH...
LOOK AT YOU. YOU'RE ABOUT DONE, AREN'T YOU? YOU'RE BURNING UP. WHY, I COULD FRY AN EGG ON YOU RIGHT NOW.

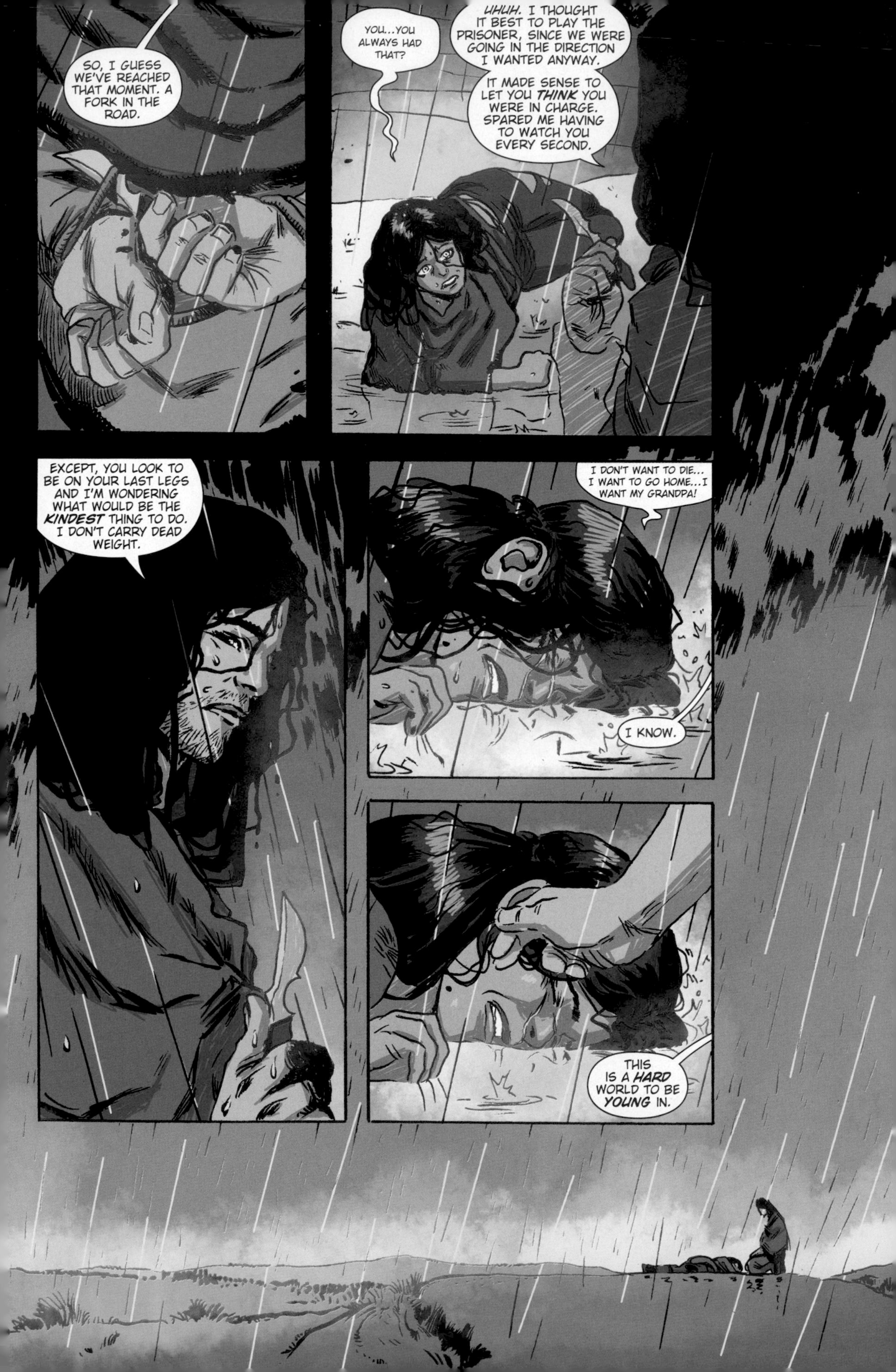
SO, I GUESS WE'VE REACHED THAT MOMENT. A FORK IN THE ROAD.
YOU...YOU ALWAYS HAD THAT?
UHUH. I THOUGHT IT BEST TO PLAY THE PRISONER, SINCE WE WERE GOING IN THE DIRECTION I WANTED ANYWAY.
IT MADE SENSE TO LET YOU THINK YOU WERE IN CHARGE. SPARED ME HAVING TO WATCH YOU EVERY SECOND.
EXCEPT, YOU LOOK TO BE ON YOUR LAST LEGS AND I'M WONDERING WHAT WOULD BE THE KINDEST THING TO DO. I DON'T CARRY DEAD WEIGHT.
I DON'T WANT TO DIE... I WANT TO GO HOME...I WANT MY GRANDPA!
I KNOW.
THIS IS A HARD WORLD TO BE YOUNG IN.

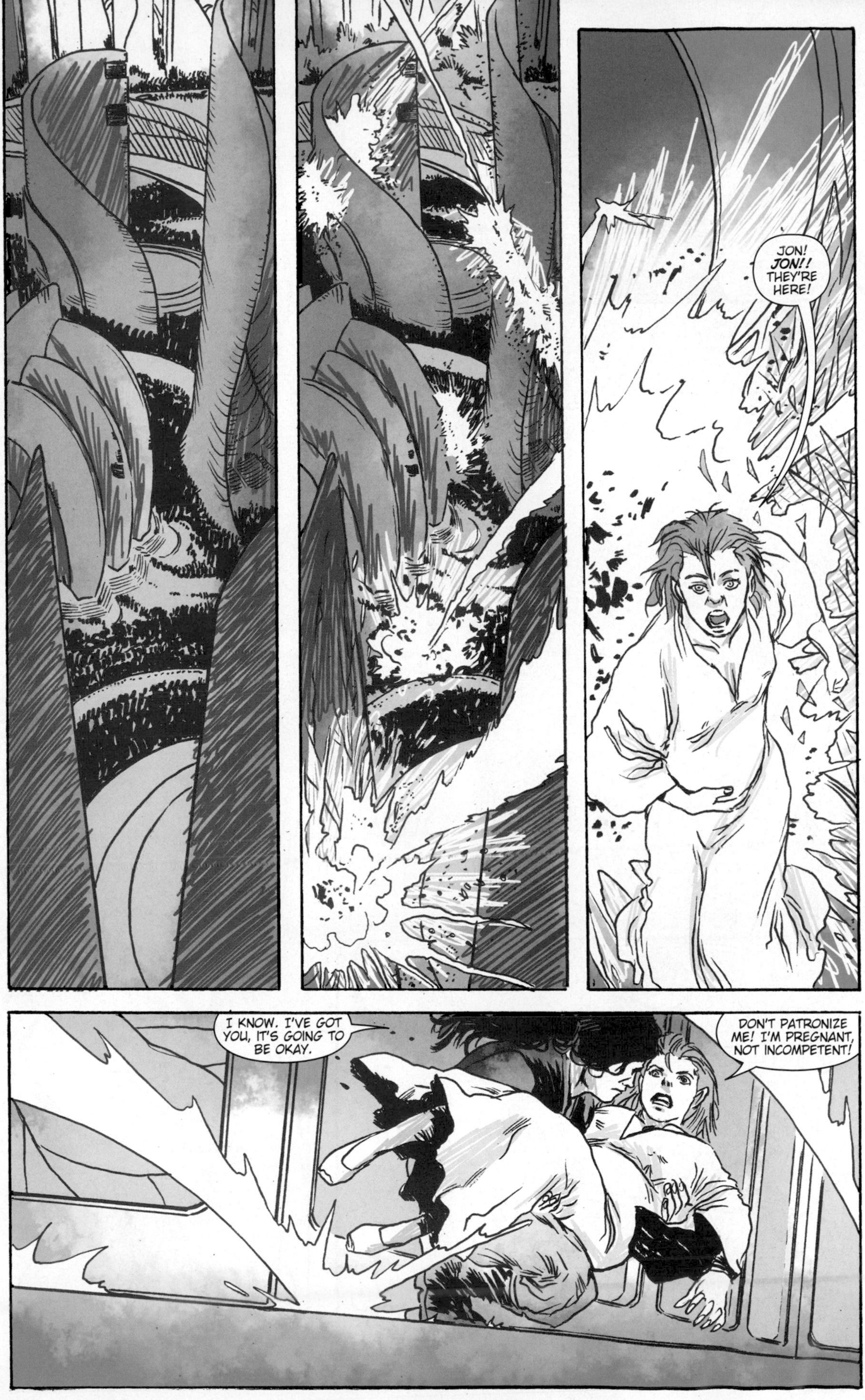
JON! JON!! THEY'RE HERE!
I KNOW. I'VE GOT YOU, IT'S GOING TO BE OKAY.
DON'T PATRONIZE ME! I'M PREGNANT, NOT INCOMPETENT!

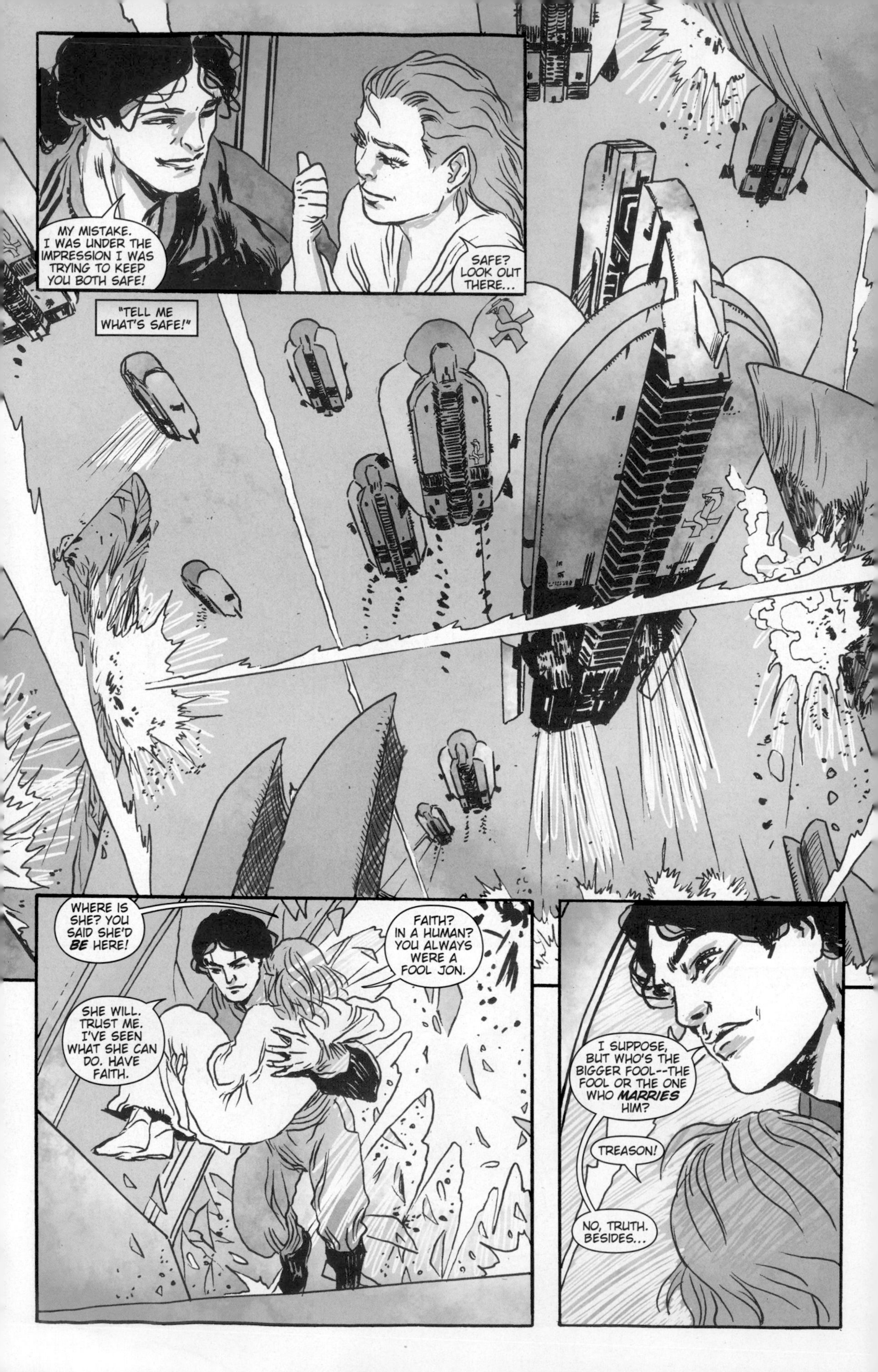
MY MISTAKE. I WAS UNDER THE IMPRESSION I WAS TRYING TO KEEP YOU BOTH SAFE!
SAFE? LOOK OUT THERE...
"TELL ME WHAT'S SAFE!"
WHERE IS SHE? YOU SAID SHE'D BE HERE!
SHE WILL. TRUST ME. I'VE SEEN WHAT SHE CAN DO. HAVE FAITH.
FAITH? IN A HUMAN? YOU ALWAYS WERE A FOOL JON.
I SUPPOSE, BUT WHO'S THE BIGGER FOOL--THE FOOL OR THE ONE WHO MARRIES HIM?
TREASON!
NO, TRUTH. BESIDES...

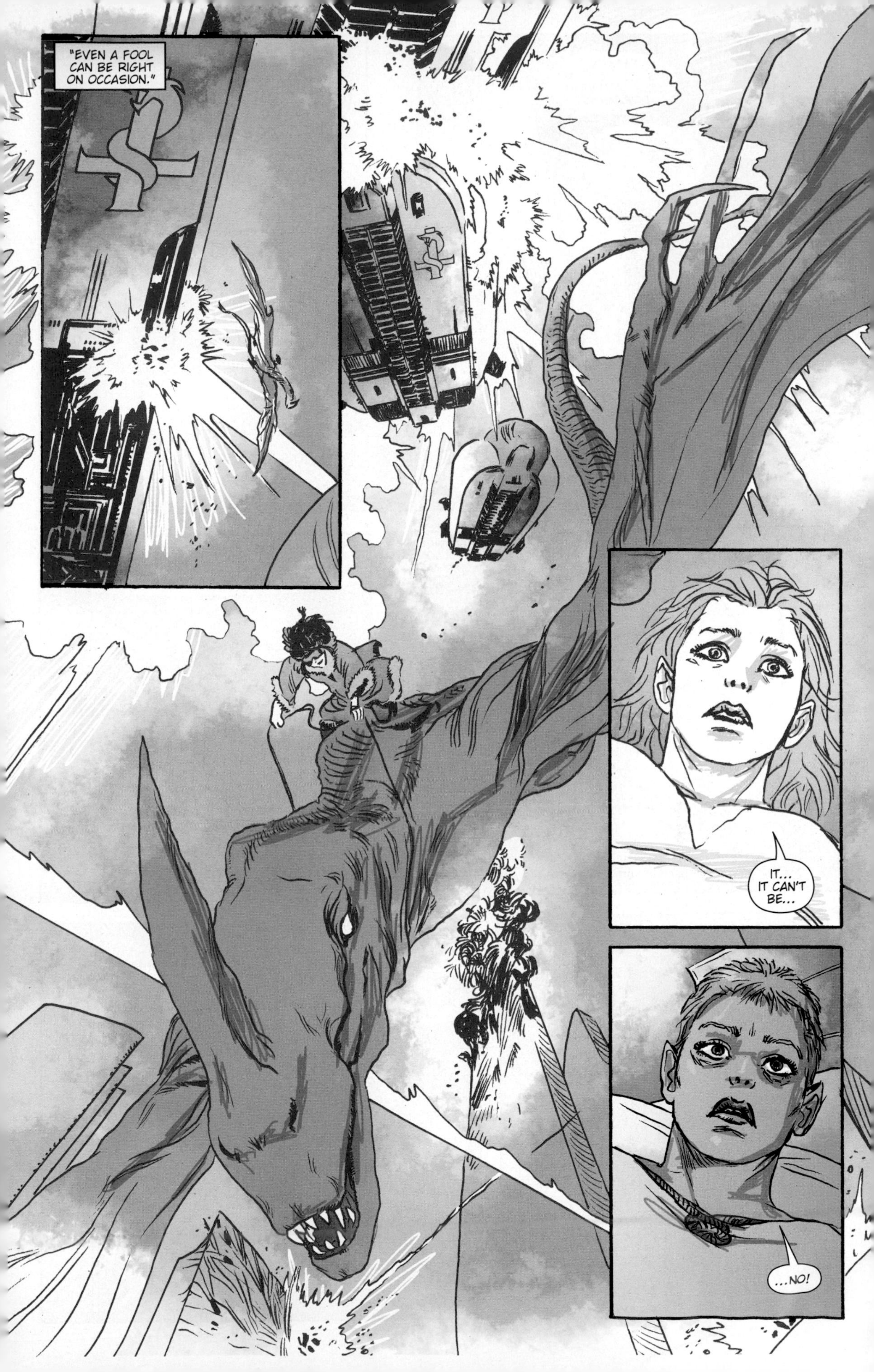
"EVEN A FOOL CAN BE RIGHT ON OCCASION."
IT... IT CAN'T BE...
...NO!

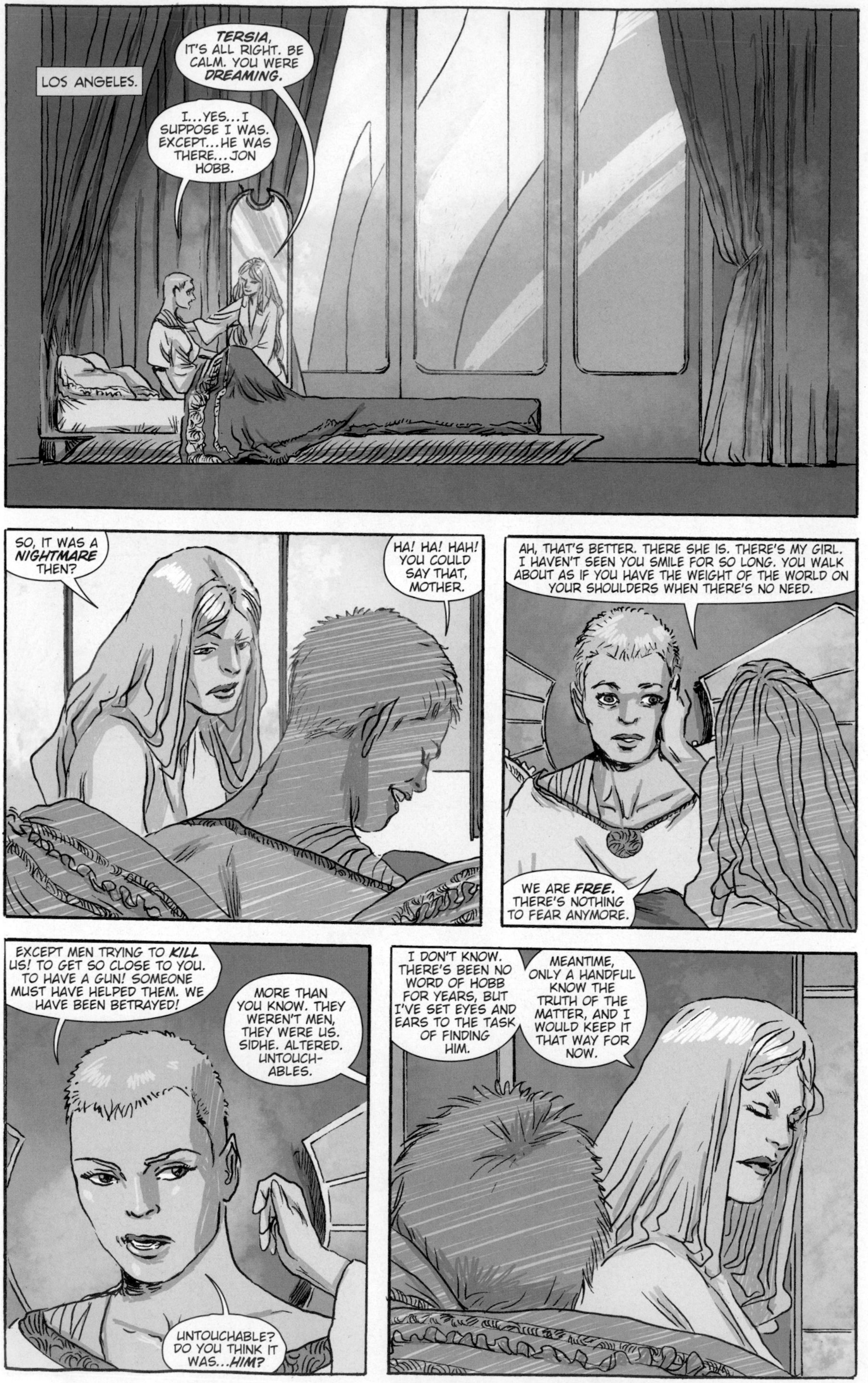
LOS ANGELES.
TERSIA, IT'S ALL RIGHT. BE CALM. YOU WERE DREAMING.
I...YES...I SUPPOSE I WAS. EXCEPT...HE WAS THERE...JON HOBB.
SO, IT WAS A NIGHTMARE THEN?
HA! HA! HAH! YOU COULD SAY THAT, MOTHER.
AH, THAT'S BETTER. THERE SHE IS. THERE'S MY GIRL. I HAVEN'T SEEN YOU SMILE FOR SO LONG. YOU WALK ABOUT AS IF YOU HAVE THE WEIGHT OF THE WORLD ON YOUR SHOULDERS WHEN THERE'S NO NEED.
WE ARE FREE. THERE'S NOTHING TO FEAR ANYMORE.
EXCEPT MEN TRYING TO KILL US! TO GET SO CLOSE TO YOU. TO HAVE A GUN! SOMEONE MUST HAVE HELPED THEM. WE HAVE BEEN BETRAYED!
MORE THAN YOU KNOW. THEY WEREN'T MEN, THEY WERE US. SIDHE. ALTERED. UNTOUCH-ABLES.
UNTOUCHABLE? DO YOU THINK IT WAS...HIM?
I DON'T KNOW. THERE'S BEEN NO WORD OF HOBB FOR YEARS, BUT I'VE SET EYES AND EARS TO THE TASK OF FINDING HIM.
MEANTIME, ONLY A HANDFUL KNOW THE TRUTH OF THE MATTER, AND I WOULD KEEP IT THAT WAY FOR NOW.

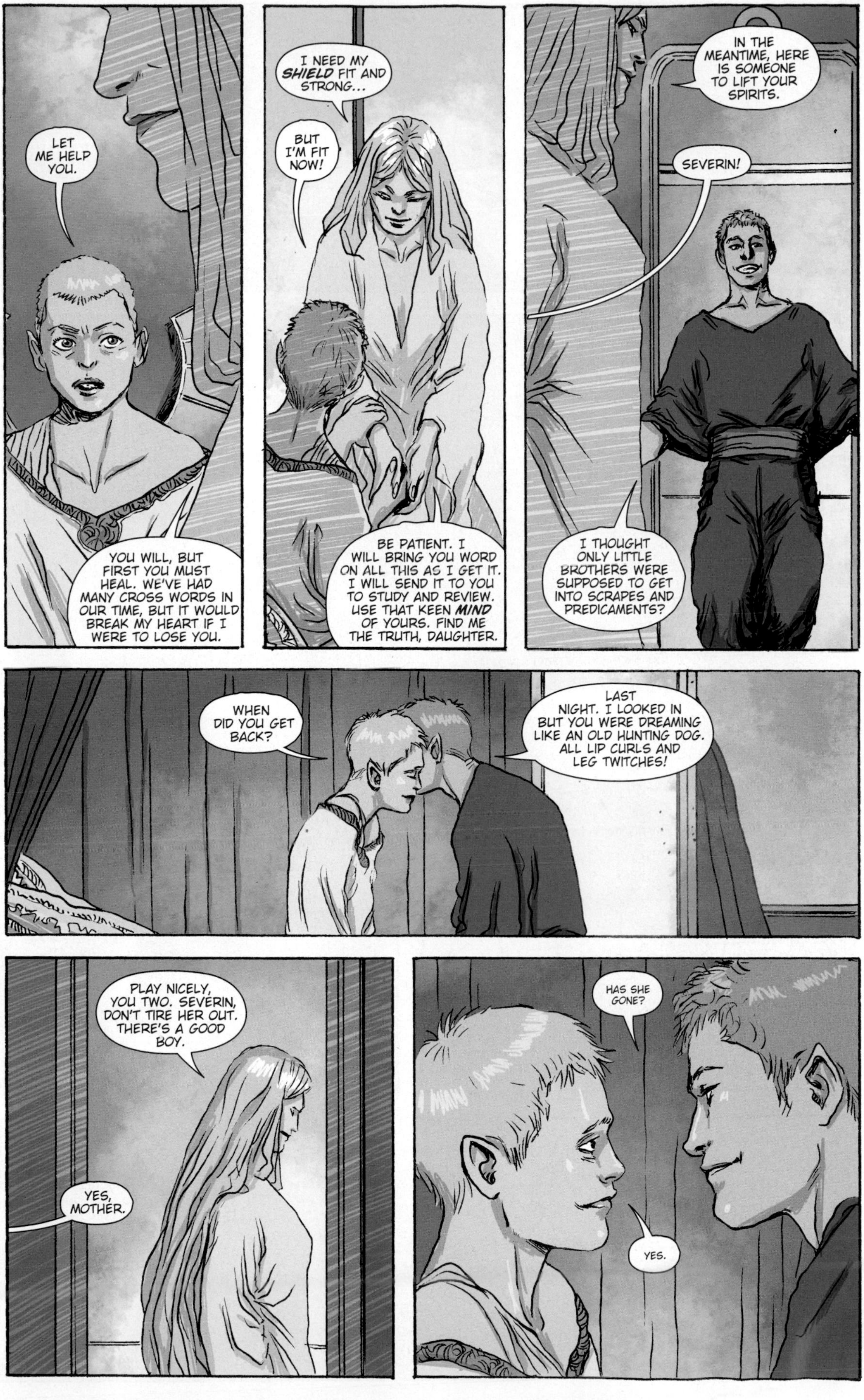
LET ME HELP YOU.
YOU WILL, BUT FIRST YOU MUST HEAL. WE'VE HAD MANY CROSS WORDS IN OUR TIME, BUT IT WOULD BREAK MY HEART IF I WERE TO LOSE YOU.
I NEED MY SHIELD FIT AND STRONG...
BUT I'M FIT NOW!
BE PATIENT. I WILL BRING YOU WORD ON ALL THIS AS I GET IT. I WILL SEND IT TO YOU TO STUDY AND REVIEW. USE THAT KEEN MIND OF YOURS. FIND ME THE TRUTH, DAUGHTER.
IN THE MEANTIME, HERE IS SOMEONE TO LIFT YOUR SPIRITS.
SEVERIN!
I THOUGHT ONLY LITTLE BROTHERS WERE SUPPOSED TO GET INTO SCRAPES AND PREDICAMENTS?
WHEN DID YOU GET BACK?
LAST NIGHT. I LOOKED IN BUT YOU WERE DREAMING LIKE AN OLD HUNTING DOG. ALL LIP CURLS AND LEG TWITCHES!
PLAY NICELY, YOU TWO. SEVERIN, DON'T TIRE HER OUT. THERE'S A GOOD BOY.
YES, MOTHER.
HAS SHE GONE?
YES.

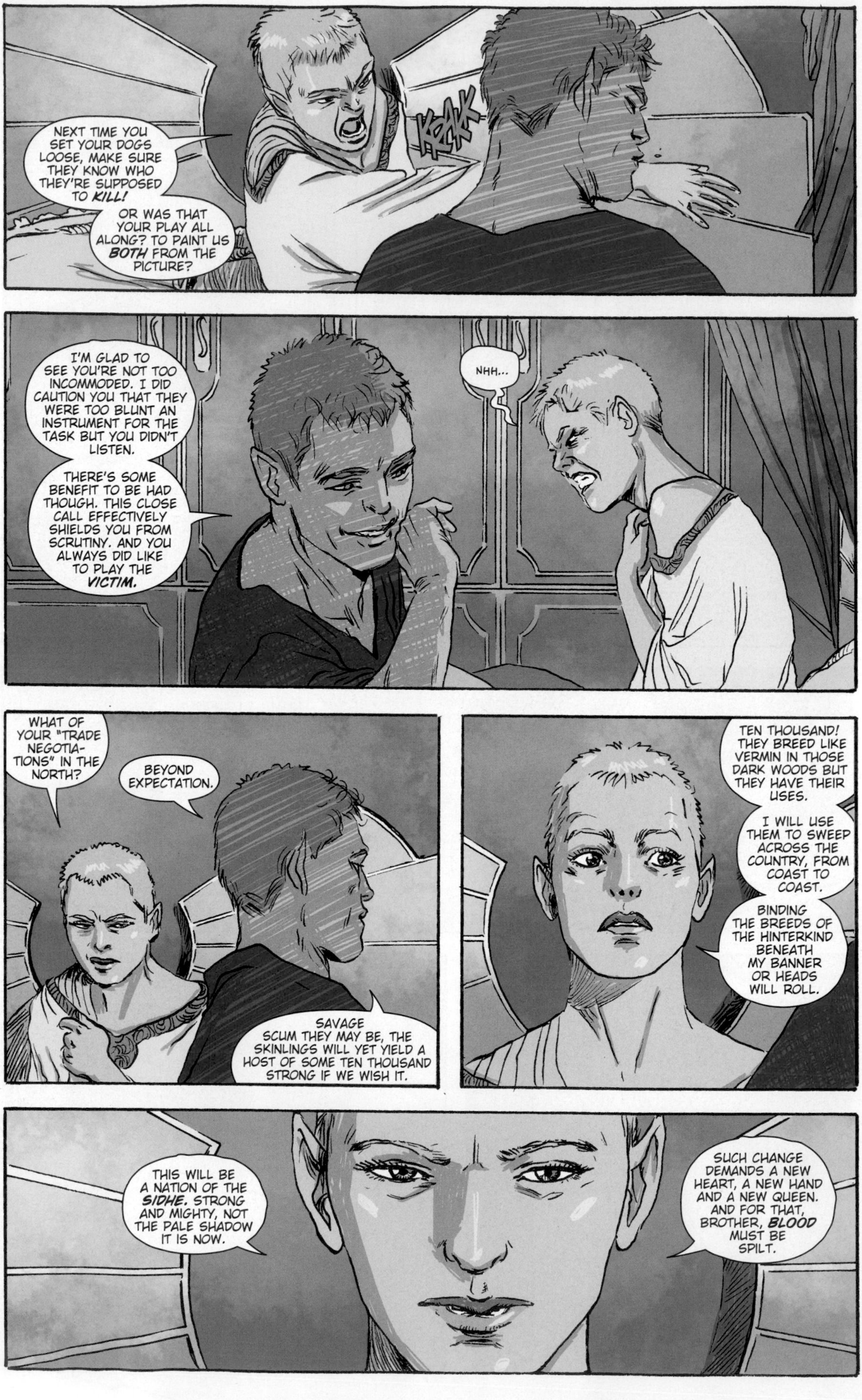

NEXT TIME YOU SET YOUR DOGS LOOSE, MAKE SURE THEY KNOW WHO THEY'RE SUPPOSED TO KILL!
KRAK
OR WAS THAT YOUR PLAY ALL ALONG? TO PAINT US BOTH FROM THE PICTURE?
I'M GLAD TO SEE YOU'RE NOT TOO INCOMMODED. I DID CAUTION YOU THAT THEY WERE TOO BLUNT AN INSTRUMENT FOR THE TASK BUT YOU DIDN'T LISTEN.
NHH...
THERE'S SOME BENEFIT TO BE HAD THOUGH. THIS CLOSE CALL EFFECTIVELY SHIELDS YOU FROM SCRUTINY. AND YOU ALWAYS DID LIKE TO PLAY THE VICTIM.
WHAT OF YOUR "TRADE NEGOTIA-TIONS" IN THE NORTH?
BEYOND EXPECTATION.
SAVAGE SCUM THEY MAY BE, THE SKINLINGS WILL YET YIELD A HOST OF SOME TEN THOUSAND STRONG IF WE WISH IT.
TEN THOUSAND! THEY BREED LIKE VERMIN IN THOSE DARK WOODS BUT THEY HAVE THEIR USES.
I WILL USE THEM TO SWEEP ACROSS THE COUNTRY, FROM COAST TO COAST.
BINDING THE BREEDS OF THE HINTERKIND BENEATH MY BANNER OR HEADS WILL ROLL.
THIS WILL BE A NATION OF THE SIDHE. STRONG AND MIGHTY, NOT THE PALE SHADOW IT IS NOW.
SUCH CHANGE DEMANDS A NEW HEART, A NEW HAND AND A NEW QUEEN. AND FOR THAT, BROTHER, BLOOD MUST BE SPILT.

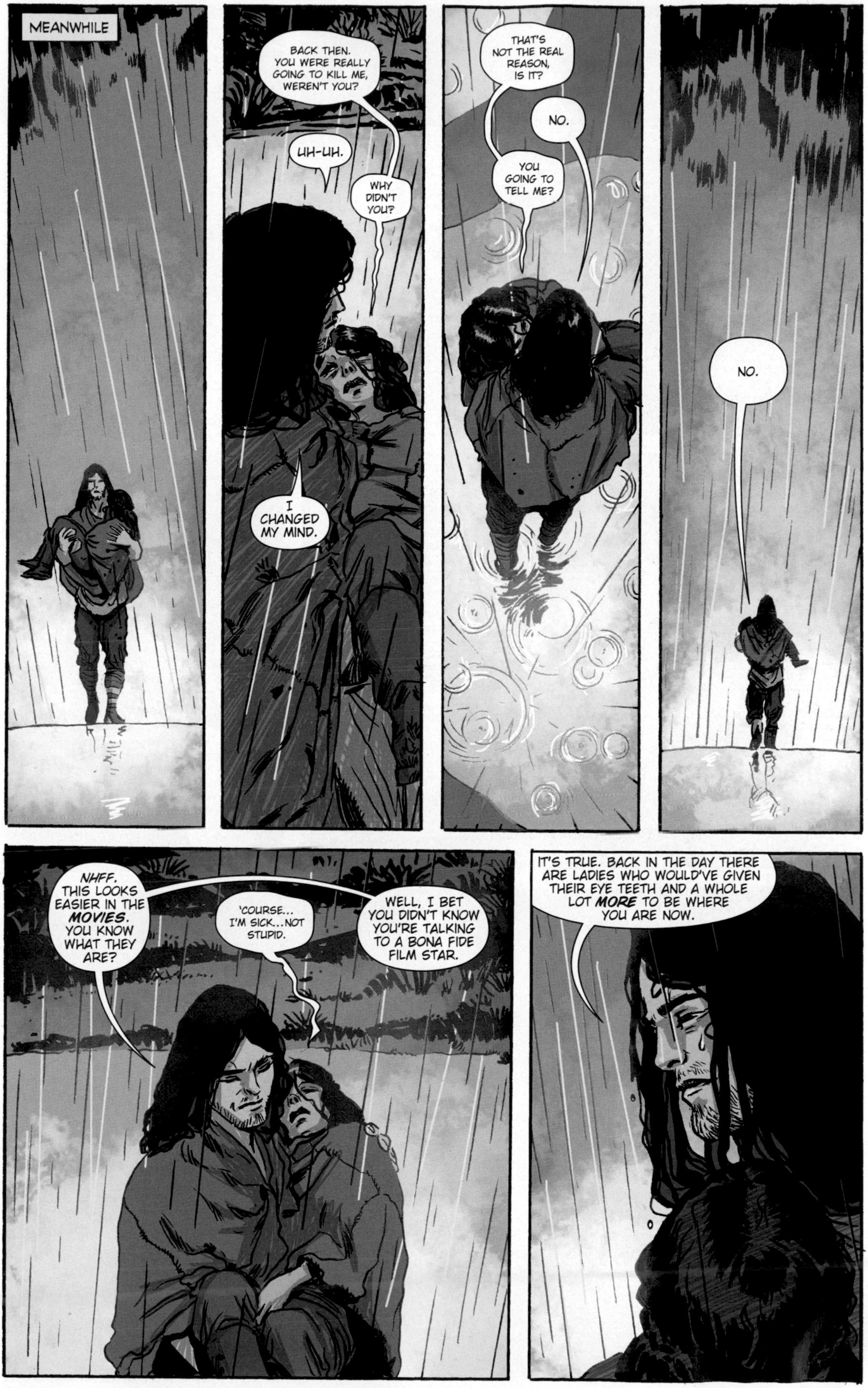
MEANWHILE
BACK THEN. YOU WERE REALLY GOING TO KILL ME, WEREN'T YOU?
UH-UH.
WHY DIDN'T YOU?
I CHANGED MY MIND.
THAT'S NOT THE REAL REASON, IS IT?
NO.
YOU GOING TO TELL ME?
NO.
NHFF. THIS LOOKS EASIER IN THE MOVIES. YOU KNOW WHAT THEY ARE?
'COURSE... I'M SICK...NOT STUPID.
WELL, I BET YOU DIDN'T KNOW YOU'RE TALKING TO A BONA FIDE FILM STAR.
IT'S TRUE. BACK IN THE DAY THERE ARE LADIES WHO WOULD'VE GIVEN THEIR EYE TEETH AND A WHOLE LOT MORE TO BE WHERE YOU ARE NOW.

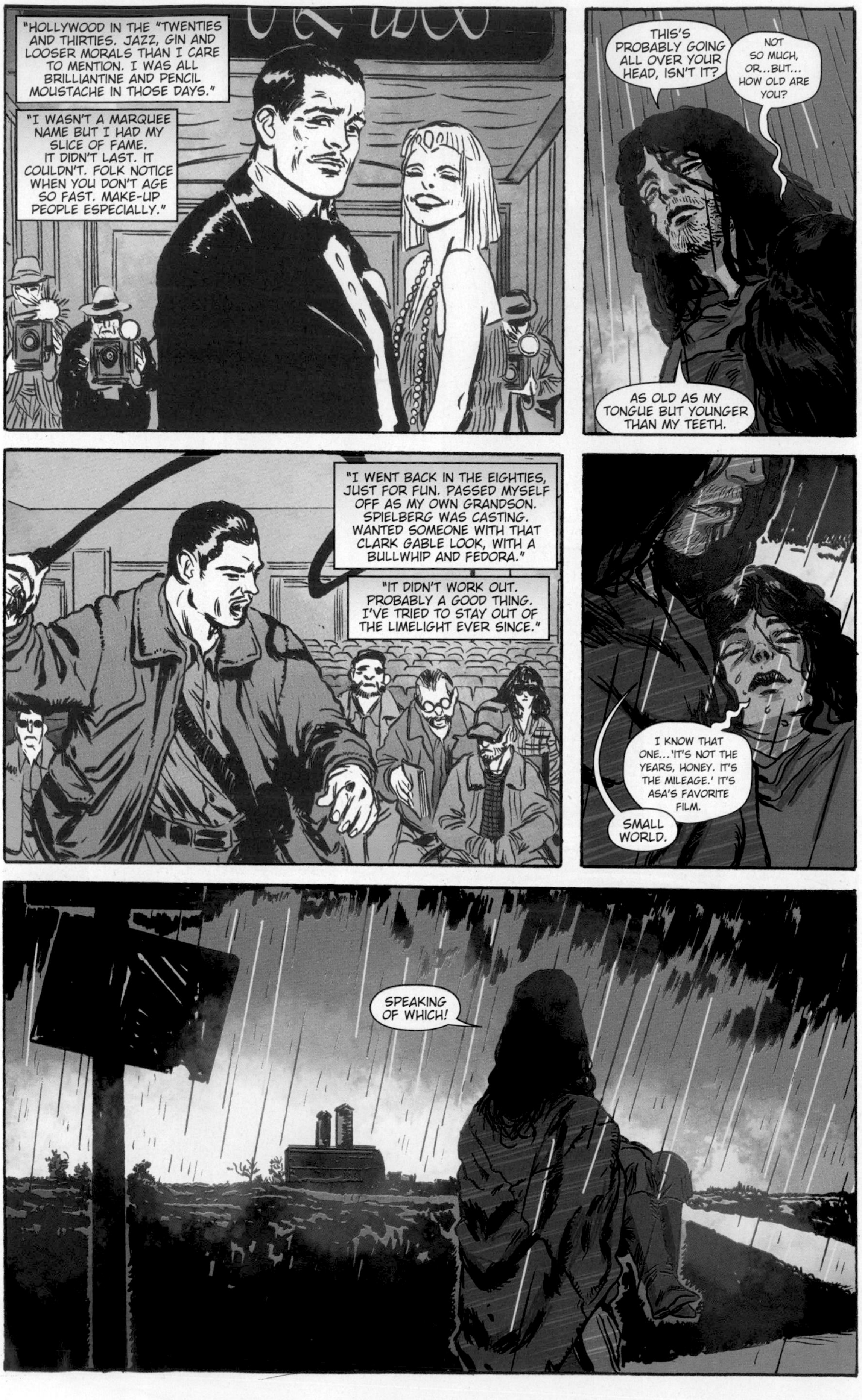
"HOLLYWOOD IN THE 'TWENTIES AND THIRTIES. JAZZ, GIN AND LOOSER MORALS THAN I CARE TO MENTION. I WAS ALL BRILLIANTINE AND PENCIL MOUSTACHE IN THOSE DAYS."
"I WASN'T A MARQUEE NAME BUT I HAD MY SLICE OF FAME. IT DIDN'T LAST. IT COULDN'T. FOLK NOTICE WHEN YOU DON'T AGE SO FAST. MAKE-UP PEOPLE ESPECIALLY."
THIS'S PROBABLY GOING ALL OVER YOUR HEAD, ISN'T IT?
NOT SO MUCH, OR...BUT... HOW OLD ARE YOU?
AS OLD AS MY TONGUE BUT YOUNGER THAN MY TEETH.
"I WENT BACK IN THE EIGHTIES, JUST FOR FUN. PASSED MYSELF OFF AS MY OWN GRANDSON. SPIELBERG WAS CASTING. WANTED SOMEONE WITH THAT CLARK GABLE LOOK, WITH A BULLWHIP AND FEDORA."
"IT DIDN'T WORK OUT. PROBABLY A GOOD THING. I'VE TRIED TO STAY OUT OF THE LIMELIGHT EVER SINCE."
I KNOW THAT ONE...'IT'S NOT THE YEARS, HONEY. IT'S THE MILEAGE.' IT'S ASA'S FAVORITE FILM.
SMALL WORLD.
SPEAKING OF WHICH!

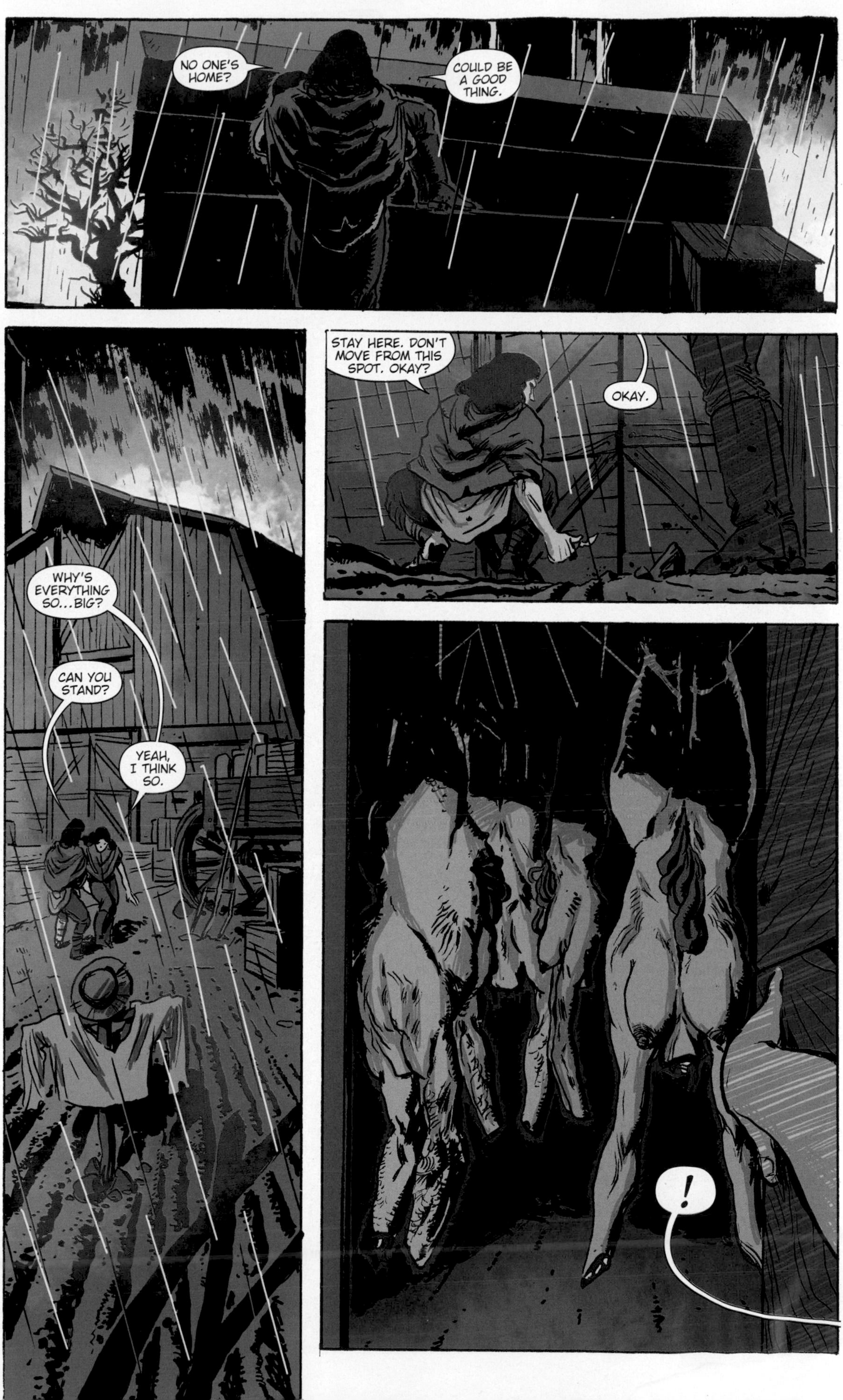
NO ONE'S HOME?
COULD BE A GOOD THING.
WHY'S EVERYTHING SO...BIG?
CAN YOU STAND?
YEAH, I THINK SO.
STAY HERE. DON'T MOVE FROM THIS SPOT. OKAY?
OKAY.
!

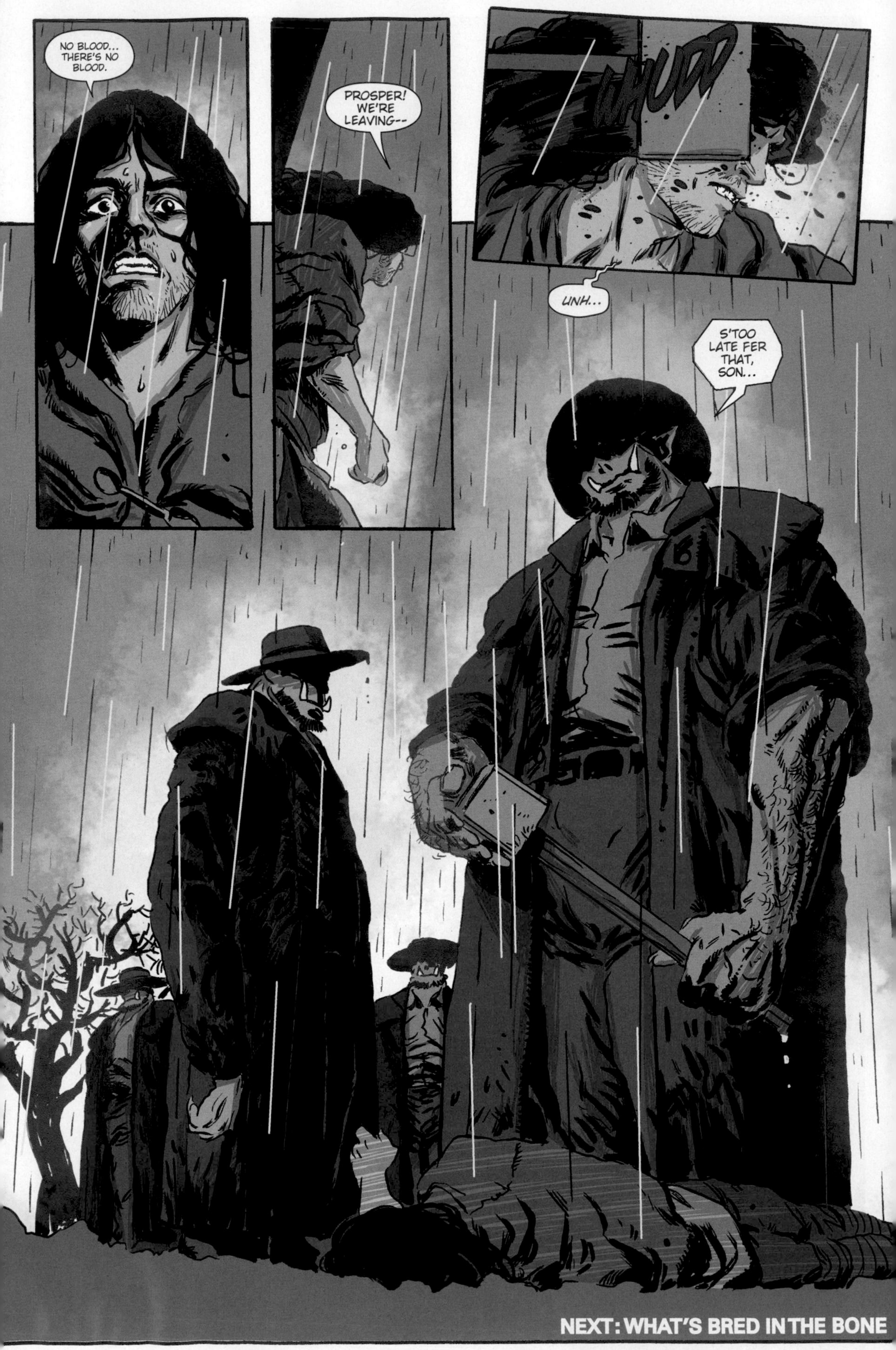
NO BLOOD... THERE'S NO BLOOD.
PROSPER! WE'RE LEAVING--
WHUDD
UNH...
S'TOO LATE FER THAT, SON...
NEXT: WHAT'S BRED IN THE BONE

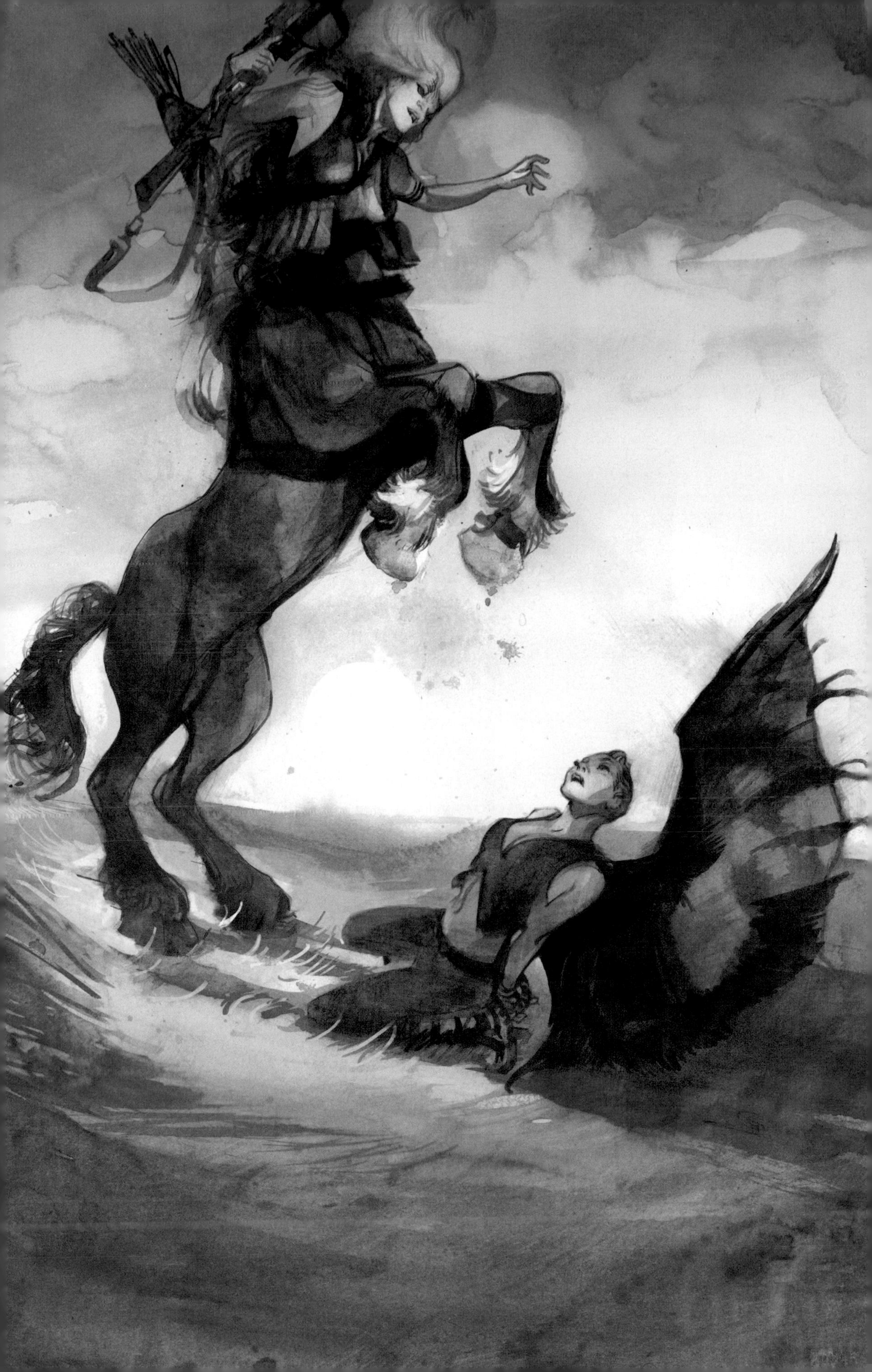

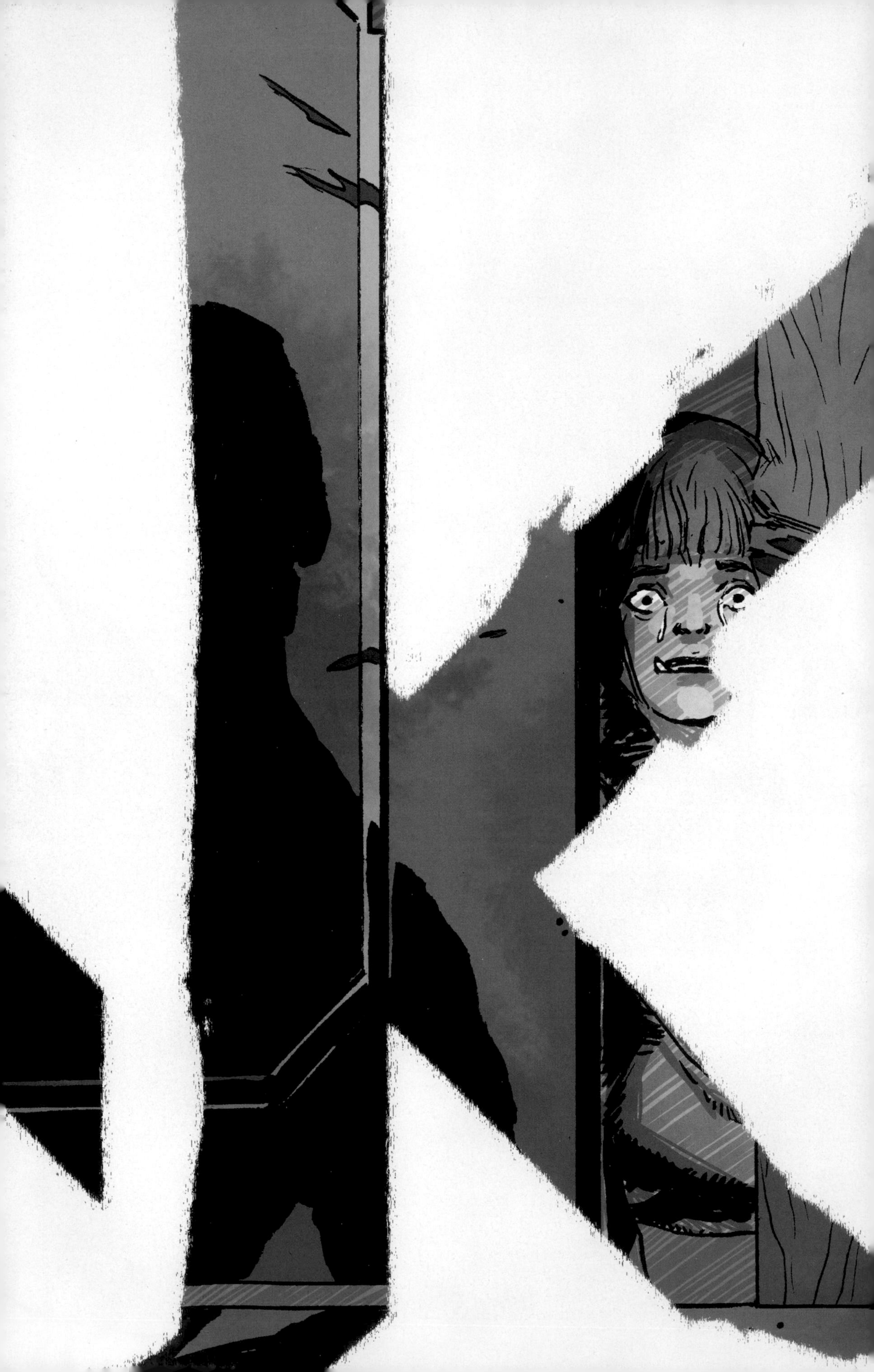

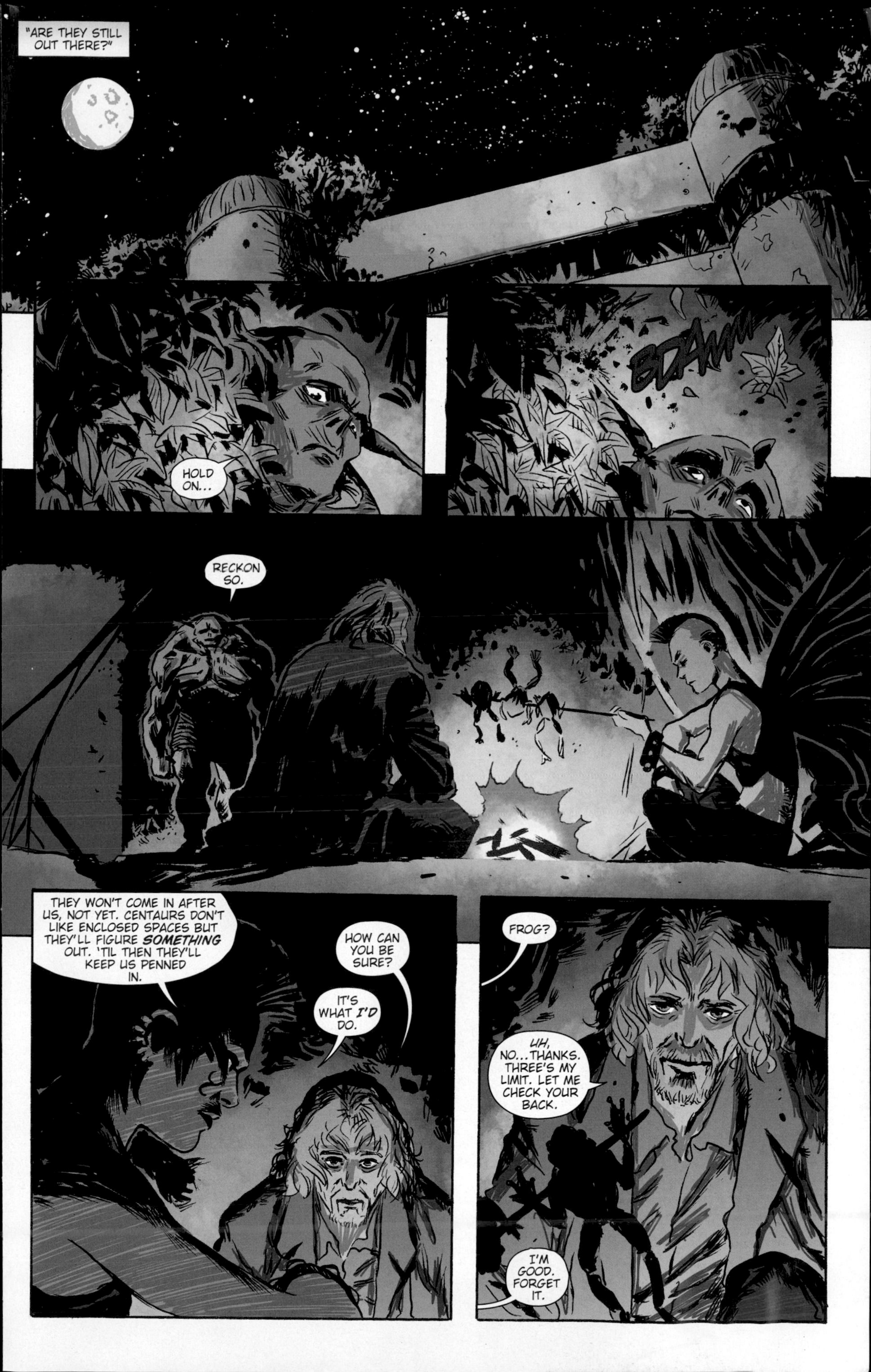
"ARE THEY STILL OUT THERE?"
HOLD ON...
BDAM!!!
RECKON SO.
THEY WON'T COME IN AFTER US, NOT YET. CENTAURS DON'T LIKE ENCLOSED SPACES BUT THEY'LL FIGURE SOMETHING OUT. 'TIL THEN THEY'LL KEEP US PENNED IN.
HOW CAN YOU BE SURE?
IT'S WHAT I'D DO.
FROG?
UH, NO...THANKS. THREE'S MY LIMIT. LET ME CHECK YOUR BACK.
I'M GOOD. FORGET IT.

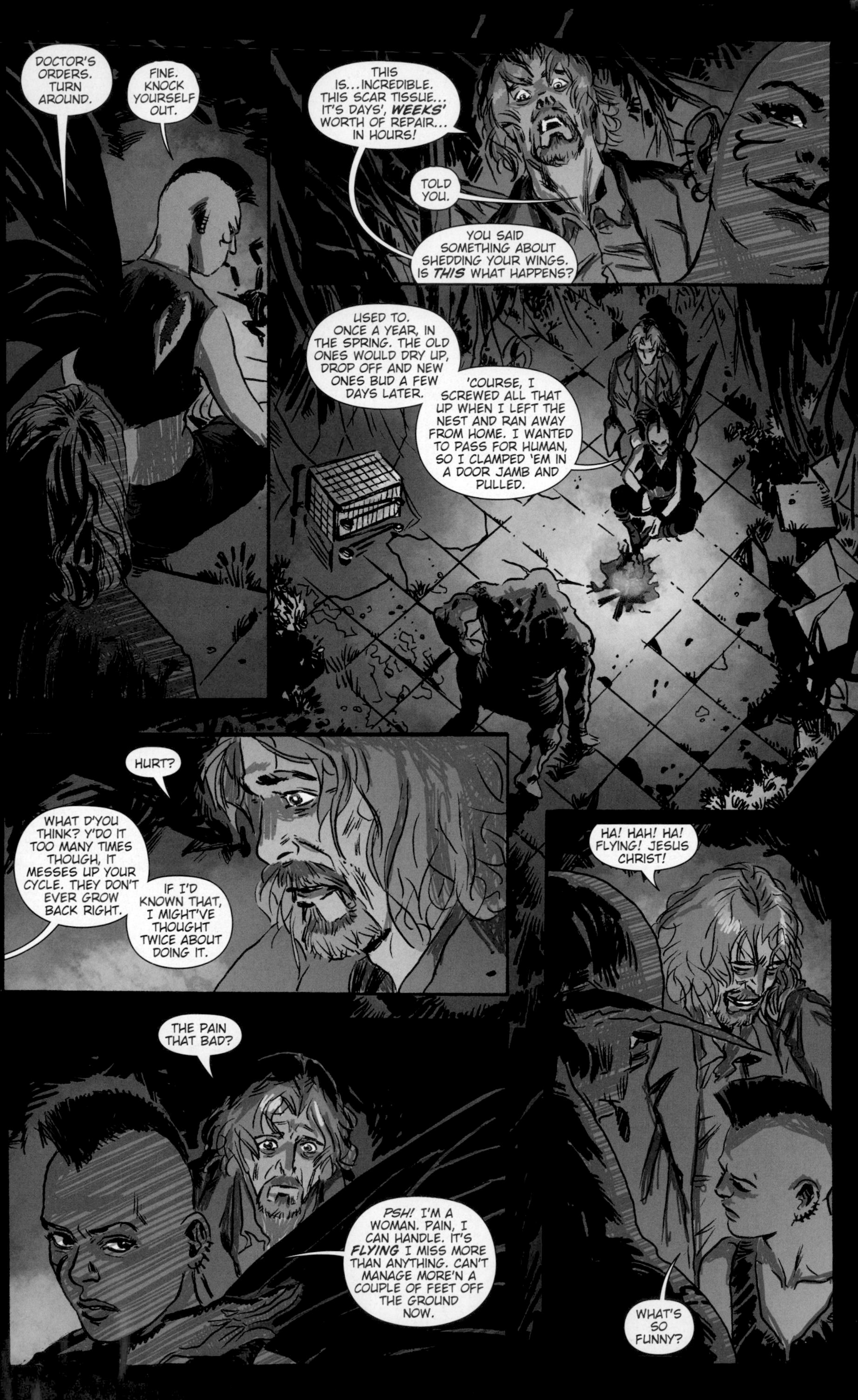
DOCTOR'S ORDERS. TURN AROUND.
FINE. KNOCK YOURSELF OUT.
THIS IS...INCREDIBLE. THIS SCAR TISSUE... IT'S DAYS', WEEKS' WORTH OF REPAIR... IN HOURS!
TOLD YOU.
YOU SAID SOMETHING ABOUT SHEDDING YOUR WINGS. IS THIS WHAT HAPPENS?
USED TO. ONCE A YEAR, IN THE SPRING. THE OLD ONES WOULD DRY UP, DROP OFF AND NEW ONES BUD A FEW DAYS LATER.
'COURSE, I SCREWED ALL THAT UP WHEN I LEFT THE NEST AND RAN AWAY FROM HOME. I WANTED TO PASS FOR HUMAN, SO I CLAMPED 'EM IN A DOOR JAMB AND PULLED.
HURT?
WHAT D'YOU THINK? Y'DO IT TOO MANY TIMES THOUGH, IT MESSES UP YOUR CYCLE. THEY DON'T EVER GROW BACK RIGHT.
IF I'D KNOWN THAT, I MIGHT'VE THOUGHT TWICE ABOUT DOING IT.
THE PAIN THAT BAD?
PSH! I'M A WOMAN. PAIN, I CAN HANDLE. IT'S FLYING I MISS MORE THAN ANYTHING. CAN'T MANAGE MORE'N A COUPLE OF FEET OFF THE GROUND NOW.
HA! HAH! HA! FLYING! JESUS CHRIST!
WHAT'S SO FUNNY?

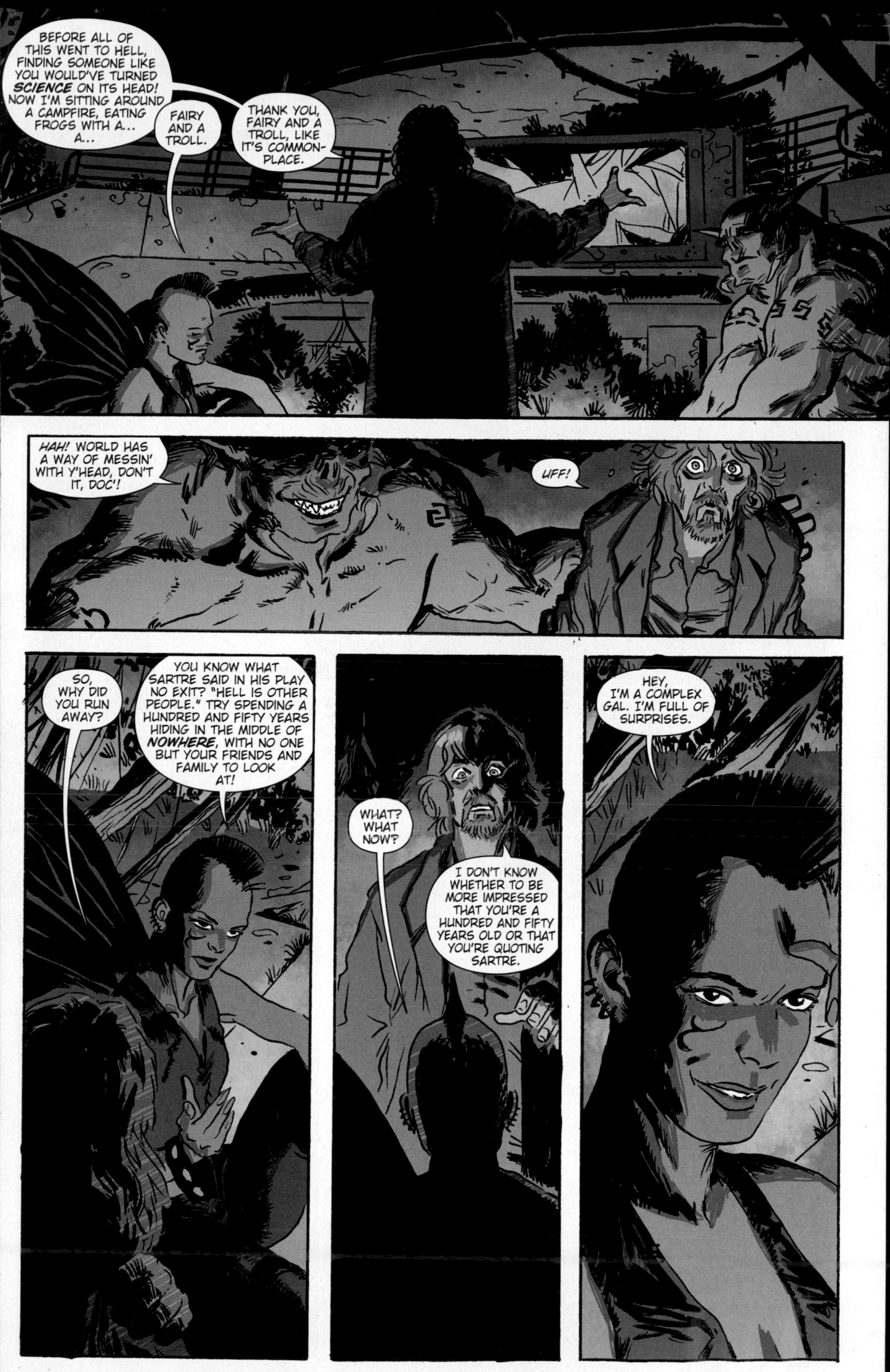
BEFORE ALL OF THIS WENT TO HELL, FINDING SOMEONE LIKE YOU WOULD'VE TURNED SCIENCE ON ITS HEAD! NOW I'M SITTING AROUND A CAMPFIRE, EATING FROGS WITH A... A...
FAIRY AND A TROLL.
THANK YOU, FAIRY AND A TROLL, LIKE IT'S COMMON-PLACE.
HAH! WORLD HAS A WAY OF MESSIN' WITH Y'HEAD, DON'T IT, DOC'!
UFF!
SO, WHY DID YOU RUN AWAY?
YOU KNOW WHAT SARTRE SAID IN HIS PLAY NO EXIT? "HELL IS OTHER PEOPLE." TRY SPENDING A HUNDRED AND FIFTY YEARS HIDING IN THE MIDDLE OF NOWHERE, WITH NO ONE BUT YOUR FRIENDS AND FAMILY TO LOOK AT!
WHAT? WHAT NOW?
I DON'T KNOW WHETHER TO BE MORE IMPRESSED THAT YOU'RE A HUNDRED AND FIFTY YEARS OLD OR THAT YOU'RE QUOTING SARTRE.
HEY, I'M A COMPLEX GAL. I'M FULL OF SURPRISES.

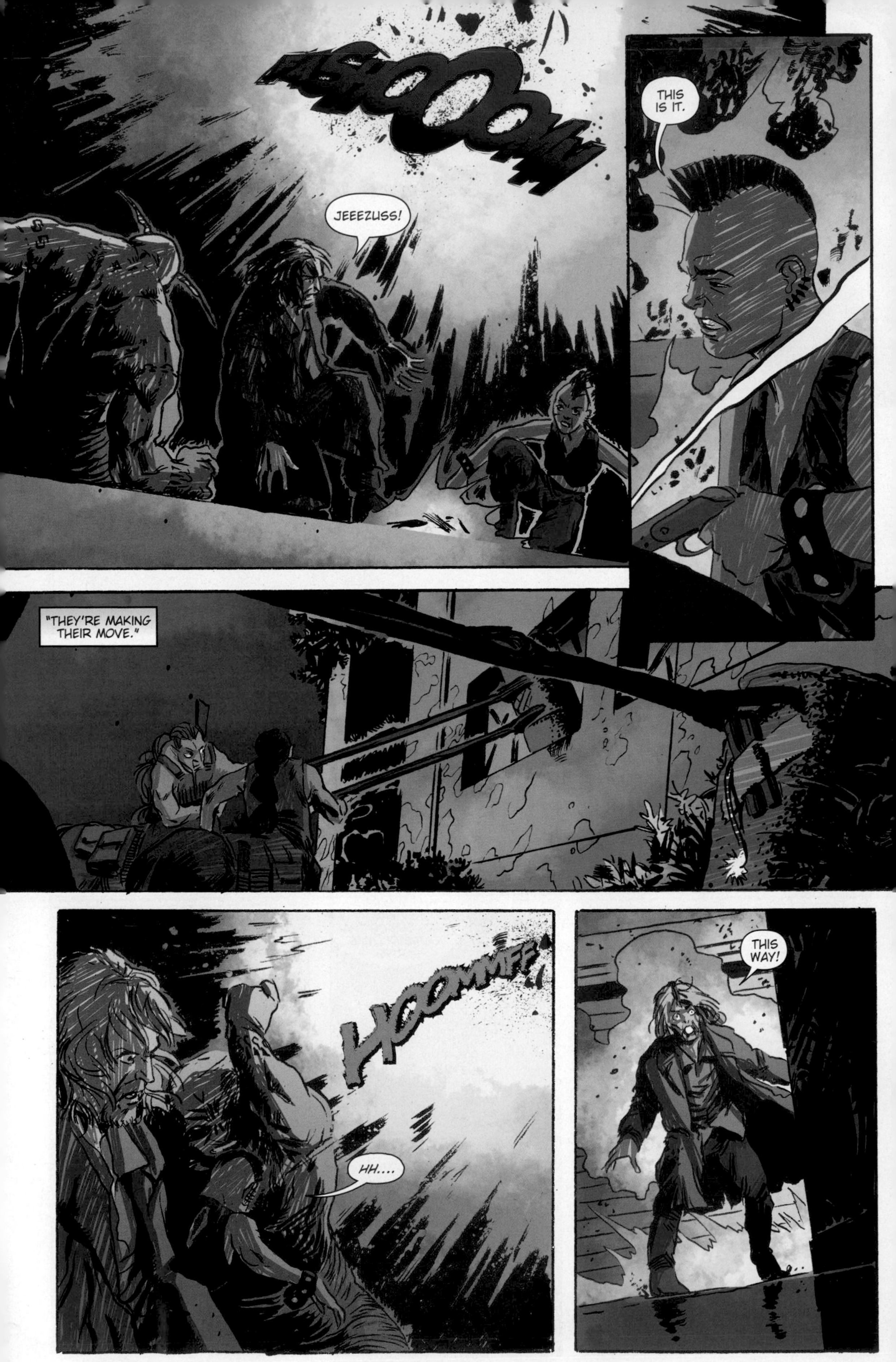

KASHOOOOM
JEEEZUSS!
THIS IS IT.
"THEY'RE MAKING THEIR MOVE."
HOOMMFF!
HH....
THIS WAY!

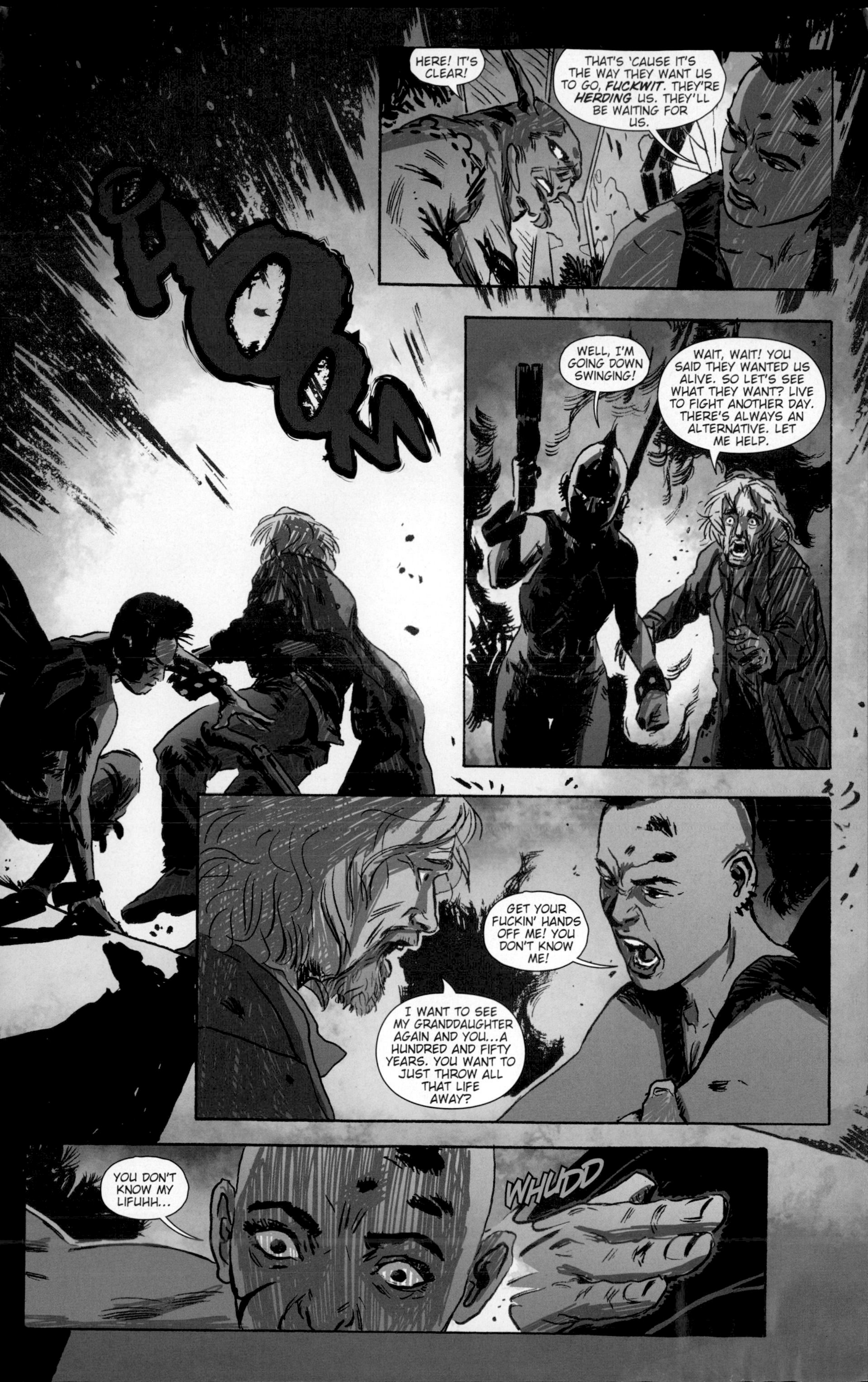
HERE! IT'S CLEAR!
THAT'S 'CAUSE IT'S THE WAY THEY WANT US TO GO, **FUCKWIT**. THEY'RE **HERDING** US. THEY'LL BE WAITING FOR US.
WOOSH
WELL, I'M GOING DOWN SWINGING!
WAIT, WAIT! YOU SAID THEY WANTED US ALIVE. SO LET'S SEE WHAT THEY WANT? LIVE TO FIGHT ANOTHER DAY. THERE'S ALWAYS AN ALTERNATIVE. LET ME HELP.
GET YOUR FUCKIN' HANDS OFF ME! YOU DON'T KNOW ME!
I WANT TO SEE MY GRANDDAUGHTER AGAIN AND YOU...A HUNDRED AND FIFTY YEARS. YOU WANT TO JUST THROW ALL THAT LIFE AWAY?
YOU DON'T KNOW MY LIFUHH...
WHUDD

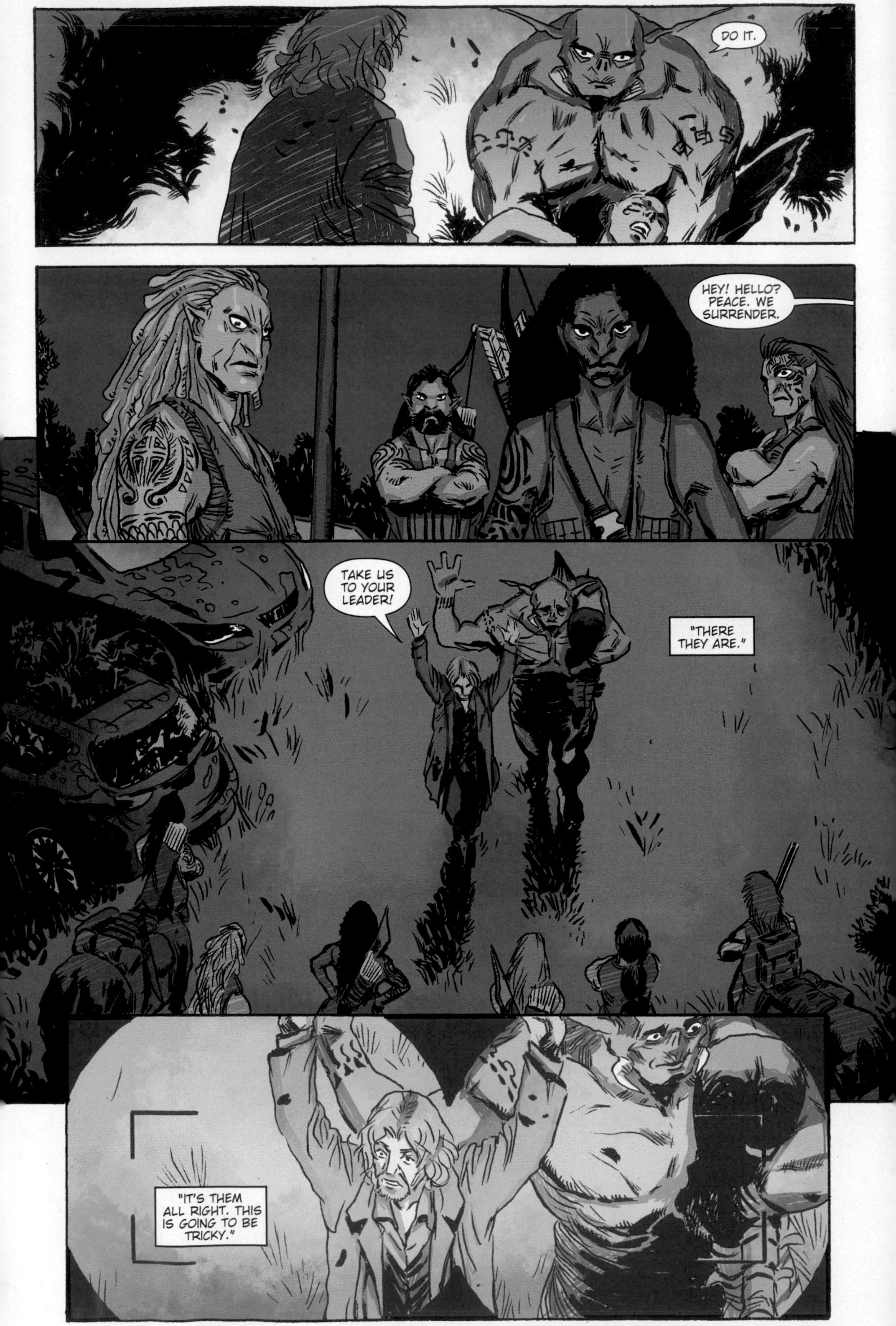
DO IT.
HEY! HELLO? PEACE. WE SURRENDER.
TAKE US TO YOUR LEADER!
"THERE THEY ARE."
"IT'S THEM ALL RIGHT. THIS IS GOING TO BE TRICKY."

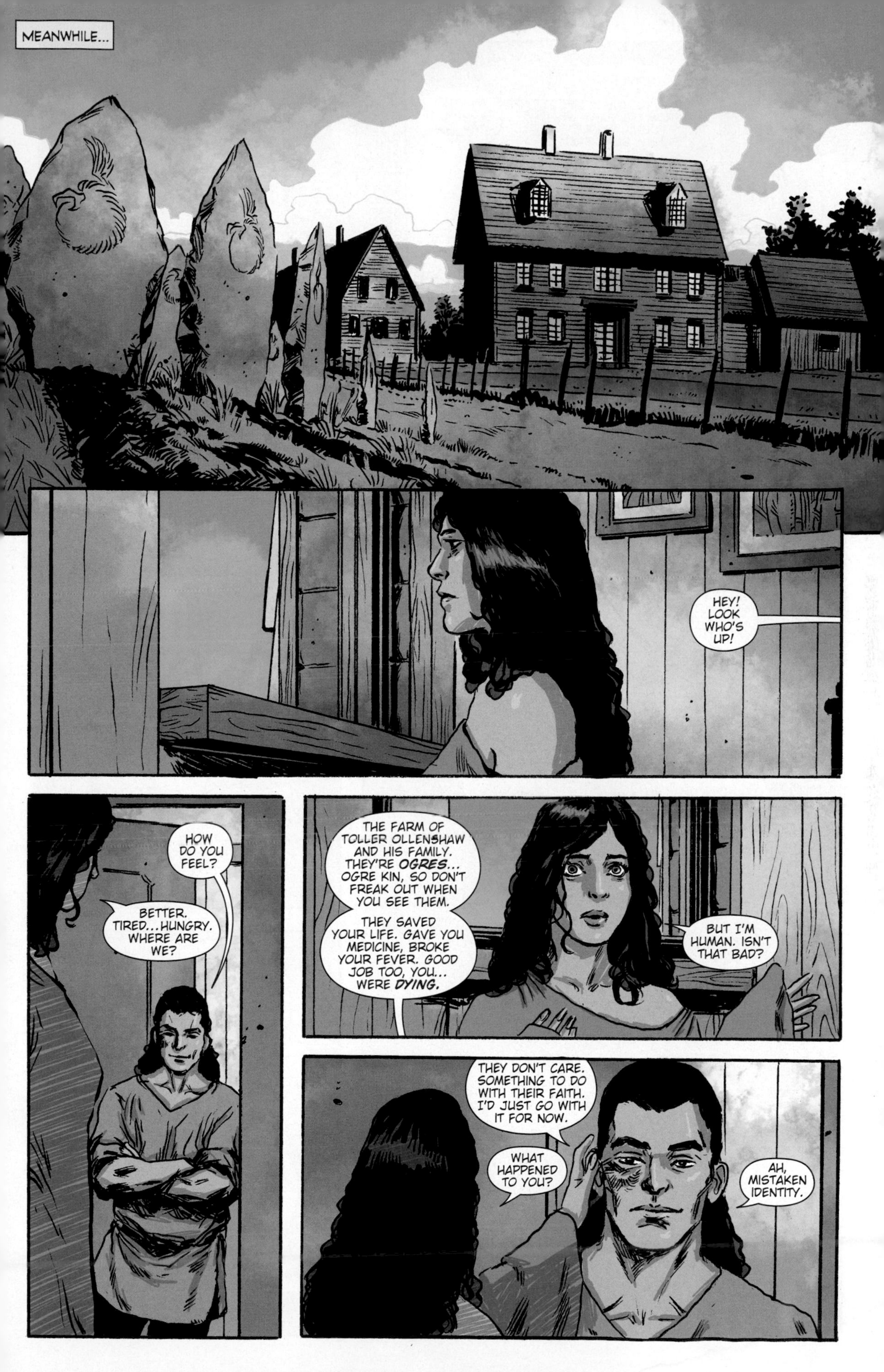
MEANWHILE...
HEY! LOOK WHO'S UP!
HOW DO YOU FEEL?
BETTER. TIRED... HUNGRY. WHERE ARE WE?
THE FARM OF TOLLER OLLENSHAW AND HIS FAMILY. THEY'RE OGRES... OGRE KIN, SO DON'T FREAK OUT WHEN YOU SEE THEM.
THEY SAVED YOUR LIFE. GAVE YOU MEDICINE, BROKE YOUR FEVER. GOOD JOB TOO, YOU... WERE DYING.
BUT I'M HUMAN. ISN'T THAT BAD?
THEY DON'T CARE. SOMETHING TO DO WITH THEIR FAITH. I'D JUST GO WITH IT FOR NOW.
WHAT HAPPENED TO YOU?
AH, MISTAKEN IDENTITY.

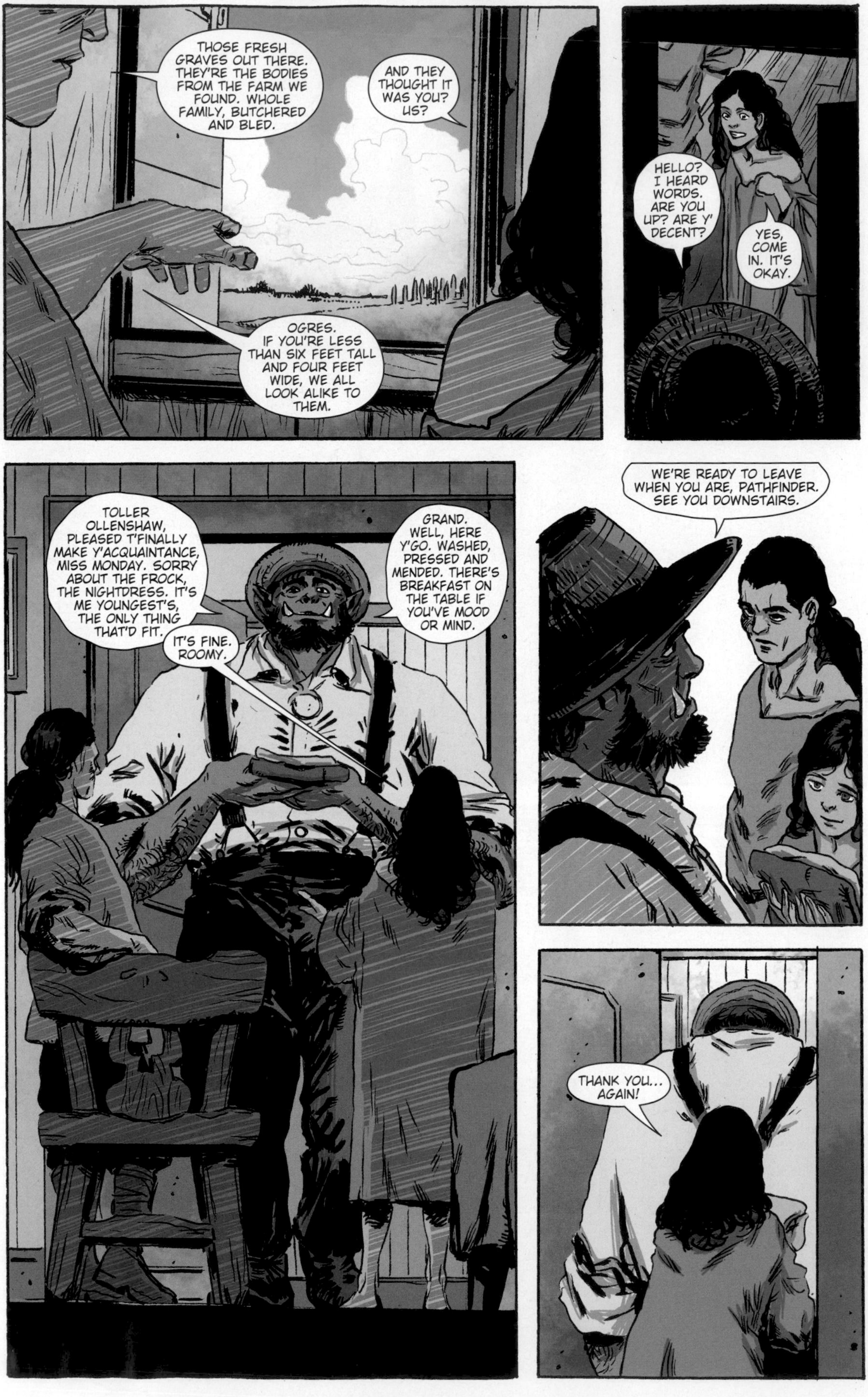
THOSE FRESH GRAVES OUT THERE. THEY'RE THE BODIES FROM THE FARM WE FOUND. WHOLE FAMILY, BUTCHERED AND BLED.
AND THEY THOUGHT IT WAS YOU? US?
OGRES. IF YOU'RE LESS THAN SIX FEET TALL AND FOUR FEET WIDE, WE ALL LOOK ALIKE TO THEM.
HELLO? I HEARD WORDS. ARE YOU UP? ARE Y' DECENT?
YES, COME IN. IT'S OKAY.
TOLLER OLLENSHAW, PLEASED T'FINALLY MAKE Y'ACQUAINTANCE, MISS MONDAY. SORRY ABOUT THE FROCK, THE NIGHTDRESS. IT'S ME YOUNGEST'S, THE ONLY THING THAT'D FIT.
IT'S FINE. ROOMY.
GRAND. WELL, HERE Y'GO. WASHED, PRESSED AND MENDED. THERE'S BREAKFAST ON THE TABLE IF YOU'VE MOOD OR MIND.
WE'RE READY TO LEAVE WHEN YOU ARE, PATHFINDER. SEE YOU DOWNSTAIRS.
THANK YOU... AGAIN!

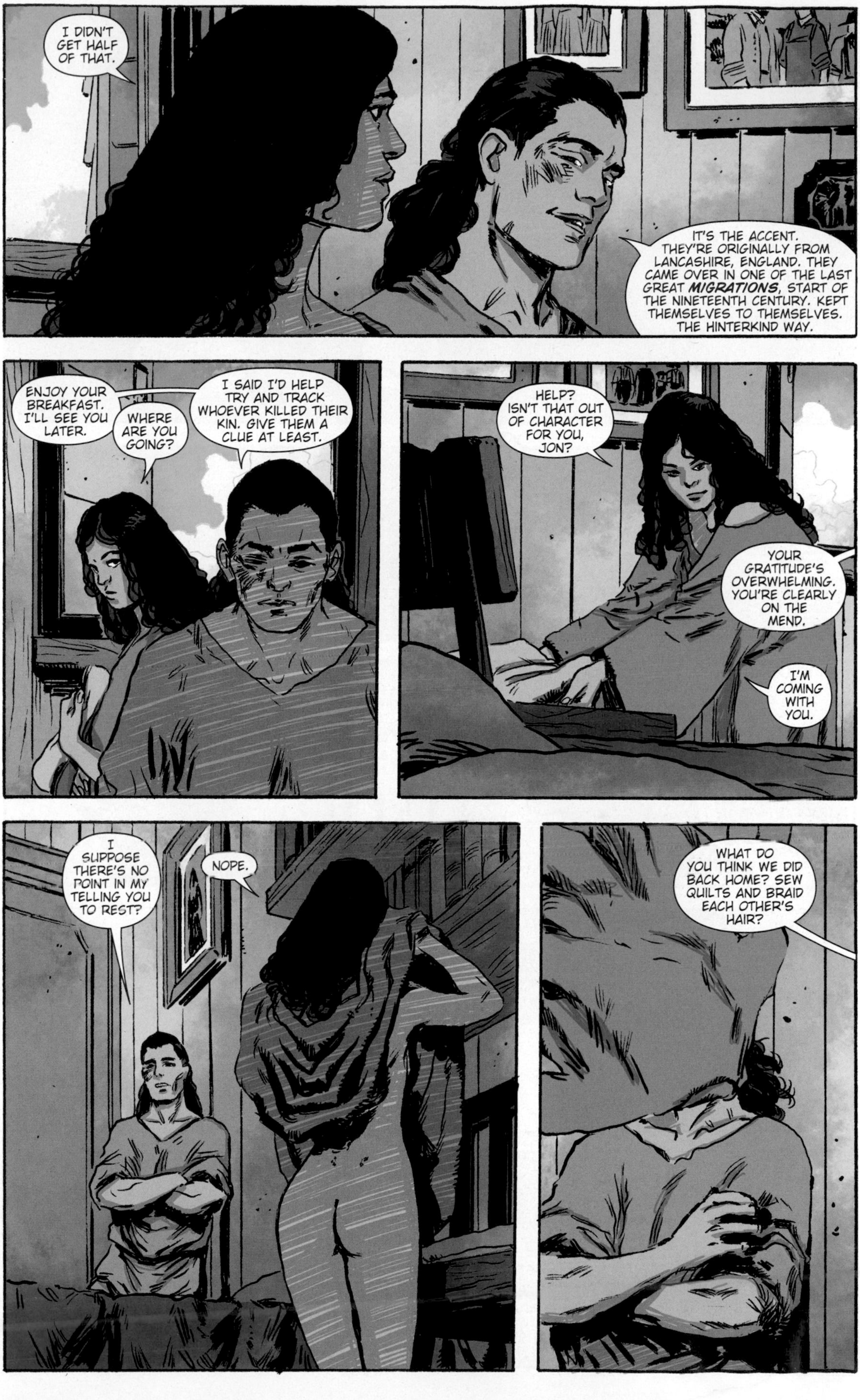
I DIDN'T GET HALF OF THAT.
IT'S THE ACCENT. THEY'RE ORIGINALLY FROM LANCASHIRE, ENGLAND. THEY CAME OVER IN ONE OF THE LAST GREAT MIGRATIONS, START OF THE NINETEENTH CENTURY. KEPT THEMSELVES TO THEMSELVES. THE HINTERKIND WAY.
ENJOY YOUR BREAKFAST. I'LL SEE YOU LATER.
WHERE ARE YOU GOING?
I SAID I'D HELP TRY AND TRACK WHOEVER KILLED THEIR KIN. GIVE THEM A CLUE AT LEAST.
HELP? ISN'T THAT OUT OF CHARACTER FOR YOU, JON?
YOUR GRATITUDE'S OVERWHELMING. YOU'RE CLEARLY ON THE MEND.
I'M COMING WITH YOU.
I SUPPOSE THERE'S NO POINT IN MY TELLING YOU TO REST?
NOPE.
WHAT DO YOU THINK WE DID BACK HOME? SEW QUILTS AND BRAID EACH OTHER'S HAIR?

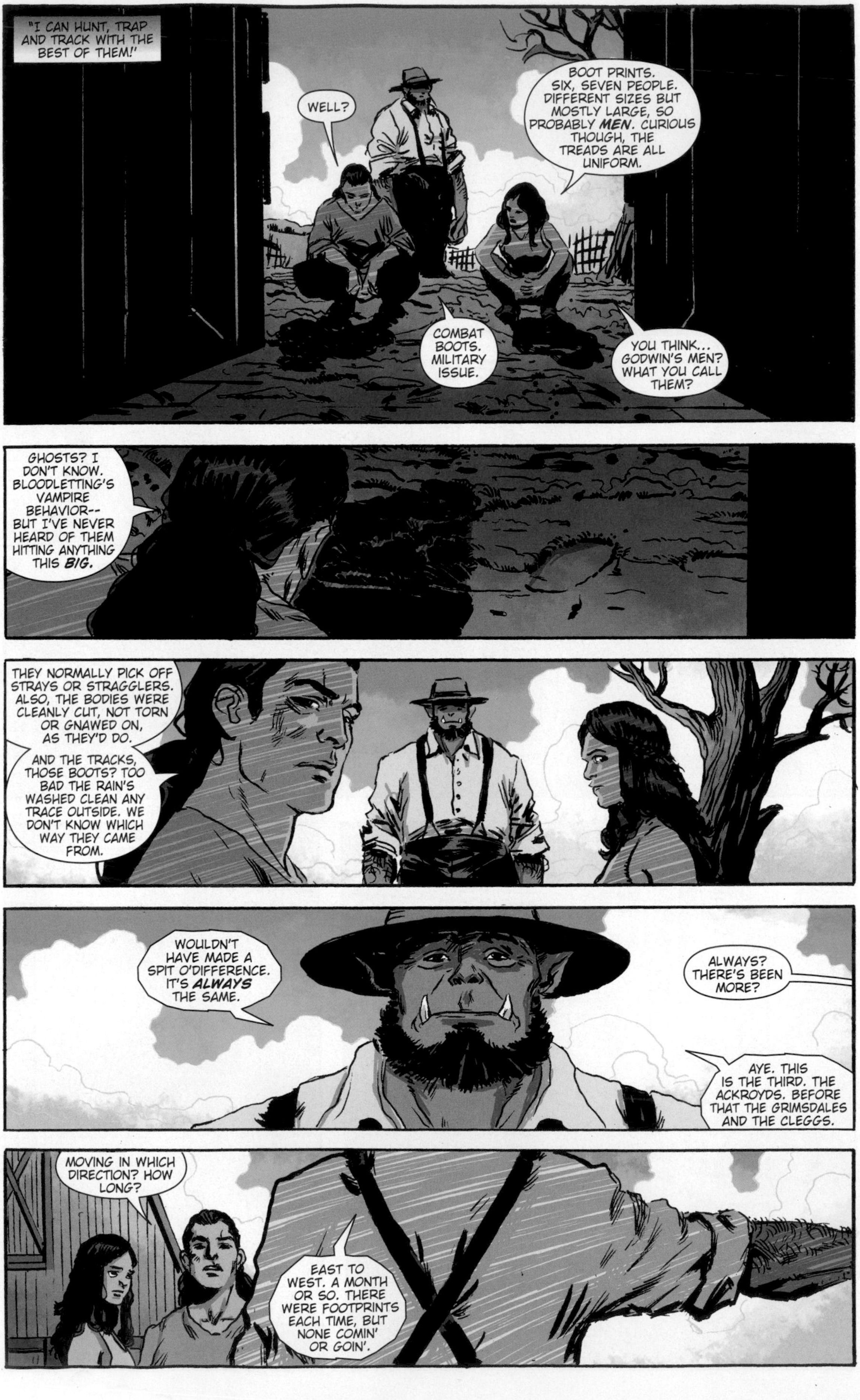
"I CAN HUNT, TRAP AND TRACK WITH THE BEST OF THEM!"
WELL?
BOOT PRINTS. SIX, SEVEN PEOPLE. DIFFERENT SIZES BUT MOSTLY LARGE, SO PROBABLY MEN. CURIOUS THOUGH, THE TREADS ARE ALL UNIFORM.
COMBAT BOOTS. MILITARY ISSUE.
YOU THINK... GODWIN'S MEN? WHAT YOU CALL THEM?
GHOSTS? I DON'T KNOW. BLOODLETTING'S VAMPIRE BEHAVIOR-- BUT I'VE NEVER HEARD OF THEM HITTING ANYTHING THIS BIG.
THEY NORMALLY PICK OFF STRAYS OR STRAGGLERS. ALSO, THE BODIES WERE CLEANLY CUT, NOT TORN OR GNAWED ON, AS THEY'D DO.
AND THE TRACKS, THOSE BOOTS? TOO BAD THE RAIN'S WASHED CLEAN ANY TRACE OUTSIDE. WE DON'T KNOW WHICH WAY THEY CAME FROM.
WOULDN'T HAVE MADE A SPIT O'DIFFERENCE. IT'S ALWAYS THE SAME.
ALWAYS? THERE'S BEEN MORE?
AYE. THIS IS THE THIRD. THE ACKROYDS. BEFORE THAT THE GRIMSDALES AND THE CLEGGS.
MOVING IN WHICH DIRECTION? HOW LONG?
EAST TO WEST. A MONTH OR SO. THERE WERE FOOTPRINTS EACH TIME, BUT NONE COMIN' OR GOIN'.

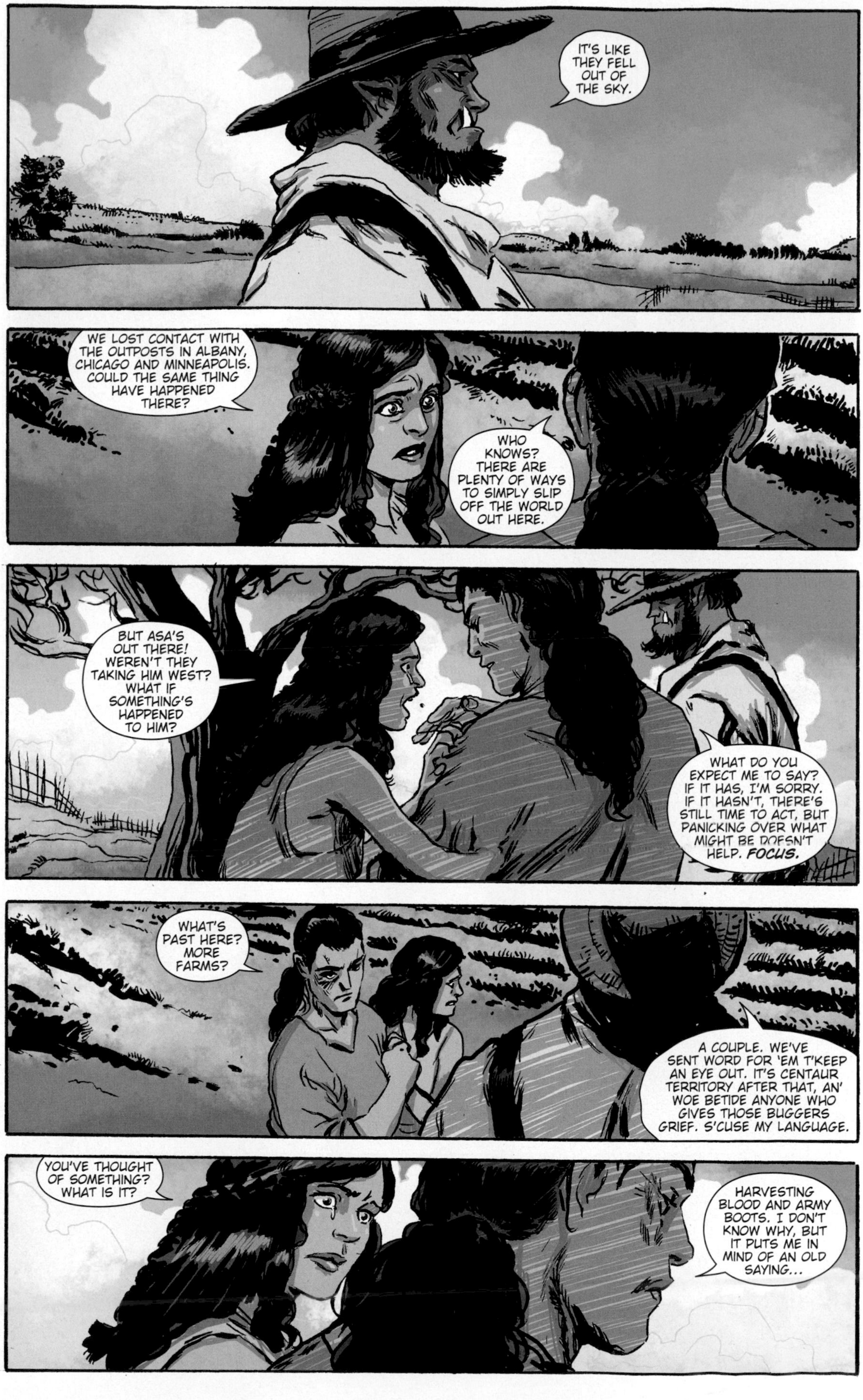
IT'S LIKE THEY FELL OUT OF THE SKY.
WE LOST CONTACT WITH THE OUTPOSTS IN ALBANY, CHICAGO AND MINNEAPOLIS. COULD THE SAME THING HAVE HAPPENED THERE?
WHO KNOWS? THERE ARE PLENTY OF WAYS TO SIMPLY SLIP OFF THE WORLD OUT HERE.
BUT ASA'S OUT THERE! WEREN'T THEY TAKING HIM WEST? WHAT IF SOMETHING'S HAPPENED TO HIM?
WHAT DO YOU EXPECT ME TO SAY? IF IT HAS, I'M SORRY. IF IT HASN'T, THERE'S STILL TIME TO ACT, BUT PANICKING OVER WHAT MIGHT BE DOESN'T HELP. FOCUS.
WHAT'S PAST HERE? MORE FARMS?
A COUPLE. WE'VE SENT WORD FOR 'EM T'KEEP AN EYE OUT. IT'S CENTAUR TERRITORY AFTER THAT, AN' WOE BETIDE ANYONE WHO GIVES THOSE BUGGERS GRIEF. S'CUSE MY LANGUAGE.
YOU'VE THOUGHT OF SOMETHING? WHAT IS IT?
HARVESTING BLOOD AND ARMY BOOTS. I DON'T KNOW WHY, BUT IT PUTS ME IN MIND OF AN OLD SAYING...

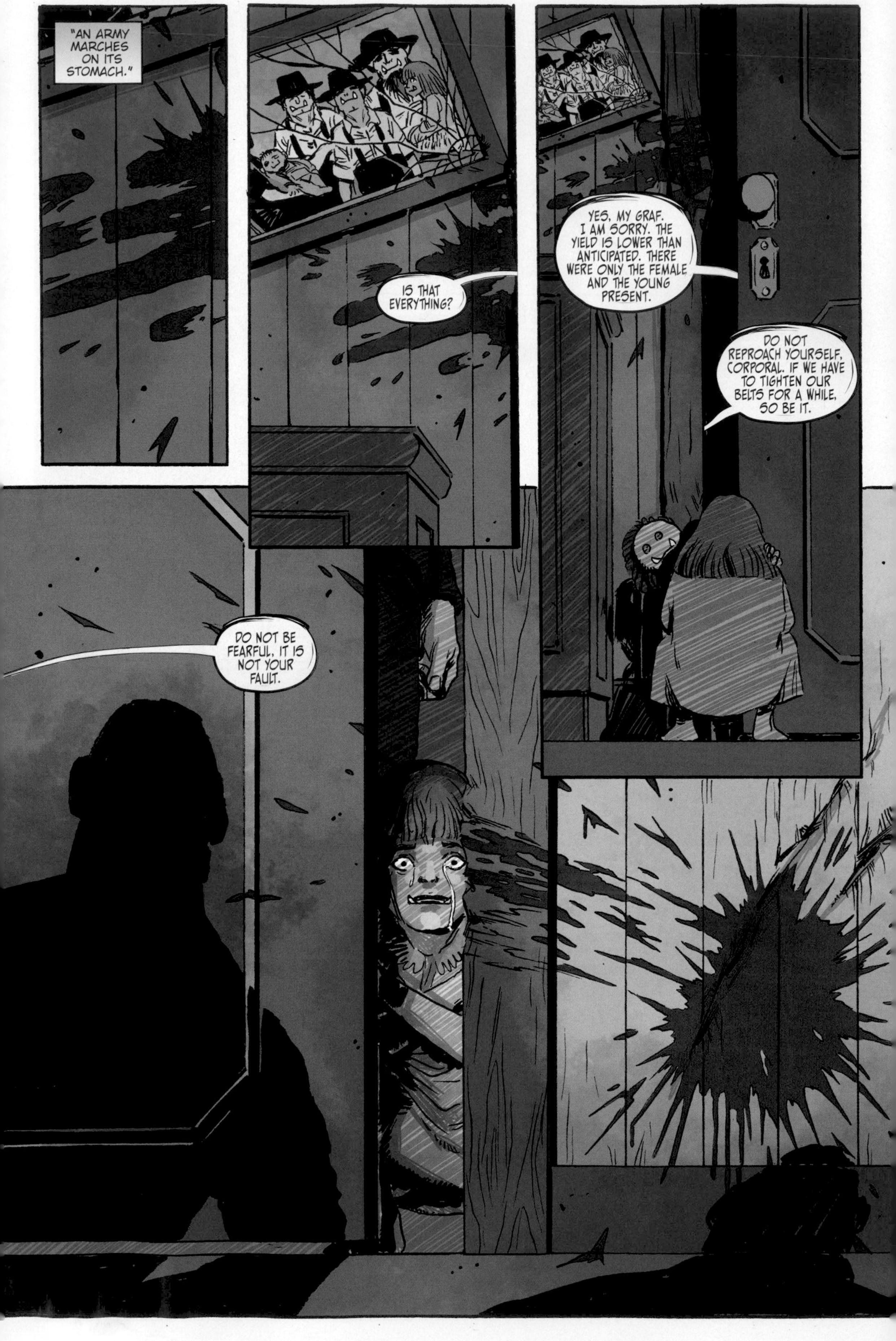
"AN ARMY MARCHES ON ITS STOMACH."
IS THAT EVERYTHING?
YES, MY GRAF. I AM SORRY. THE YIELD IS LOWER THAN ANTICIPATED. THERE WERE ONLY THE FEMALE AND THE YOUNG PRESENT.
DO NOT REPROACH YOURSELF, CORPORAL. IF WE HAVE TO TIGHTEN OUR BELTS FOR A WHILE, SO BE IT.
DO NOT BE FEARFUL, IT IS NOT YOUR FAULT.

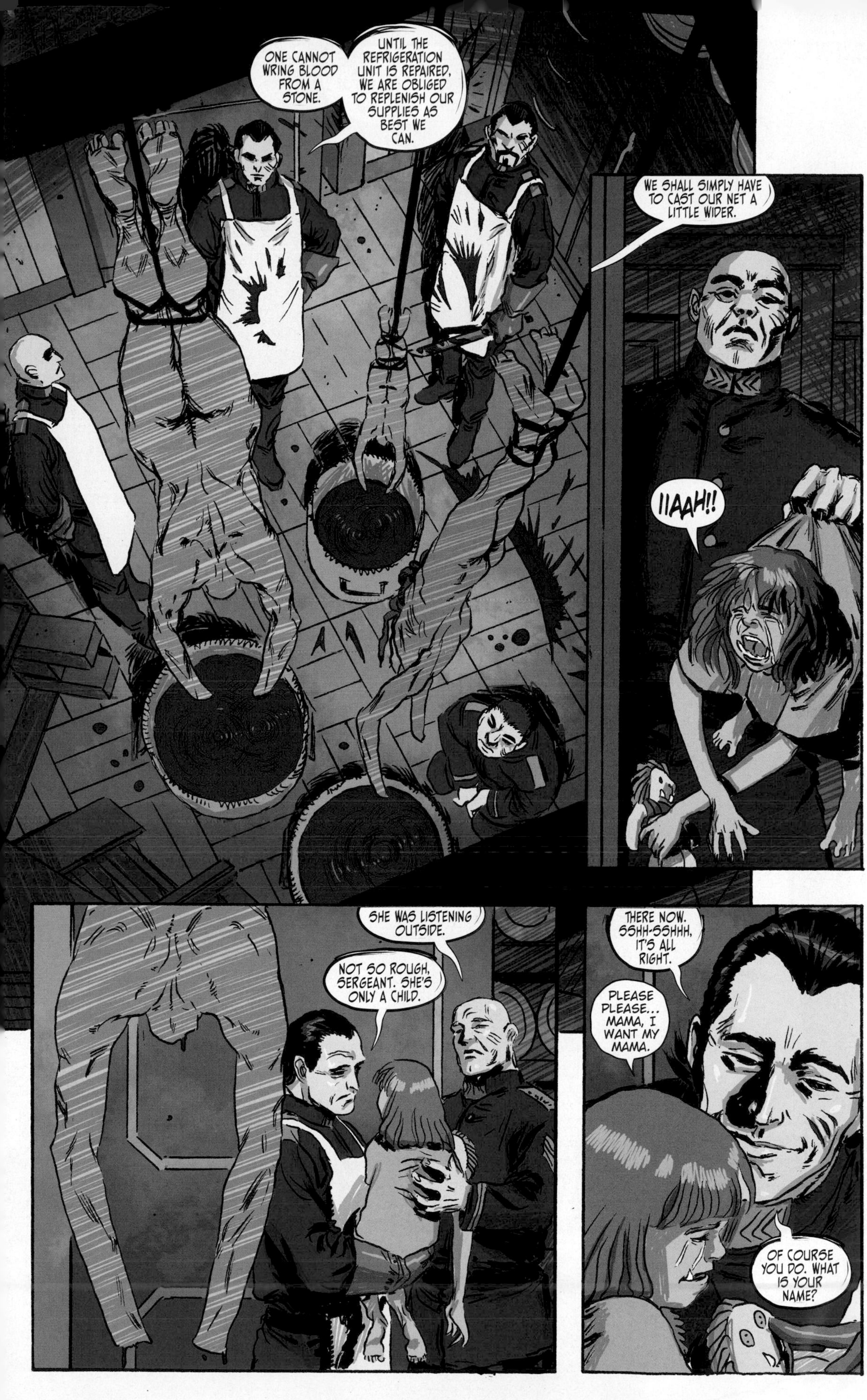
ONE CANNOT WRING BLOOD FROM A STONE.
UNTIL THE REFRIGERATION UNIT IS REPAIRED, WE ARE OBLIGED TO REPLENISH OUR SUPPLIES AS BEST WE CAN.
WE SHALL SIMPLY HAVE TO CAST OUR NET A LITTLE WIDER.
IIAAH!!
SHE WAS LISTENING OUTSIDE.
NOT SO ROUGH, SERGEANT. SHE'S ONLY A CHILD.
THERE NOW. SSHH-SSHHH, IT'S ALL RIGHT.
PLEASE PLEASE... MAMA, I WANT MY MAMA.
OF COURSE YOU DO. WHAT IS YOUR NAME?

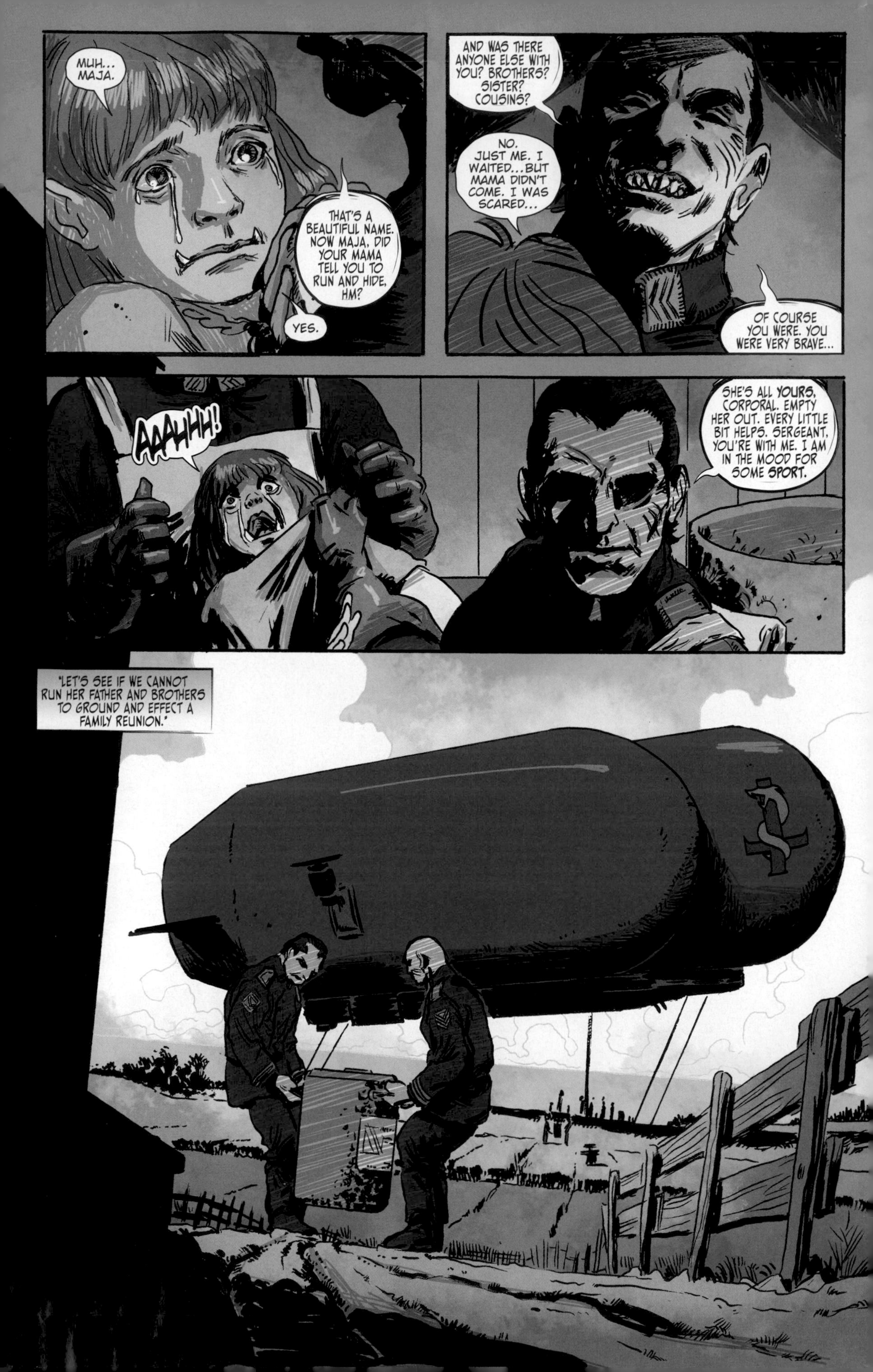
MUH... MAJA.
THAT'S A BEAUTIFUL NAME. NOW MAJA, DID YOUR MAMA TELL YOU TO RUN AND HIDE, HM?
YES.
AND WAS THERE ANYONE ELSE WITH YOU? BROTHERS? SISTER? COUSINS?
NO. JUST ME. I WAITED...BUT MAMA DIDN'T COME. I WAS SCARED...
OF COURSE YOU WERE. YOU WERE VERY BRAVE...
AAAHHH!
SHE'S ALL YOURS, CORPORAL. EMPTY HER OUT. EVERY LITTLE BIT HELPS. SERGEANT, YOU'RE WITH ME. I AM IN THE MOOD FOR SOME SPORT.
"LET'S SEE IF WE CANNOT RUN HER FATHER AND BROTHERS TO GROUND AND EFFECT A FAMILY REUNION."

CALIFORNIA.

"PURE BLOOD, MAJESTY, THAT IS THE KEY."

PURE BLOOD HEALS THE FASTEST AND YOUR FAMILY'S IS THE PUREST OF ALL. WHY, IN A FEW MONTHS, I DOUBT THERE WILL EVEN BE A BLEMISH TO SHOW FOR WHAT'S PASSED.

YOUR MOTHER SHRUGGED OFF HER WOUND IN A MATTER OF *WEEKS*, ALTHOUGH YOURS WAS CONSIDERABLY MORE TRAUMATIC.

I SHUDDER TO THINK THAT WE ALMOST LOST YOU.

YOUR CONCERN AND MINISTRATIONS ARE MUCH APPRECIATED, MAGISTER GRAYLE. HOWEVER, I HAVE QUESTIONS ON ANOTHER MATTER.

WHAT DO YOU KNOW OF *THE FORE-SIGHTERS*?

THAT, *UH*... IS A TITLE I'VE NOT HEARD IN AN AGE. HOW DID YOU COME BY IT, MAY I ASK?

IT BEHOOVES THE QUEEN-IN-WAITING TO ACQUAINT HERSELF WITH HER PEOPLE'S HISTORY, DOES IT NOT, NO MATTER HOW OBSCURE?

SO, GOOD MAGISTER, TELL ME WHAT YOU KNOW.

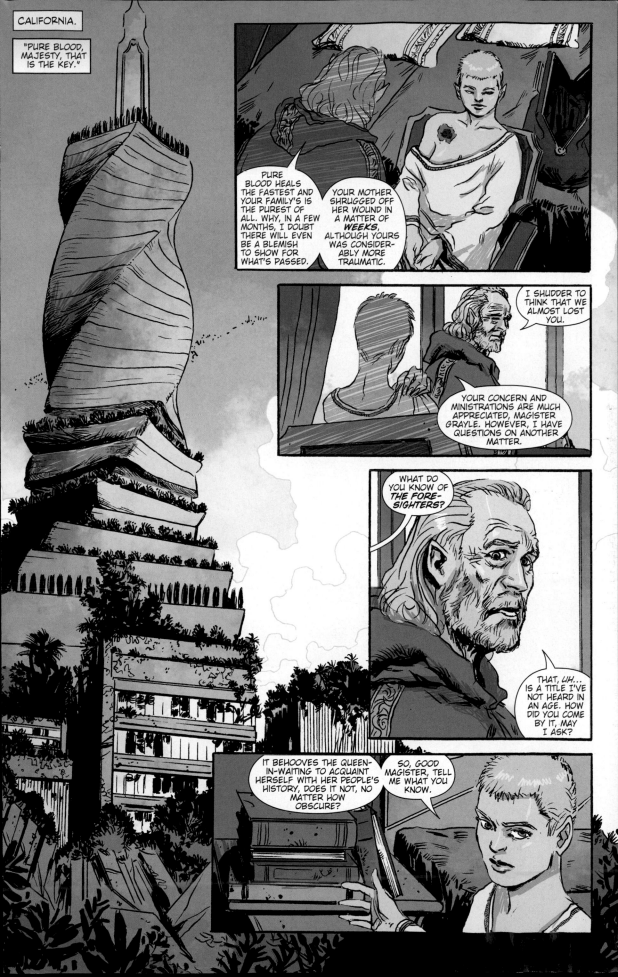

WELL, THE FIRST FORESIGHTERS WERE IN FACT THE MAGISTERS OF OLD...

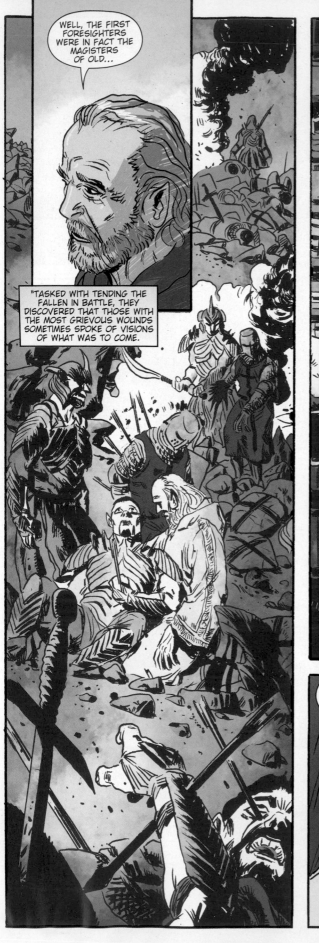

"TASKED WITH TENDING THE FALLEN IN BATTLE, THEY DISCOVERED THAT THOSE WITH THE MOST GRIEVOUS WOUNDS SOMETIMES SPOKE OF VISIONS OF WHAT WAS TO COME.

"NATURALLY, BEING SEEKERS AFTER TRUTH, THEY BEGAN TO EXPERIMENT. THEY FOUND THE GIFT WAS UNIQUE TO THE *SIDHE*, BUT ONLY SOME, NOT ALL.

"DRINKING MEASURED TEARS OF MORPHEUS, THEY PURPOSEFULLY WALKED UNDER THE SHADOW OF DEATH. BY SKIRTING THAT GREAT ETERNAL MYSTERY, THEY SOUGHT TO GLIMPSE INTO WHAT LAY BEYOND."

AREN'T THE TEARS OF MORPHEUS POISONOUS?

INDEED, AND MANY DIED. IT WAS A PERILOUS PROCESS. SO MUCH SO, IN THE THIRD AGE, THE BLIND QUEEN SORCHA PROHIBITED THE PRACTICE ALTOGETHER.

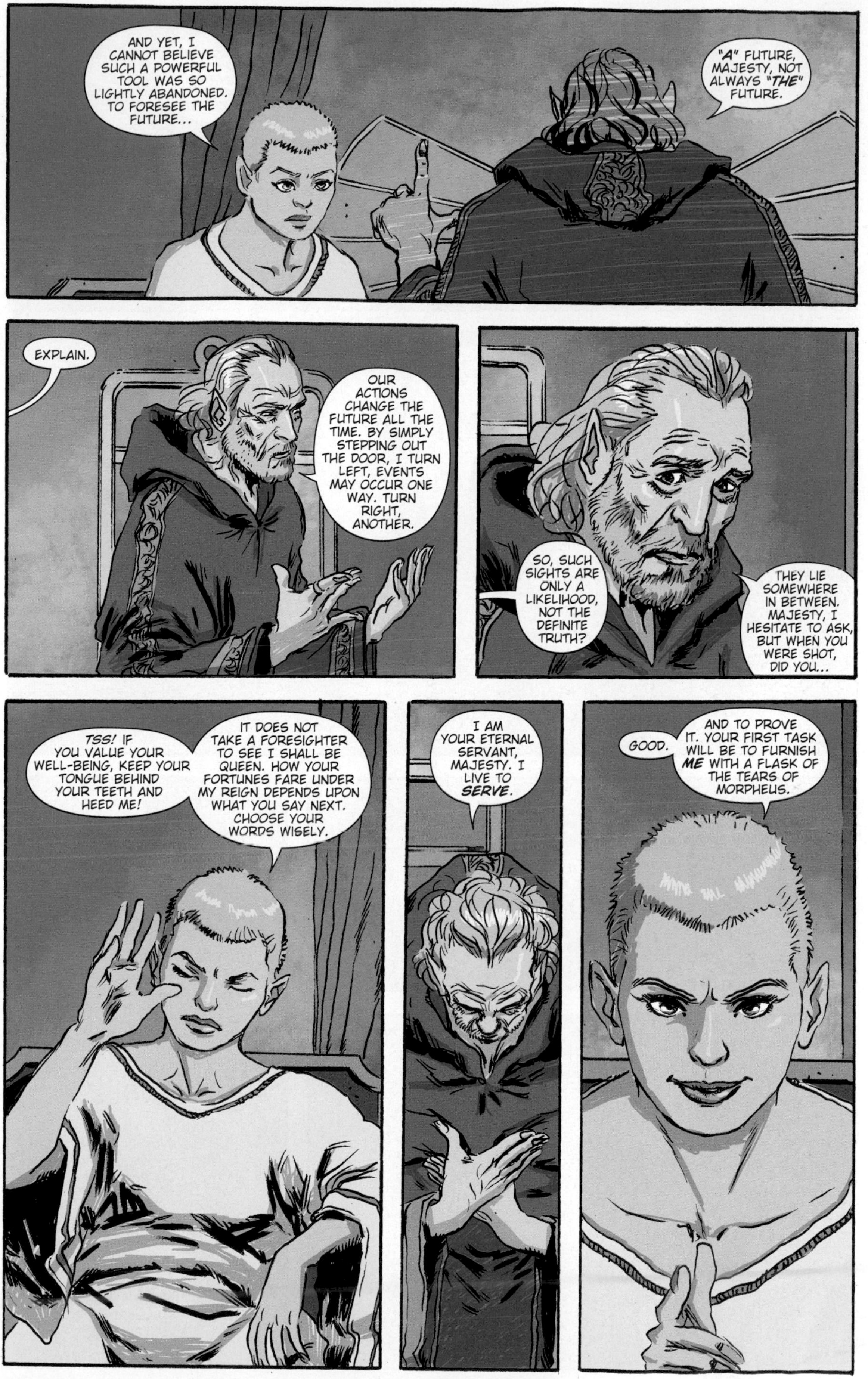
AND YET, I CANNOT BELIEVE SUCH A POWERFUL TOOL WAS SO LIGHTLY ABANDONED. TO FORESEE THE FUTURE...
"A" FUTURE, MAJESTY, NOT ALWAYS "THE" FUTURE.
EXPLAIN.
OUR ACTIONS CHANGE THE FUTURE ALL THE TIME. BY SIMPLY STEPPING OUT THE DOOR, I TURN LEFT, EVENTS MAY OCCUR ONE WAY. TURN RIGHT, ANOTHER.
SO, SUCH SIGHTS ARE ONLY A LIKELIHOOD, NOT THE DEFINITE TRUTH?
THEY LIE SOMEWHERE IN BETWEEN. MAJESTY, I HESITATE TO ASK, BUT WHEN YOU WERE SHOT, DID YOU...
TSS! IF YOU VALUE YOUR WELL-BEING, KEEP YOUR TONGUE BEHIND YOUR TEETH AND HEED ME!
IT DOES NOT TAKE A FORESIGHTER TO SEE I SHALL BE QUEEN. HOW YOUR FORTUNES FARE UNDER MY REIGN DEPENDS UPON WHAT YOU SAY NEXT. CHOOSE YOUR WORDS WISELY.
I AM YOUR ETERNAL SERVANT, MAJESTY. I LIVE TO SERVE.
GOOD.
AND TO PROVE IT. YOUR FIRST TASK WILL BE TO FURNISH ME WITH A FLASK OF THE TEARS OF MORPHEUS.

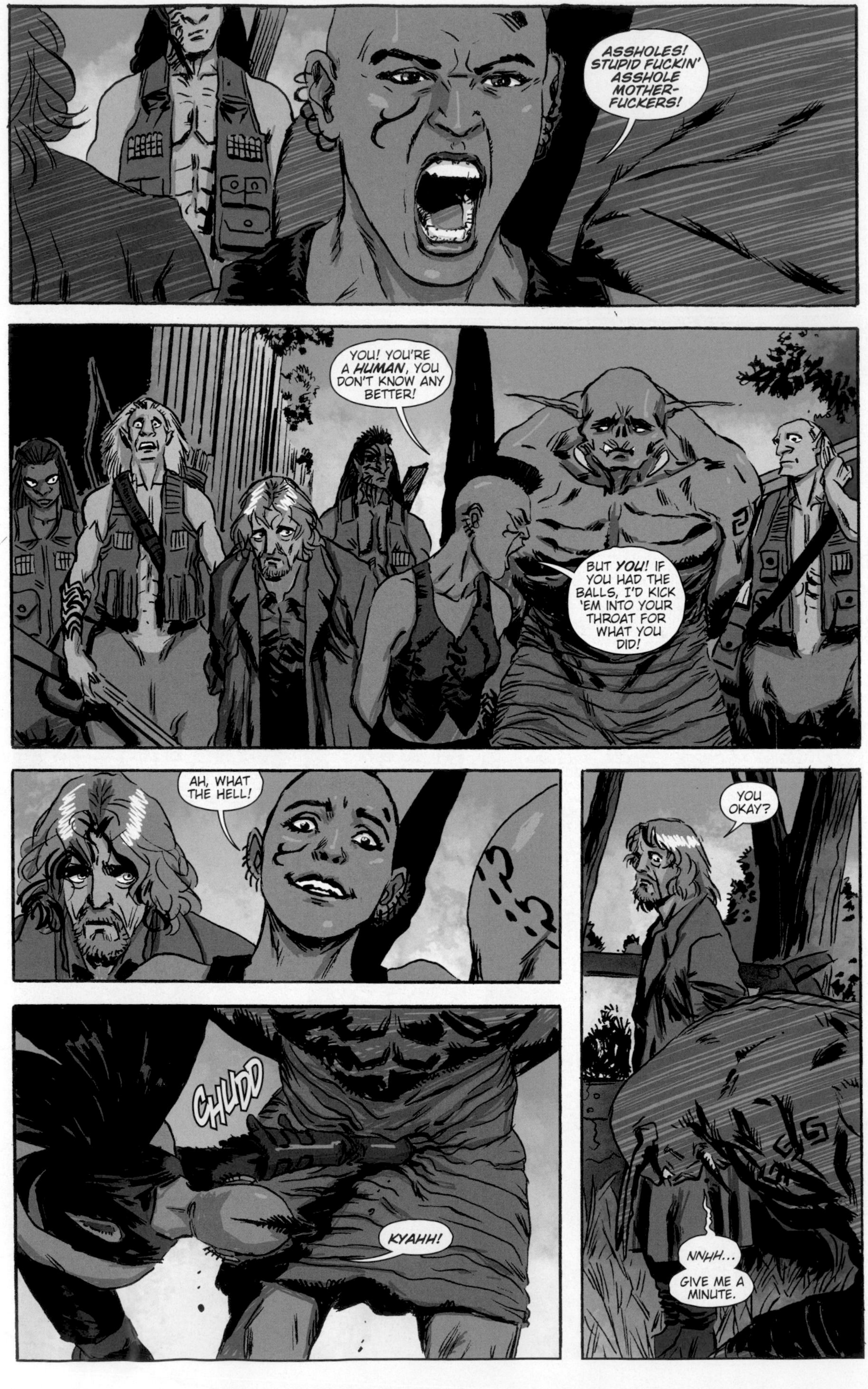
ASSHOLES! STUPID FUCKIN' ASSHOLE MOTHER-FUCKERS!
YOU! YOU'RE A **HUMAN**, YOU DON'T KNOW ANY BETTER!
BUT **YOU**! IF YOU HAD THE BALLS, I'D KICK 'EM INTO YOUR THROAT FOR WHAT YOU DID!
AH, WHAT THE HELL!
CHUDD
KYAHH!
YOU OKAY?
NNHH...
GIVE ME A MINUTE.

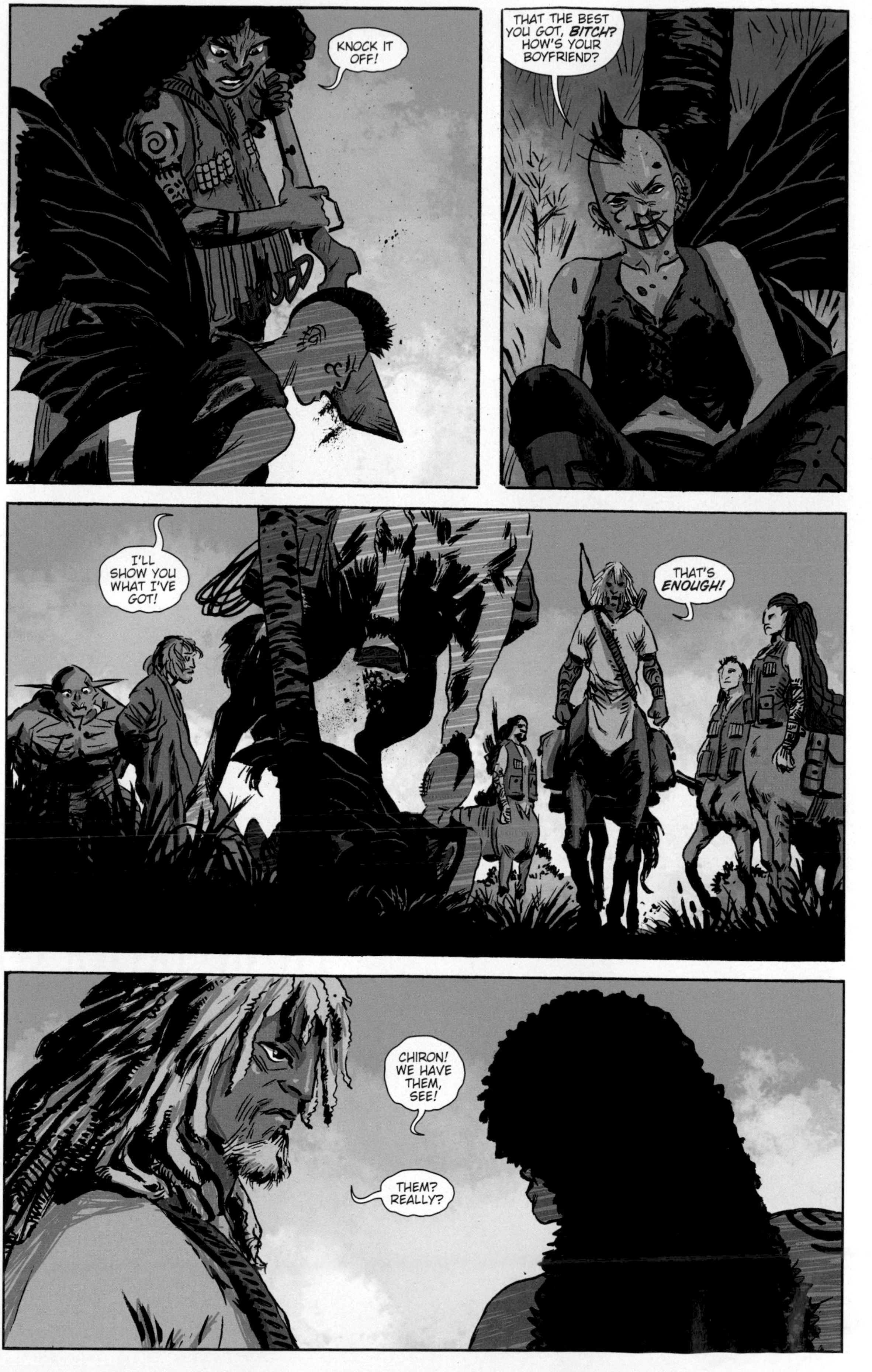
KNOCK IT OFF!
WHUDD
THAT THE BEST YOU GOT, *BITCH?* HOW'S YOUR BOYFRIEND?
I'LL SHOW YOU WHAT I'VE GOT!
THAT'S *ENOUGH!*
CHIRON! WE HAVE THEM, SEE!
THEM? REALLY?

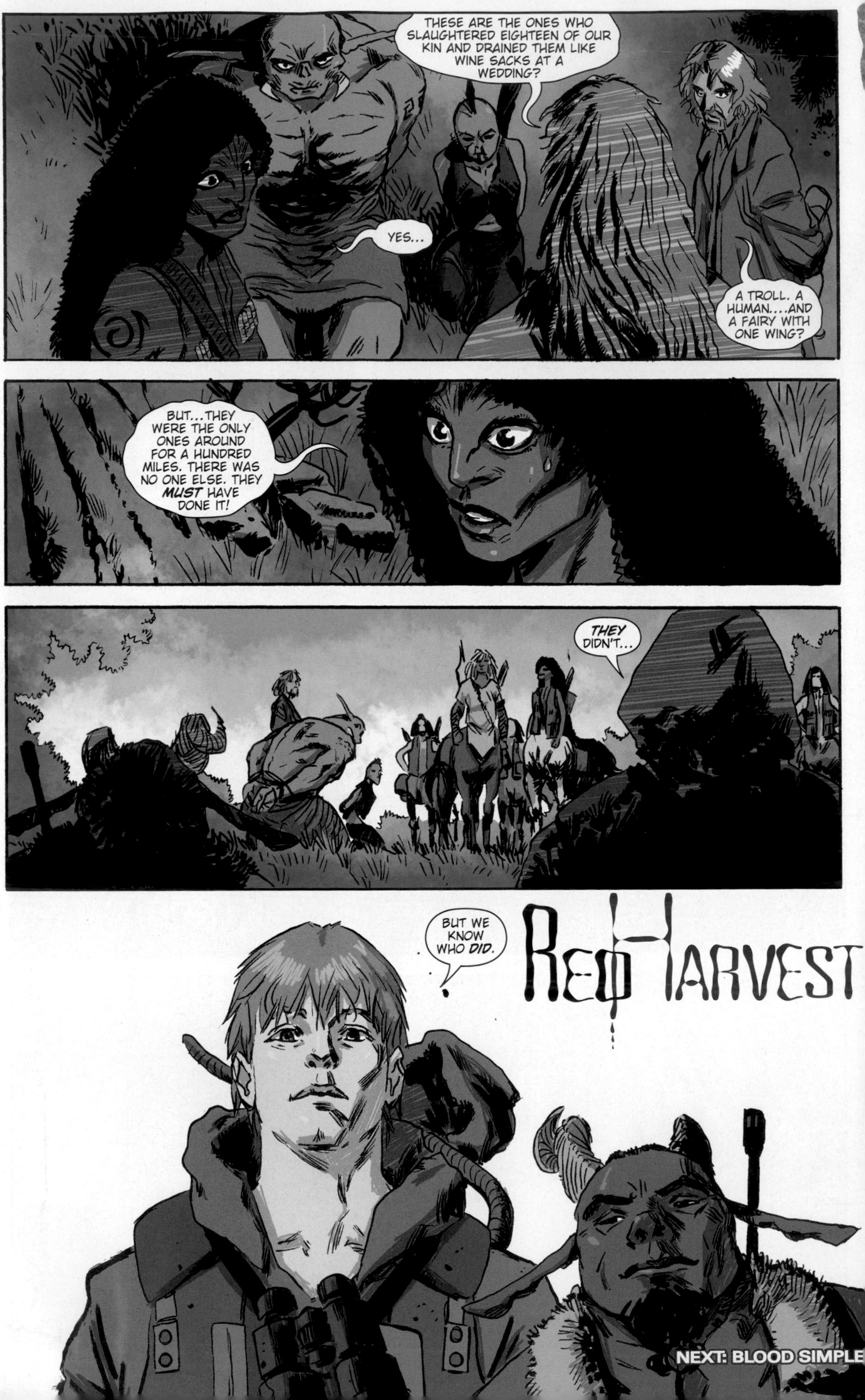
THESE ARE THE ONES WHO SLAUGHTERED EIGHTEEN OF OUR KIN AND DRAINED THEM LIKE WINE SACKS AT A WEDDING?
YES...
A TROLL. A HUMAN....AND A FAIRY WITH ONE WING?
BUT...THEY WERE THE ONLY ONES AROUND FOR A HUNDRED MILES. THERE WAS NO ONE ELSE. THEY MUST HAVE DONE IT!
THEY DIDN'T...
BUT WE KNOW WHO DID.
RED HARVEST
NEXT: BLOOD SIMPLE

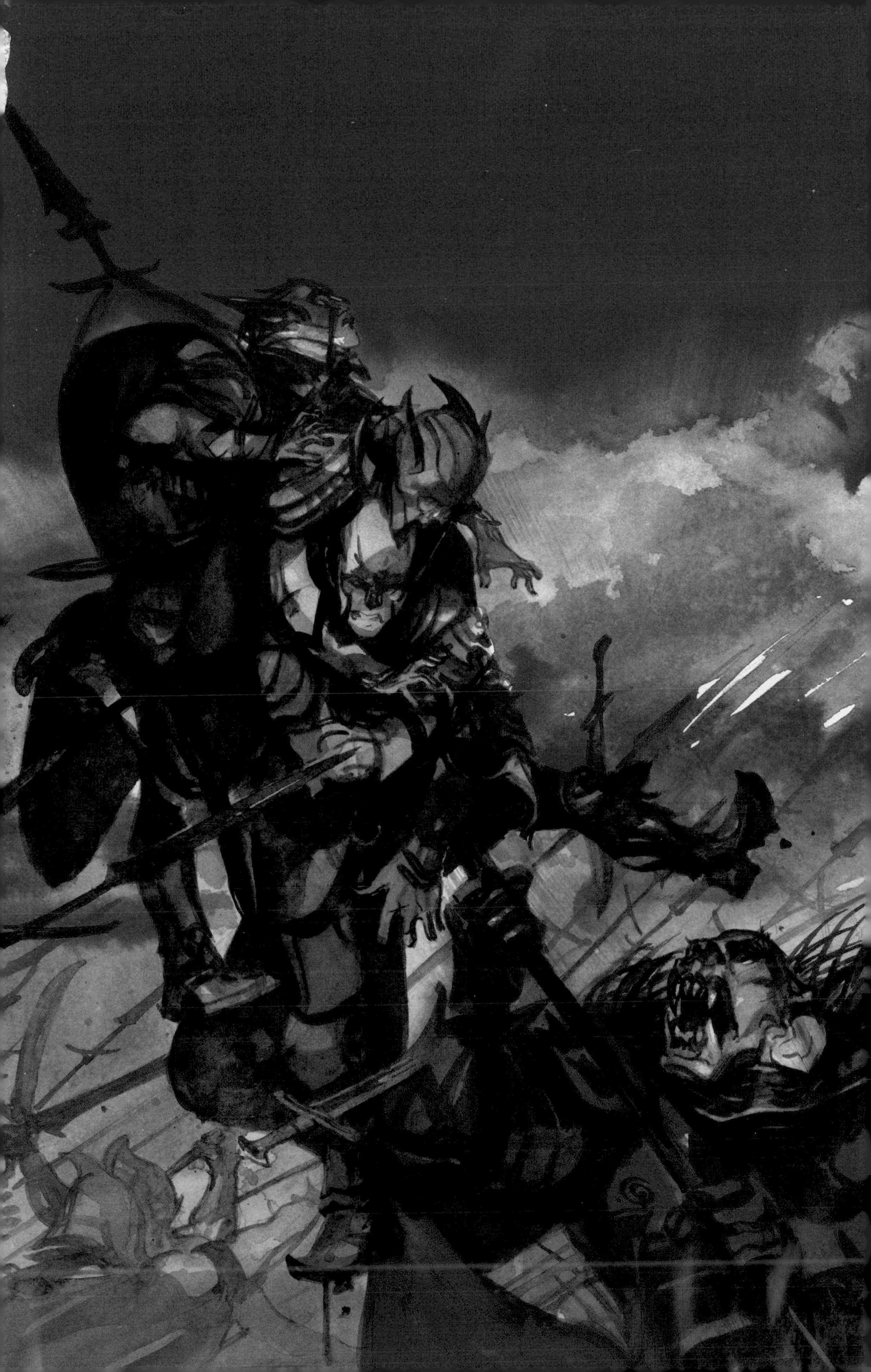

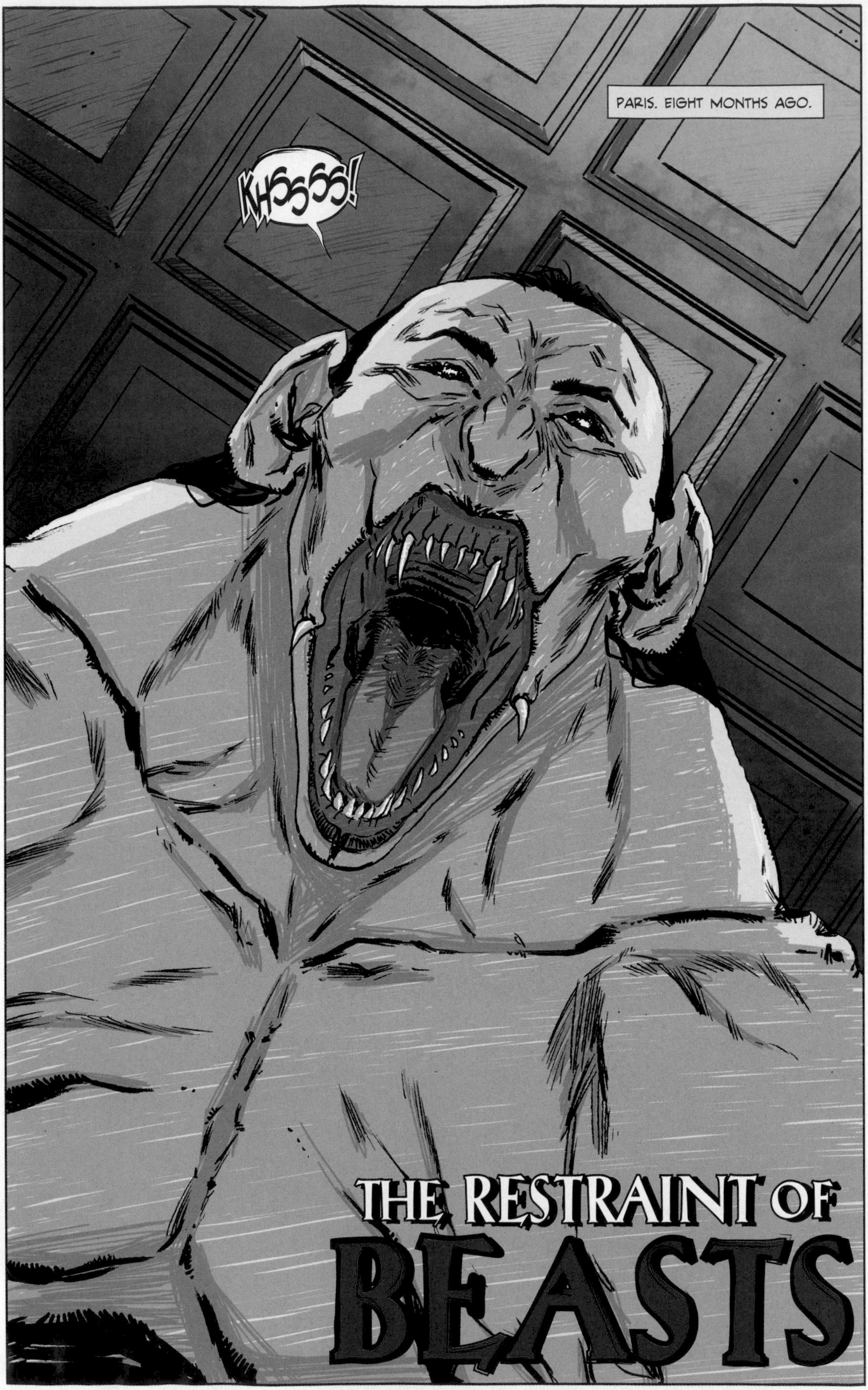
PARIS. EIGHT MONTHS AGO.
KHSSSS!
THE RESTRAINT OF
BEASTS

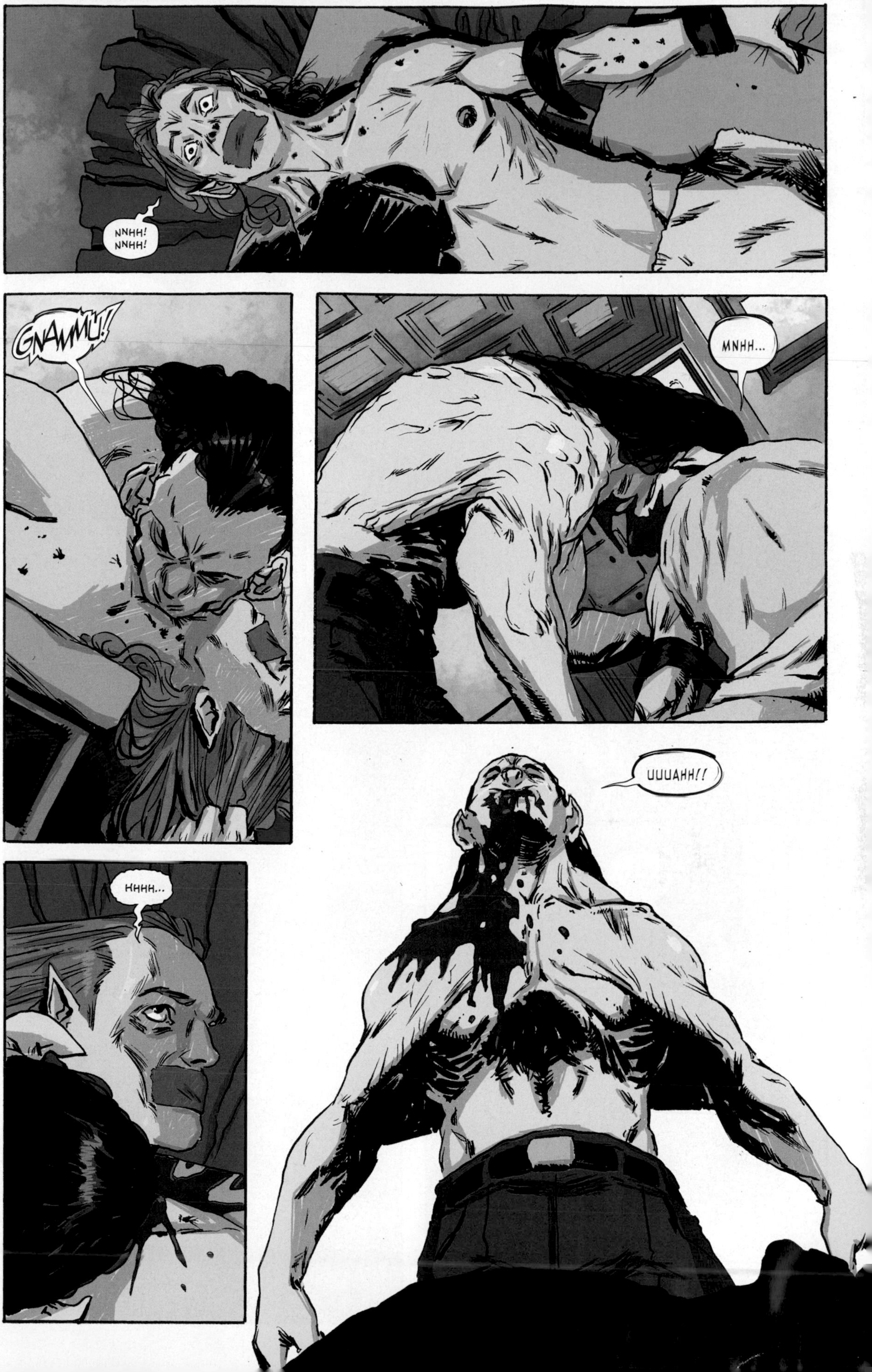
NNHH!
NNHH!
GNAMMU!!
MNHH...
HHHH...
UUUAHH!!

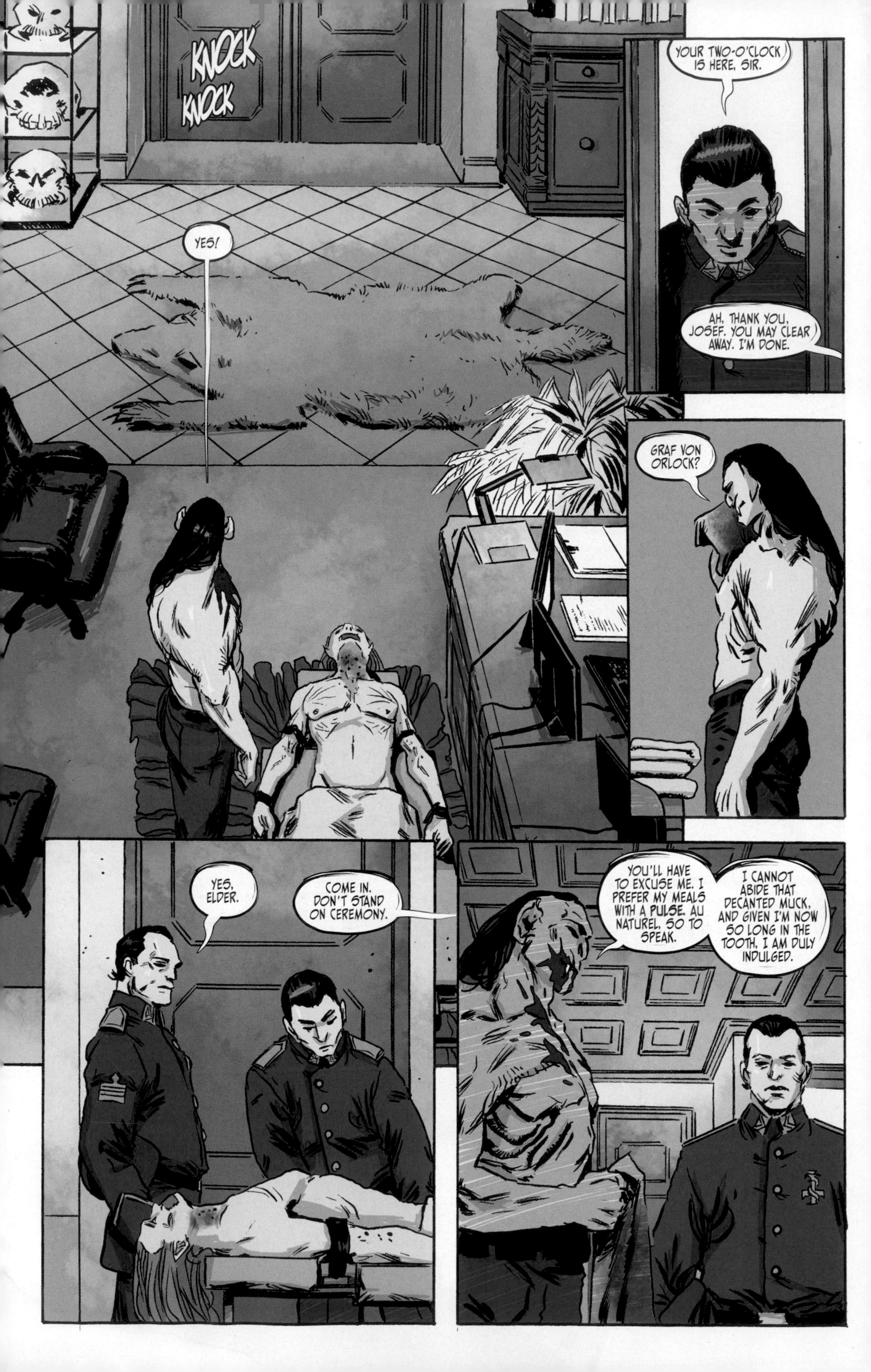
KNOCK KNOCK
YOUR TWO-O'CLOCK IS HERE, SIR.
AH, THANK YOU, JOSEF. YOU MAY CLEAR AWAY. I'M DONE.
YES!
GRAF VON ORLOCK?
YES, ELDER.
COME IN. DON'T STAND ON CEREMONY.
YOU'LL HAVE TO EXCUSE ME. I PREFER MY MEALS WITH A PULSE. AU NATUREL, SO TO SPEAK.
I CANNOT ABIDE THAT DECANTED MUCK, AND GIVEN I'M NOW SO LONG IN THE TOOTH, I AM DULY INDULGED.

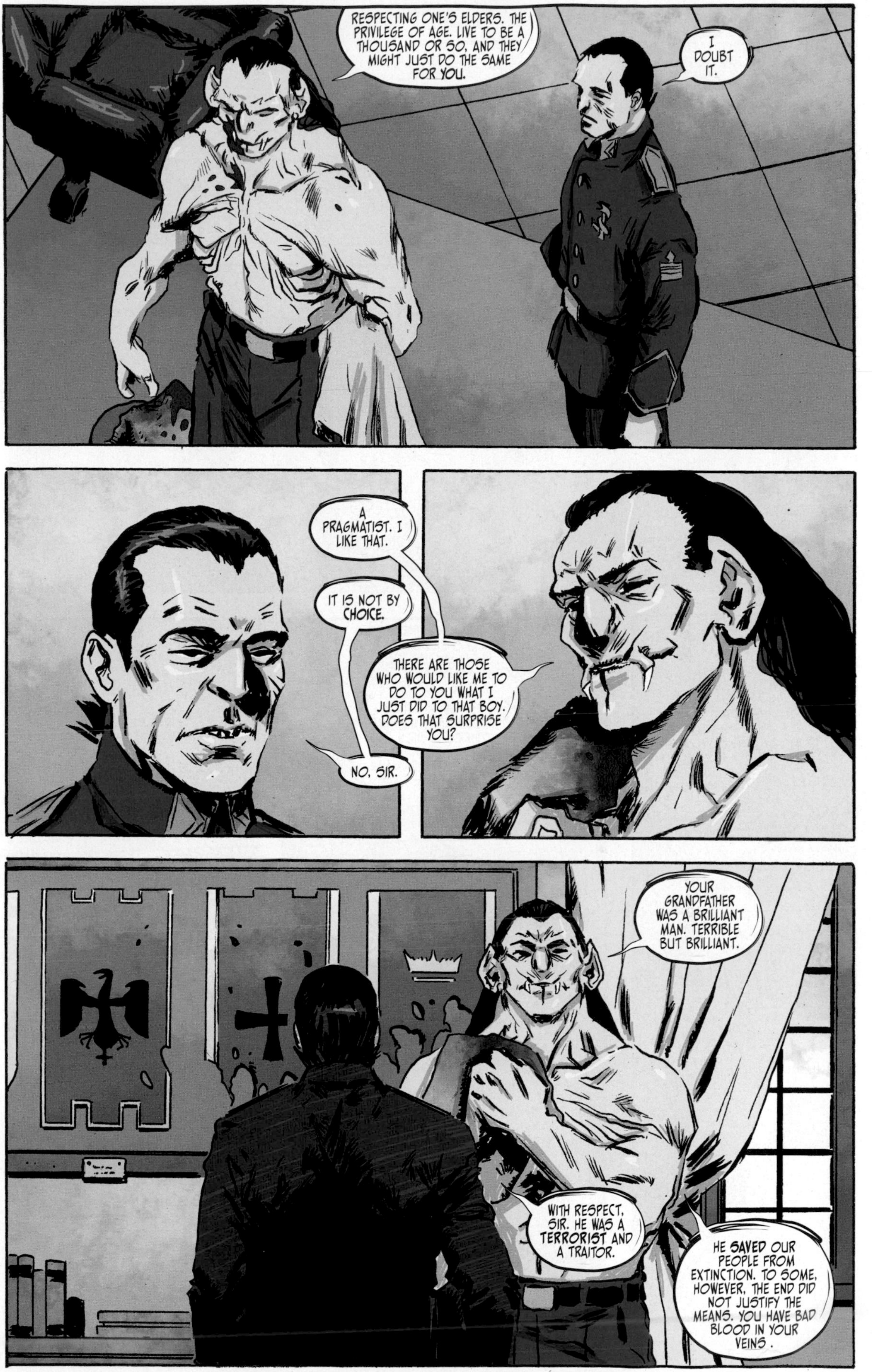
RESPECTING ONE'S ELDERS. THE PRIVILEGE OF AGE. LIVE TO BE A THOUSAND OR SO, AND THEY MIGHT JUST DO THE SAME FOR YOU.
I DOUBT IT.
A PRAGMATIST. I LIKE THAT.
IT IS NOT BY CHOICE.
THERE ARE THOSE WHO WOULD LIKE ME TO DO TO YOU WHAT I JUST DID TO THAT BOY. DOES THAT SURPRISE YOU?
NO, SIR.
YOUR GRANDFATHER WAS A BRILLIANT MAN. TERRIBLE BUT BRILLIANT.
WITH RESPECT, SIR. HE WAS A TERRORIST AND A TRAITOR.
HE SAVED OUR PEOPLE FROM EXTINCTION. TO SOME, HOWEVER, THE END DID NOT JUSTIFY THE MEANS. YOU HAVE BAD BLOOD IN YOUR VEINS.

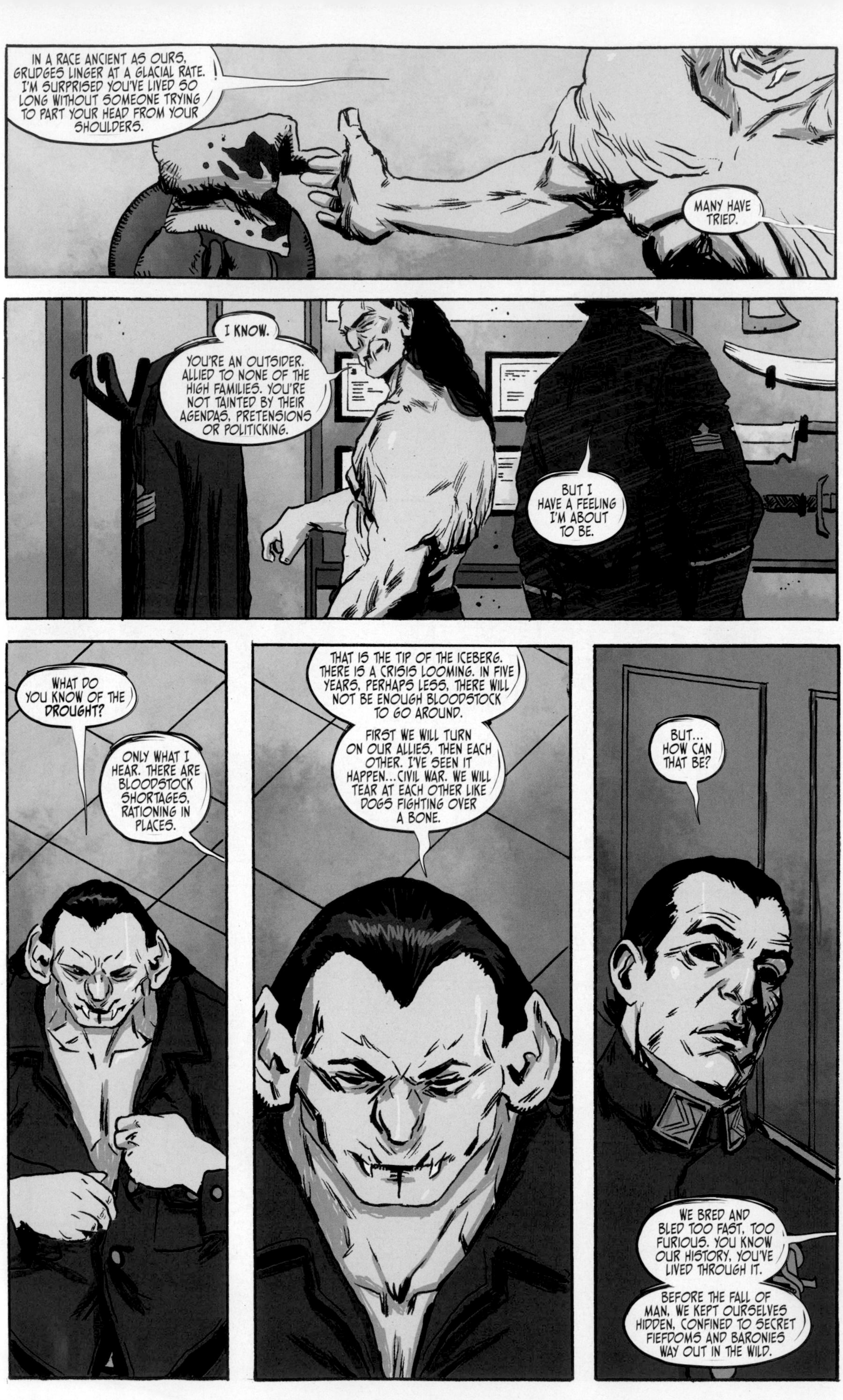
IN A RACE ANCIENT AS OURS, GRUDGES LINGER AT A GLACIAL RATE. I'M SURPRISED YOU'VE LIVED SO LONG WITHOUT SOMEONE TRYING TO PART YOUR HEAD FROM YOUR SHOULDERS.
MANY HAVE TRIED.
I KNOW.
YOU'RE AN OUTSIDER. ALLIED TO NONE OF THE HIGH FAMILIES. YOU'RE NOT TAINTED BY THEIR AGENDAS, PRETENSIONS OR POLITICKING.
BUT I HAVE A FEELING I'M ABOUT TO BE.
WHAT DO YOU KNOW OF THE DROUGHT?
ONLY WHAT I HEAR. THERE ARE BLOODSTOCK SHORTAGES, RATIONING IN PLACES.
THAT IS THE TIP OF THE ICEBERG. THERE IS A CRISIS LOOMING. IN FIVE YEARS, PERHAPS LESS, THERE WILL NOT BE ENOUGH BLOODSTOCK TO GO AROUND.
FIRST WE WILL TURN ON OUR ALLIES, THEN EACH OTHER. I'VE SEEN IT HAPPEN...CIVIL WAR. WE WILL TEAR AT EACH OTHER LIKE DOGS FIGHTING OVER A BONE.
BUT... HOW CAN THAT BE?
WE BRED AND BLED TOO FAST, TOO FURIOUS. YOU KNOW OUR HISTORY, YOU'VE LIVED THROUGH IT.
BEFORE THE FALL OF MAN, WE KEPT OURSELVES HIDDEN, CONFINED TO SECRET FIEFDOMS AND BARONIES WAY OUT IN THE WILD.

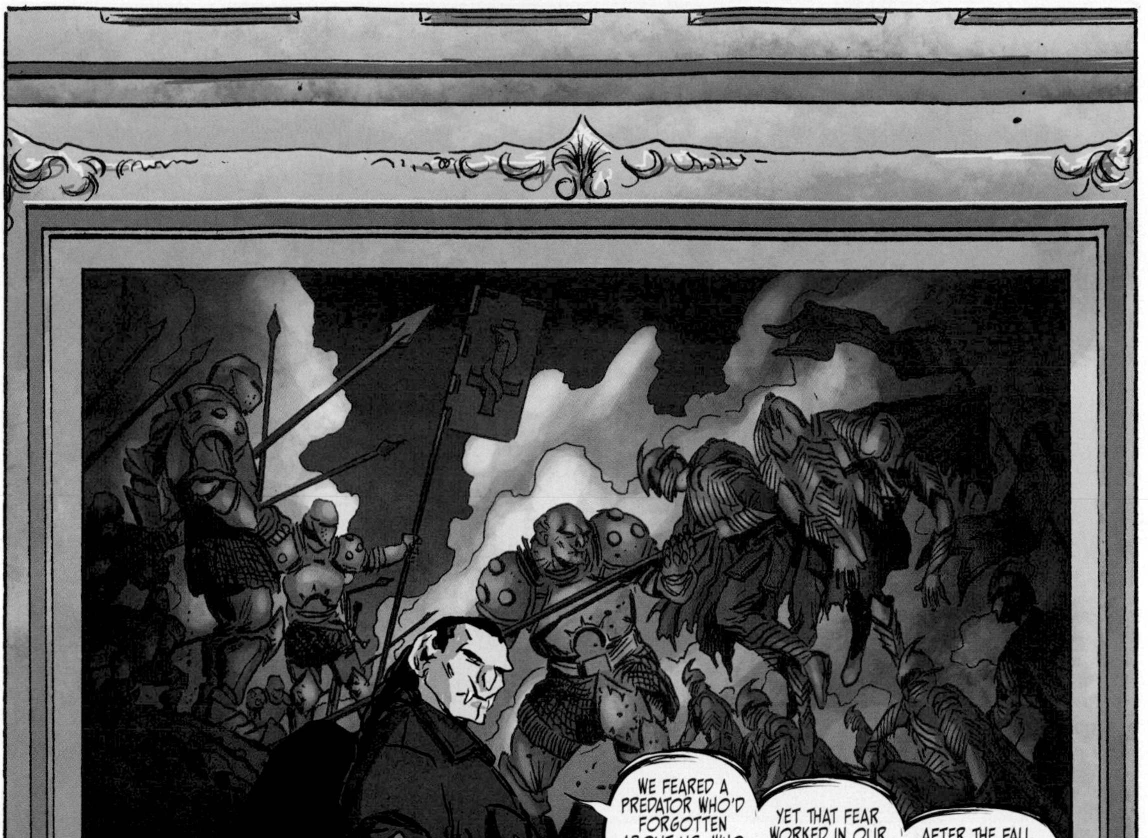
WE FEARED A PREDATOR WHO'D FORGOTTEN ABOUT US. WHO CONSIGNED US TO FICTION AND FILM.
YET THAT FEAR WORKED IN OUR FAVOR. IT KEPT US SPARE, SHARP AND WATCHFUL.
AFTER THE FALL, THE SIDHE SOUGHT TO FILL THE VACUUM...

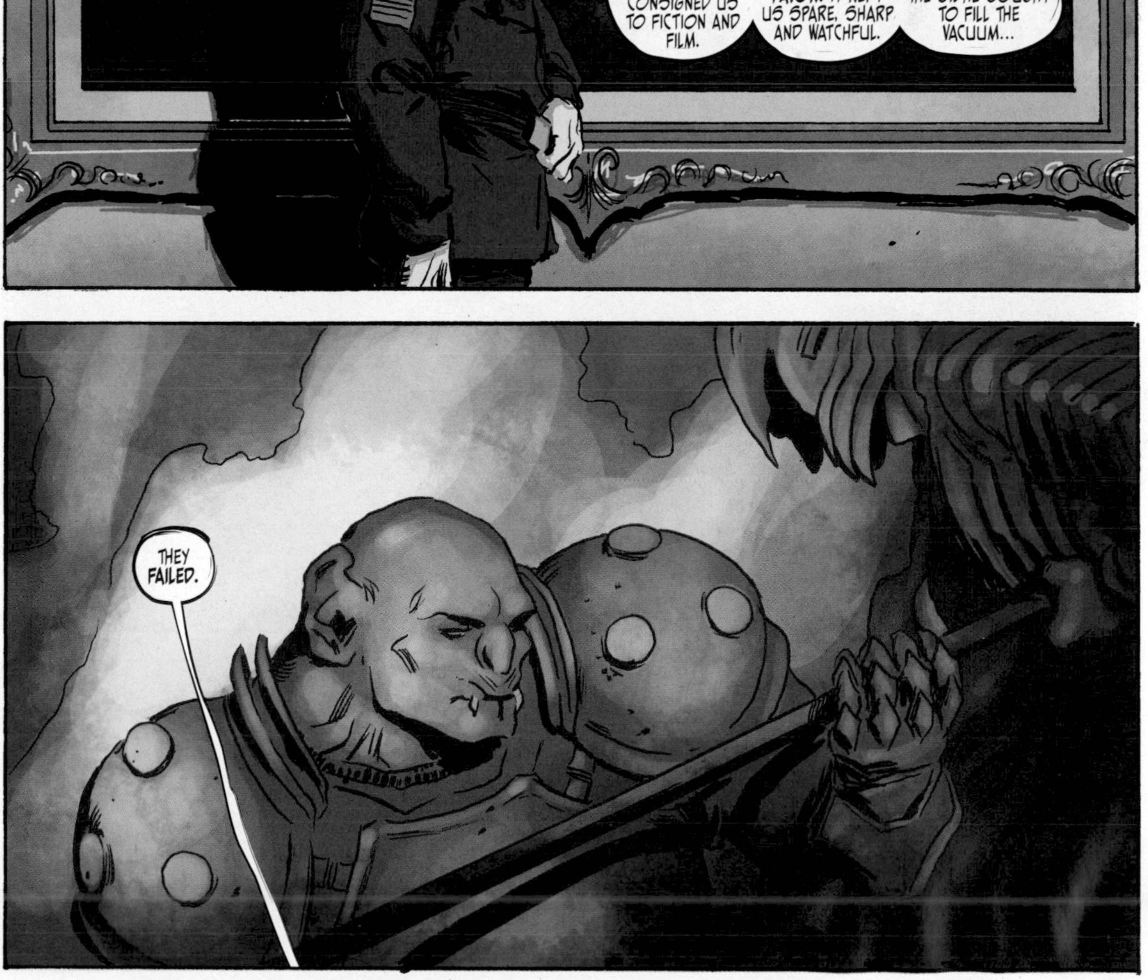
THEY FAILED.

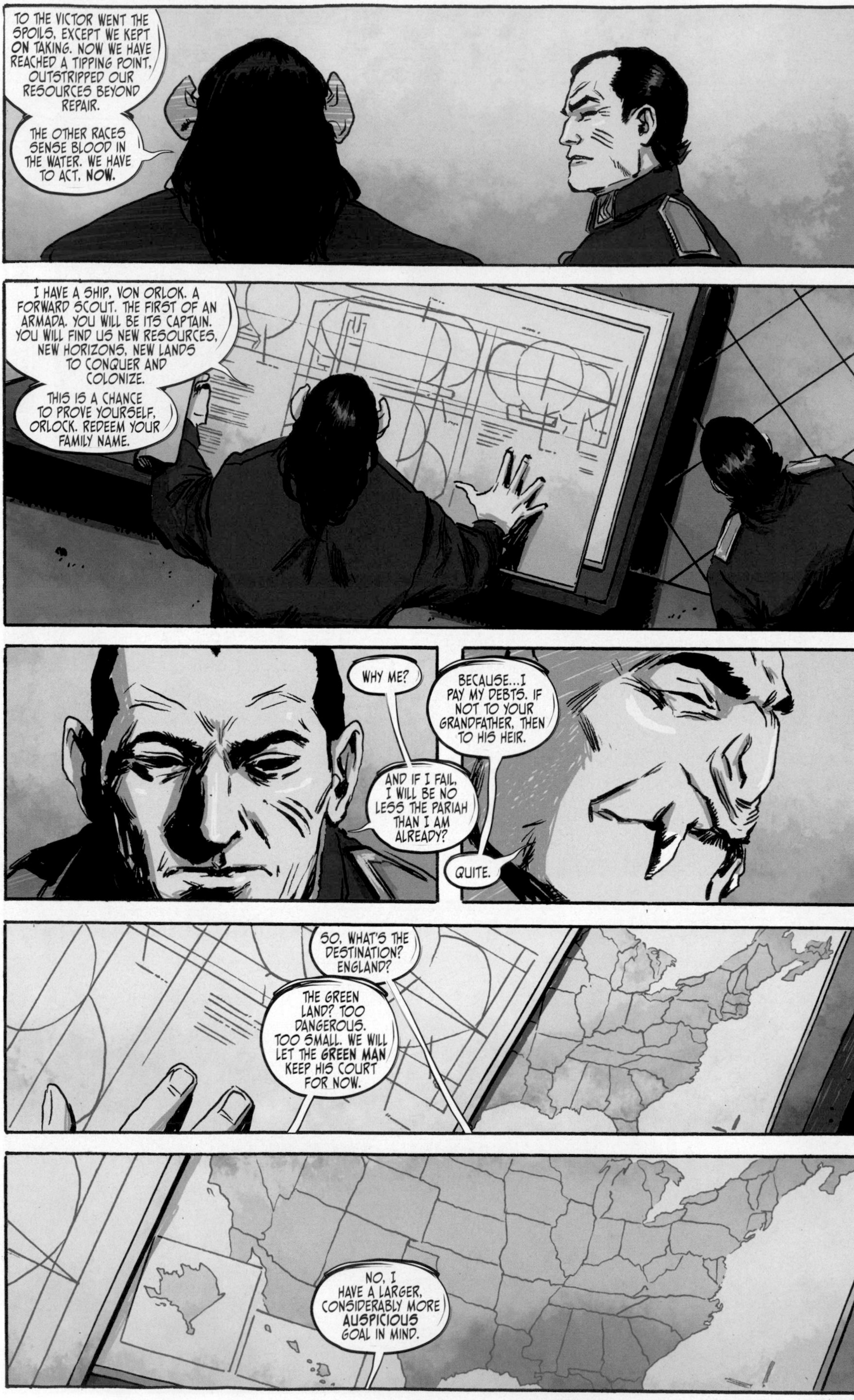
TO THE VICTOR WENT THE SPOILS, EXCEPT WE KEPT ON TAKING. NOW WE HAVE REACHED A TIPPING POINT, OUTSTRIPPED OUR RESOURCES BEYOND REPAIR.
THE OTHER RACES SENSE BLOOD IN THE WATER. WE HAVE TO ACT, NOW.
I HAVE A SHIP, VON ORLOK. A FORWARD SCOUT. THE FIRST OF AN ARMADA. YOU WILL BE ITS CAPTAIN. YOU WILL FIND US NEW RESOURCES, NEW HORIZONS, NEW LANDS TO CONQUER AND COLONIZE.
THIS IS A CHANCE TO PROVE YOURSELF, ORLOCK. REDEEM YOUR FAMILY NAME.
WHY ME?
BECAUSE...I PAY MY DEBTS. IF NOT TO YOUR GRANDFATHER, THEN TO HIS HEIR.
AND IF I FAIL, I WILL BE NO LESS THE PARIAH THAN I AM ALREADY?
QUITE.
SO, WHAT'S THE DESTINATION? ENGLAND?
THE GREEN LAND? TOO DANGEROUS. TOO SMALL. WE WILL LET THE GREEN MAN KEEP HIS COURT FOR NOW.
NO, I HAVE A LARGER, CONSIDERABLY MORE AUSPICIOUS GOAL IN MIND.

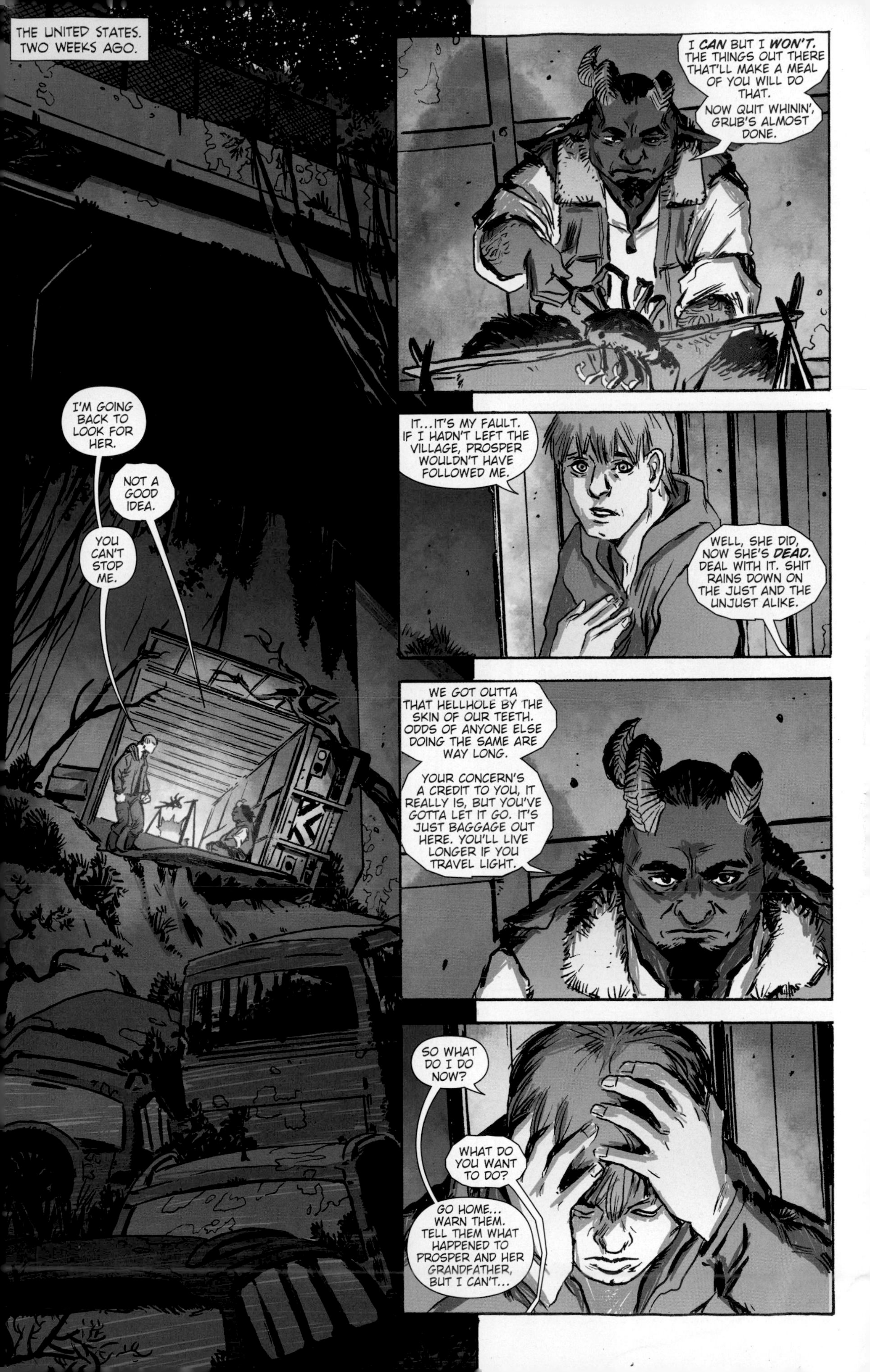
THE UNITED STATES. TWO WEEKS AGO.
I CAN BUT I WON'T. THE THINGS OUT THERE THAT'LL MAKE A MEAL OF YOU WILL DO THAT.
NOW QUIT WHININ', GRUB'S ALMOST DONE.
I'M GOING BACK TO LOOK FOR HER.
NOT A GOOD IDEA.
YOU CAN'T STOP ME.
IT...IT'S MY FAULT. IF I HADN'T LEFT THE VILLAGE, PROSPER WOULDN'T HAVE FOLLOWED ME.
WELL, SHE DID, NOW SHE'S DEAD. DEAL WITH IT. SHIT RAINS DOWN ON THE JUST AND THE UNJUST ALIKE.
WE GOT OUTTA THAT HELLHOLE BY THE SKIN OF OUR TEETH. ODDS OF ANYONE ELSE DOING THE SAME ARE WAY LONG.
YOUR CONCERN'S A CREDIT TO YOU, IT REALLY IS, BUT YOU'VE GOTTA LET IT GO. IT'S JUST BAGGAGE OUT HERE. YOU'LL LIVE LONGER IF YOU TRAVEL LIGHT.
SO WHAT DO I DO NOW?
WHAT DO YOU WANT TO DO?
GO HOME... WARN THEM. TELL THEM WHAT HAPPENED TO PROSPER AND HER GRANDFATHER, BUT I CAN'T...

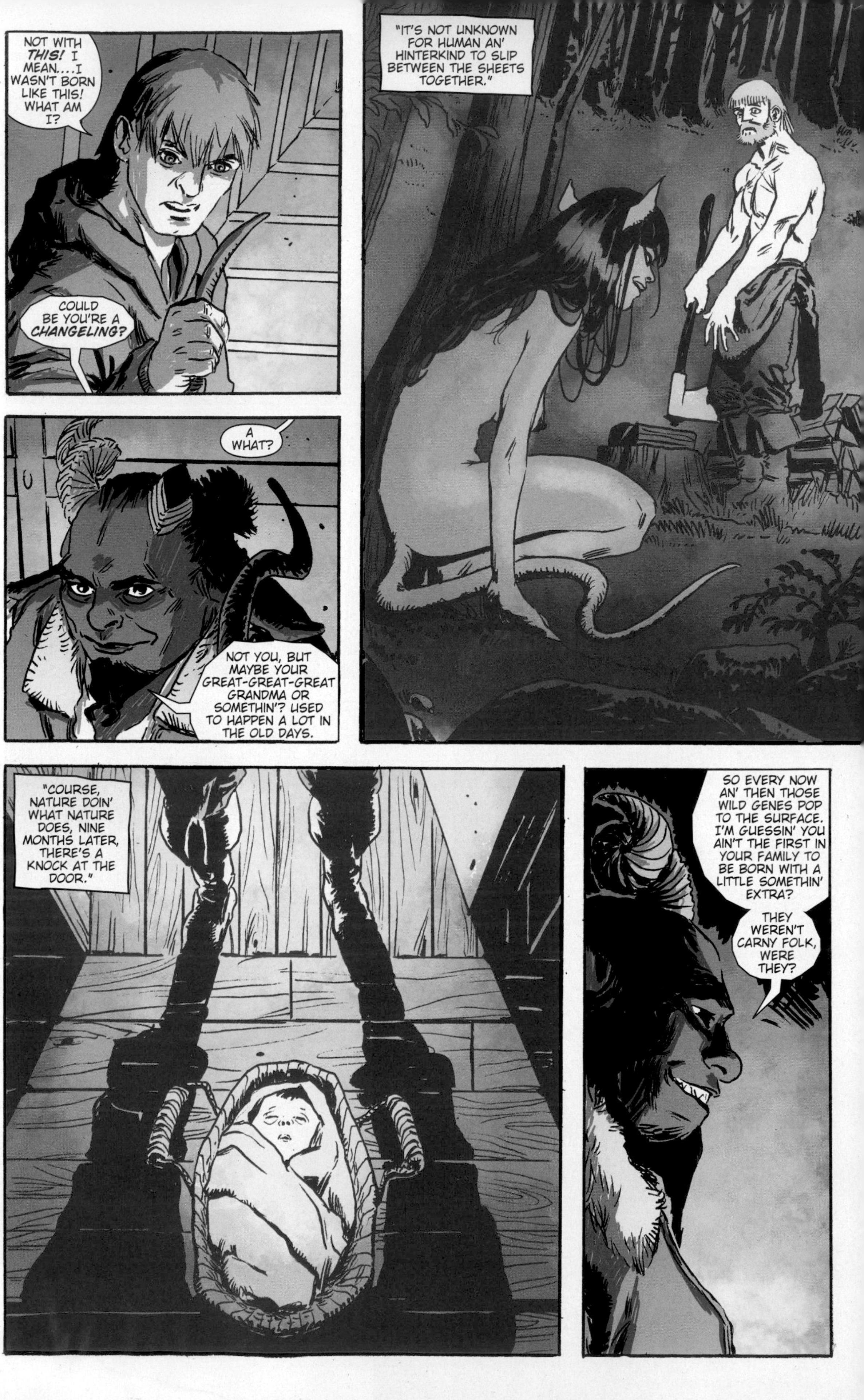
NOT WITH THIS! I MEAN....I WASN'T BORN LIKE THIS! WHAT AM I?
COULD BE YOU'RE A CHANGELING?
A WHAT?
NOT YOU, BUT MAYBE YOUR GREAT-GREAT-GREAT GRANDMA OR SOMETHIN'? USED TO HAPPEN A LOT IN THE OLD DAYS.
"IT'S NOT UNKNOWN FOR HUMAN AN' HINTERKIND TO SLIP BETWEEN THE SHEETS TOGETHER."
"COURSE, NATURE DOIN' WHAT NATURE DOES, NINE MONTHS LATER, THERE'S A KNOCK AT THE DOOR."
SO EVERY NOW AN' THEN THOSE WILD GENES POP TO THE SURFACE. I'M GUESSIN' YOU AIN'T THE FIRST IN YOUR FAMILY TO BE BORN WITH A LITTLE SOMETHIN' EXTRA?
THEY WEREN'T CARNY FOLK, WERE THEY?

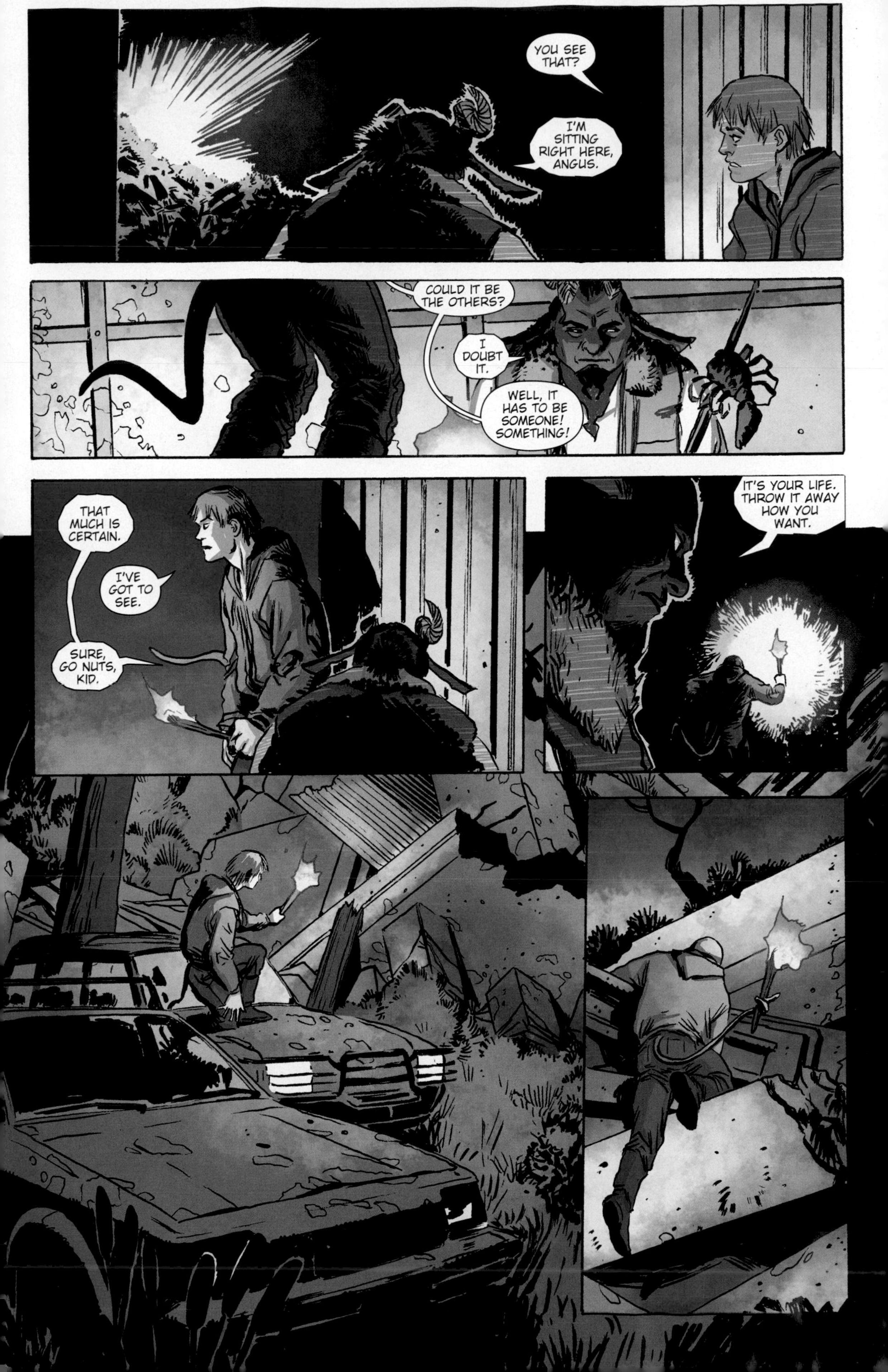
YOU SEE THAT?
I'M SITTING RIGHT HERE, ANGUS.
COULD IT BE THE OTHERS?
I DOUBT IT.
WELL, IT HAS TO BE SOMEONE! SOMETHING!
THAT MUCH IS CERTAIN.
I'VE GOT TO SEE.
SURE, GO NUTS, KID.
IT'S YOUR LIFE. THROW IT AWAY HOW YOU WANT.

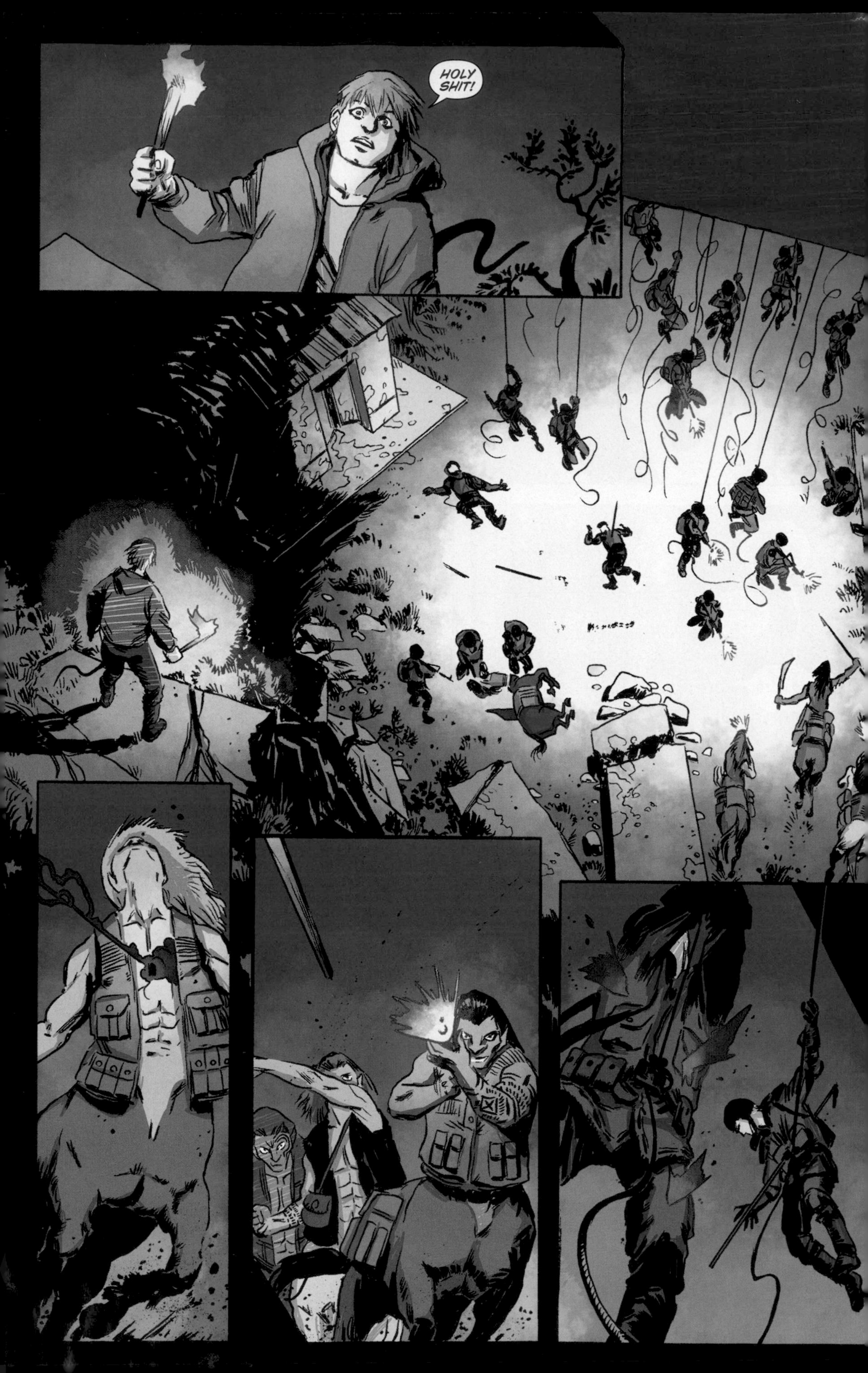
HOLY SHIT!

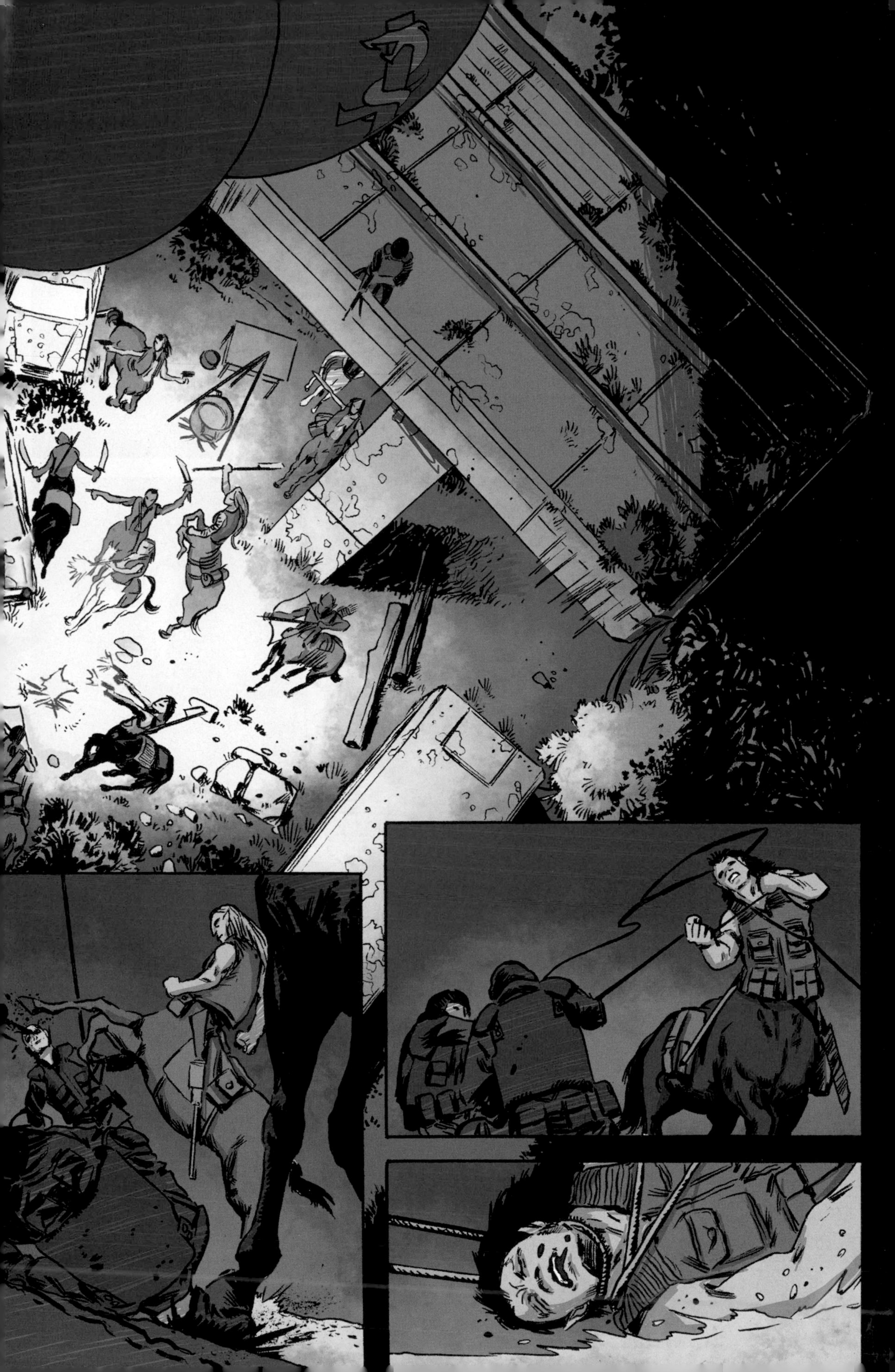

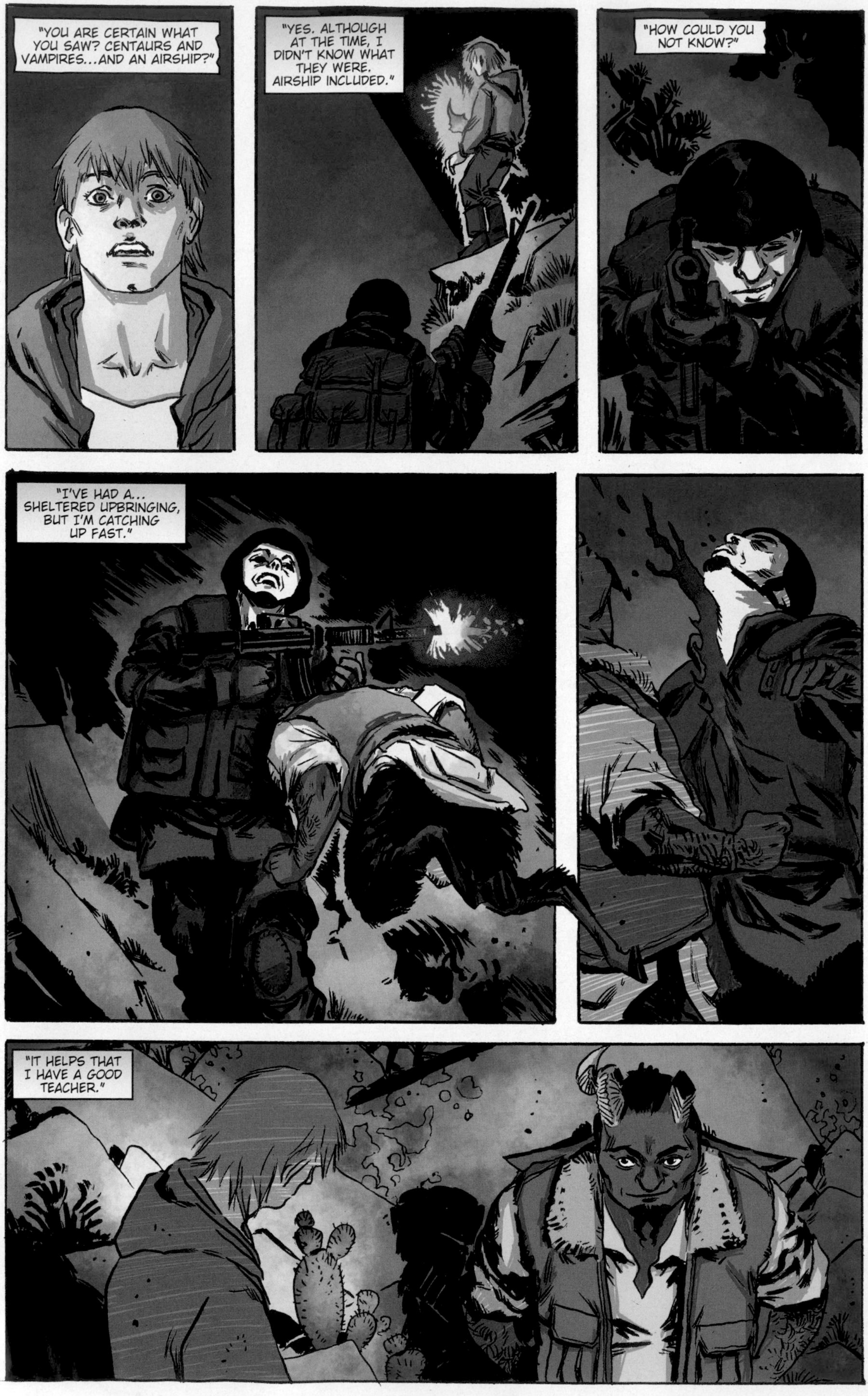
"YOU ARE CERTAIN WHAT YOU SAW? CENTAURS AND VAMPIRES...AND AN AIRSHIP?"
"YES. ALTHOUGH AT THE TIME, I DIDN'T KNOW WHAT THEY WERE. AIRSHIP INCLUDED."
"HOW COULD YOU NOT KNOW?"
"I'VE HAD A... SHELTERED UPBRINGING, BUT I'M CATCHING UP FAST."
"IT HELPS THAT I HAVE A GOOD TEACHER."

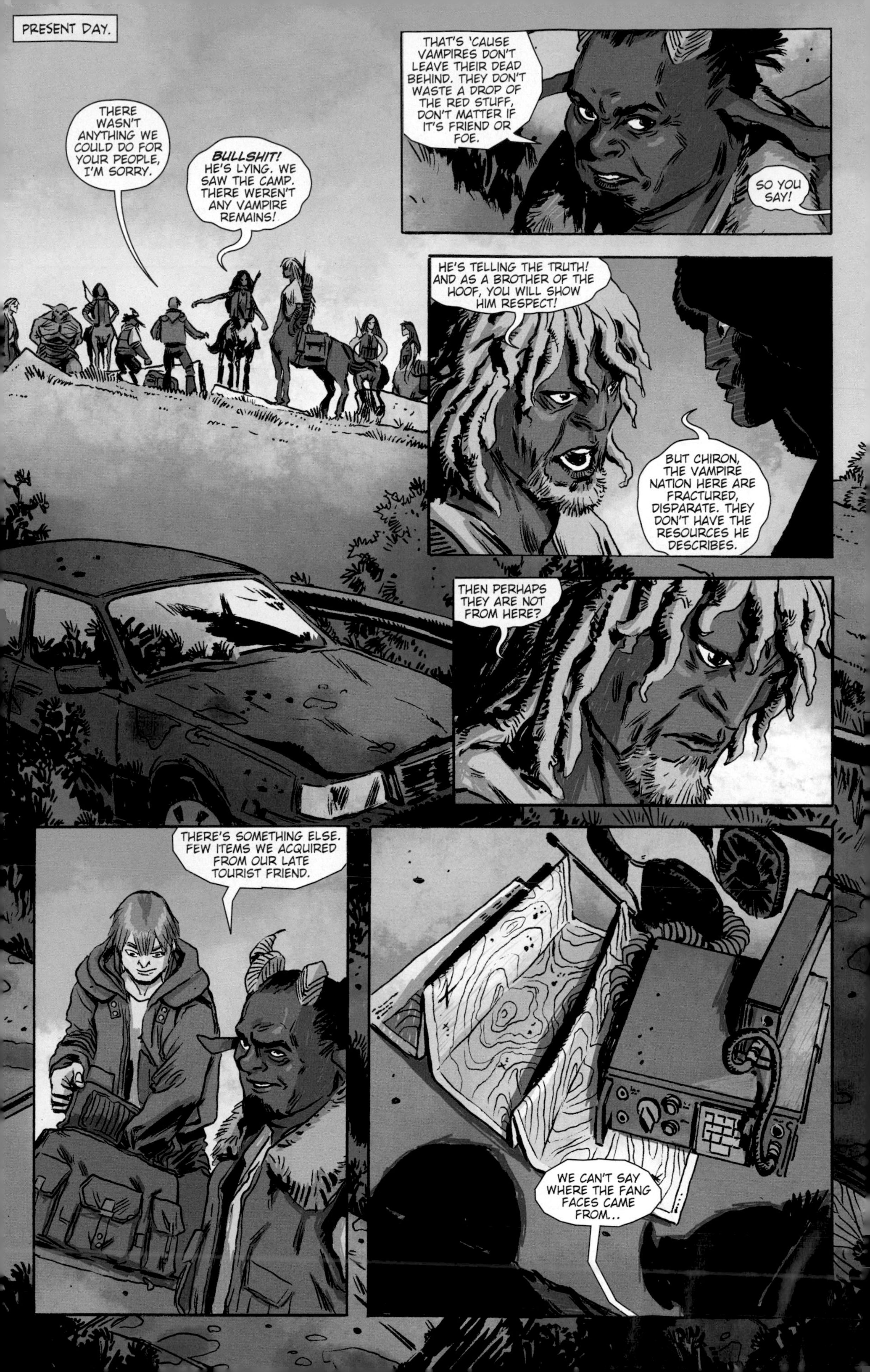
PRESENT DAY.
THERE WASN'T ANYTHING WE COULD DO FOR YOUR PEOPLE, I'M SORRY.
BULLSHIT! HE'S LYING. WE SAW THE CAMP. THERE WEREN'T ANY VAMPIRE REMAINS!
THAT'S 'CAUSE VAMPIRES DON'T LEAVE THEIR DEAD BEHIND. THEY DON'T WASTE A DROP OF THE RED STUFF, DON'T MATTER IF IT'S FRIEND OR FOE.
SO YOU SAY!
HE'S TELLING THE TRUTH! AND AS A BROTHER OF THE HOOF, YOU WILL SHOW HIM RESPECT!
BUT CHIRON, THE VAMPIRE NATION HERE ARE FRACTURED, DISPARATE. THEY DON'T HAVE THE RESOURCES HE DESCRIBES.
THEN PERHAPS THEY ARE NOT FROM HERE?
THERE'S SOMETHING ELSE. FEW ITEMS WE ACQUIRED FROM OUR LATE TOURIST FRIEND.
WE CAN'T SAY WHERE THE FANG FACES CAME FROM...

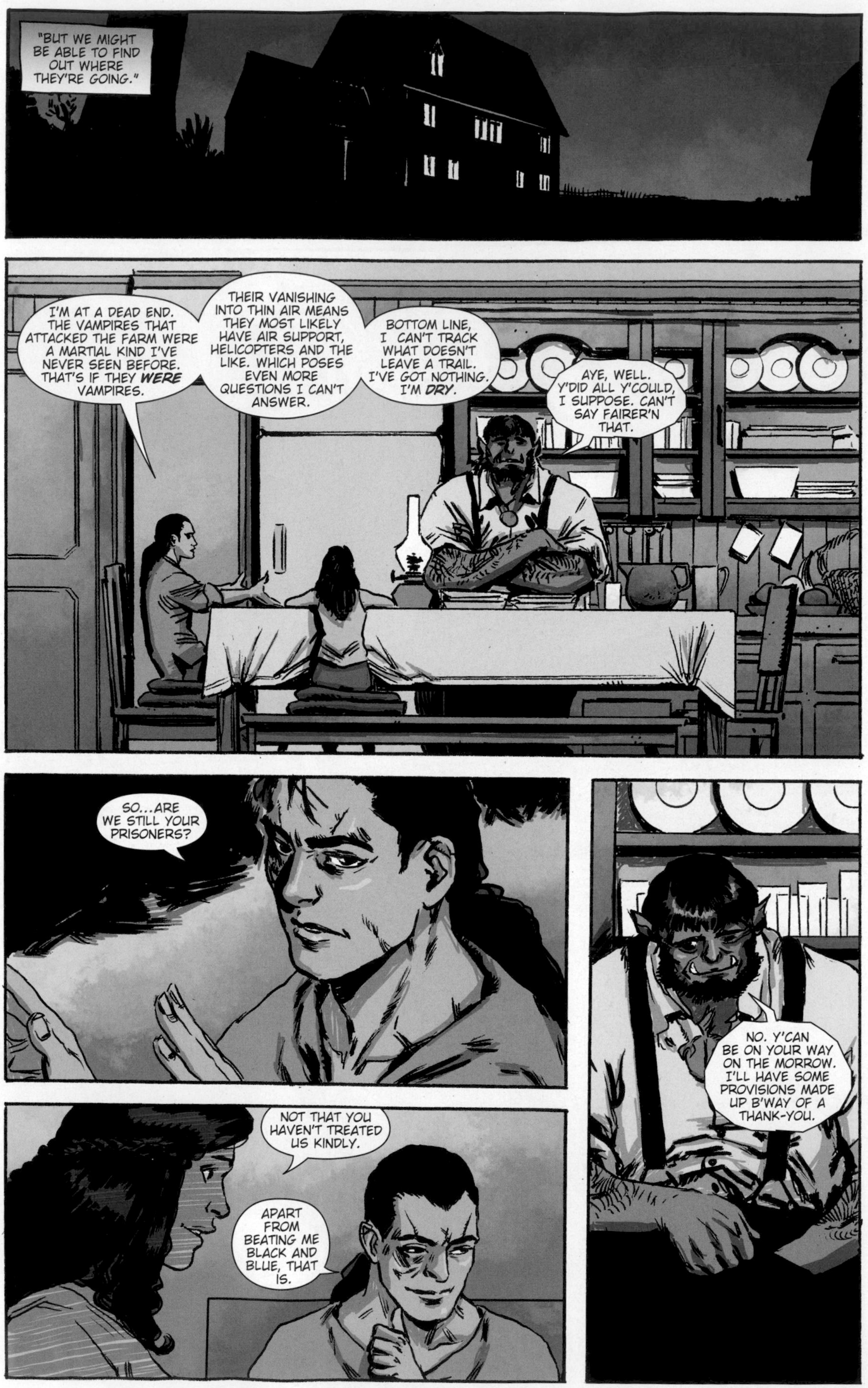
"BUT WE MIGHT BE ABLE TO FIND OUT WHERE THEY'RE GOING."
I'M AT A DEAD END. THE VAMPIRES THAT ATTACKED THE FARM WERE A MARTIAL KIND I'VE NEVER SEEN BEFORE. THAT'S IF THEY WERE VAMPIRES.
THEIR VANISHING INTO THIN AIR MEANS THEY MOST LIKELY HAVE AIR SUPPORT, HELICOPTERS AND THE LIKE. WHICH POSES EVEN MORE QUESTIONS I CAN'T ANSWER.
BOTTOM LINE, I CAN'T TRACK WHAT DOESN'T LEAVE A TRAIL. I'VE GOT NOTHING. I'M DRY.
AYE, WELL. Y'DID ALL Y'COULD, I SUPPOSE. CAN'T SAY FAIRER'N THAT.
SO...ARE WE STILL YOUR PRISONERS?
NO. Y'CAN BE ON YOUR WAY ON THE MORROW. I'LL HAVE SOME PROVISIONS MADE UP B'WAY OF A THANK-YOU.
NOT THAT YOU HAVEN'T TREATED US KINDLY.
APART FROM BEATING ME BLACK AND BLUE, THAT IS.

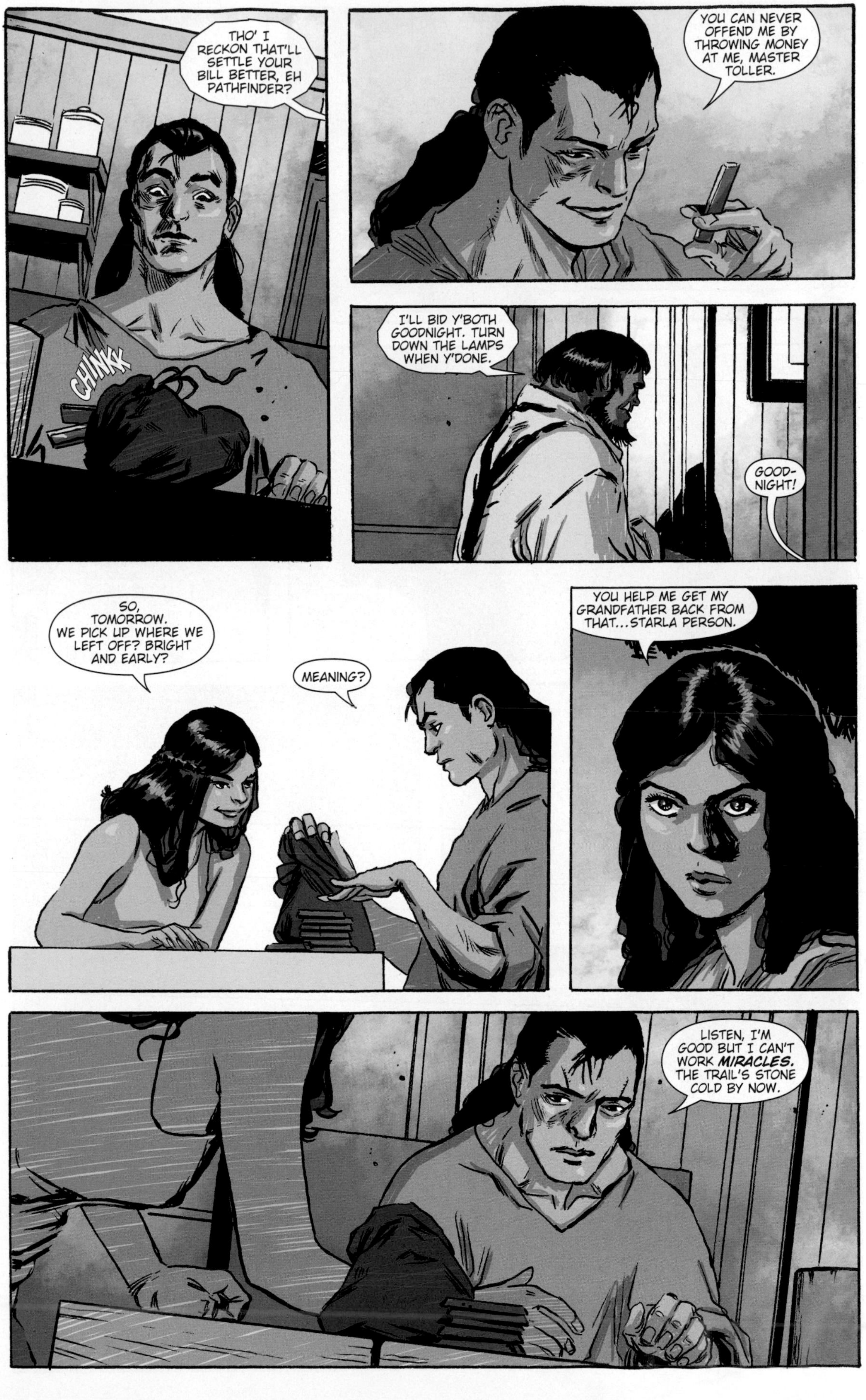

THO' I RECKON THAT'LL SETTLE YOUR BILL BETTER, EH PATHFINDER?
CHINKK
YOU CAN NEVER OFFEND ME BY THROWING MONEY AT ME, MASTER TOLLER.
I'LL BID Y'BOTH GOODNIGHT. TURN DOWN THE LAMPS WHEN Y'DONE.
GOOD-NIGHT!
SO, TOMORROW. WE PICK UP WHERE WE LEFT OFF? BRIGHT AND EARLY?
MEANING?
YOU HELP ME GET MY GRANDFATHER BACK FROM THAT...STARLA PERSON.
LISTEN, I'M GOOD BUT I CAN'T WORK MIRACLES. THE TRAIL'S STONE COLD BY NOW.

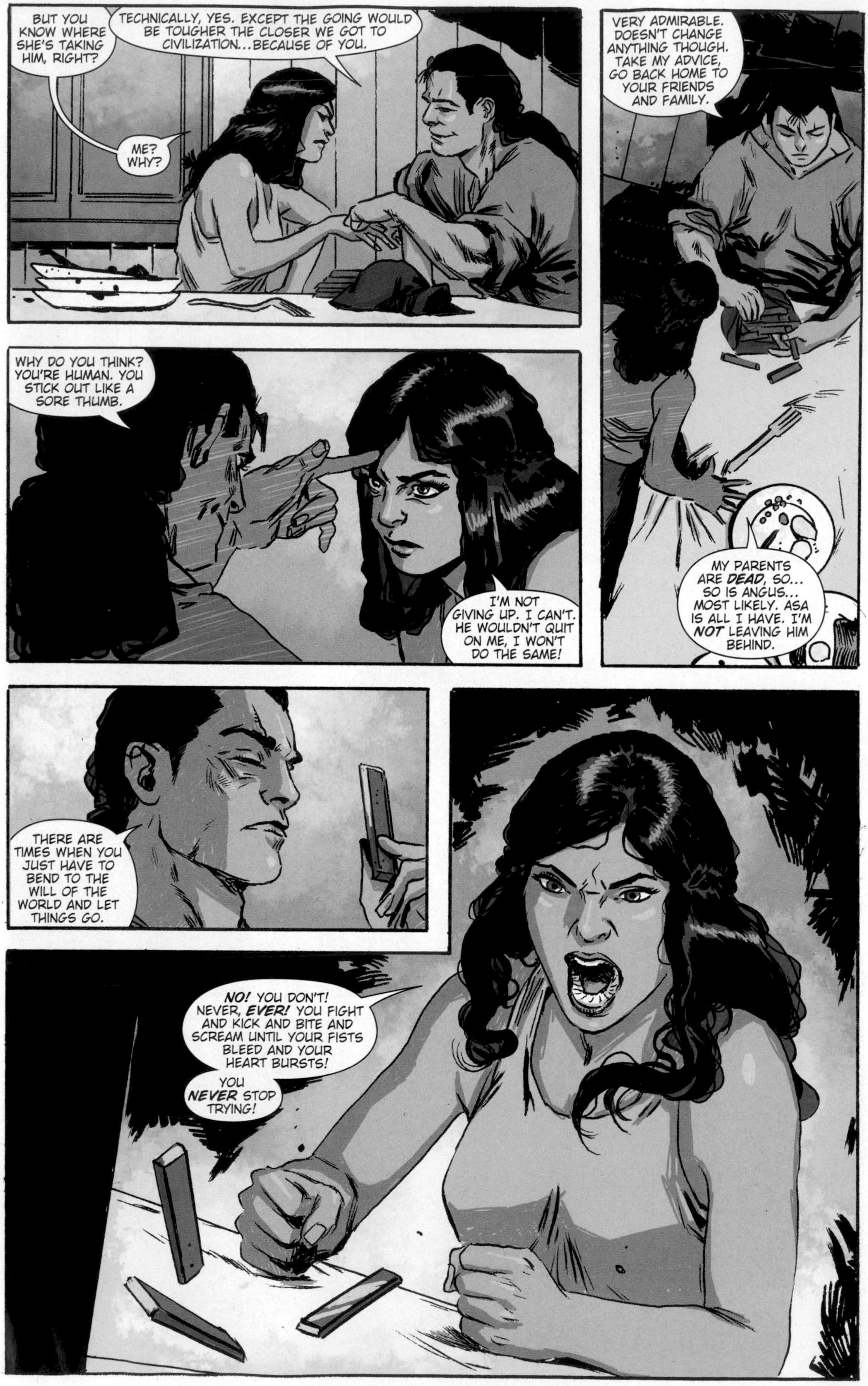
BUT YOU KNOW WHERE SHE'S TAKING HIM, RIGHT?
TECHNICALLY, YES. EXCEPT THE GOING WOULD BE TOUGHER THE CLOSER WE GOT TO CIVILIZATION...BECAUSE OF YOU.
ME? WHY?
WHY DO YOU THINK? YOU'RE HUMAN. YOU STICK OUT LIKE A SORE THUMB.
I'M NOT GIVING UP. I CAN'T. HE WOULDN'T QUIT ON ME, I WON'T DO THE SAME!
VERY ADMIRABLE. DOESN'T CHANGE ANYTHING THOUGH. TAKE MY ADVICE, GO BACK HOME TO YOUR FRIENDS AND FAMILY.
MY PARENTS ARE **DEAD**, SO... SO IS ANGUS... MOST LIKELY. ASA IS ALL I HAVE. I'M **NOT** LEAVING HIM BEHIND.
THERE ARE TIMES WHEN YOU JUST HAVE TO BEND TO THE WILL OF THE WORLD AND LET THINGS GO.
NO! YOU DON'T! NEVER, **EVER!** YOU FIGHT AND KICK AND BITE AND SCREAM UNTIL YOUR FISTS BLEED AND YOUR HEART BURSTS!
YOU **NEVER** STOP TRYING!

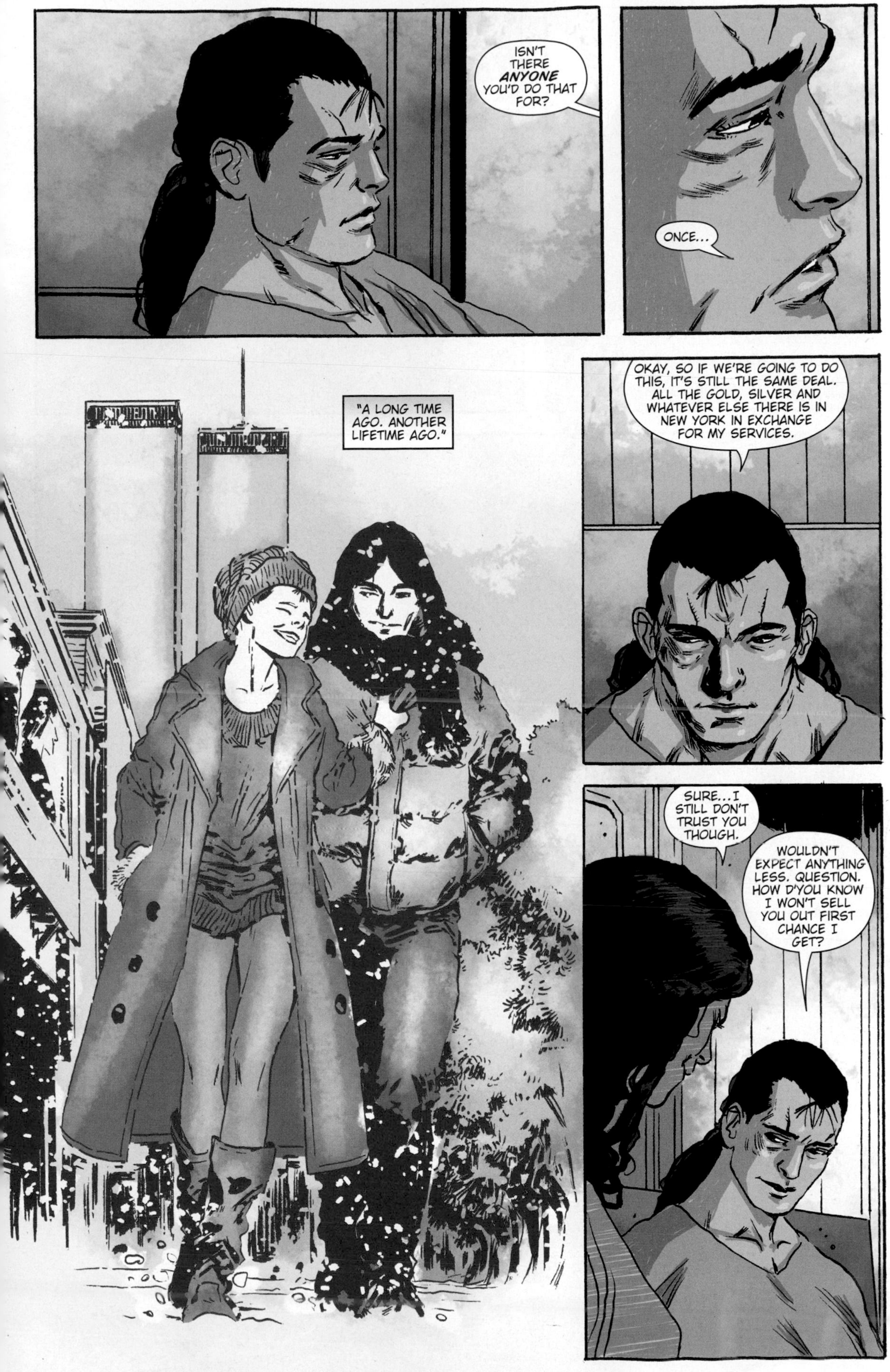
ISN'T THERE ANYONE YOU'D DO THAT FOR?
ONCE...
"A LONG TIME AGO. ANOTHER LIFETIME AGO."
OKAY, SO IF WE'RE GOING TO DO THIS, IT'S STILL THE SAME DEAL. ALL THE GOLD, SILVER AND WHATEVER ELSE THERE IS IN NEW YORK IN EXCHANGE FOR MY SERVICES.
SURE...I STILL DON'T TRUST YOU THOUGH.
WOULDN'T EXPECT ANYTHING LESS. QUESTION. HOW D'YOU KNOW I WON'T SELL YOU OUT FIRST CHANCE I GET?

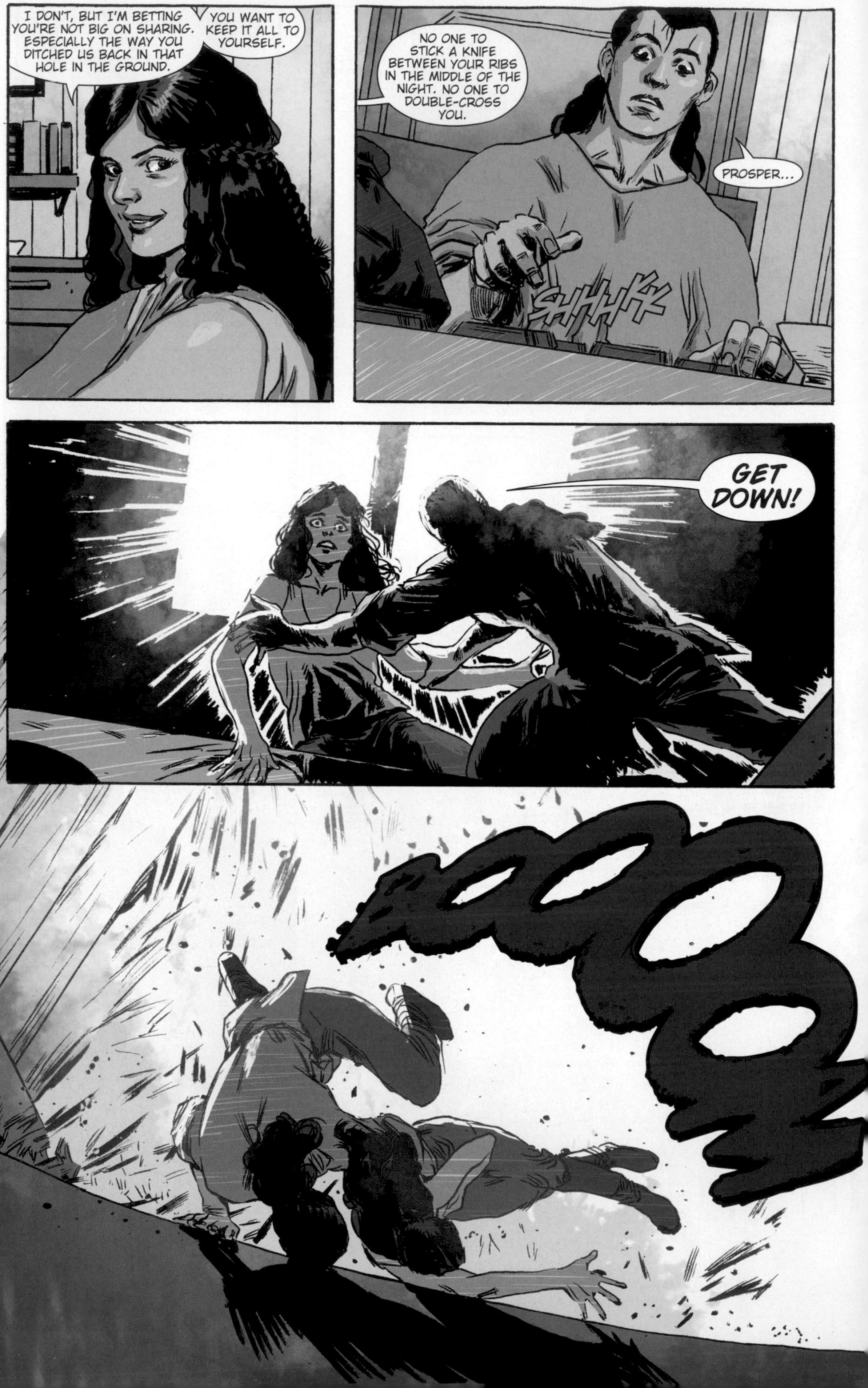
I DON'T, BUT I'M BETTING YOU'RE NOT BIG ON SHARING. ESPECIALLY THE WAY YOU DITCHED US BACK IN THAT HOLE IN THE GROUND.
YOU WANT TO KEEP IT ALL TO YOURSELF.
NO ONE TO STICK A KNIFE BETWEEN YOUR RIBS IN THE MIDDLE OF THE NIGHT. NO ONE TO DOUBLE-CROSS YOU.
PROSPER...
SHHHK
GET DOWN!

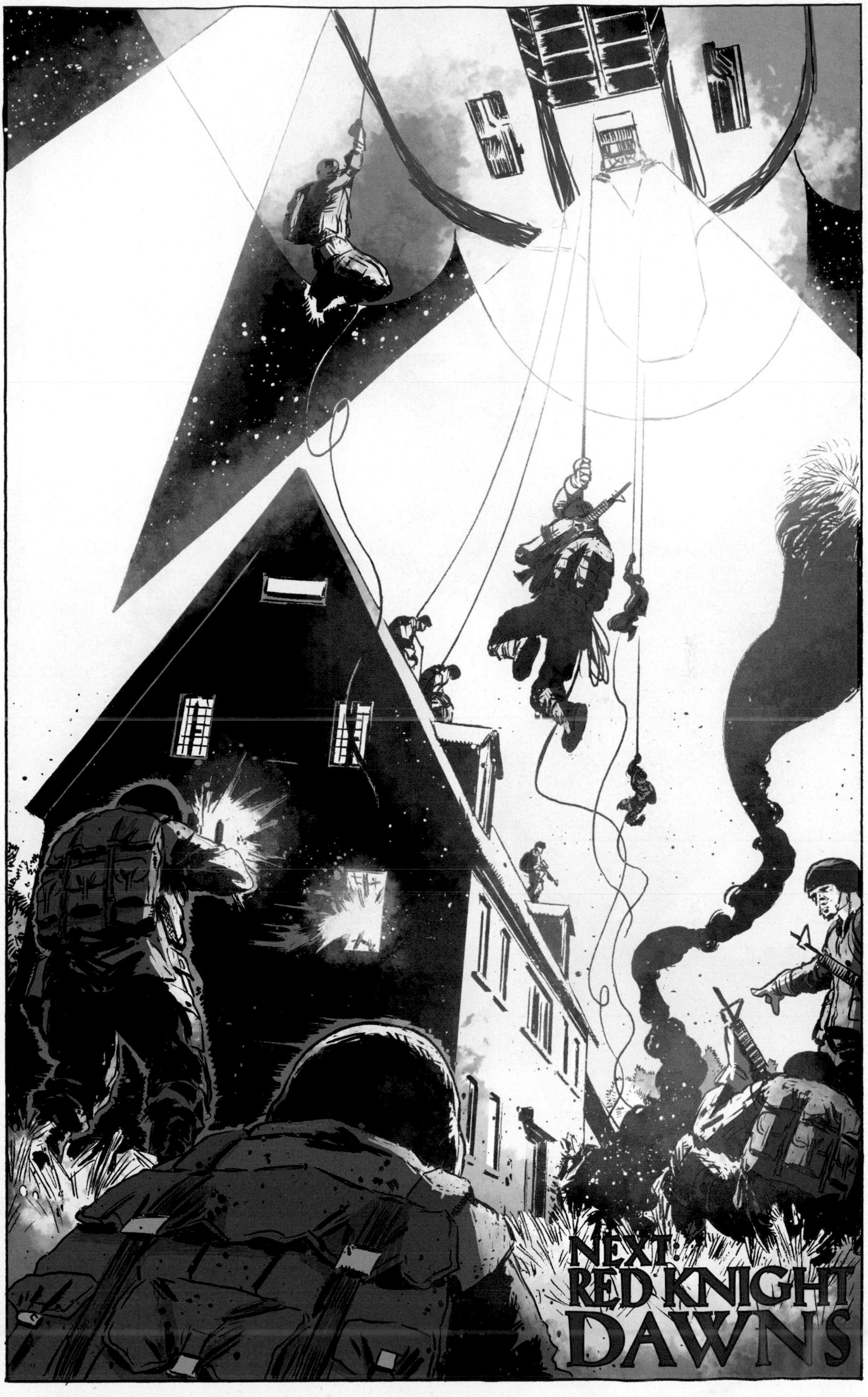
NEXT:
RED KNIGHT
DAWNS

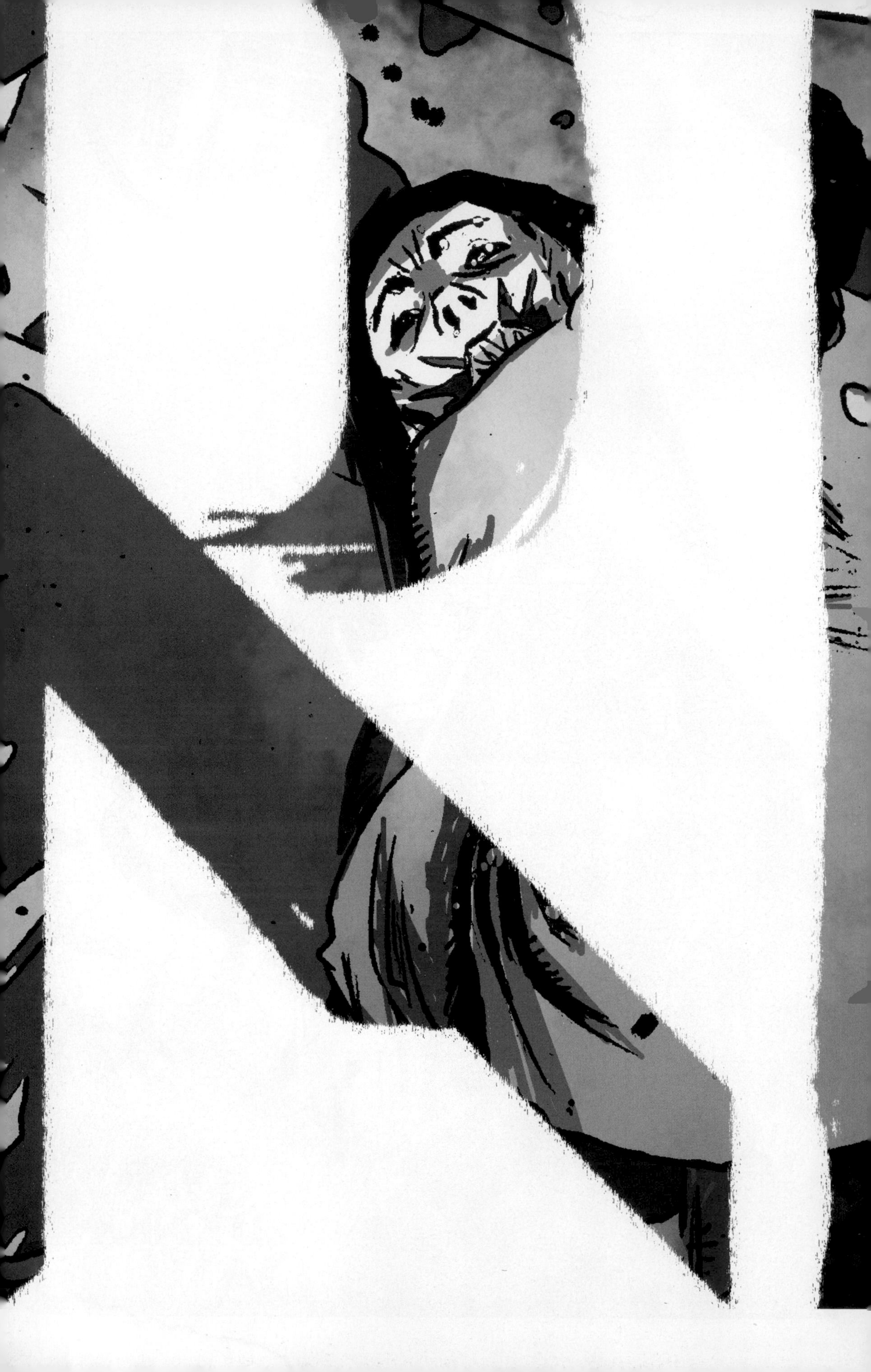

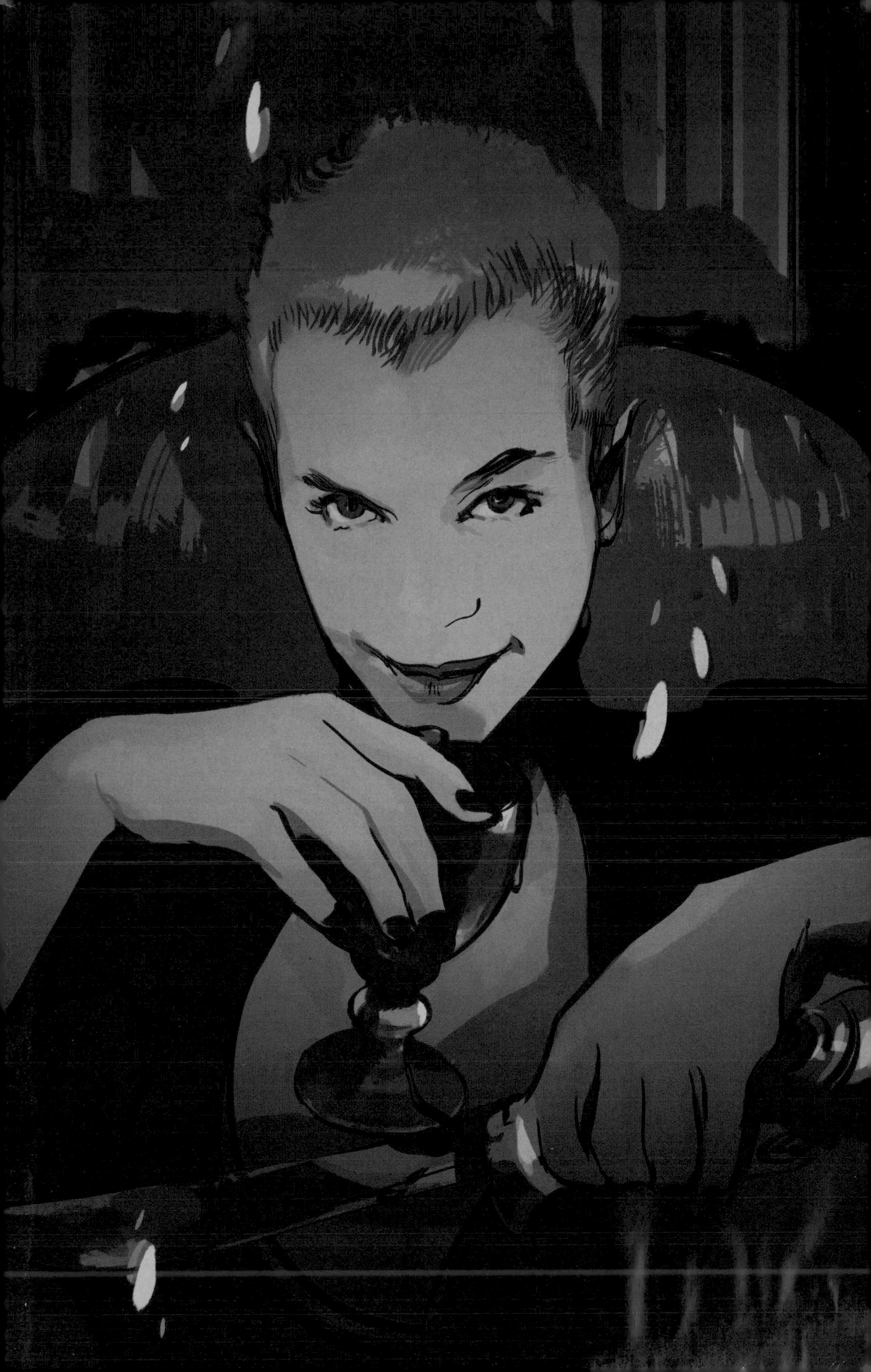

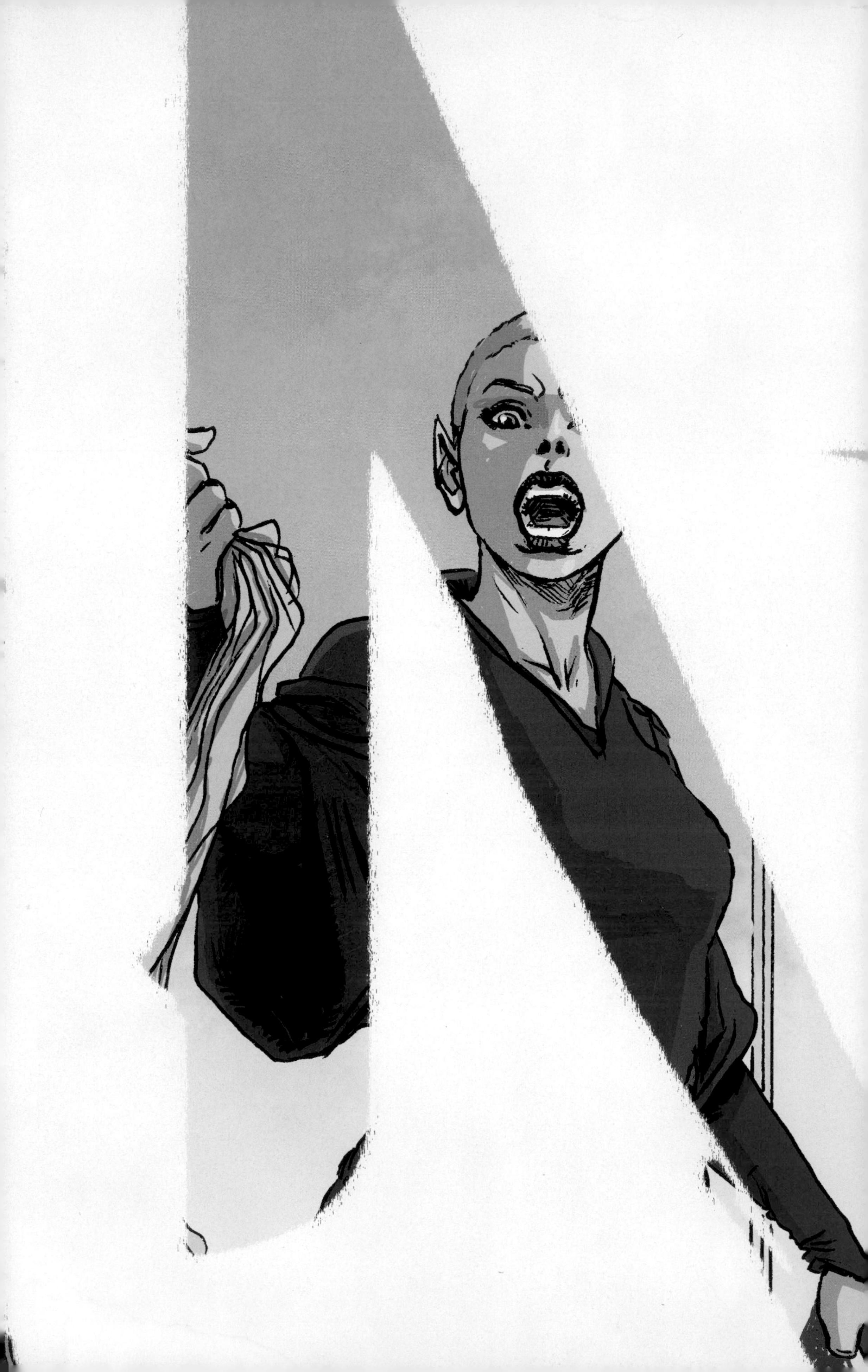

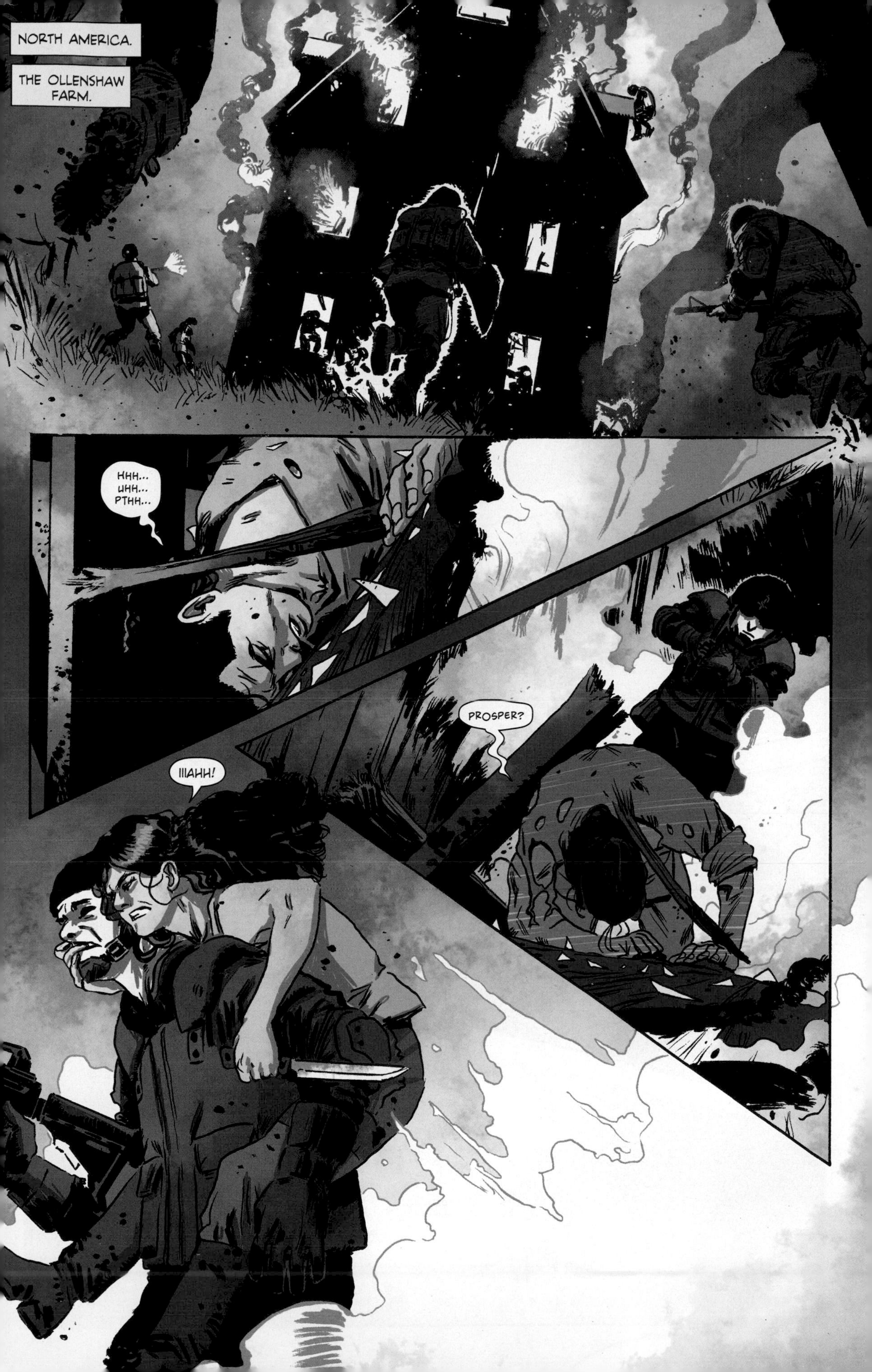
NORTH AMERICA.
THE OLLENSHAW FARM.
HHH... UHH... PTHH...
PROSPER?
IIIAHH!

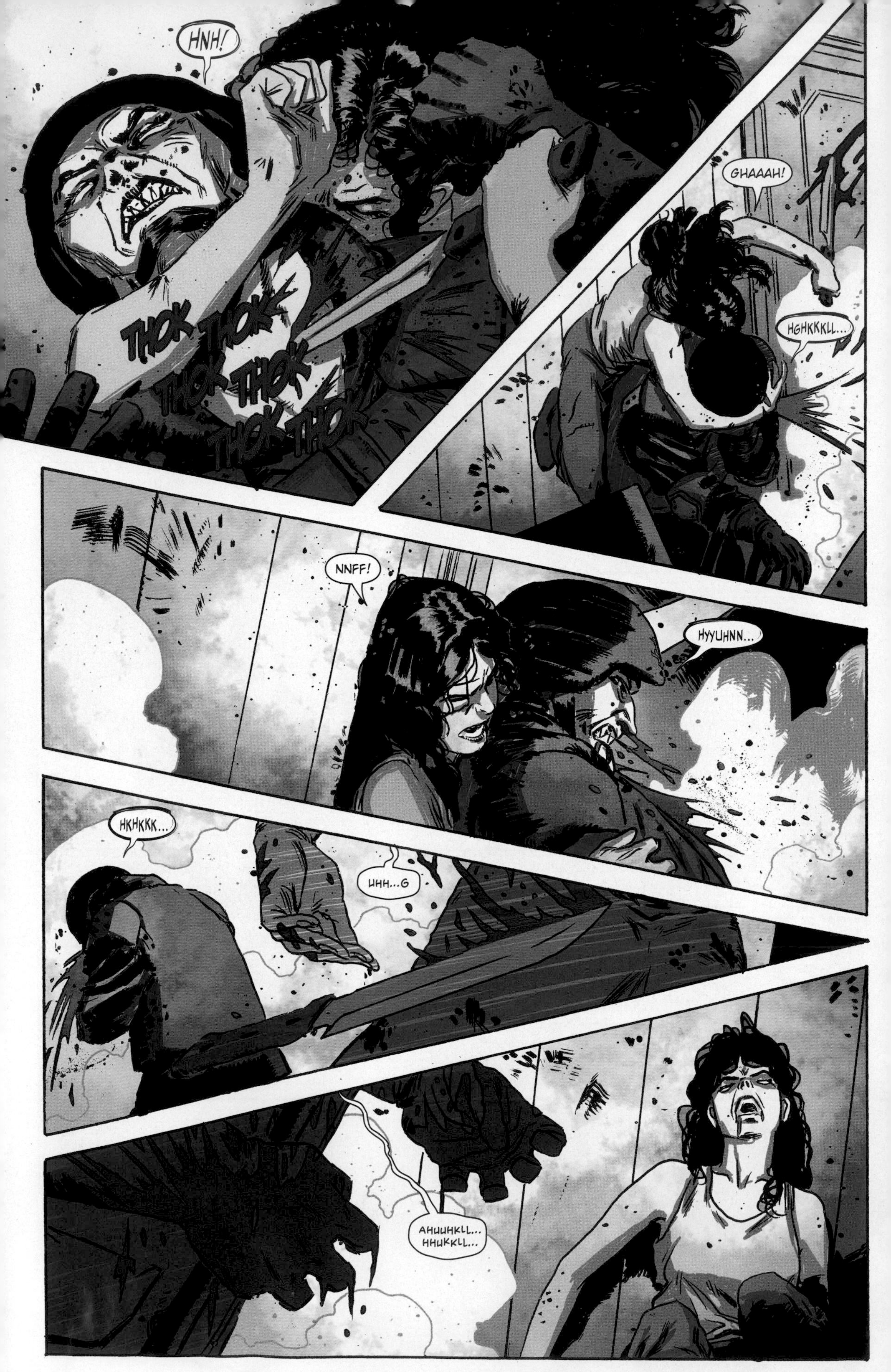
HNH!
THOK THOK THOK THOK THOK THOK
GHAAAH!
HGHKKKLL...
NNFF!
HYYUHNN...
HKHKKK...
UHH...G
AHUUHKLL... HHUKKLL...

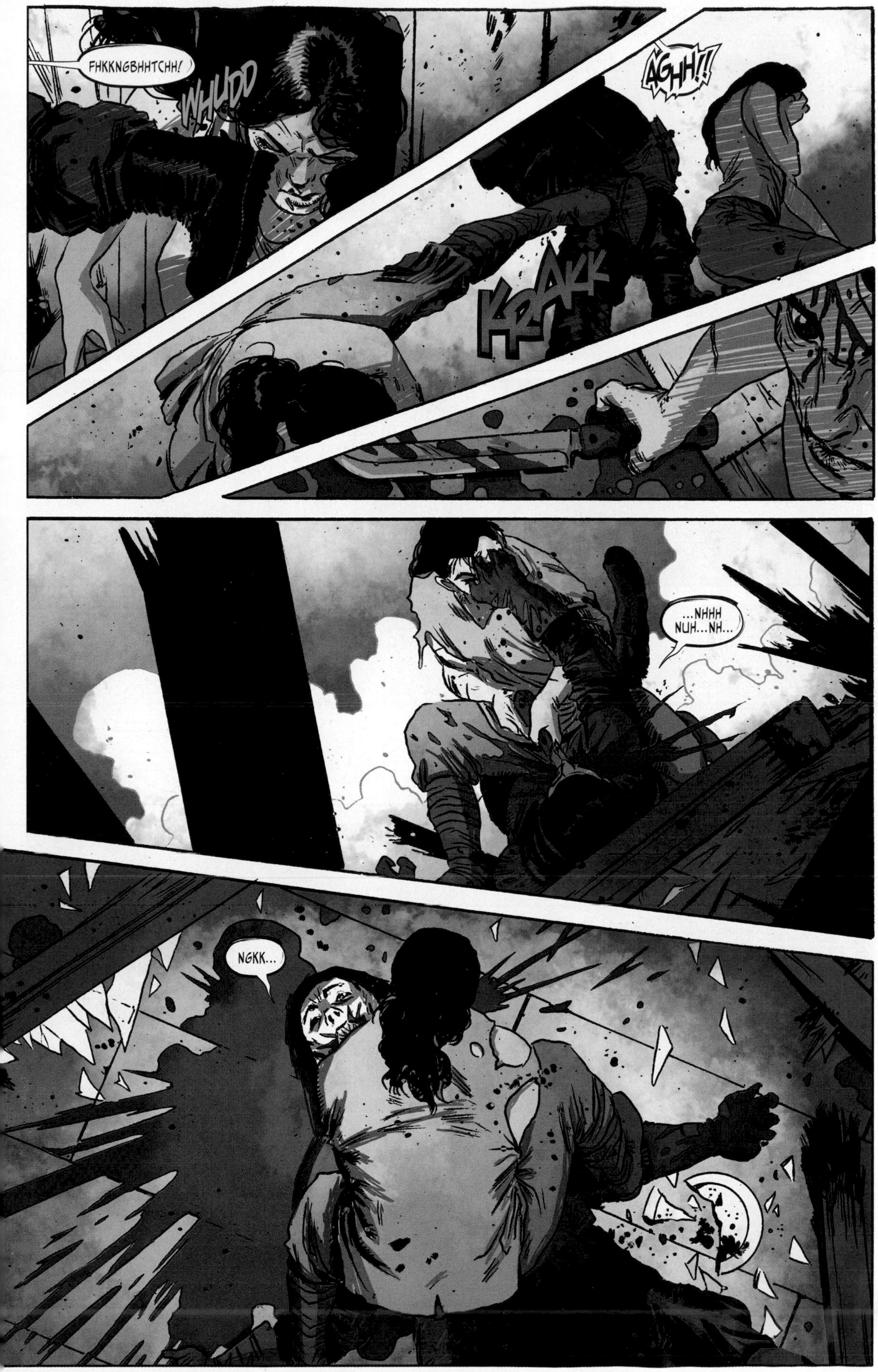
FHKKNGBHHTCHH!
WHUDD
AGHH!!
KRAKK
...NHHH NUH...NH...
NGKK...

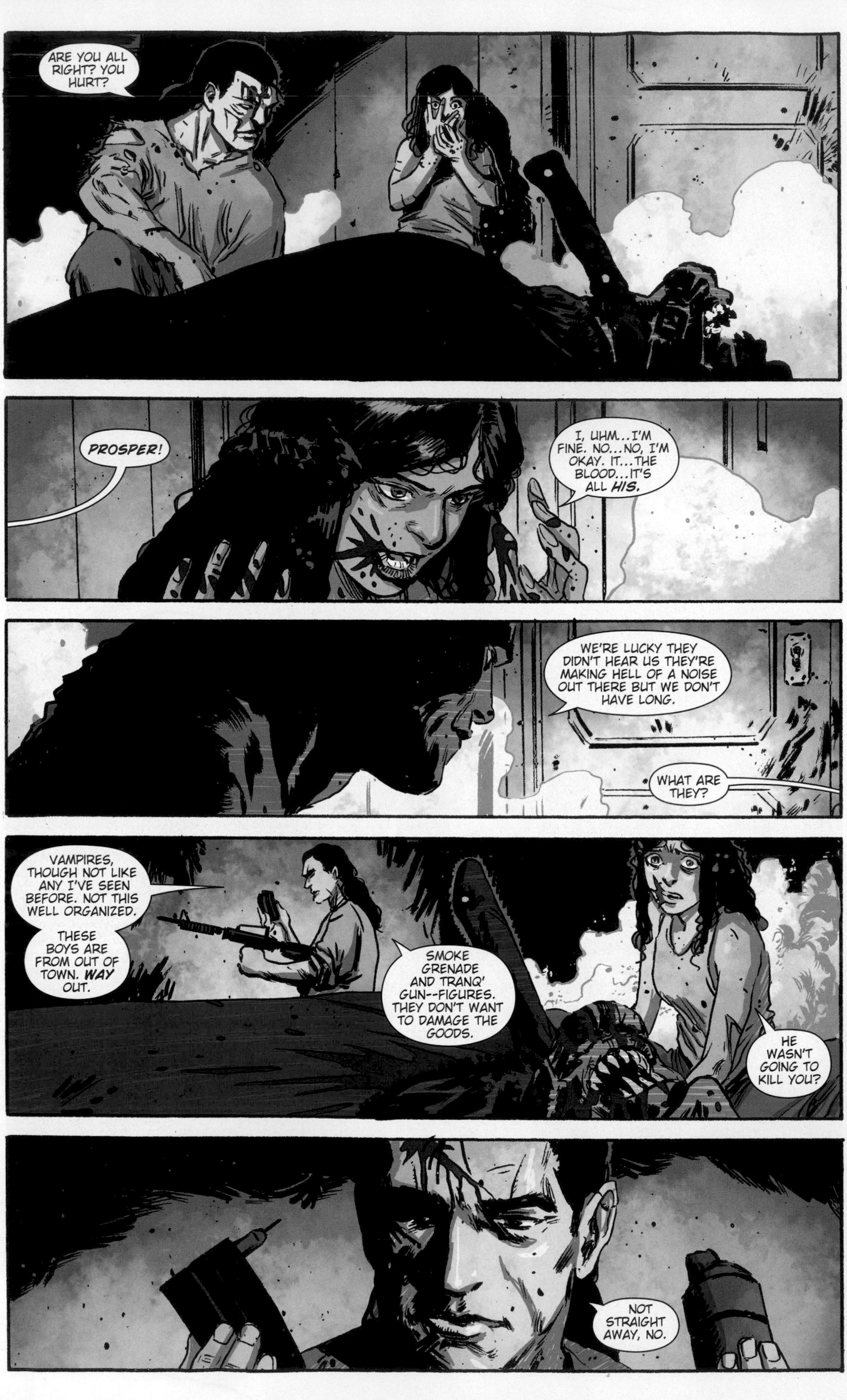
ARE YOU ALL RIGHT? YOU HURT?
PROSPER!
I, UHM...I'M FINE. NO...NO, I'M OKAY. IT...THE BLOOD...IT'S ALL HIS.
WE'RE LUCKY THEY DIDN'T HEAR US THEY'RE MAKING HELL OF A NOISE OUT THERE BUT WE DON'T HAVE LONG.
WHAT ARE THEY?
VAMPIRES, THOUGH NOT LIKE ANY I'VE SEEN BEFORE. NOT THIS WELL ORGANIZED.
THESE BOYS ARE FROM OUT OF TOWN. WAY OUT.
SMOKE GRENADE AND TRANQ' GUN--FIGURES. THEY DON'T WANT TO DAMAGE THE GOODS.
HE WASN'T GOING TO KILL YOU?
NOT STRAIGHT AWAY, NO.

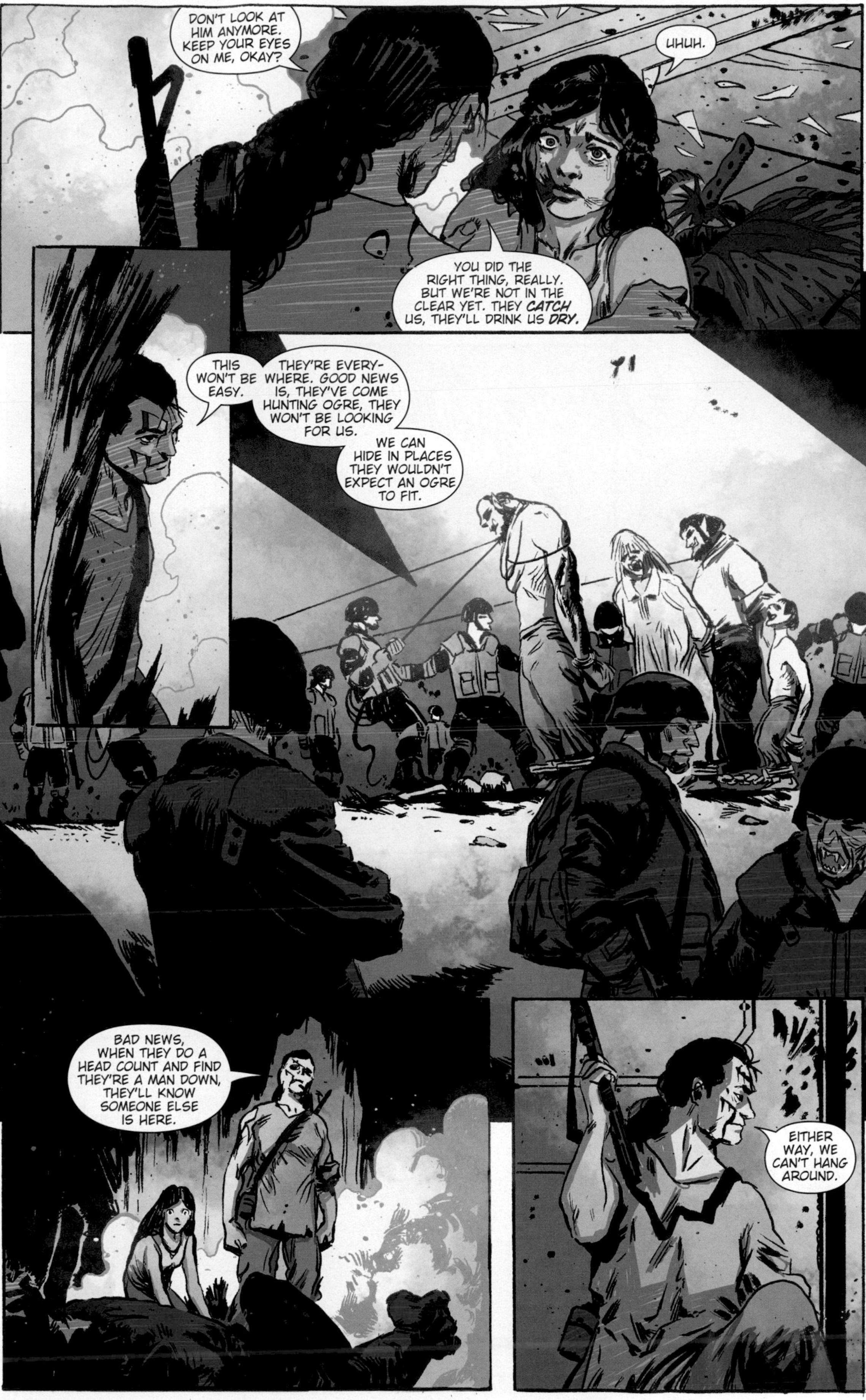
DON'T LOOK AT HIM ANYMORE. KEEP YOUR EYES ON ME, OKAY?
UHUH.
YOU DID THE RIGHT THING, REALLY. BUT WE'RE NOT IN THE CLEAR YET. THEY CATCH US, THEY'LL DRINK US DRY.
THIS WON'T BE EASY.
THEY'RE EVERY-WHERE. GOOD NEWS IS, THEY'VE COME HUNTING OGRE, THEY WON'T BE LOOKING FOR US.
WE CAN HIDE IN PLACES THEY WOULDN'T EXPECT AN OGRE TO FIT.
BAD NEWS, WHEN THEY DO A HEAD COUNT AND FIND THEY'RE A MAN DOWN, THEY'LL KNOW SOMEONE ELSE IS HERE.
EITHER WAY, WE CAN'T HANG AROUND.

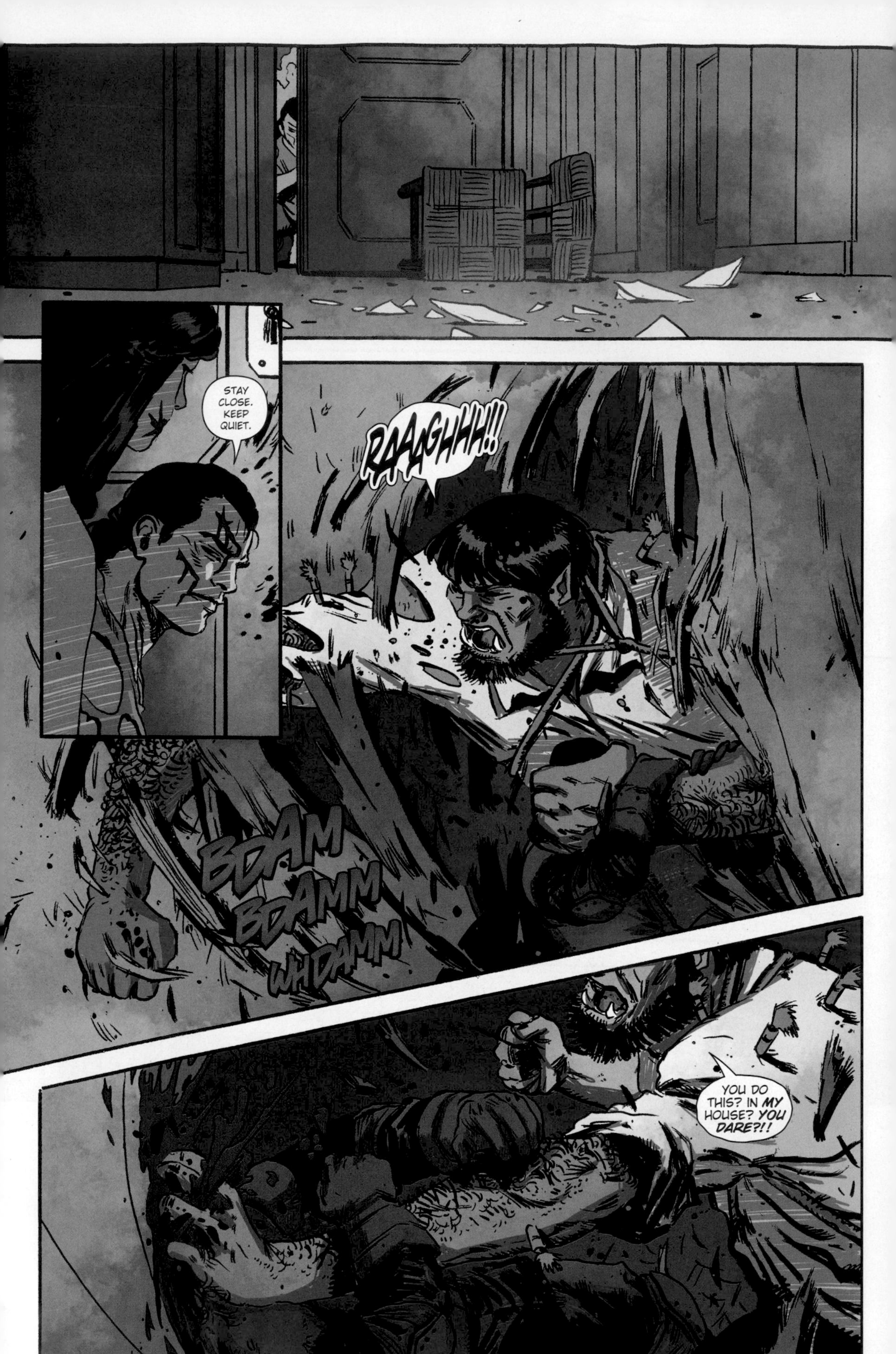

STAY CLOSE. KEEP QUIET.
RAAAGHHH!!
BDAM
BDAMM
WHDAMM
YOU DO THIS? IN MY HOUSE? YOU DARE?!!

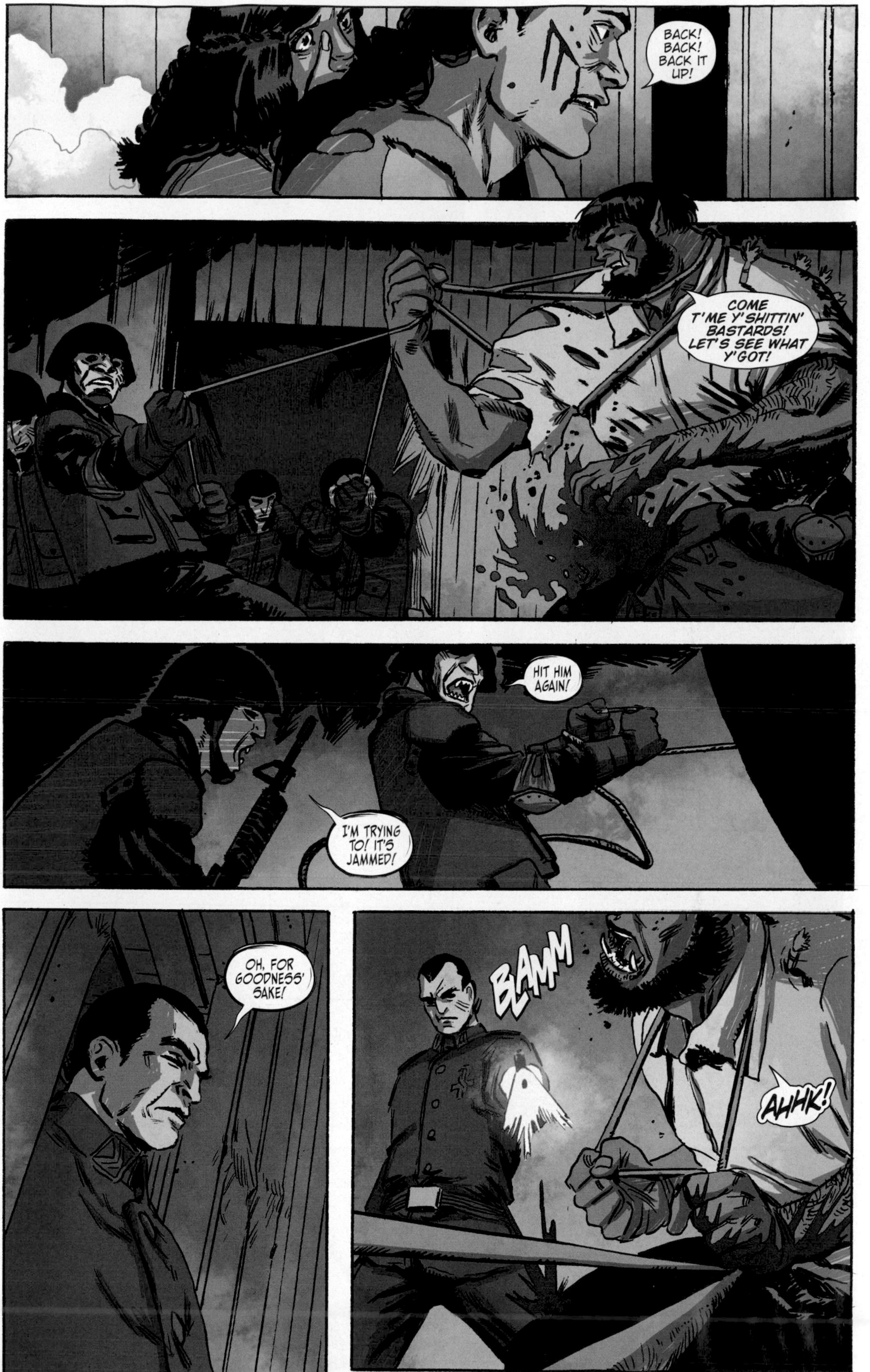
BACK! BACK! BACK IT UP!
COME T'ME Y'SHITTIN' BASTARDS! LET'S SEE WHAT Y'GOT!
HIT HIM AGAIN!
I'M TRYING TO! IT'S JAMMED!
OH, FOR GOODNESS' SAKE!
BLAMM
AHHK!

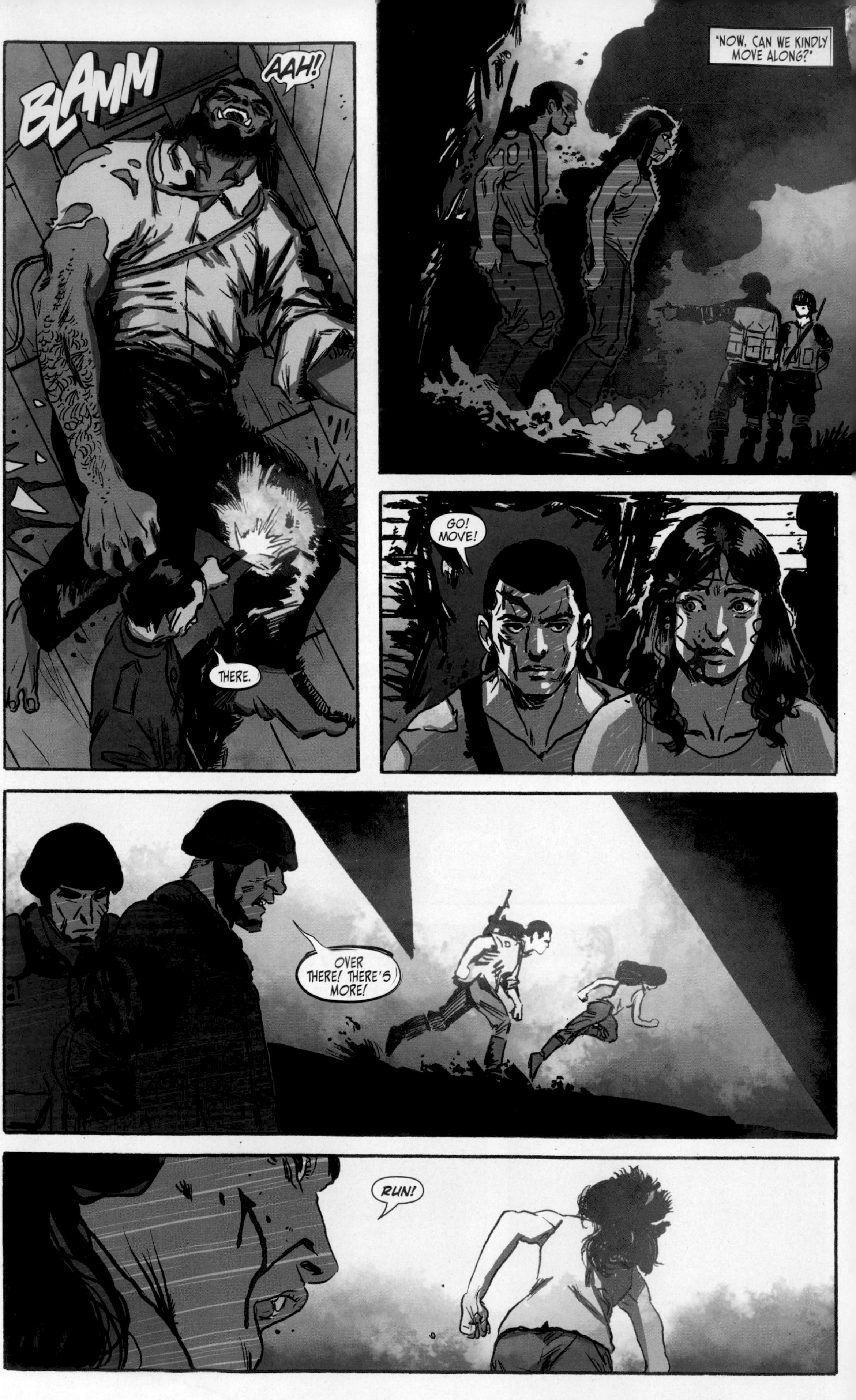
BLAMM
AAH!
THERE.
"NOW, CAN WE KINDLY MOVE ALONG?"
GO! MOVE!
OVER THERE! THERE'S MORE!
RUN!

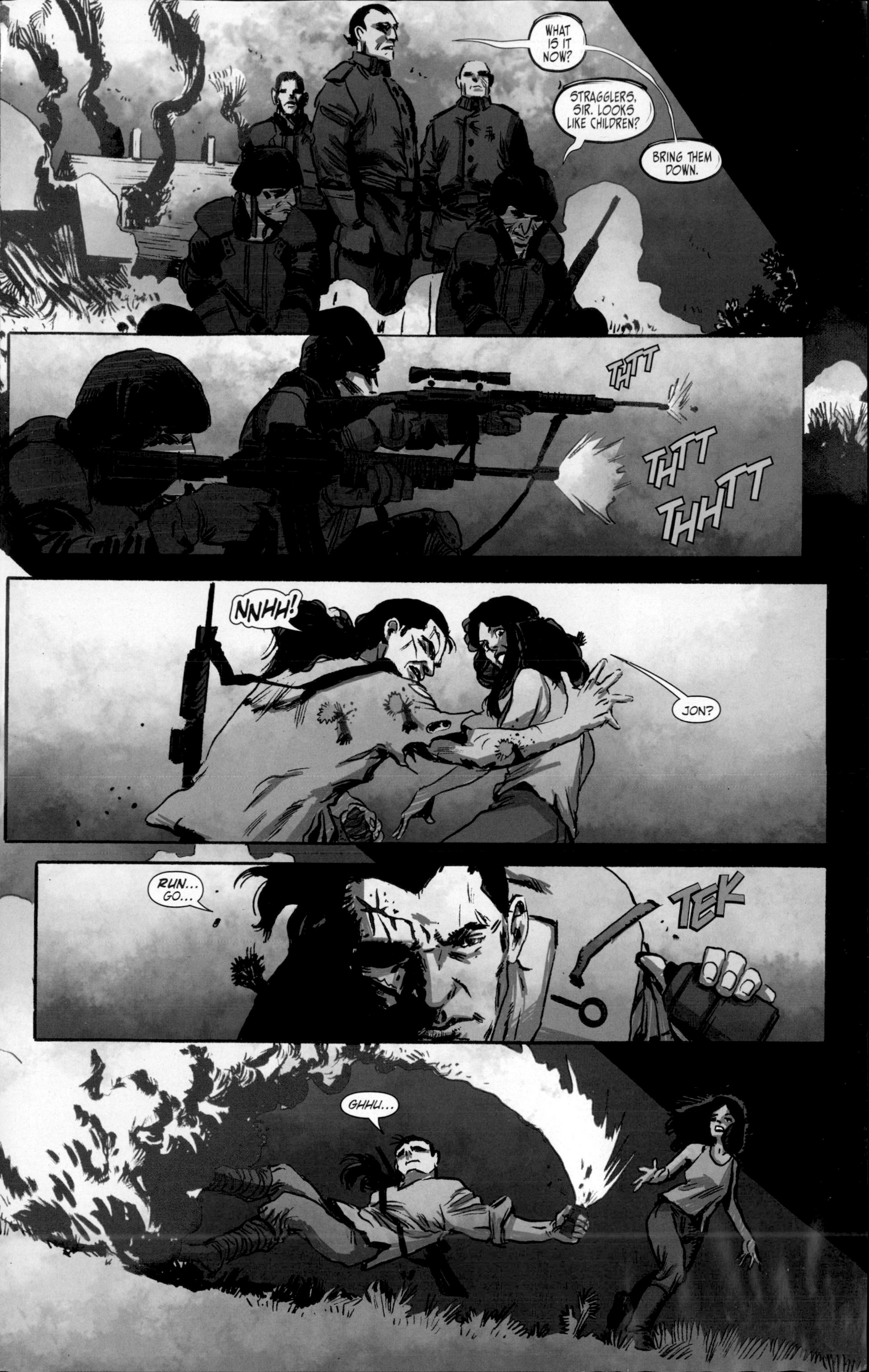
WHAT IS IT NOW?
STRAGGLERS, SIR. LOOKS LIKE CHILDREN?
BRING THEM DOWN.
THTT
THTT
THHTT
NNHH!
JON?
RUN... GO...
TEK
GHHU...

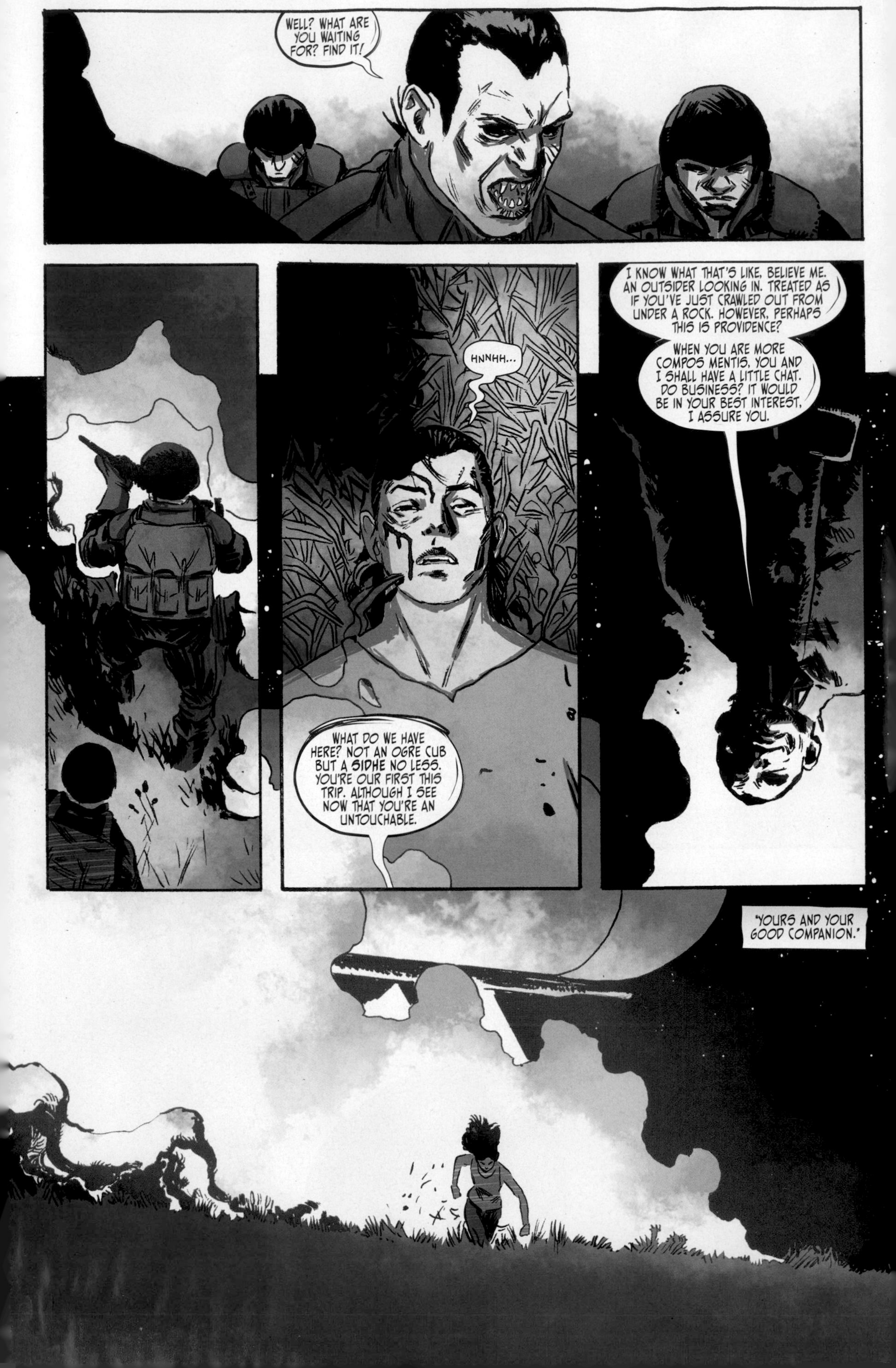

WELL? WHAT ARE YOU WAITING FOR? FIND IT!
HNNHH...
WHAT DO WE HAVE HERE? NOT AN OGRE CUB BUT A SIDHE NO LESS. YOU'RE OUR FIRST THIS TRIP. ALTHOUGH I SEE NOW THAT YOU'RE AN UNTOUCHABLE.
I KNOW WHAT THAT'S LIKE, BELIEVE ME. AN OUTSIDER LOOKING IN. TREATED AS IF YOU'VE JUST CRAWLED OUT FROM UNDER A ROCK. HOWEVER, PERHAPS THIS IS PROVIDENCE?
WHEN YOU ARE MORE COMPOS MENTIS, YOU AND I SHALL HAVE A LITTLE CHAT. DO BUSINESS? IT WOULD BE IN YOUR BEST INTEREST, I ASSURE YOU.
"YOURS AND YOUR GOOD COMPANION."

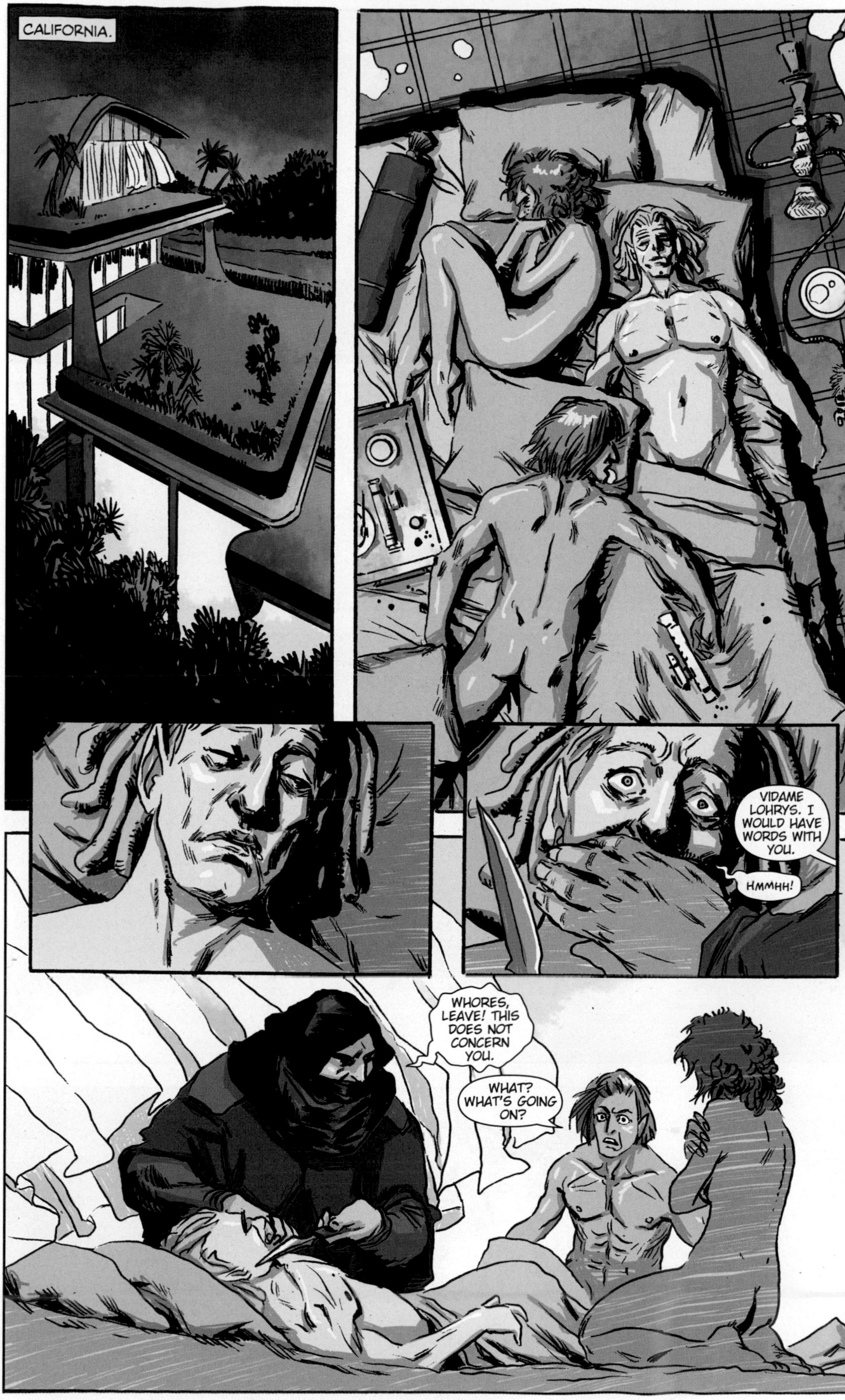
CALIFORNIA.
VIDAME LOHRYS. I WOULD HAVE WORDS WITH YOU.
HMMHH!
WHORES, LEAVE! THIS DOES NOT CONCERN YOU.
WHAT? WHAT'S GOING ON?

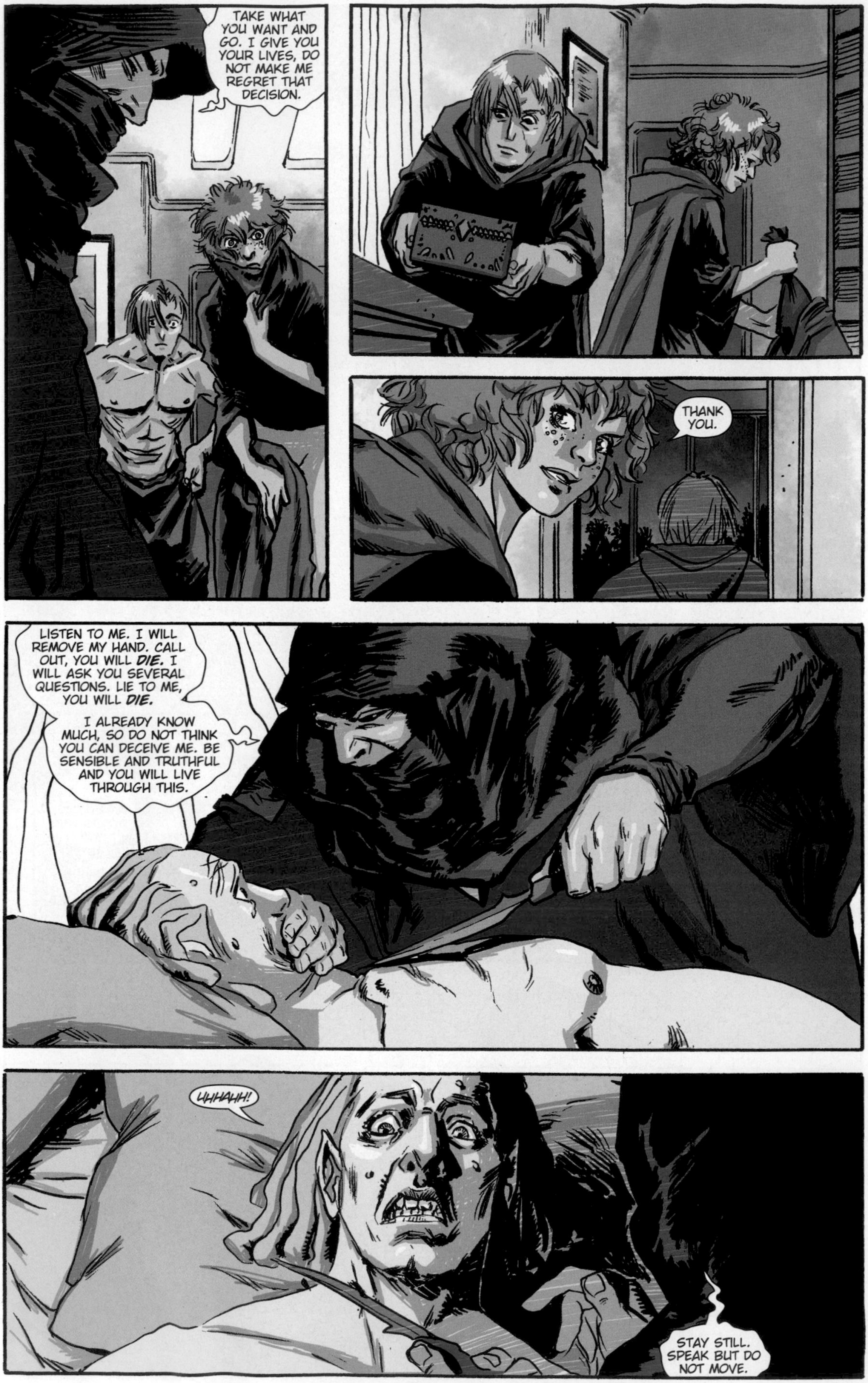
TAKE WHAT YOU WANT AND GO. I GIVE YOU YOUR LIVES, DO NOT MAKE ME REGRET THAT DECISION.
THANK YOU.
LISTEN TO ME. I WILL REMOVE MY HAND. CALL OUT, YOU WILL DIE. I WILL ASK YOU SEVERAL QUESTIONS. LIE TO ME, YOU WILL DIE.
I ALREADY KNOW MUCH, SO DO NOT THINK YOU CAN DECEIVE ME. BE SENSIBLE AND TRUTHFUL AND YOU WILL LIVE THROUGH THIS.
UHHAHH!
STAY STILL. SPEAK BUT DO NOT MOVE.

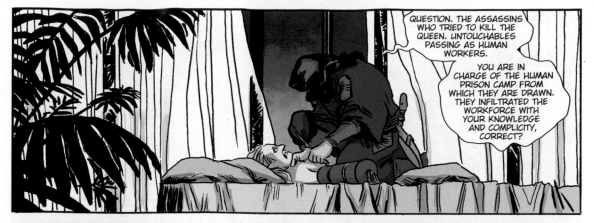

QUESTION. THE ASSASSINS WHO TRIED TO KILL THE QUEEN. UNTOUCHABLES PASSING AS HUMAN WORKERS.

YOU ARE IN CHARGE OF THE HUMAN PRISON CAMP FROM WHICH THEY ARE DRAWN. THEY INFILTRATED THE WORKFORCE WITH YOUR KNOWLEDGE AND COMPLICITY, CORRECT?

I...YES, BUT...

PLEASE, I CAN'T...

QUESTION. WHO ORDERED THIS ACTION? WHO DO YOU SERVE?

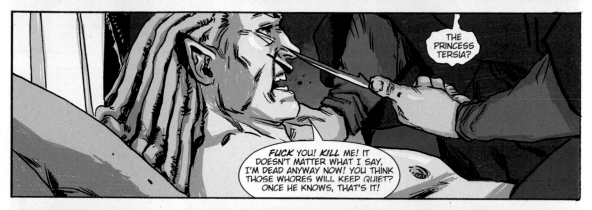

THE PRINCESS TERSIA?

FUCK YOU! *KILL* ME! IT DOESN'T MATTER WHAT I SAY, I'M DEAD ANYWAY NOW! YOU THINK THOSE WHORES WILL KEEP QUIET? ONCE HE KNOWS, THAT'S IT!

HE? SEVERIN?

AND OF COURSE, HE ANSWERS TO HIS OLDER SISTER.

FOR NOW. ALTHOUGH I HEAR HE HAS HIS OWN GAME IN PLAY.

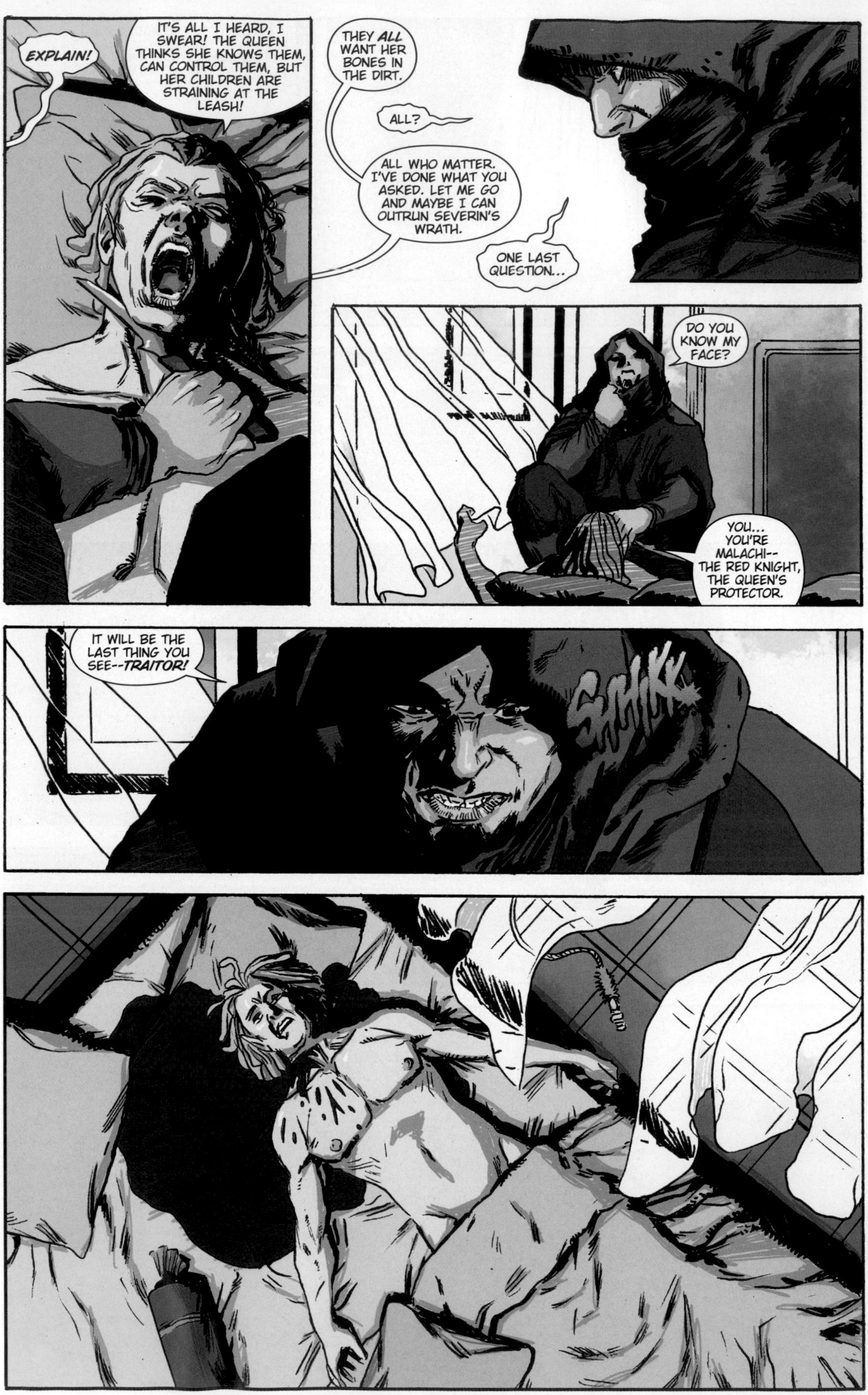
EXPLAIN!
IT'S ALL I HEARD, I SWEAR! THE QUEEN THINKS SHE KNOWS THEM, CAN CONTROL THEM, BUT HER CHILDREN ARE STRAINING AT THE LEASH!
THEY ALL WANT HER BONES IN THE DIRT.
ALL?
ALL WHO MATTER. I'VE DONE WHAT YOU ASKED. LET ME GO AND MAYBE I CAN OUTRUN SEVERIN'S WRATH.
ONE LAST QUESTION...
DO YOU KNOW MY FACE?
YOU... YOU'RE MALACHI-- THE RED KNIGHT, THE QUEEN'S PROTECTOR.
IT WILL BE THE LAST THING YOU SEE--TRAITOR!
SHKK

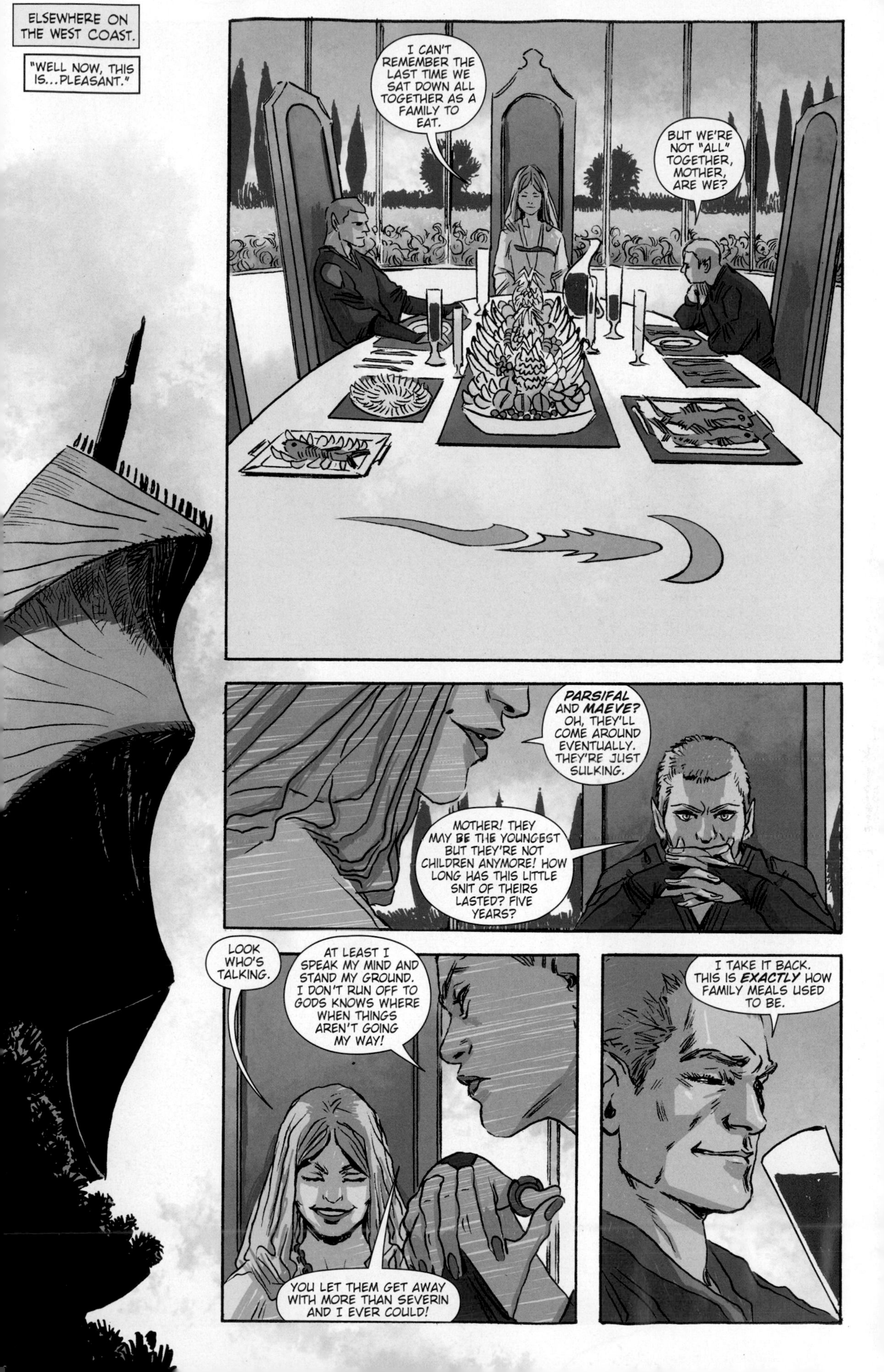
ELSEWHERE ON THE WEST COAST.
"WELL NOW, THIS IS...PLEASANT."
I CAN'T REMEMBER THE LAST TIME WE SAT DOWN ALL TOGETHER AS A FAMILY TO EAT.
BUT WE'RE NOT "ALL" TOGETHER, MOTHER, ARE WE?
PARSIFAL AND MAEVE? OH, THEY'LL COME AROUND EVENTUALLY. THEY'RE JUST SULKING.
MOTHER! THEY MAY BE THE YOUNGEST BUT THEY'RE NOT CHILDREN ANYMORE! HOW LONG HAS THIS LITTLE SNIT OF THEIRS LASTED? FIVE YEARS?
LOOK WHO'S TALKING.
AT LEAST I SPEAK MY MIND AND STAND MY GROUND. I DON'T RUN OFF TO GODS KNOWS WHERE WHEN THINGS AREN'T GOING MY WAY!
YOU LET THEM GET AWAY WITH MORE THAN SEVERIN AND I EVER COULD!
I TAKE IT BACK. THIS IS EXACTLY HOW FAMILY MEALS USED TO BE.

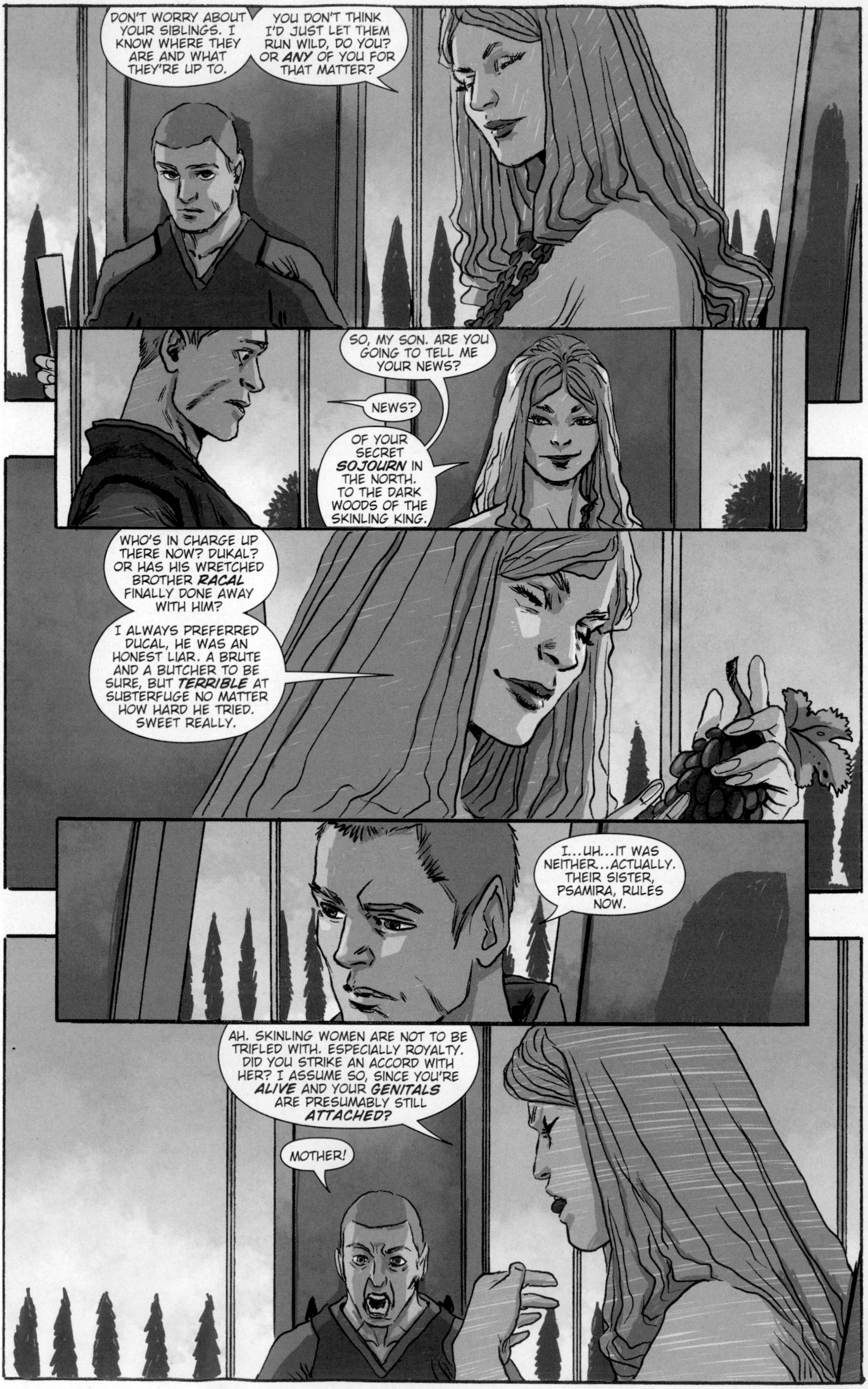
DON'T WORRY ABOUT YOUR SIBLINGS. I KNOW WHERE THEY ARE AND WHAT THEY'RE UP TO.
YOU DON'T THINK I'D JUST LET THEM RUN WILD, DO YOU? OR ANY OF YOU FOR THAT MATTER?
SO, MY SON. ARE YOU GOING TO TELL ME YOUR NEWS?
NEWS?
OF YOUR SECRET SOJOURN IN THE NORTH. TO THE DARK WOODS OF THE SKINLING KING.
WHO'S IN CHARGE UP THERE NOW? DUKAL? OR HAS HIS WRETCHED BROTHER RACAL FINALLY DONE AWAY WITH HIM?
I ALWAYS PREFERRED DUCAL, HE WAS AN HONEST LIAR. A BRUTE AND A BUTCHER TO BE SURE, BUT TERRIBLE AT SUBTERFUGE NO MATTER HOW HARD HE TRIED. SWEET REALLY.
I...UH...IT WAS NEITHER...ACTUALLY. THEIR SISTER, PSAMIRA, RULES NOW.
AH. SKINLING WOMEN ARE NOT TO BE TRIFLED WITH. ESPECIALLY ROYALTY. DID YOU STRIKE AN ACCORD WITH HER? I ASSUME SO, SINCE YOU'RE ALIVE AND YOUR GENITALS ARE PRESUMABLY STILL ATTACHED?
MOTHER!

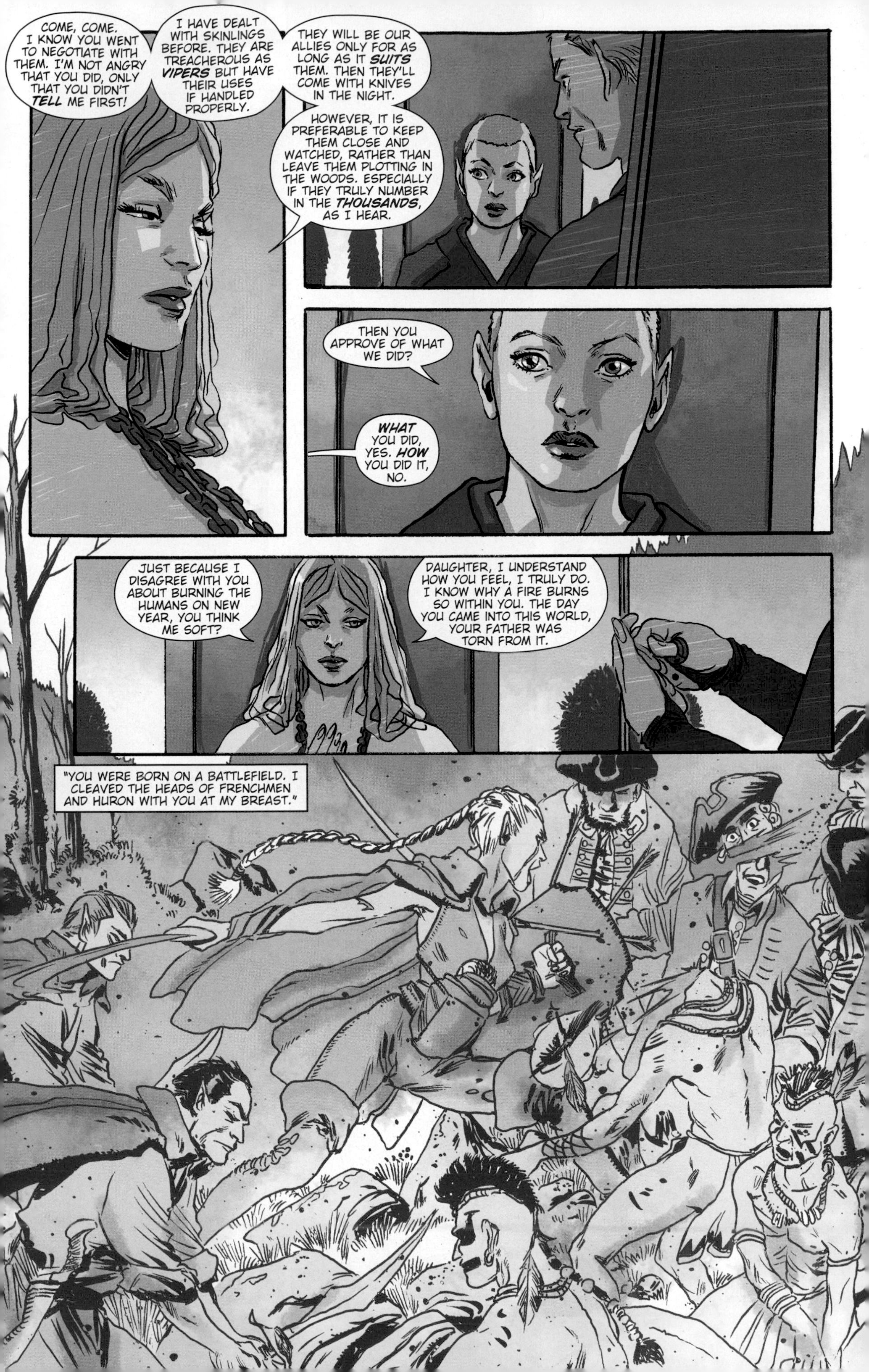
COME, COME. I KNOW YOU WENT TO NEGOTIATE WITH THEM. I'M NOT ANGRY THAT YOU DID, ONLY THAT YOU DIDN'T TELL ME FIRST!
I HAVE DEALT WITH SKINLINGS BEFORE. THEY ARE TREACHEROUS AS VIPERS BUT HAVE THEIR USES IF HANDLED PROPERLY.
THEY WILL BE OUR ALLIES ONLY FOR AS LONG AS IT SUITS THEM. THEN THEY'LL COME WITH KNIVES IN THE NIGHT.
HOWEVER, IT IS PREFERABLE TO KEEP THEM CLOSE AND WATCHED, RATHER THAN LEAVE THEM PLOTTING IN THE WOODS. ESPECIALLY IF THEY TRULY NUMBER IN THE THOUSANDS, AS I HEAR.
THEN YOU APPROVE OF WHAT WE DID?
WHAT YOU DID, YES. HOW YOU DID IT, NO.
JUST BECAUSE I DISAGREE WITH YOU ABOUT BURNING THE HUMANS ON NEW YEAR, YOU THINK ME SOFT?
DAUGHTER, I UNDERSTAND HOW YOU FEEL, I TRULY DO. I KNOW WHY A FIRE BURNS SO WITHIN YOU. THE DAY YOU CAME INTO THIS WORLD, YOUR FATHER WAS TORN FROM IT.
"YOU WERE BORN ON A BATTLEFIELD. I CLEAVED THE HEADS OF FRENCHMEN AND HURON WITH YOU AT MY BREAST."

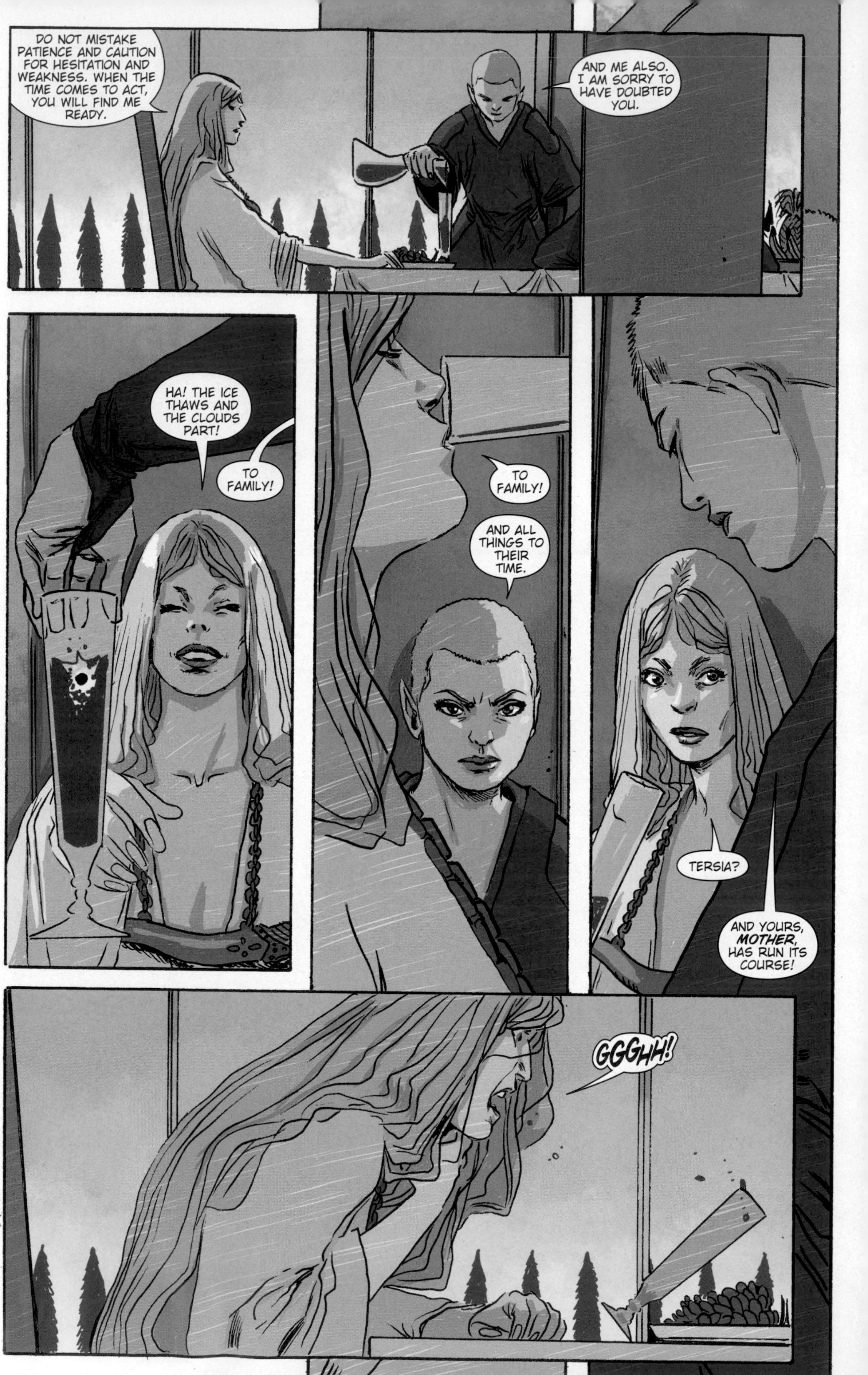
DO NOT MISTAKE PATIENCE AND CAUTION FOR HESITATION AND WEAKNESS. WHEN THE TIME COMES TO ACT, YOU WILL FIND ME READY.
AND ME ALSO. I AM SORRY TO HAVE DOUBTED YOU.
HA! THE ICE THAWS AND THE CLOUDS PART!
TO FAMILY!
TO FAMILY!
AND ALL THINGS TO THEIR TIME.
TERSIA?
AND YOURS, *MOTHER*, HAS RUN ITS COURSE!
GGGHH!

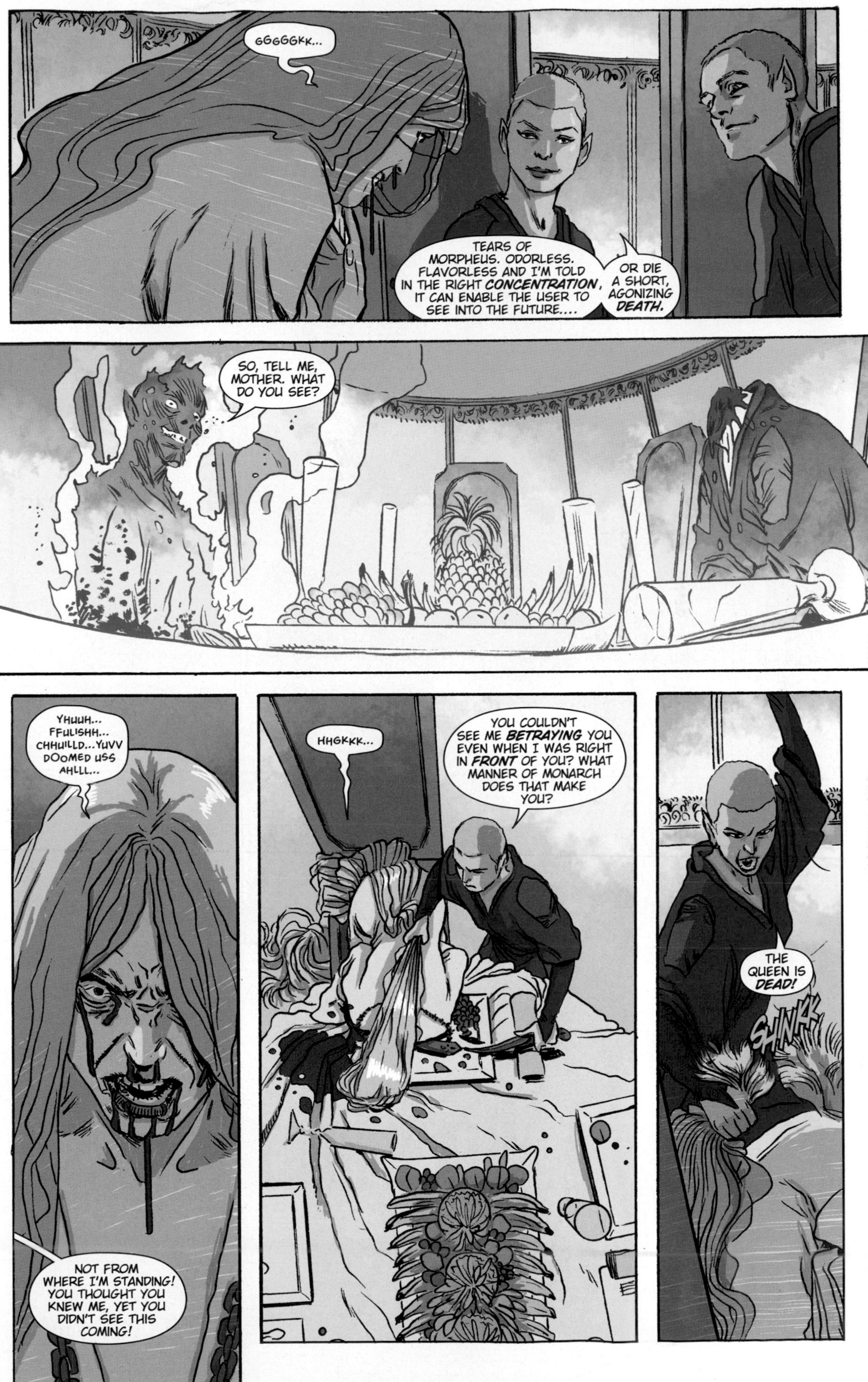
GGGGGKK...
TEARS OF MORPHEUS. ODORLESS. FLAVORLESS AND I'M TOLD IN THE RIGHT CONCENTRATION, IT CAN ENABLE THE USER TO SEE INTO THE FUTURE....
OR DIE A SHORT, AGONIZING DEATH.
SO, TELL ME, MOTHER. WHAT DO YOU SEE?
YHUUH... FFULISHH... CHHUILLD...YUVV DOOMED USS AHLLL...
NOT FROM WHERE I'M STANDING! YOU THOUGHT YOU KNEW ME, YET YOU DIDN'T SEE THIS COMING!
HHGKKK...
YOU COULDN'T SEE ME BETRAYING YOU EVEN WHEN I WAS RIGHT IN FRONT OF YOU? WHAT MANNER OF MONARCH DOES THAT MAKE YOU?
THE QUEEN IS DEAD!
SHINK!

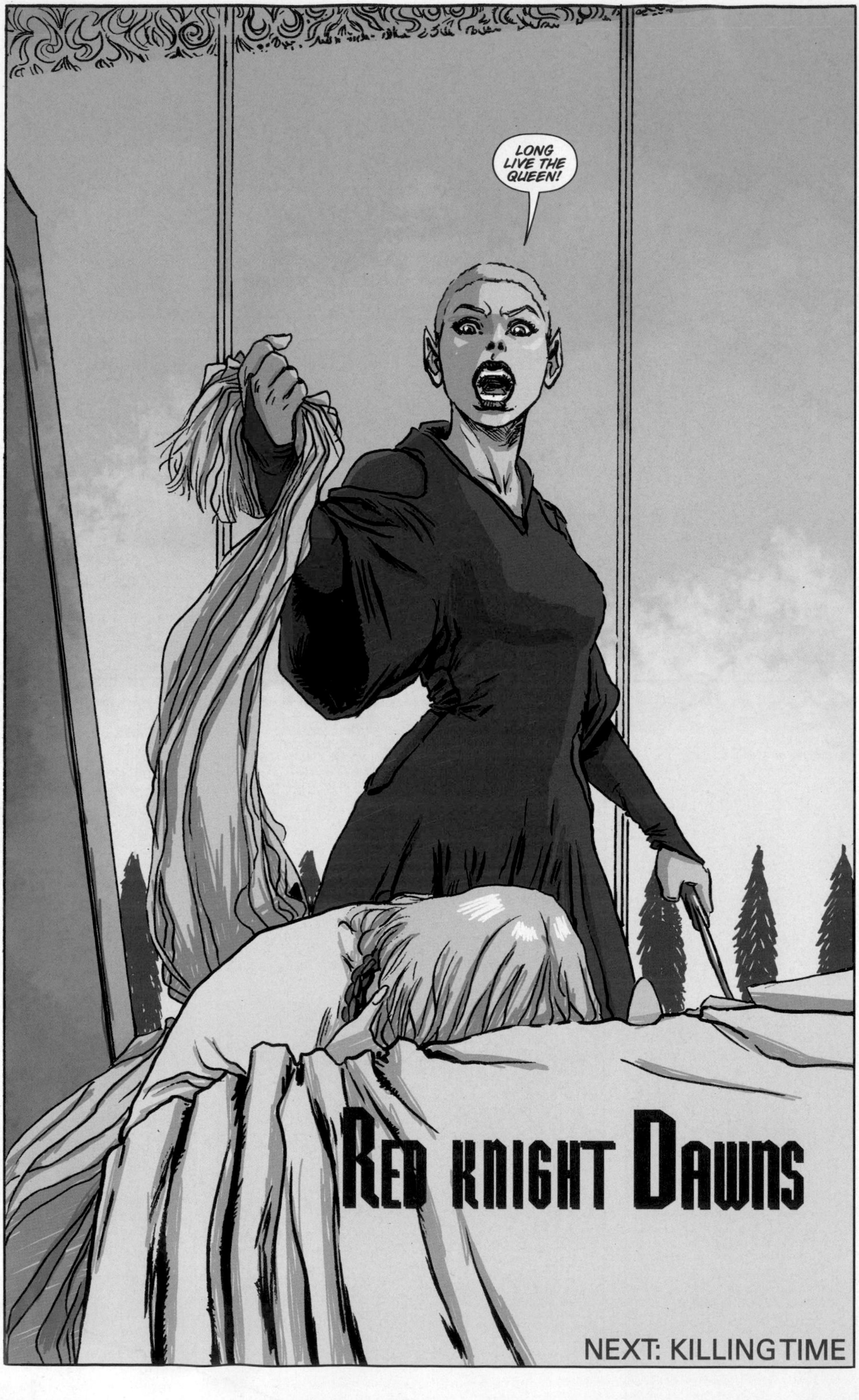
LONG LIVE THE QUEEN!
RED KNIGHT DAWNS
NEXT: KILLING TIME

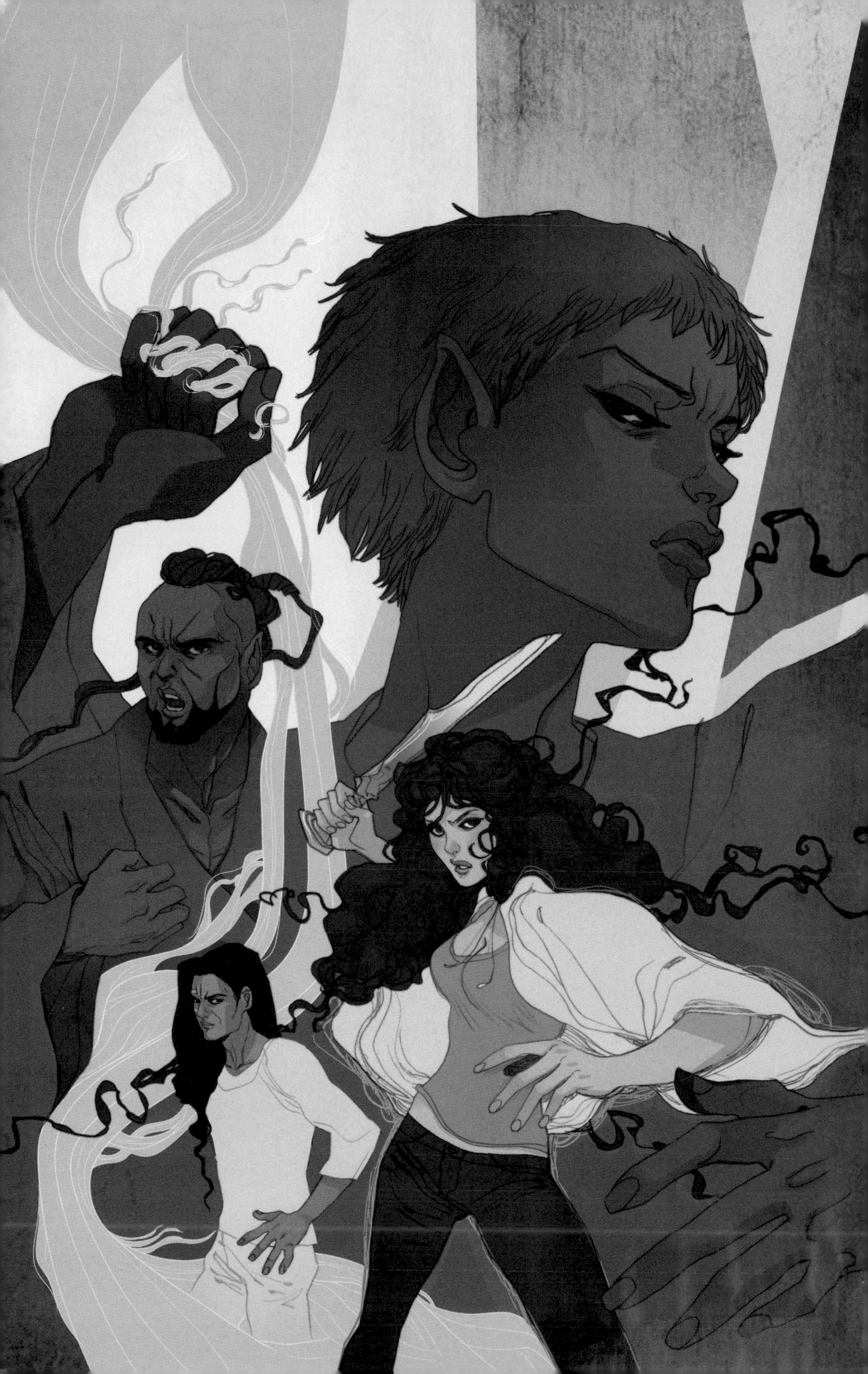

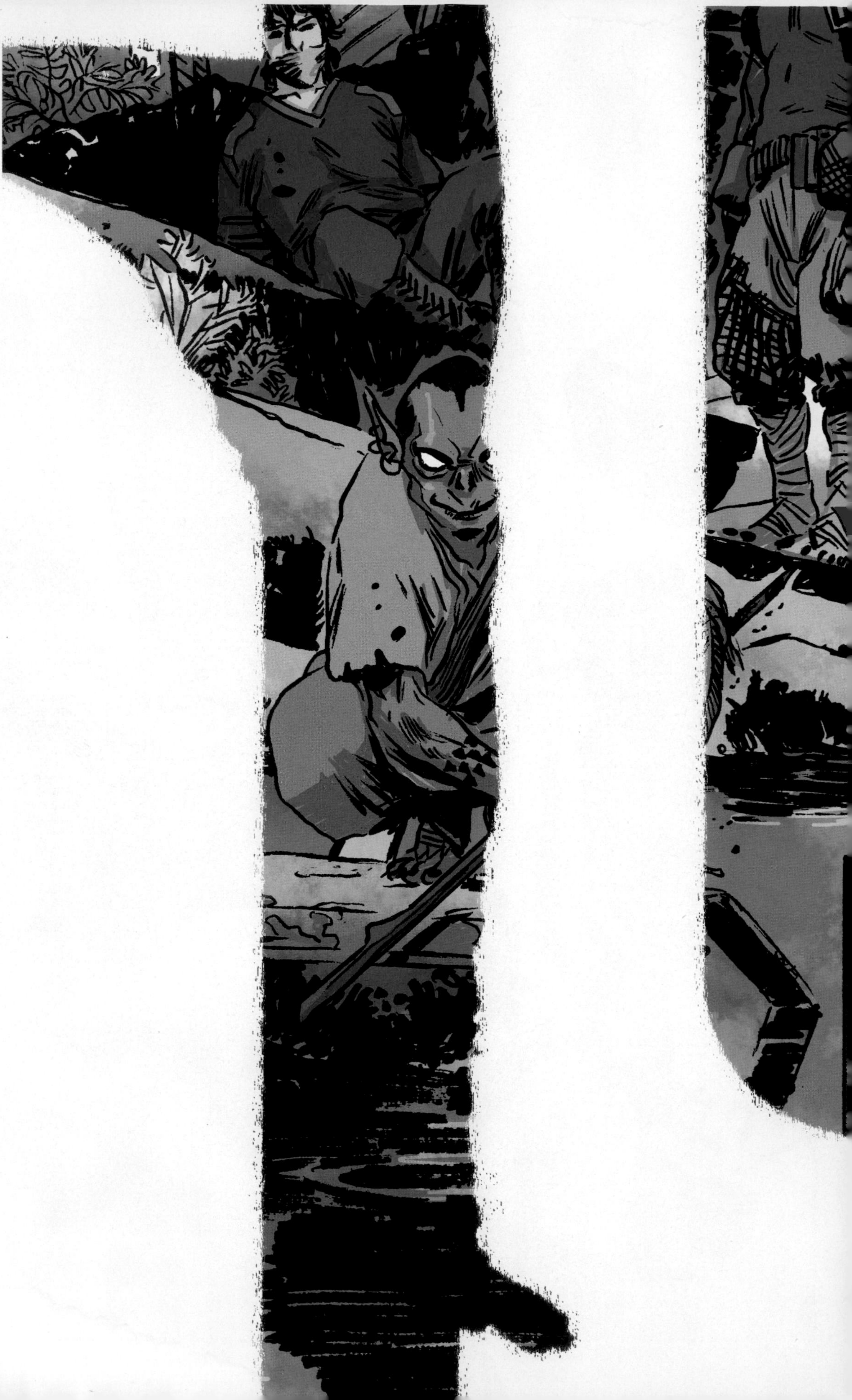

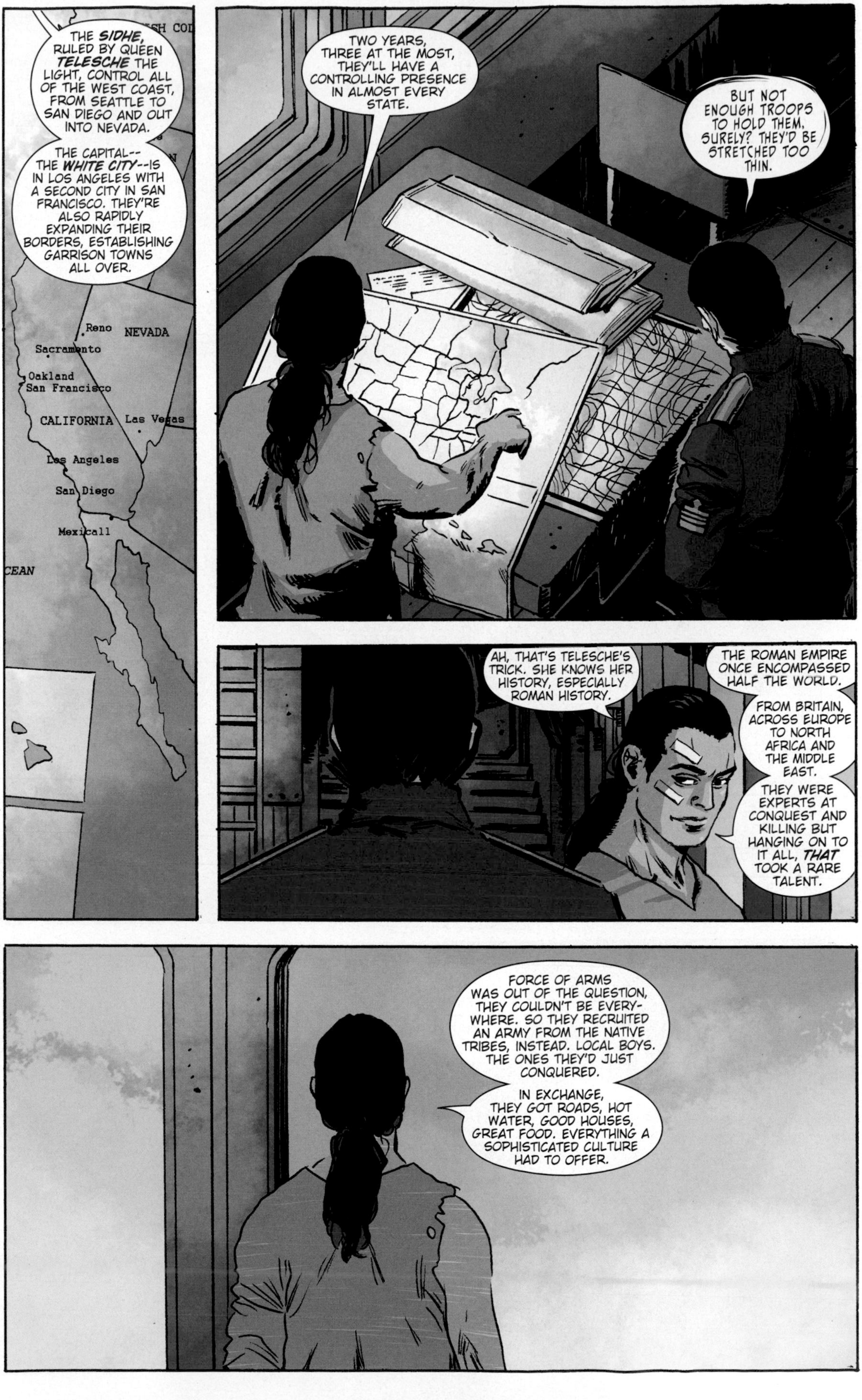
THE SIDHE, RULED BY QUEEN TELESCHE THE LIGHT, CONTROL ALL OF THE WEST COAST, FROM SEATTLE TO SAN DIEGO AND OUT INTO NEVADA.
THE CAPITAL-- THE WHITE CITY--IS IN LOS ANGELES WITH A SECOND CITY IN SAN FRANCISCO. THEY'RE ALSO RAPIDLY EXPANDING THEIR BORDERS, ESTABLISHING GARRISON TOWNS ALL OVER.
Reno
NEVADA
Sacramento
Oakland
San Francisco
CALIFORNIA
Las Vegas
Los Angeles
San Diego
Mexicali
CEAN
TWO YEARS, THREE AT THE MOST, THEY'LL HAVE A CONTROLLING PRESENCE IN ALMOST EVERY STATE.
BUT NOT ENOUGH TROOPS TO HOLD THEM, SURELY? THEY'D BE STRETCHED TOO THIN.
AH, THAT'S TELESCHE'S TRICK. SHE KNOWS HER HISTORY, ESPECIALLY ROMAN HISTORY.
THE ROMAN EMPIRE ONCE ENCOMPASSED HALF THE WORLD.
FROM BRITAIN, ACROSS EUROPE TO NORTH AFRICA AND THE MIDDLE EAST.
THEY WERE EXPERTS AT CONQUEST AND KILLING BUT HANGING ON TO IT ALL, THAT TOOK A RARE TALENT.
FORCE OF ARMS WAS OUT OF THE QUESTION, THEY COULDN'T BE EVERY-WHERE. SO THEY RECRUITED AN ARMY FROM THE NATIVE TRIBES, INSTEAD. LOCAL BOYS. THE ONES THEY'D JUST CONQUERED.
IN EXCHANGE, THEY GOT ROADS, HOT WATER, GOOD HOUSES, GREAT FOOD. EVERYTHING A SOPHISTICATED CULTURE HAD TO OFFER.

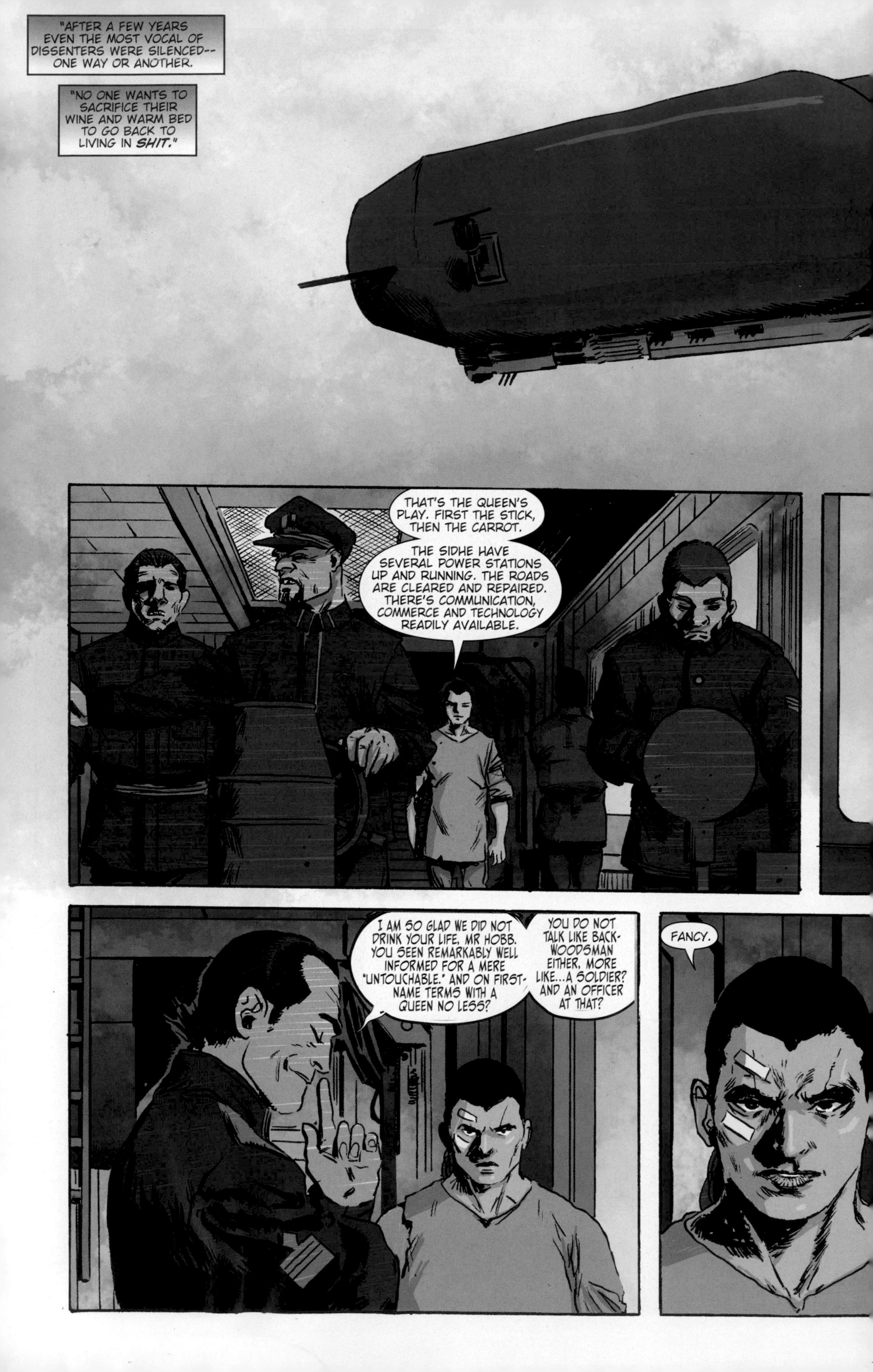
"AFTER A FEW YEARS EVEN THE MOST VOCAL OF DISSENTERS WERE SILENCED-- ONE WAY OR ANOTHER.
"NO ONE WANTS TO SACRIFICE THEIR WINE AND WARM BED TO GO BACK TO LIVING IN *SHIT*."
THAT'S THE QUEEN'S PLAY. FIRST THE STICK, THEN THE CARROT.
THE SIDHE HAVE SEVERAL POWER STATIONS UP AND RUNNING. THE ROADS ARE CLEARED AND REPAIRED. THERE'S COMMUNICATION, COMMERCE AND TECHNOLOGY READILY AVAILABLE.
I AM SO GLAD WE DID NOT DRINK YOUR LIFE, MR HOBB. YOU SEEN REMARKABLY WELL INFORMED FOR A MERE "UNTOUCHABLE." AND ON FIRST-NAME TERMS WITH A QUEEN NO LESS?
YOU DO NOT TALK LIKE BACK-WOODSMAN EITHER, MORE LIKE...A SOLDIER? AND AN OFFICER AT THAT?
FANCY.

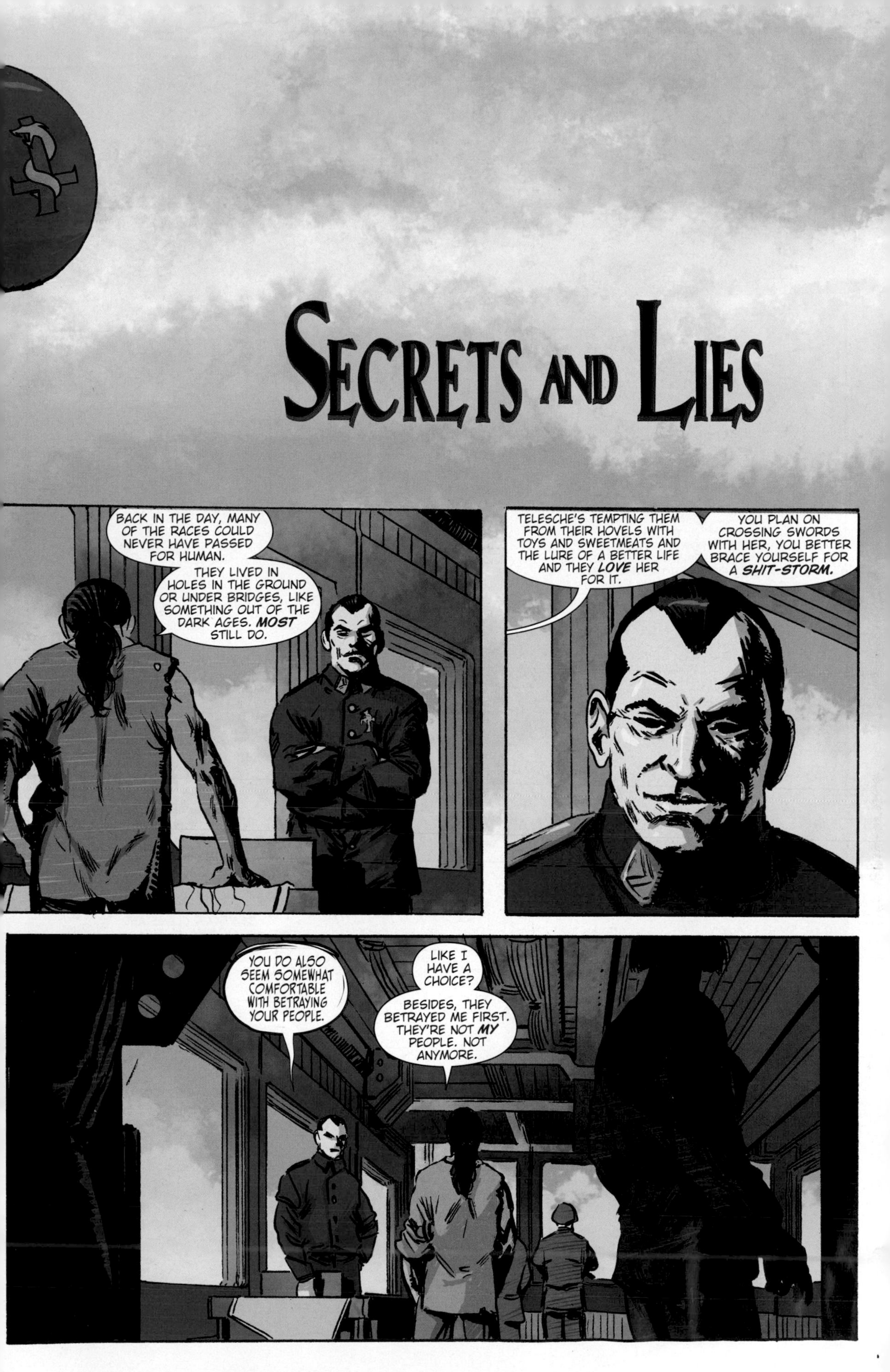
SECRETS AND LIES
BACK IN THE DAY, MANY OF THE RACES COULD NEVER HAVE PASSED FOR HUMAN.
THEY LIVED IN HOLES IN THE GROUND OR UNDER BRIDGES, LIKE SOMETHING OUT OF THE DARK AGES. MOST STILL DO.
TELESCHE'S TEMPTING THEM FROM THEIR HOVELS WITH TOYS AND SWEETMEATS AND THE LURE OF A BETTER LIFE AND THEY LOVE HER FOR IT.
YOU PLAN ON CROSSING SWORDS WITH HER, YOU BETTER BRACE YOURSELF FOR A SHIT-STORM.
YOU DO ALSO SEEM SOMEWHAT COMFORTABLE WITH BETRAYING YOUR PEOPLE.
LIKE I HAVE A CHOICE?
BESIDES, THEY BETRAYED ME FIRST. THEY'RE NOT MY PEOPLE. NOT ANYMORE.

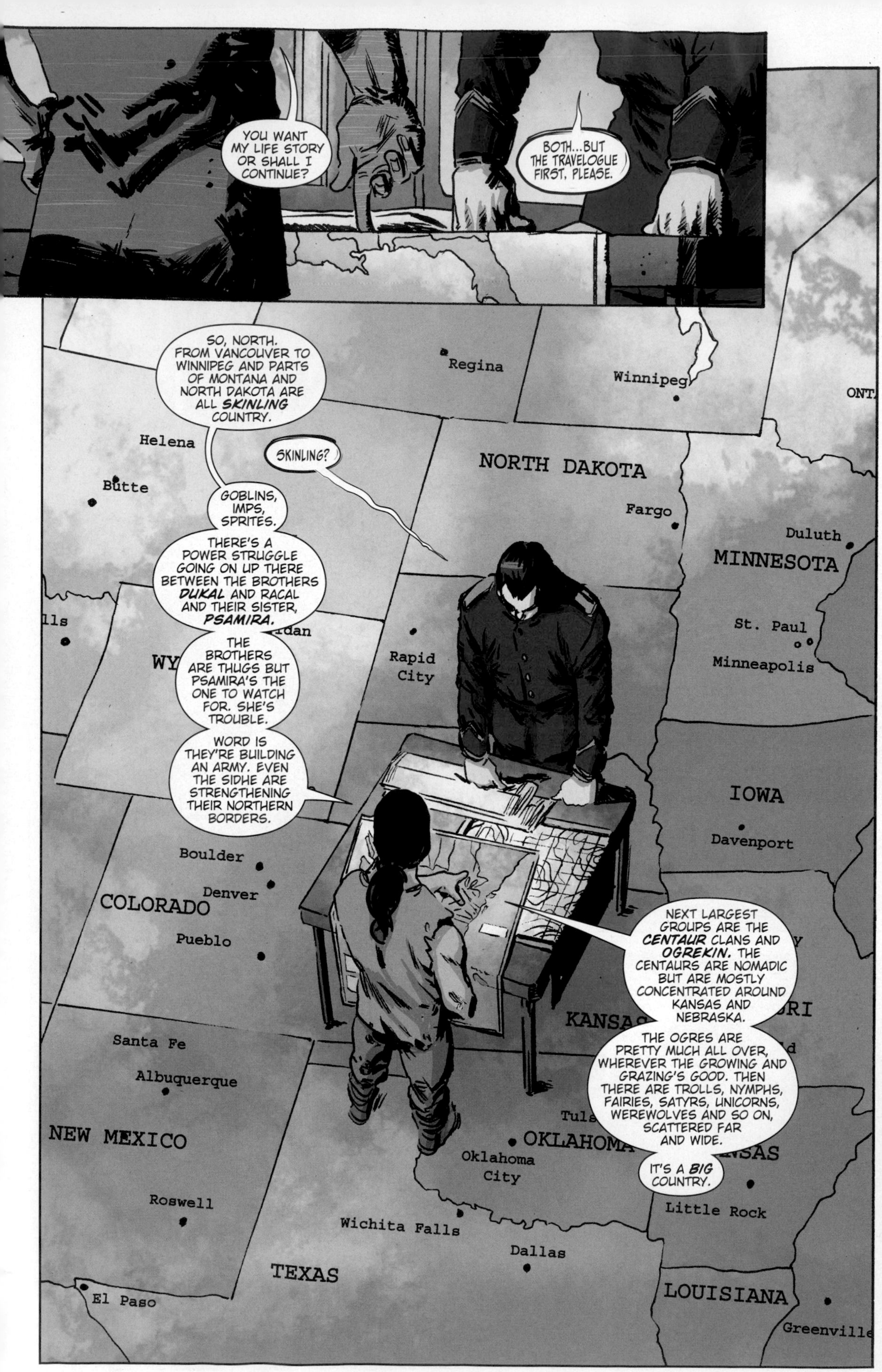

YOU WANT MY LIFE STORY OR SHALL I CONTINUE?
BOTH...BUT THE TRAVELOGUE FIRST, PLEASE.
SO, NORTH. FROM VANCOUVER TO WINNIPEG AND PARTS OF MONTANA AND NORTH DAKOTA ARE ALL SKINLING COUNTRY.
SKINLING?
GOBLINS, IMPS, SPRITES.
THERE'S A POWER STRUGGLE GOING ON UP THERE BETWEEN THE BROTHERS DUKAL AND RACAL AND THEIR SISTER, PSAMIRA.
THE BROTHERS ARE THUGS BUT PSAMIRA'S THE ONE TO WATCH FOR. SHE'S TROUBLE.
WORD IS THEY'RE BUILDING AN ARMY. EVEN THE SIDHE ARE STRENGTHENING THEIR NORTHERN BORDERS.
NEXT LARGEST GROUPS ARE THE CENTAUR CLANS AND OGREKIN. THE CENTAURS ARE NOMADIC BUT ARE MOSTLY CONCENTRATED AROUND KANSAS AND NEBRASKA.
THE OGRES ARE PRETTY MUCH ALL OVER, WHEREVER THE GROWING AND GRAZING'S GOOD. THEN THERE ARE TROLLS, NYMPHS, FAIRIES, SATYRS, UNICORNS, WEREWOLVES AND SO ON, SCATTERED FAR AND WIDE.
IT'S A BIG COUNTRY.
Regina
Winnipeg
Helena
Butte
NORTH DAKOTA
Fargo
Duluth
MINNESOTA
St. Paul
Minneapolis
Rapid City
IOWA
Davenport
Boulder
Denver
COLORADO
Pueblo
KANSAS
Santa Fe
Albuquerque
NEW MEXICO
OKLAHOMA
Oklahoma City
Roswell
Wichita Falls
Little Rock
Dallas
TEXAS
LOUISIANA
El Paso
Greenville

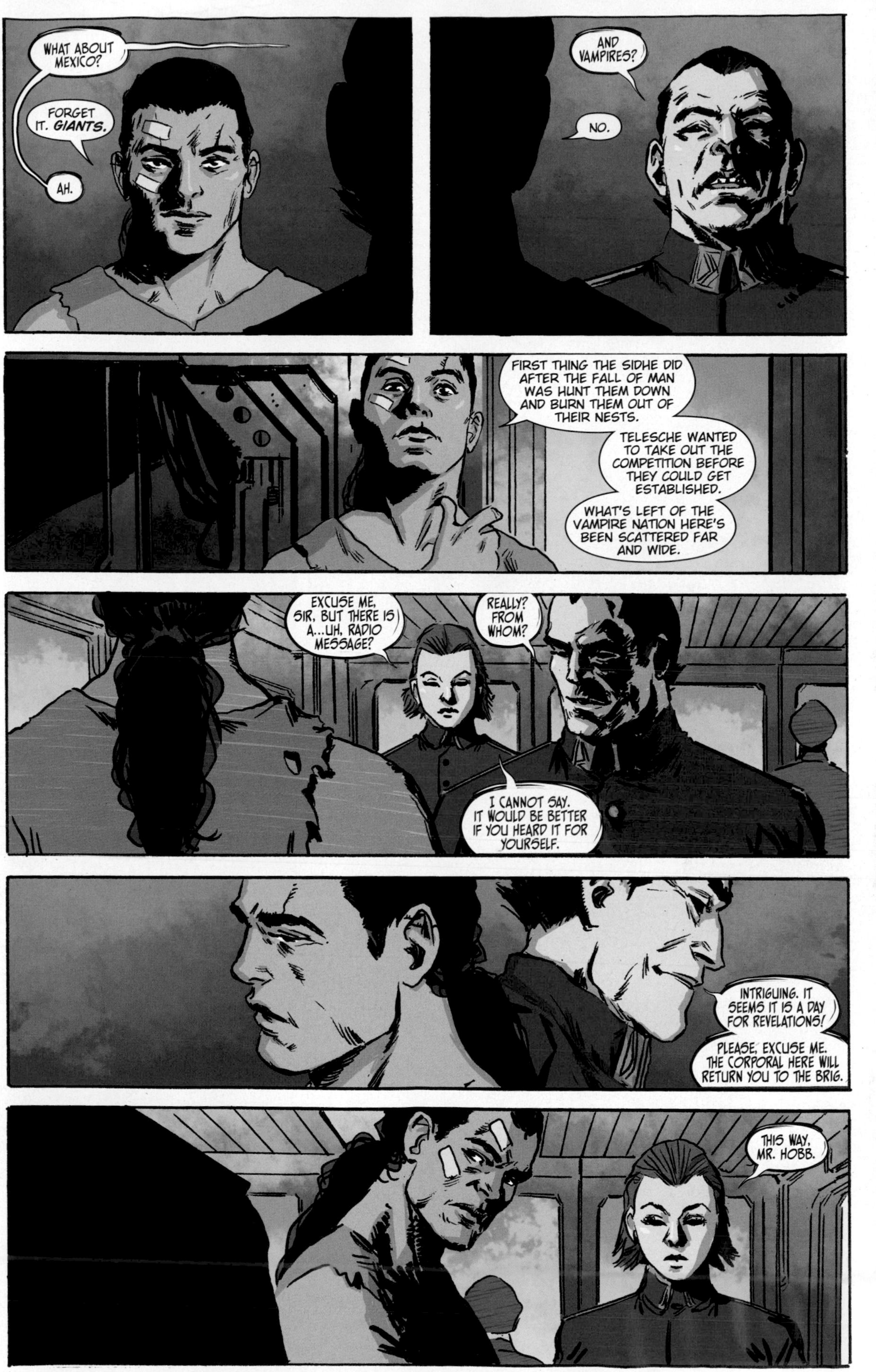
WHAT ABOUT MEXICO?
FORGET IT. GIANTS.
AH.
AND VAMPIRES?
NO.
FIRST THING THE SIDHE DID AFTER THE FALL OF MAN WAS HUNT THEM DOWN AND BURN THEM OUT OF THEIR NESTS.
TELESCHE WANTED TO TAKE OUT THE COMPETITION BEFORE THEY COULD GET ESTABLISHED.
WHAT'S LEFT OF THE VAMPIRE NATION HERE'S BEEN SCATTERED FAR AND WIDE.
EXCUSE ME, SIR, BUT THERE IS A...UH, RADIO MESSAGE?
REALLY? FROM WHOM?
I CANNOT SAY. IT WOULD BE BETTER IF YOU HEARD IT FOR YOURSELF.
INTRIGUING. IT SEEMS IT IS A DAY FOR REVELATIONS!
PLEASE, EXCUSE ME. THE CORPORAL HERE WILL RETURN YOU TO THE BRIG.
THIS WAY, MR. HOBB.

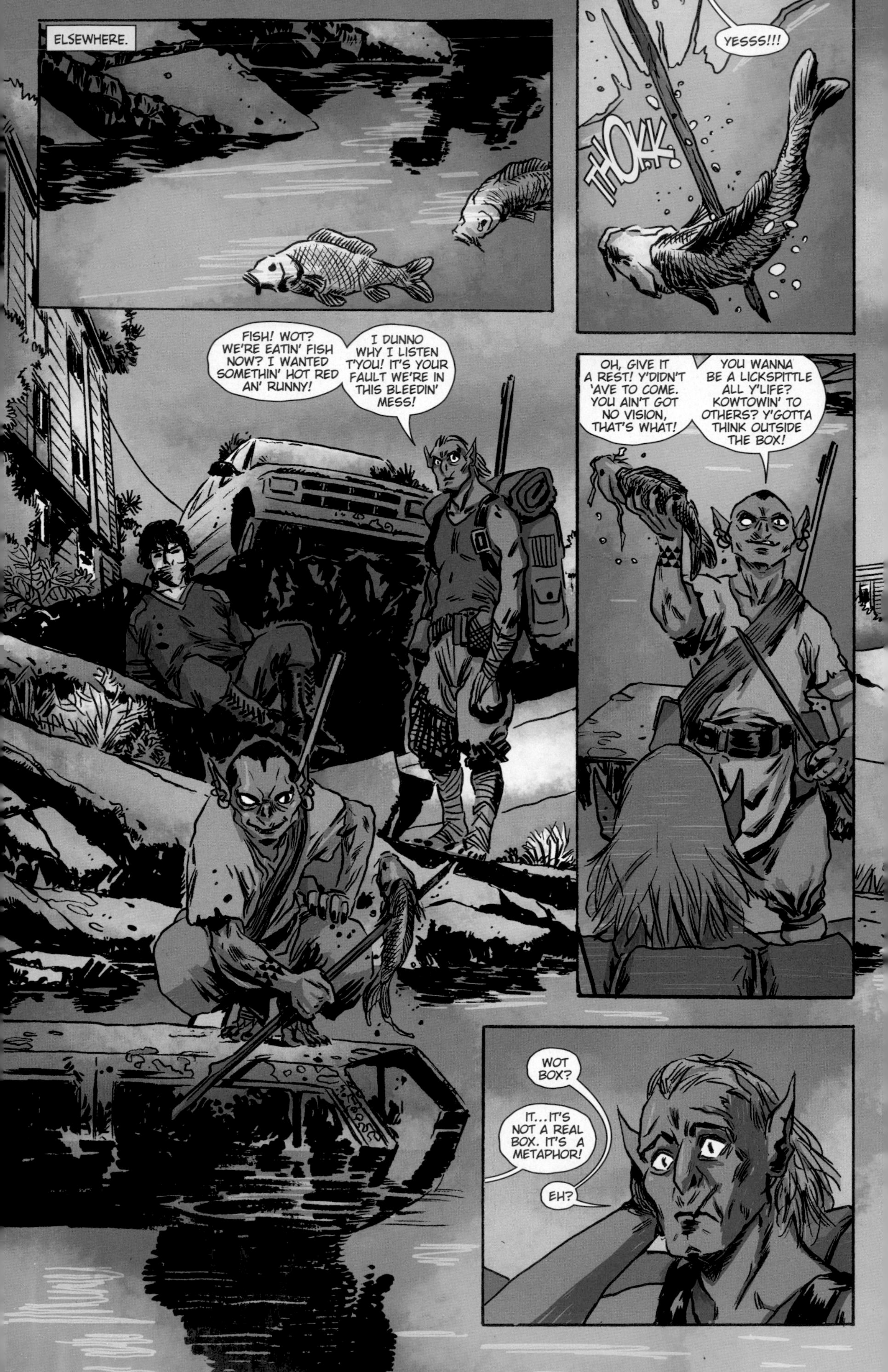
ELSEWHERE.
THOKK!
YESSS!!!
FISH! WOT? WE'RE EATIN' FISH NOW? I WANTED SOMETHIN' HOT RED AN' RUNNY!
I DUNNO WHY I LISTEN T'YOU! IT'S YOUR FAULT WE'RE IN THIS BLEEDIN' MESS!
OH, GIVE IT A REST! Y'DIDN'T 'AVE TO COME. YOU AIN'T GOT NO VISION, THAT'S WHAT!
YOU WANNA BE A LICKSPITTLE ALL Y'LIFE? KOWTOWIN' TO OTHERS? Y'GOTTA THINK OUTSIDE THE BOX!
WOT BOX?
IT...IT'S NOT A REAL BOX. IT'S A METAPHOR!
EH?

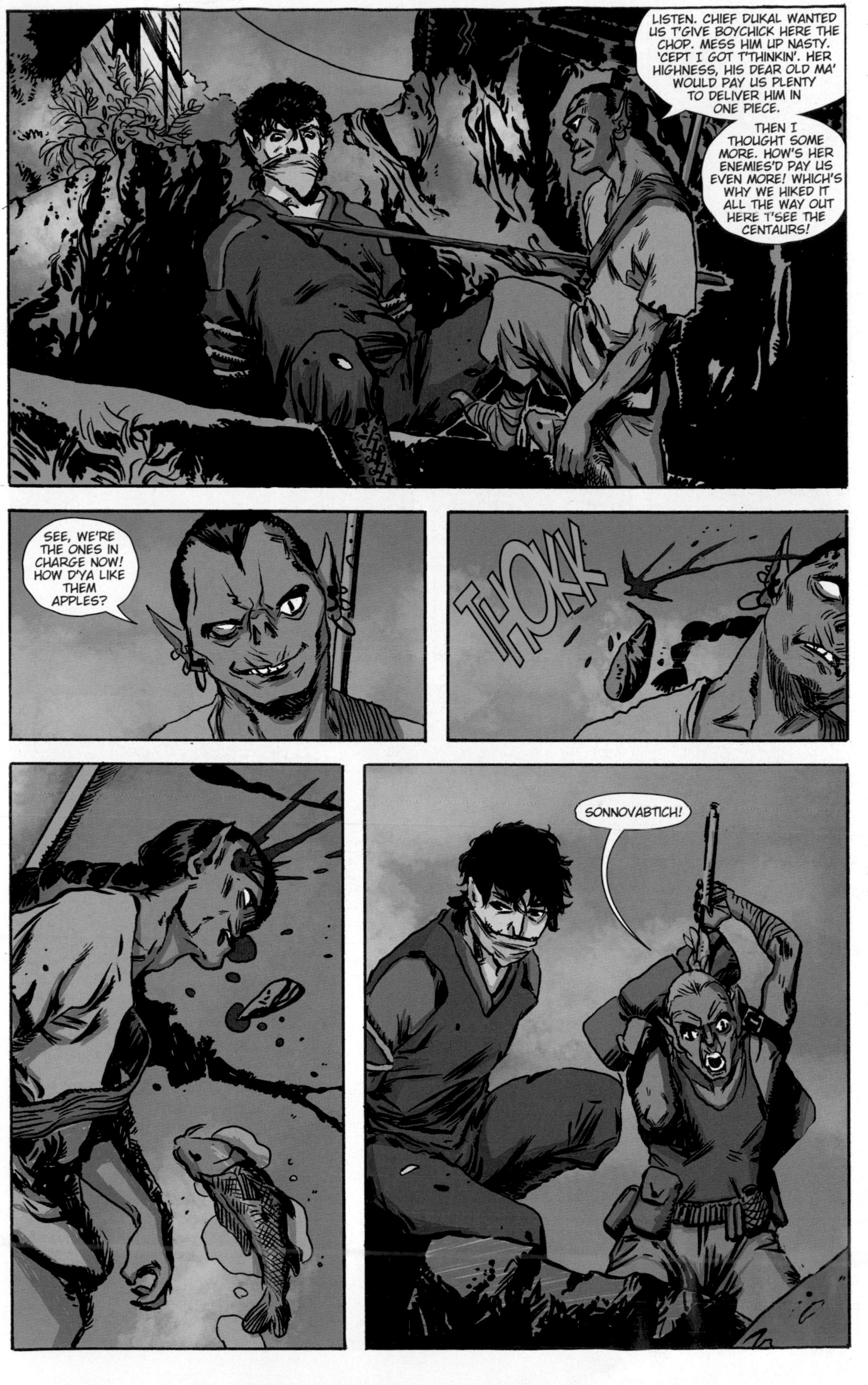
LISTEN. CHIEF DUKAL WANTED US T'GIVE BOYCHICK HERE THE CHOP. MESS HIM UP NASTY. 'CEPT I GOT T'THINKIN'. HER HIGHNESS, HIS DEAR OLD MA' WOULD PAY US PLENTY TO DELIVER HIM IN ONE PIECE.
THEN I THOUGHT SOME MORE. HOW'S HER ENEMIES'D PAY US EVEN MORE! WHICH'S WHY WE HIKED IT ALL THE WAY OUT HERE T'SEE THE CENTAURS!
SEE, WE'RE THE ONES IN CHARGE NOW! HOW D'YA LIKE THEM APPLES?
THOKK
SONNOVABTICH!

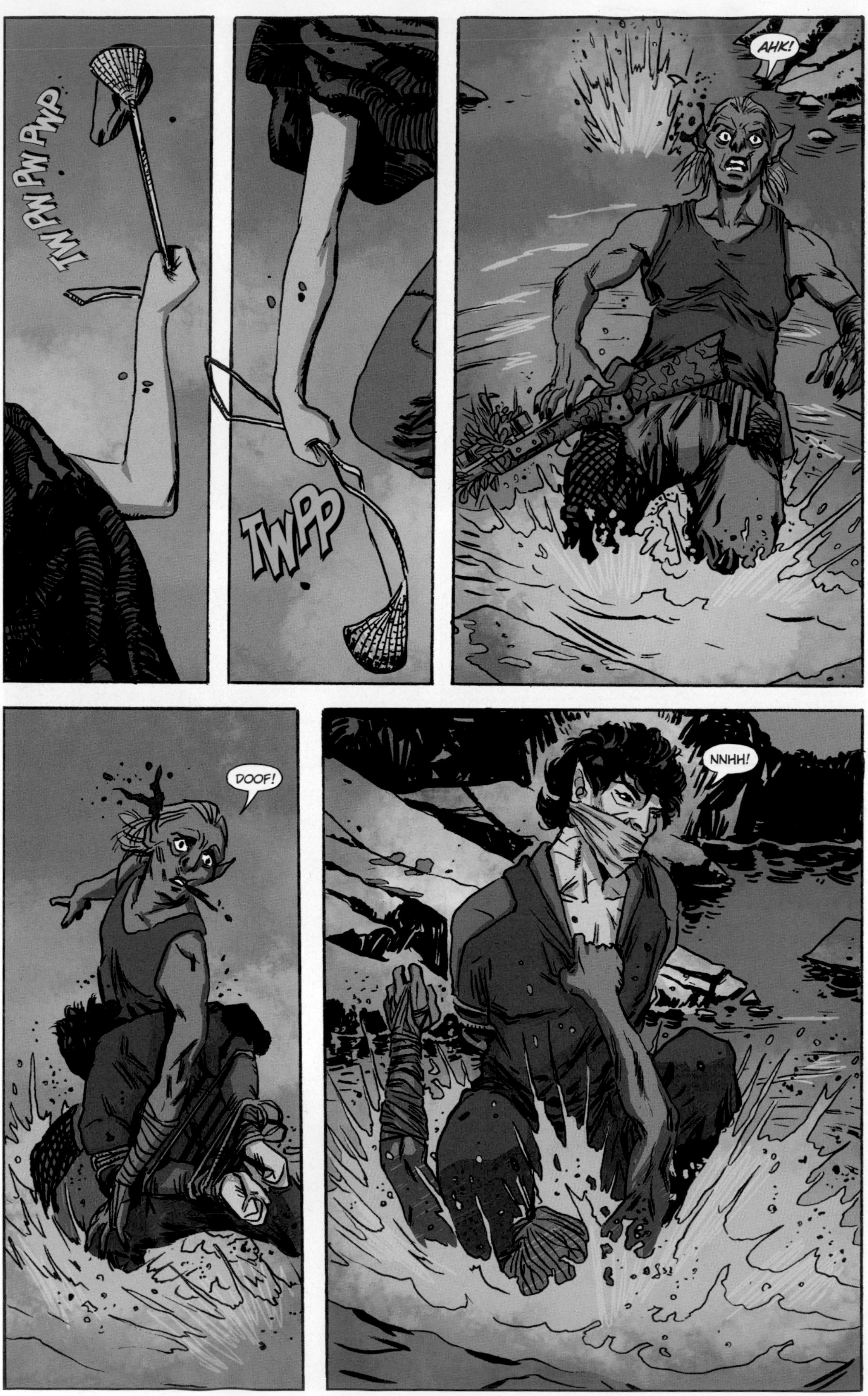
TW PW PW PWP
TWPP
AHK!
DOOF!
NNHH!

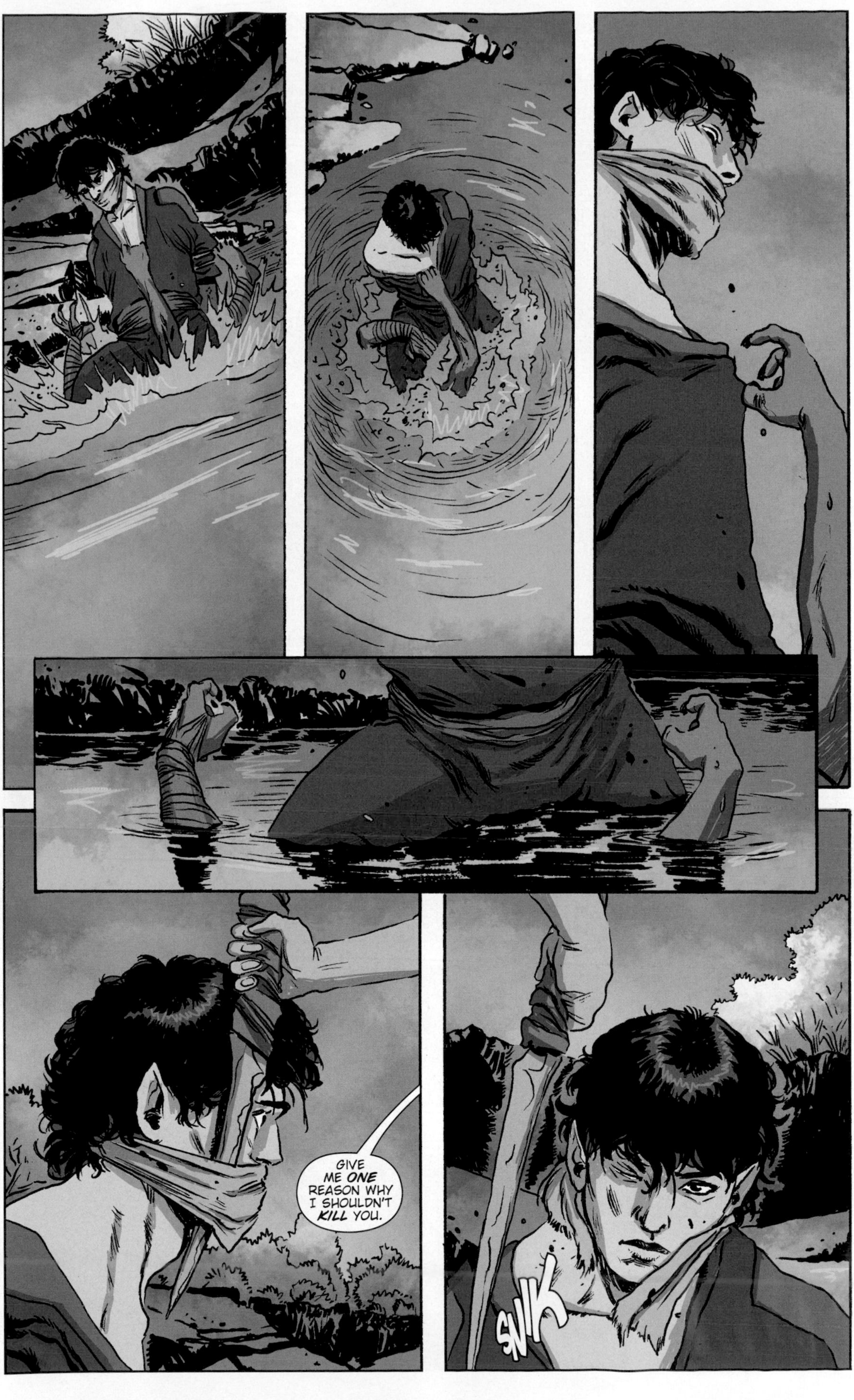
GIVE ME ONE REASON WHY I SHOULDN'T KILL YOU.
SNIK

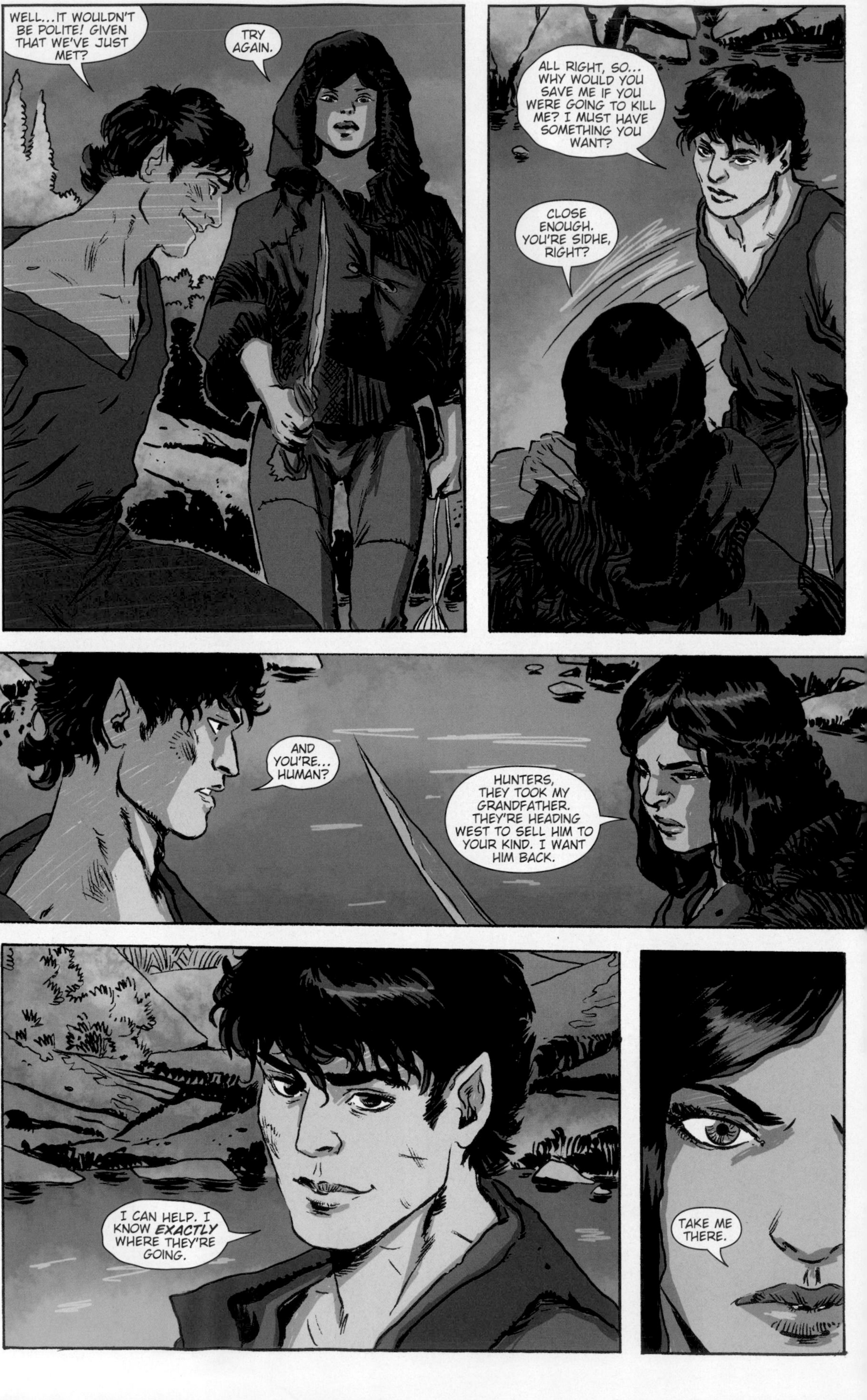
WELL...IT WOULDN'T BE POLITE! GIVEN THAT WE'VE JUST MET?
TRY AGAIN.
ALL RIGHT, SO... WHY WOULD YOU SAVE ME IF YOU WERE GOING TO KILL ME? I MUST HAVE SOMETHING YOU WANT?
CLOSE ENOUGH. YOU'RE SIDHE, RIGHT?
AND YOU'RE... HUMAN?
HUNTERS, THEY TOOK MY GRANDFATHER. THEY'RE HEADING WEST TO SELL HIM TO YOUR KIND. I WANT HIM BACK.
I CAN HELP. I KNOW *EXACTLY* WHERE THEY'RE GOING.
TAKE ME THERE.

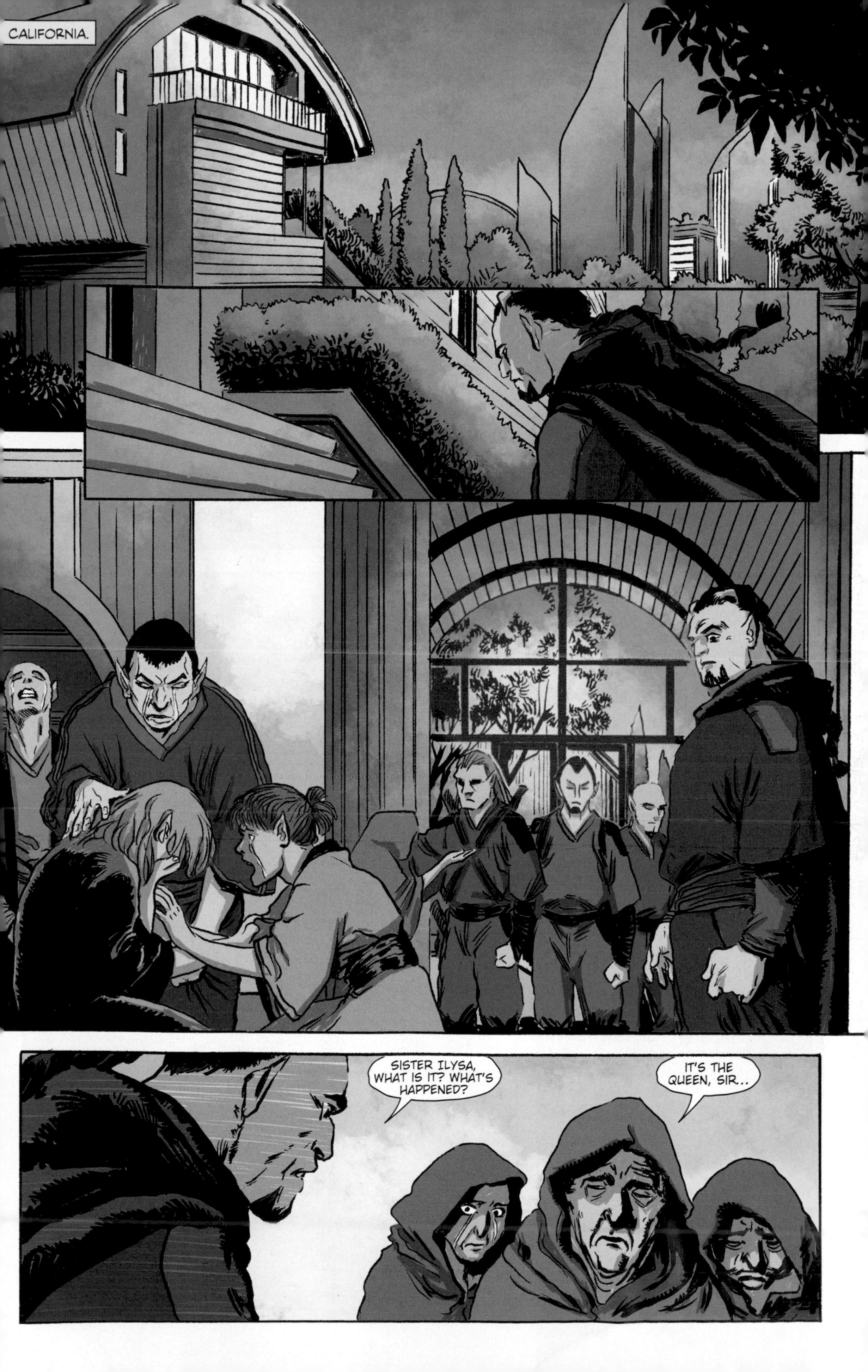
CALIFORNIA.
SISTER ILYSA, WHAT IS IT? WHAT'S HAPPENED?
IT'S THE QUEEN, SIR...

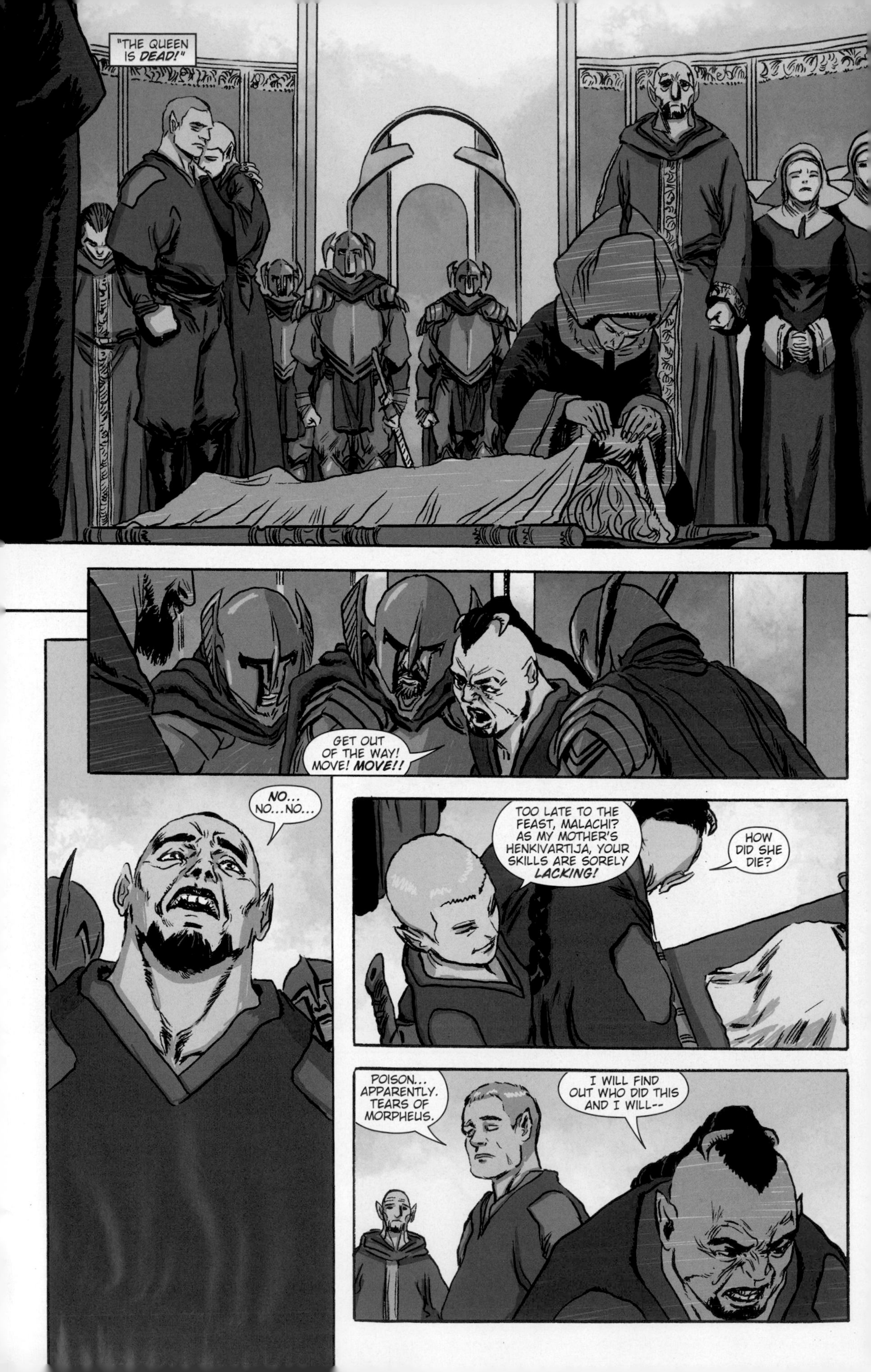
"THE QUEEN IS DEAD!"
GET OUT OF THE WAY! MOVE! MOVE!!
NO... NO...NO...
TOO LATE TO THE FEAST, MALACHI? AS MY MOTHER'S HENKIVARTIJA, YOUR SKILLS ARE SORELY LACKING!
HOW DID SHE DIE?
POISON... APPARENTLY. TEARS OF MORPHEUS.
I WILL FIND OUT WHO DID THIS AND I WILL--

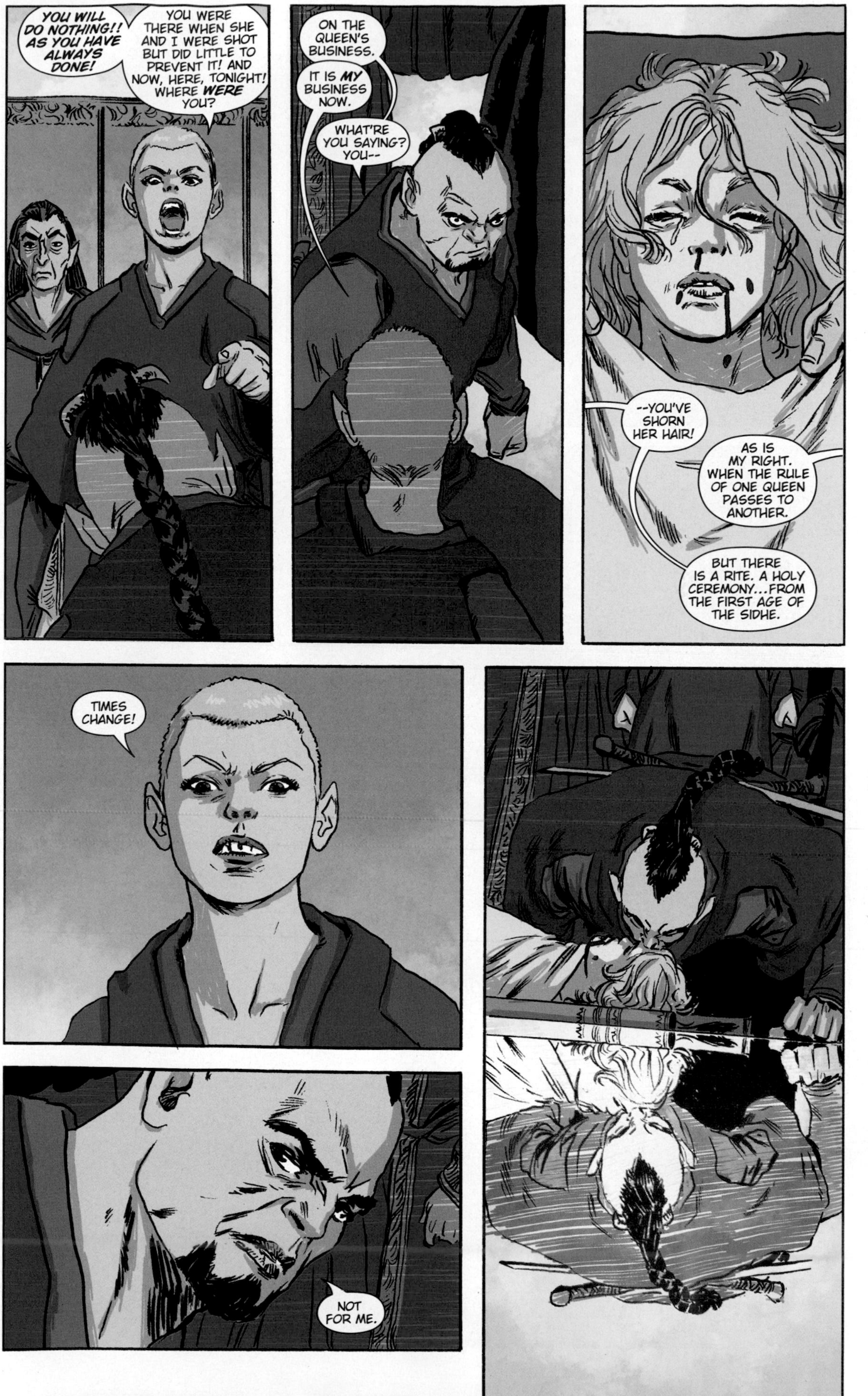
YOU WILL DO NOTHING!! AS YOU HAVE ALWAYS DONE!
YOU WERE THERE WHEN SHE AND I WERE SHOT BUT DID LITTLE TO PREVENT IT! AND NOW, HERE, TONIGHT! WHERE WERE YOU?
ON THE QUEEN'S BUSINESS.
IT IS MY BUSINESS NOW.
WHAT'RE YOU SAYING? YOU--
--YOU'VE SHORN HER HAIR!
AS IS MY RIGHT. WHEN THE RULE OF ONE QUEEN PASSES TO ANOTHER.
BUT THERE IS A RITE. A HOLY CEREMONY...FROM THE FIRST AGE OF THE SIDHE.
TIMES CHANGE!
NOT FOR ME.

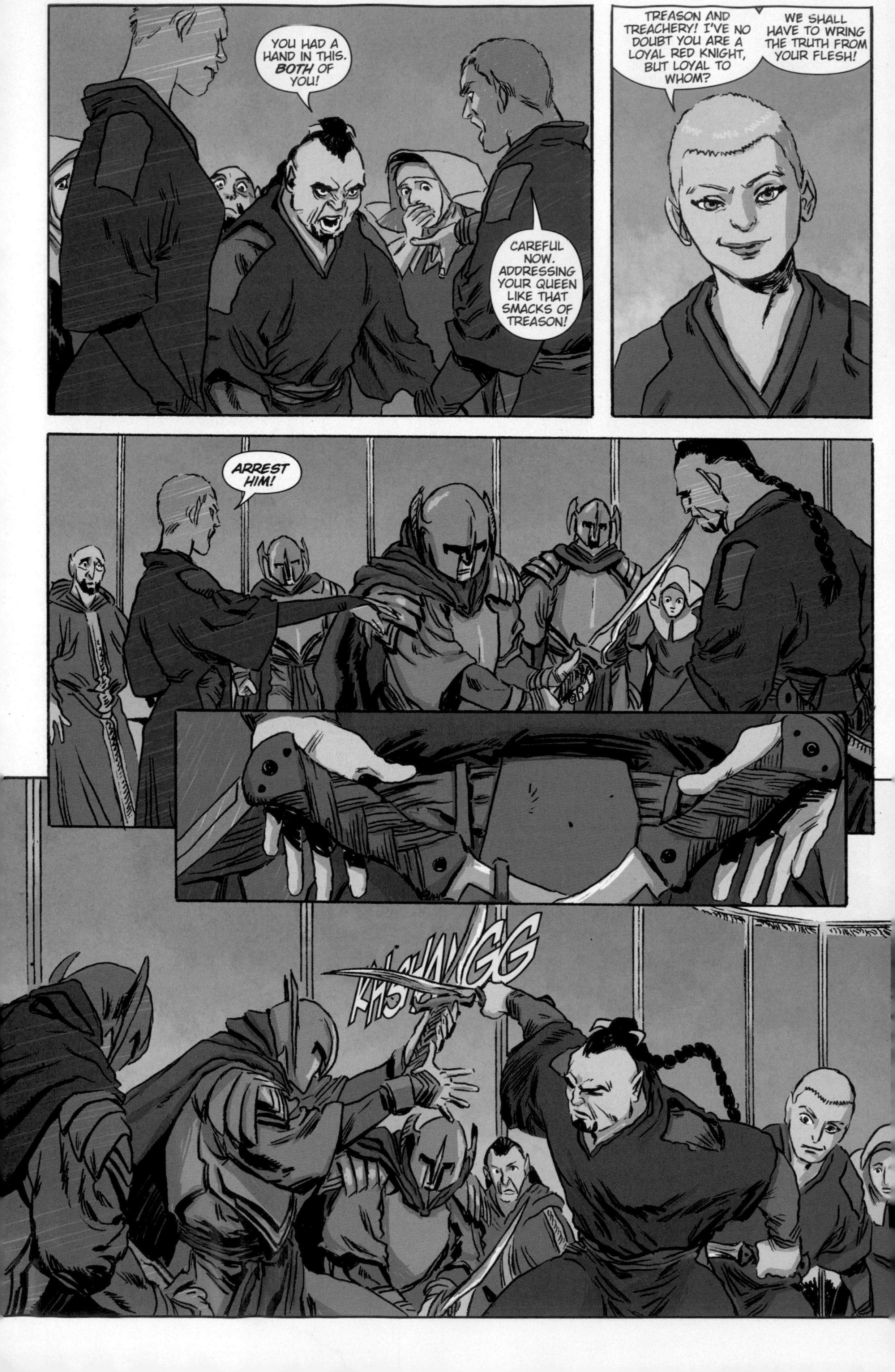
YOU HAD A HAND IN THIS. BOTH OF YOU!
CAREFUL NOW. ADDRESSING YOUR QUEEN LIKE THAT SMACKS OF TREASON!
TREASON AND TREACHERY! I'VE NO DOUBT YOU ARE A LOYAL RED KNIGHT, BUT LOYAL TO WHOM?
WE SHALL HAVE TO WRING THE TRUTH FROM YOUR FLESH!
ARREST HIM!

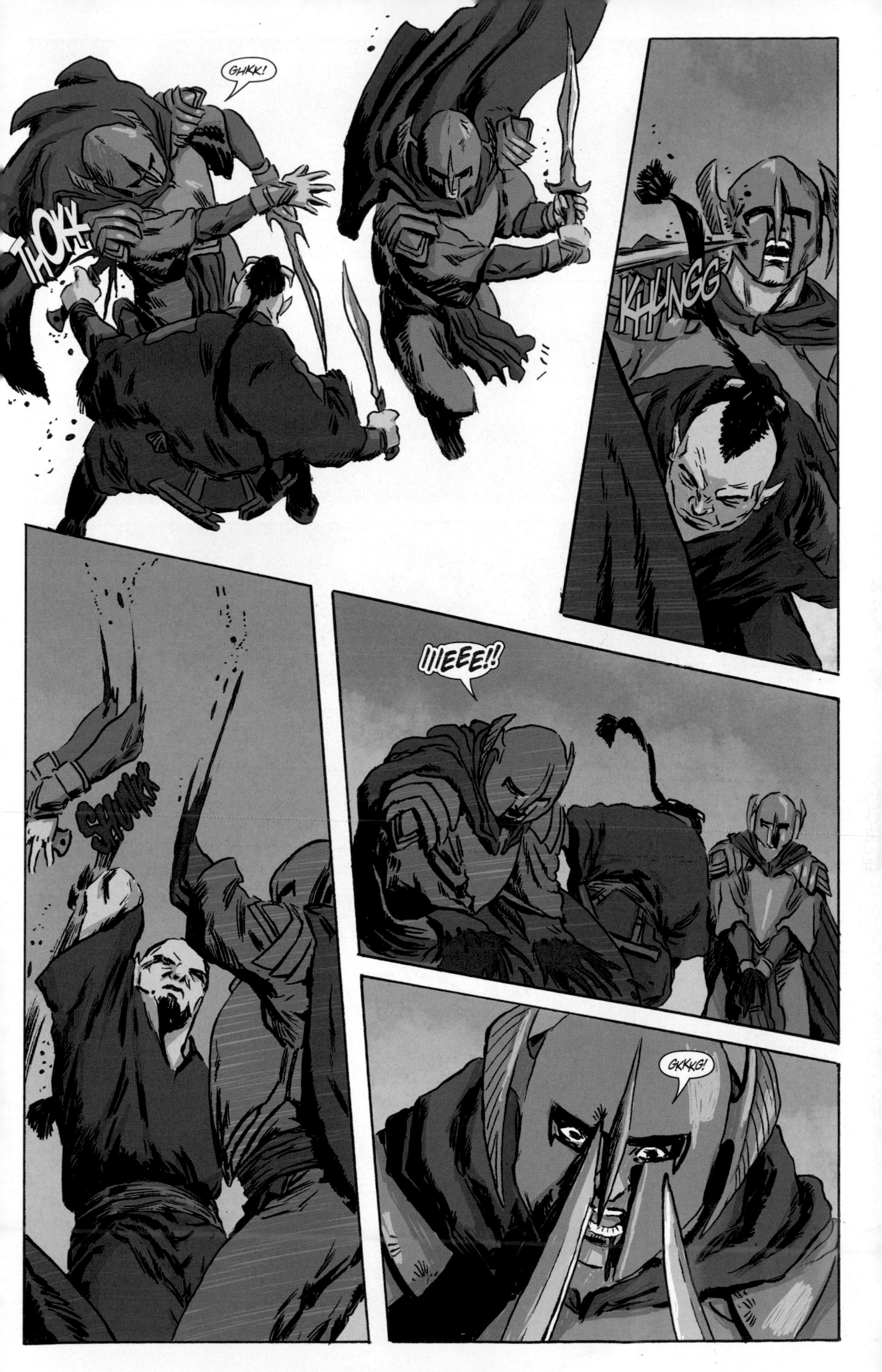
GHKK!
THOKK
KHUNGG
SHUNKK
IIIEEE!!
GKKKG!

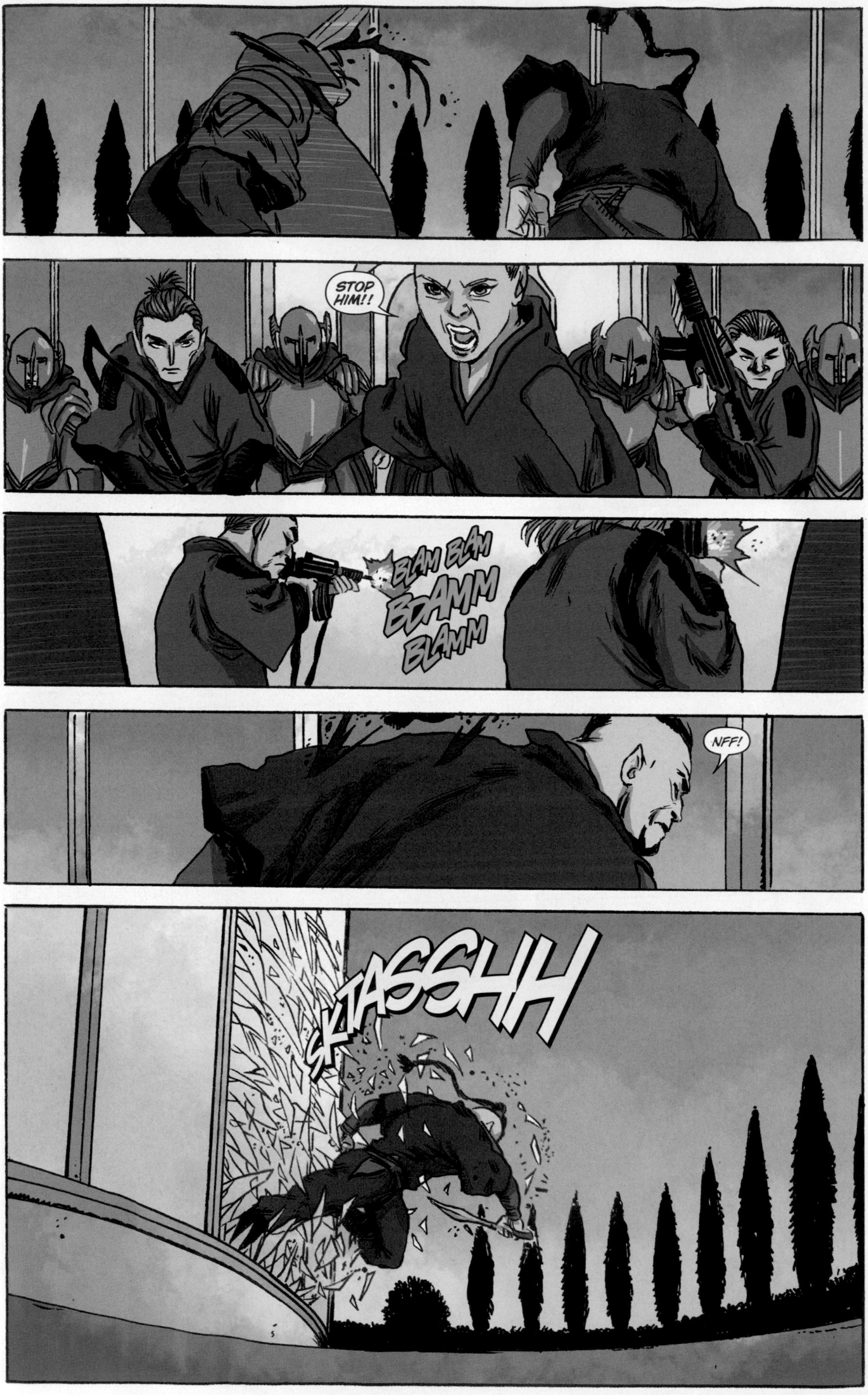
STOP HIM!!
BLAM BLAM
BDAMM
BLAMM
NFF!
SKTASSHH

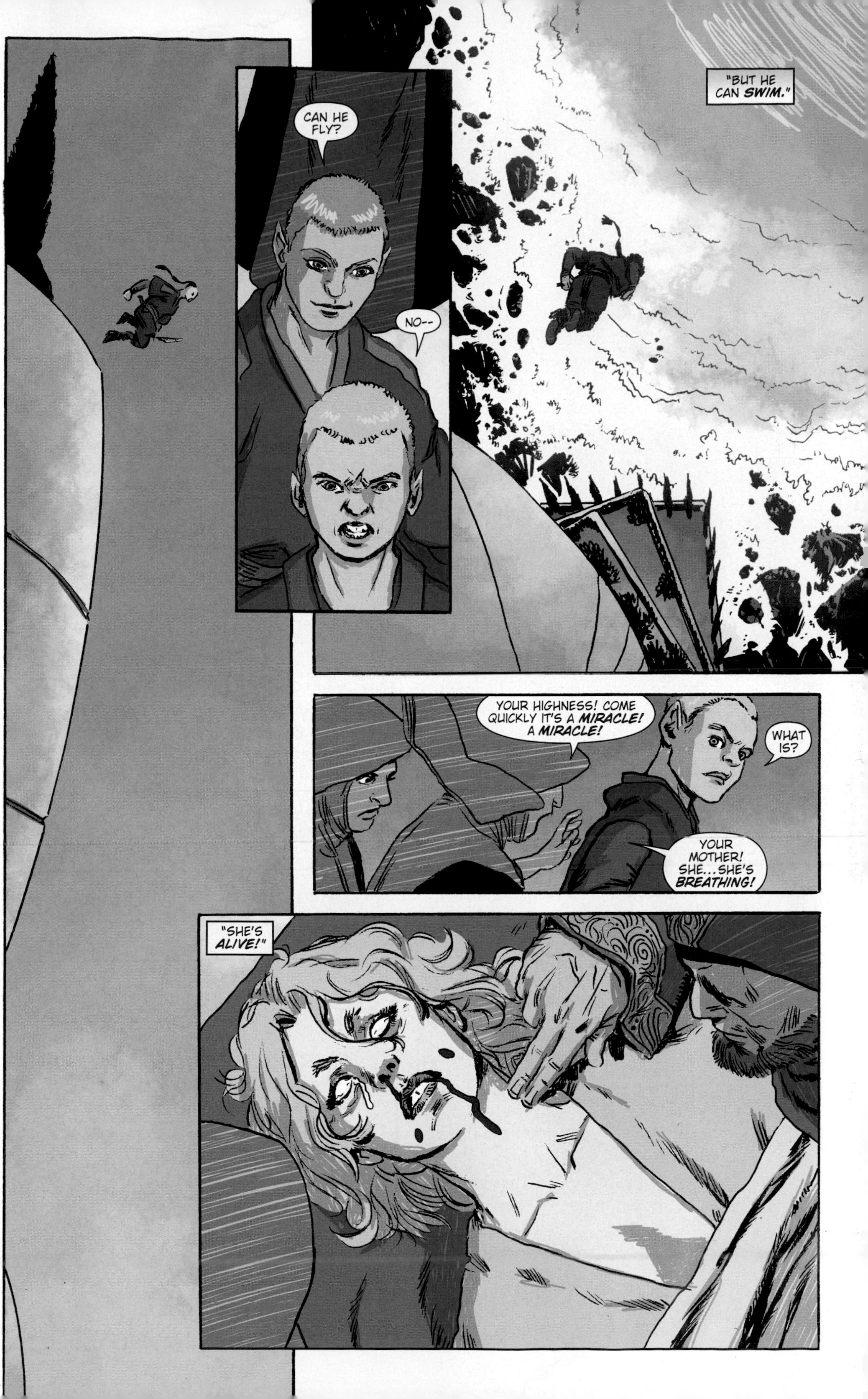
CAN HE FLY?
NO--
"BUT HE CAN SWIM."
YOUR HIGHNESS! COME QUICKLY IT'S A MIRACLE! A MIRACLE!
WHAT IS?
YOUR MOTHER! SHE...SHE'S BREATHING!
"SHE'S ALIVE!"

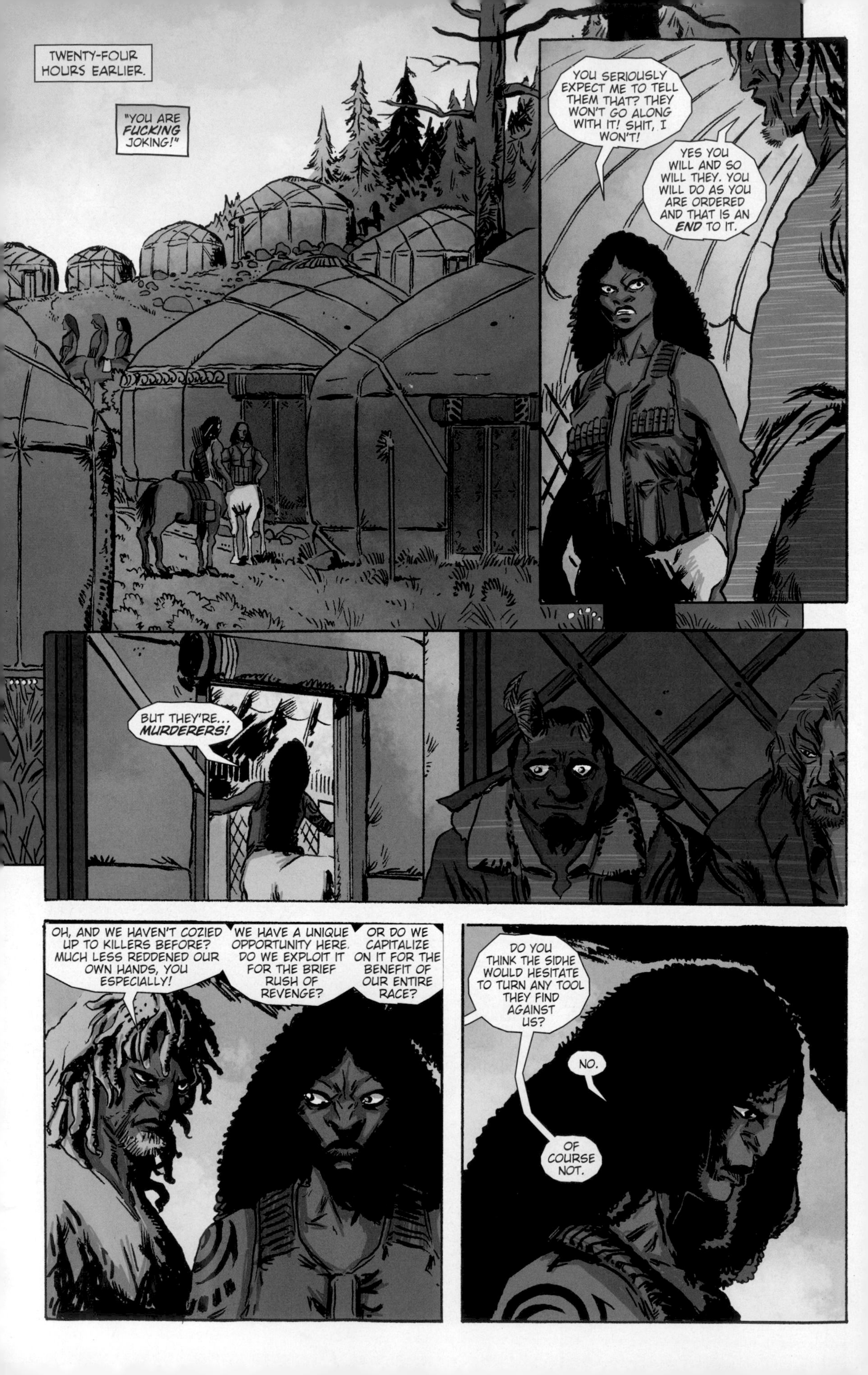
TWENTY-FOUR HOURS EARLIER.
"YOU ARE *FUCKING* JOKING!"
YOU SERIOUSLY EXPECT ME TO TELL THEM THAT? THEY WON'T GO ALONG WITH IT! SHIT, I WON'T!
YES YOU WILL AND SO WILL THEY. YOU WILL DO AS YOU ARE ORDERED AND THAT IS AN *END* TO IT.
BUT THEY'RE... *MURDERERS!*
OH, AND WE HAVEN'T COZIED UP TO KILLERS BEFORE? MUCH LESS REDDENED OUR OWN HANDS, YOU ESPECIALLY!
WE HAVE A UNIQUE OPPORTUNITY HERE. DO WE EXPLOIT IT FOR THE BRIEF RUSH OF REVENGE?
OR DO WE CAPITALIZE ON IT FOR THE BENEFIT OF OUR ENTIRE RACE?
DO YOU THINK THE SIDHE WOULD HESITATE TO TURN ANY TOOL THEY FIND AGAINST US?
NO.
OF COURSE NOT.

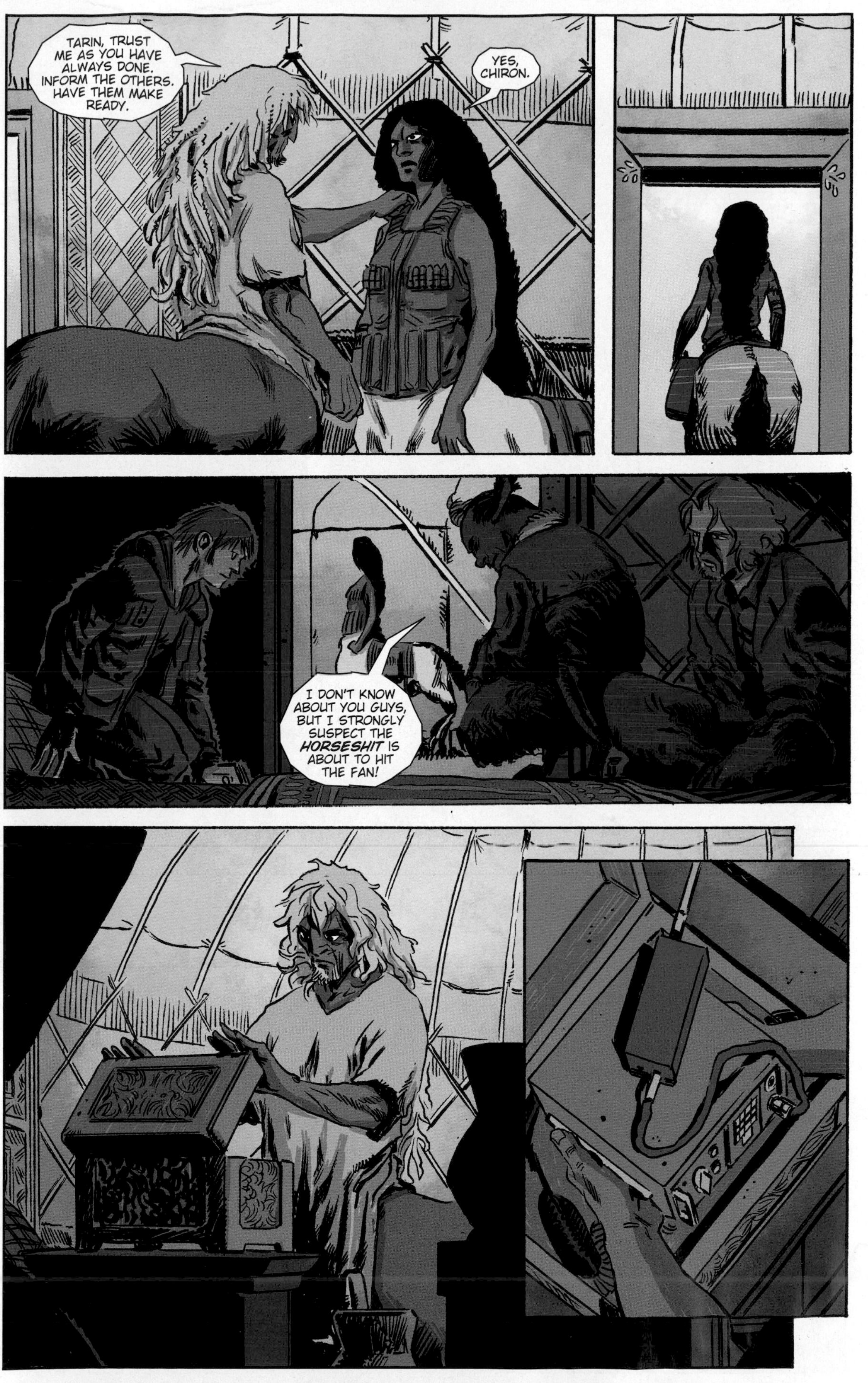
TARIN, TRUST ME AS YOU HAVE ALWAYS DONE. INFORM THE OTHERS. HAVE THEM MAKE READY.
YES, CHIRON.
I DON'T KNOW ABOUT YOU GUYS, BUT I STRONGLY SUSPECT THE HORSESHIT IS ABOUT TO HIT THE FAN!

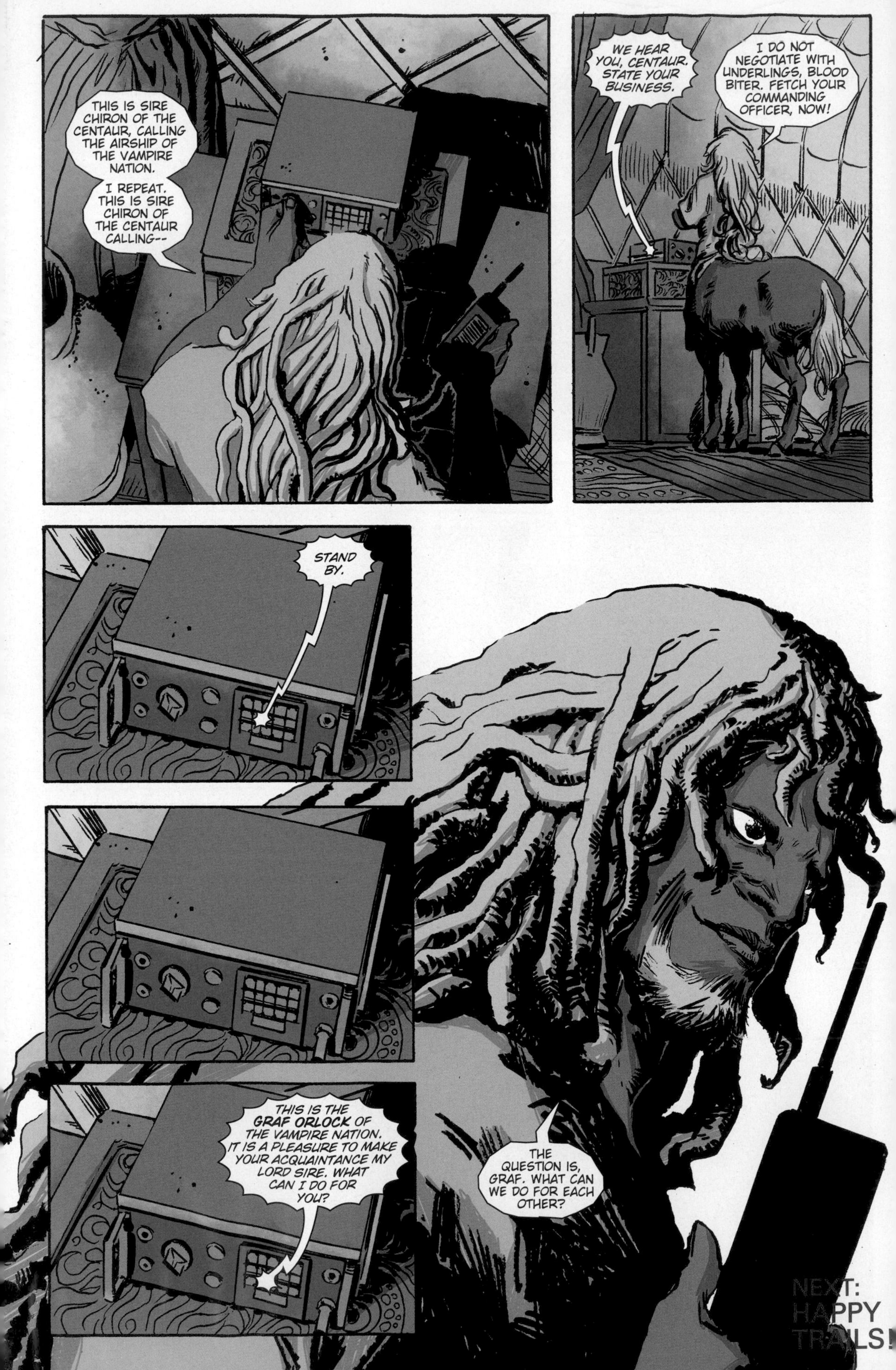
THIS IS SIRE CHIRON OF THE CENTAUR, CALLING THE AIRSHIP OF THE VAMPIRE NATION.
I REPEAT. THIS IS SIRE CHIRON OF THE CENTAUR CALLING--
WE HEAR YOU, CENTAUR. STATE YOUR BUSINESS.
I DO NOT NEGOTIATE WITH UNDERLINGS, BLOOD BITER. FETCH YOUR COMMANDING OFFICER, NOW!
STAND BY.
THIS IS THE GRAF ORLOCK OF THE VAMPIRE NATION. IT IS A PLEASURE TO MAKE YOUR ACQUAINTANCE MY LORD SIRE. WHAT CAN I DO FOR YOU?
THE QUESTION IS, GRAF. WHAT CAN WE DO FOR EACH OTHER?
NEXT: HAPPY TRAILS!

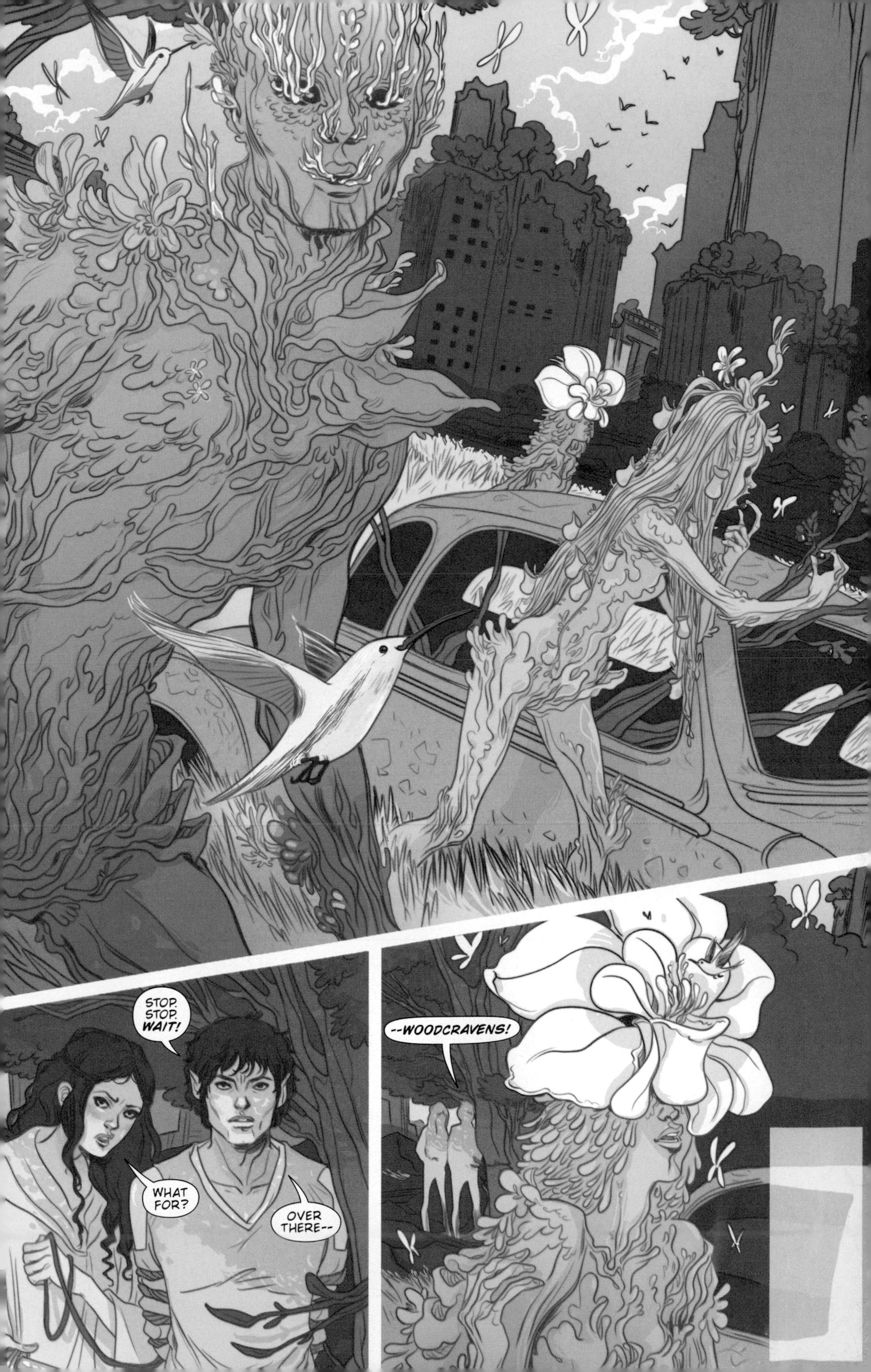
STOP. STOP. WAIT!
WHAT FOR?
OVER THERE--
--WOODCRAVENS!

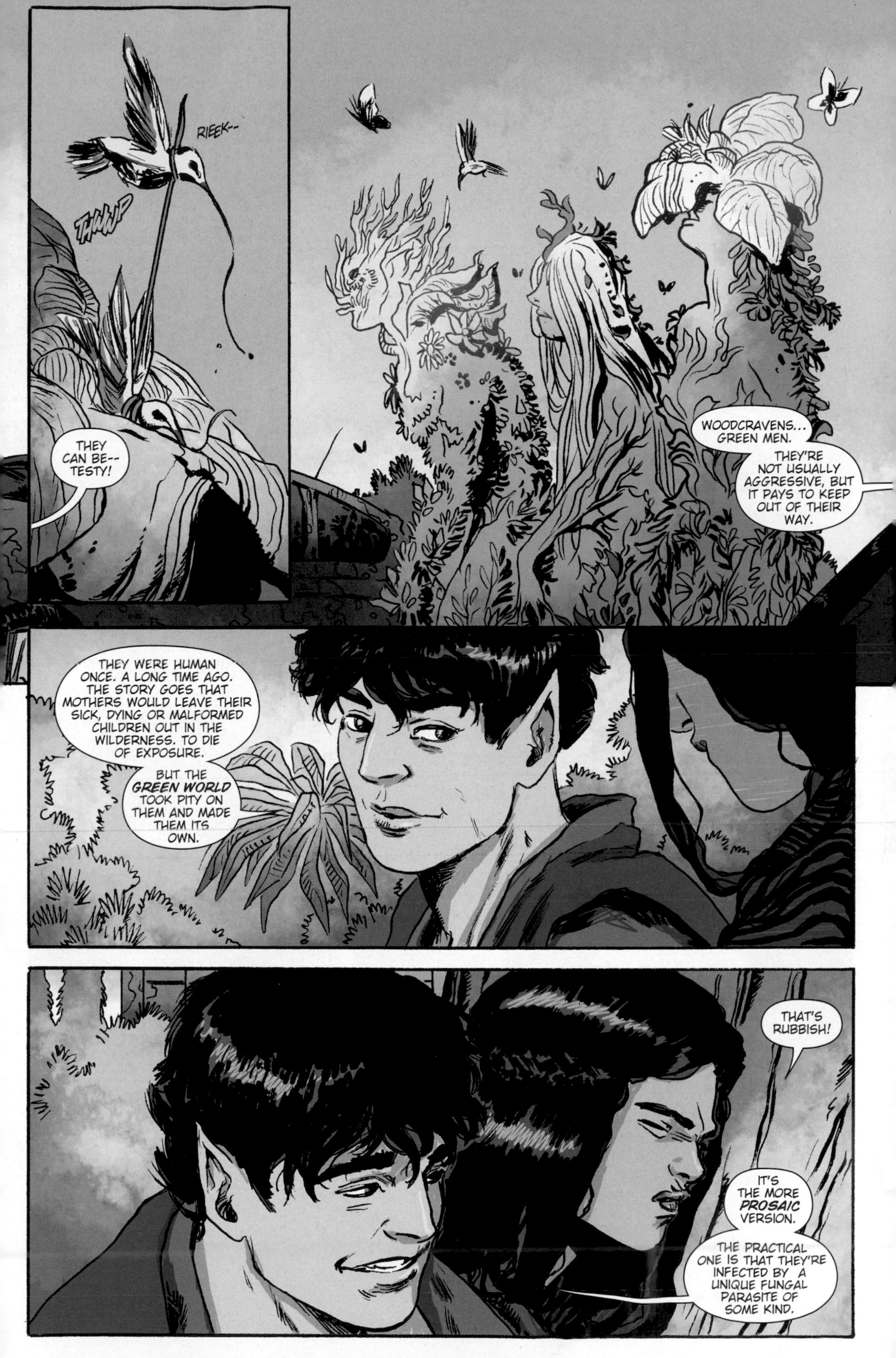
RIEEK--
THWP
THEY CAN BE-- TESTY!
WOODCRAVENS... GREEN MEN.
THEY'RE NOT USUALLY AGGRESSIVE, BUT IT PAYS TO KEEP OUT OF THEIR WAY.
THEY WERE HUMAN ONCE. A LONG TIME AGO. THE STORY GOES THAT MOTHERS WOULD LEAVE THEIR SICK, DYING OR MALFORMED CHILDREN OUT IN THE WILDERNESS. TO DIE OF EXPOSURE.
BUT THE *GREEN WORLD* TOOK PITY ON THEM AND MADE THEM ITS OWN.
THAT'S RUBBISH!
IT'S THE MORE *PROSAIC* VERSION.
THE PRACTICAL ONE IS THAT THEY'RE INFECTED BY A UNIQUE FUNGAL PARASITE OF SOME KIND.

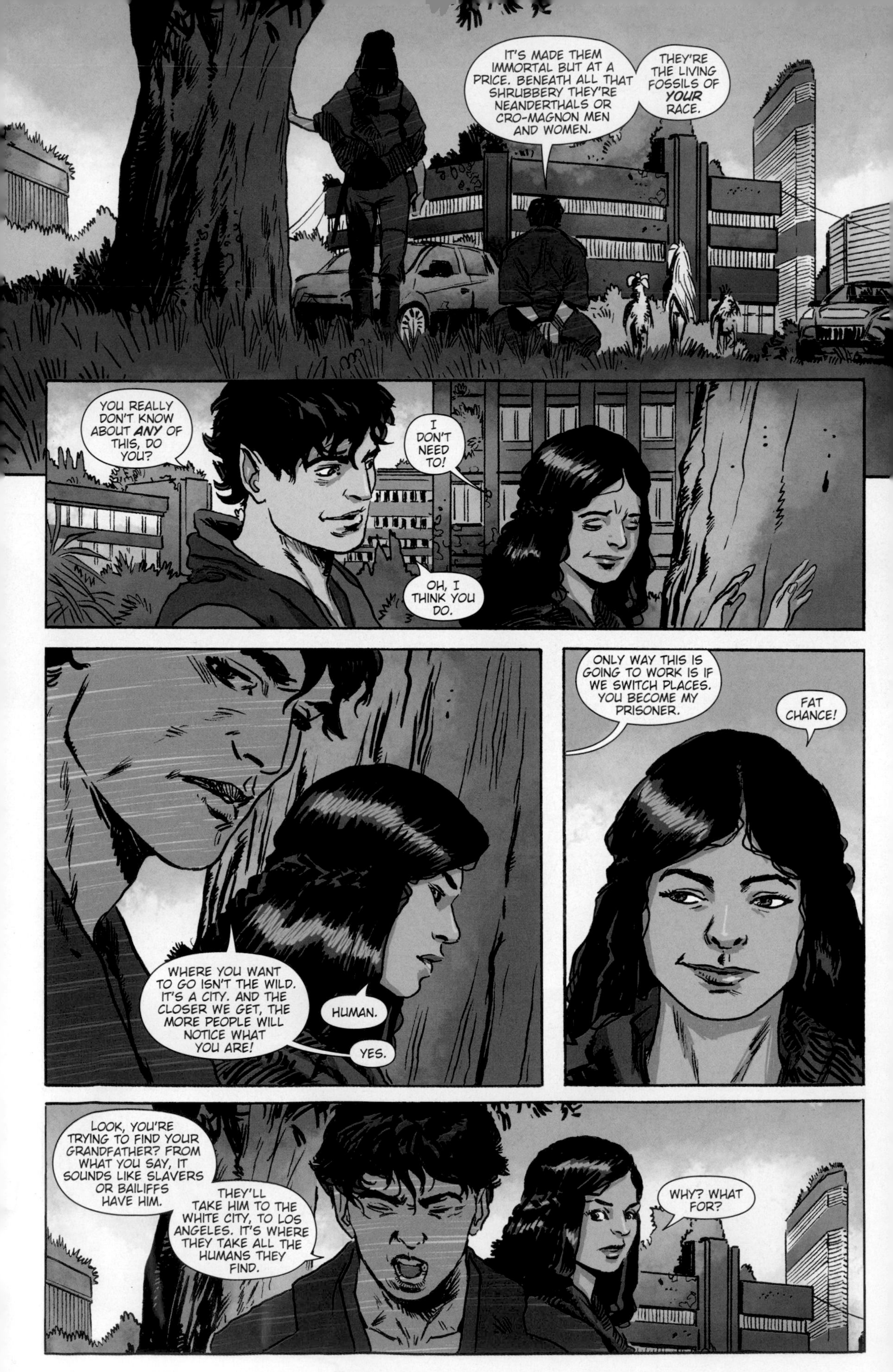
IT'S MADE THEM IMMORTAL BUT AT A PRICE. BENEATH ALL THAT SHRUBBERY THEY'RE NEANDERTHALS OR CRO-MAGNON MEN AND WOMEN.
THEY'RE THE LIVING FOSSILS OF *YOUR* RACE.
YOU REALLY DON'T KNOW ABOUT *ANY* OF THIS, DO YOU?
I DON'T NEED TO!
OH, I THINK YOU DO.
WHERE YOU WANT TO GO ISN'T THE WILD. IT'S A CITY. AND THE CLOSER WE GET, THE MORE PEOPLE WILL NOTICE WHAT YOU ARE!
HUMAN.
YES.
ONLY WAY THIS IS GOING TO WORK IS IF WE SWITCH PLACES. YOU BECOME MY PRISONER.
FAT CHANCE!
LOOK, YOU'RE TRYING TO FIND YOUR GRANDFATHER? FROM WHAT YOU SAY, IT SOUNDS LIKE SLAVERS OR BAILIFFS HAVE HIM.
THEY'LL TAKE HIM TO THE WHITE CITY, TO LOS ANGELES. IT'S WHERE THEY TAKE ALL THE HUMANS THEY FIND.
WHY? WHAT FOR?

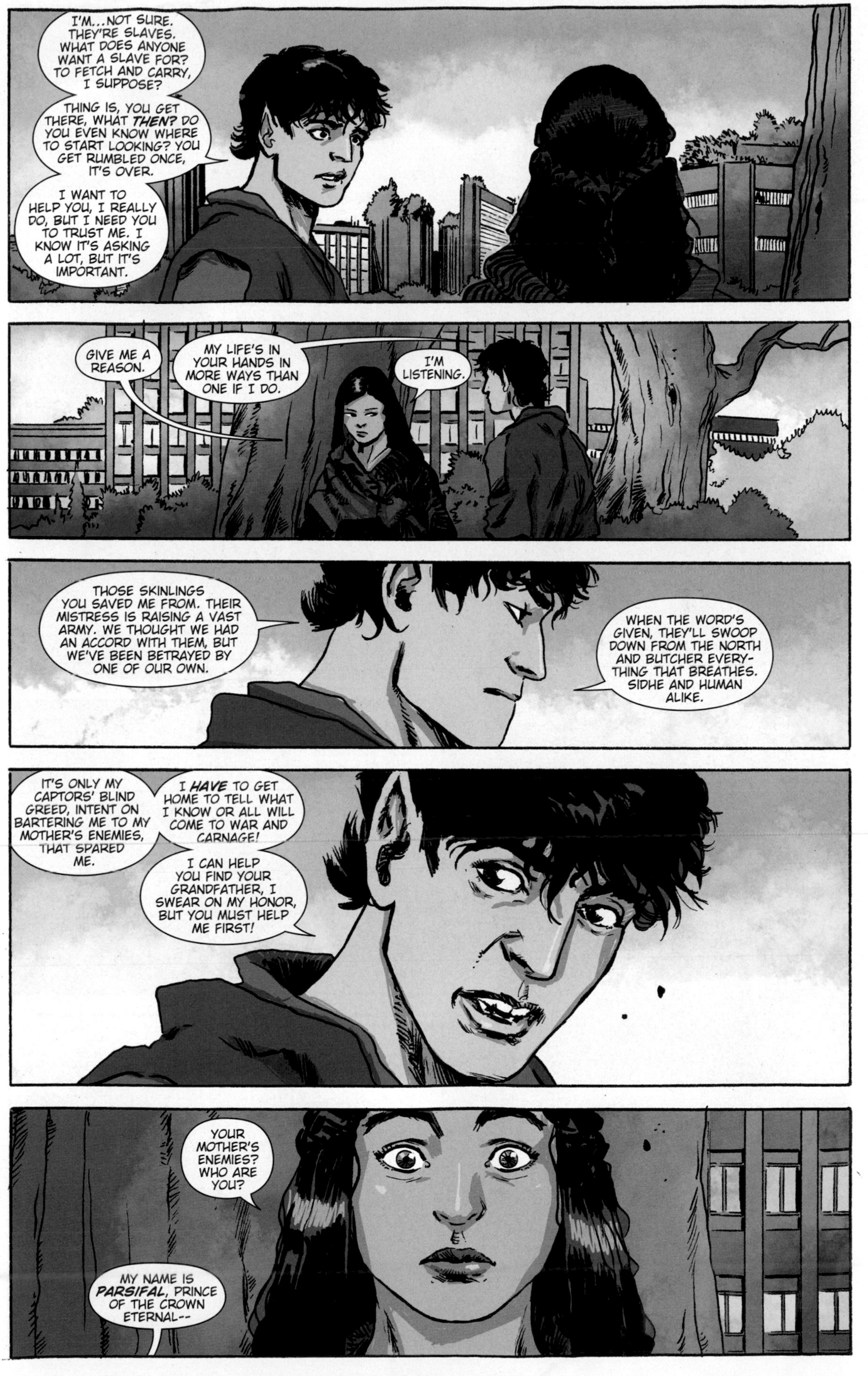
I'M...NOT SURE. THEY'RE SLAVES. WHAT DOES ANYONE WANT A SLAVE FOR? TO FETCH AND CARRY, I SUPPOSE?
THING IS, YOU GET THERE, WHAT *THEN?* DO YOU EVEN KNOW WHERE TO START LOOKING? YOU GET RUMBLED ONCE, IT'S OVER.
I WANT TO HELP YOU, I REALLY DO, BUT I NEED YOU TO TRUST ME. I KNOW IT'S ASKING A LOT, BUT IT'S IMPORTANT.
GIVE ME A REASON.
MY LIFE'S IN YOUR HANDS IN MORE WAYS THAN ONE IF I DO.
I'M LISTENING.
THOSE SKINLINGS YOU SAVED ME FROM. THEIR MISTRESS IS RAISING A VAST ARMY. WE THOUGHT WE HAD AN ACCORD WITH THEM, BUT WE'VE BEEN BETRAYED BY ONE OF OUR OWN.
WHEN THE WORD'S GIVEN, THEY'LL SWOOP DOWN FROM THE NORTH AND BUTCHER EVERY-THING THAT BREATHES. SIDHE AND HUMAN ALIKE.
IT'S ONLY MY CAPTORS' BLIND GREED, INTENT ON BARTERING ME TO MY MOTHER'S ENEMIES, THAT SPARED ME.
I *HAVE* TO GET HOME TO TELL WHAT I KNOW OR ALL WILL COME TO WAR AND CARNAGE!
I CAN HELP YOU FIND YOUR GRANDFATHER, I SWEAR ON MY HONOR, BUT YOU MUST HELP ME FIRST!
YOUR MOTHER'S ENEMIES? WHO ARE YOU?
MY NAME IS *PARSIFAL*, PRINCE OF THE CROWN ETERNAL--

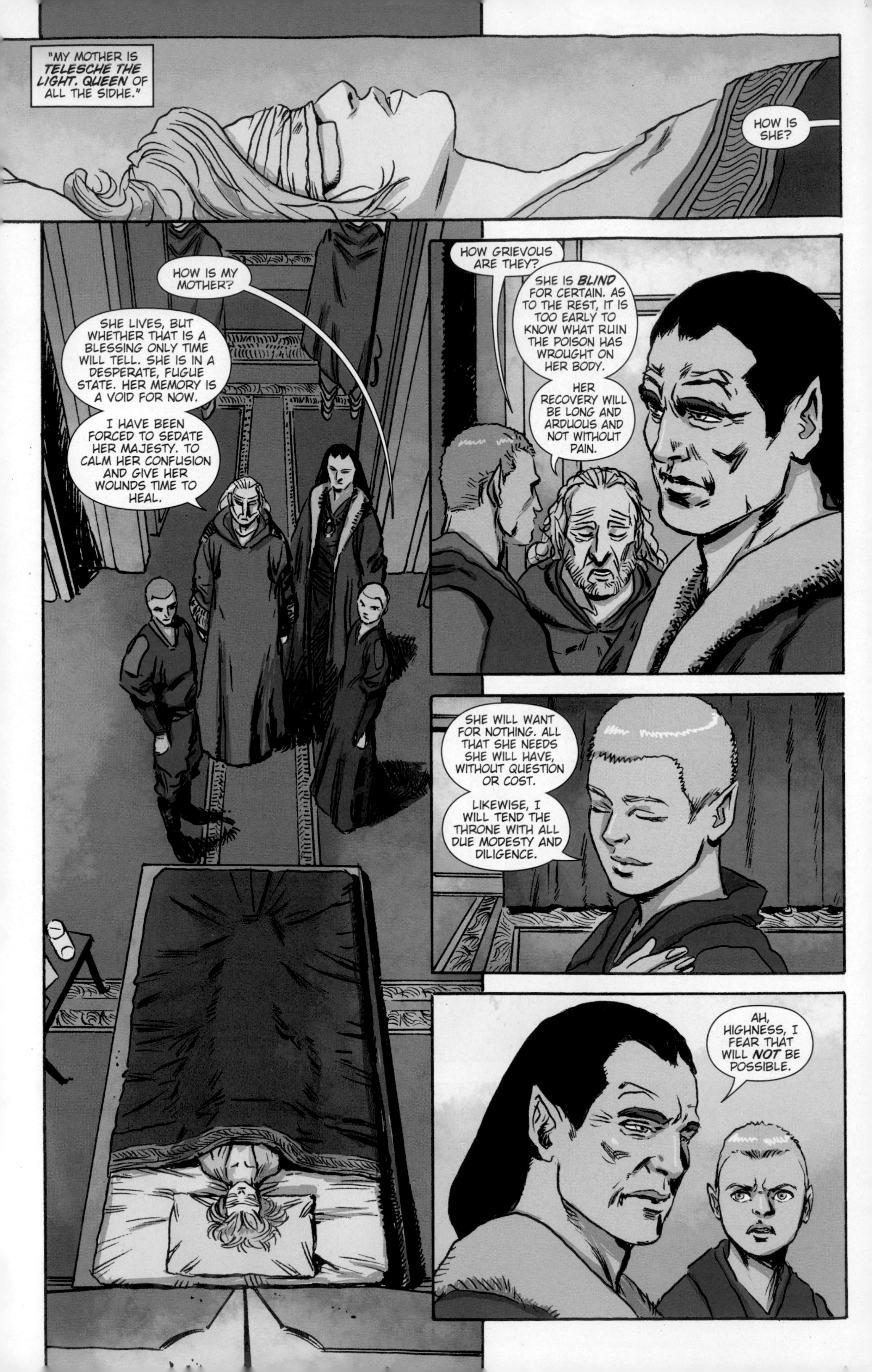
"MY MOTHER IS TELESCHE THE LIGHT, QUEEN OF ALL THE SIDHE."
HOW IS SHE?
HOW IS MY MOTHER?
SHE LIVES, BUT WHETHER THAT IS A BLESSING ONLY TIME WILL TELL. SHE IS IN A DESPERATE, FUGUE STATE. HER MEMORY IS A VOID FOR NOW.
I HAVE BEEN FORCED TO SEDATE HER MAJESTY. TO CALM HER CONFUSION AND GIVE HER WOUNDS TIME TO HEAL.
HOW GRIEVOUS ARE THEY?
SHE IS BLIND FOR CERTAIN. AS TO THE REST, IT IS TOO EARLY TO KNOW WHAT RUIN THE POISON HAS WROUGHT ON HER BODY.
HER RECOVERY WILL BE LONG AND ARDUOUS AND NOT WITHOUT PAIN.
SHE WILL WANT FOR NOTHING. ALL THAT SHE NEEDS SHE WILL HAVE, WITHOUT QUESTION OR COST.
LIKEWISE, I WILL TEND THE THRONE WITH ALL DUE MODESTY AND DILIGENCE.
AH, HIGHNESS, I FEAR THAT WILL NOT BE POSSIBLE.

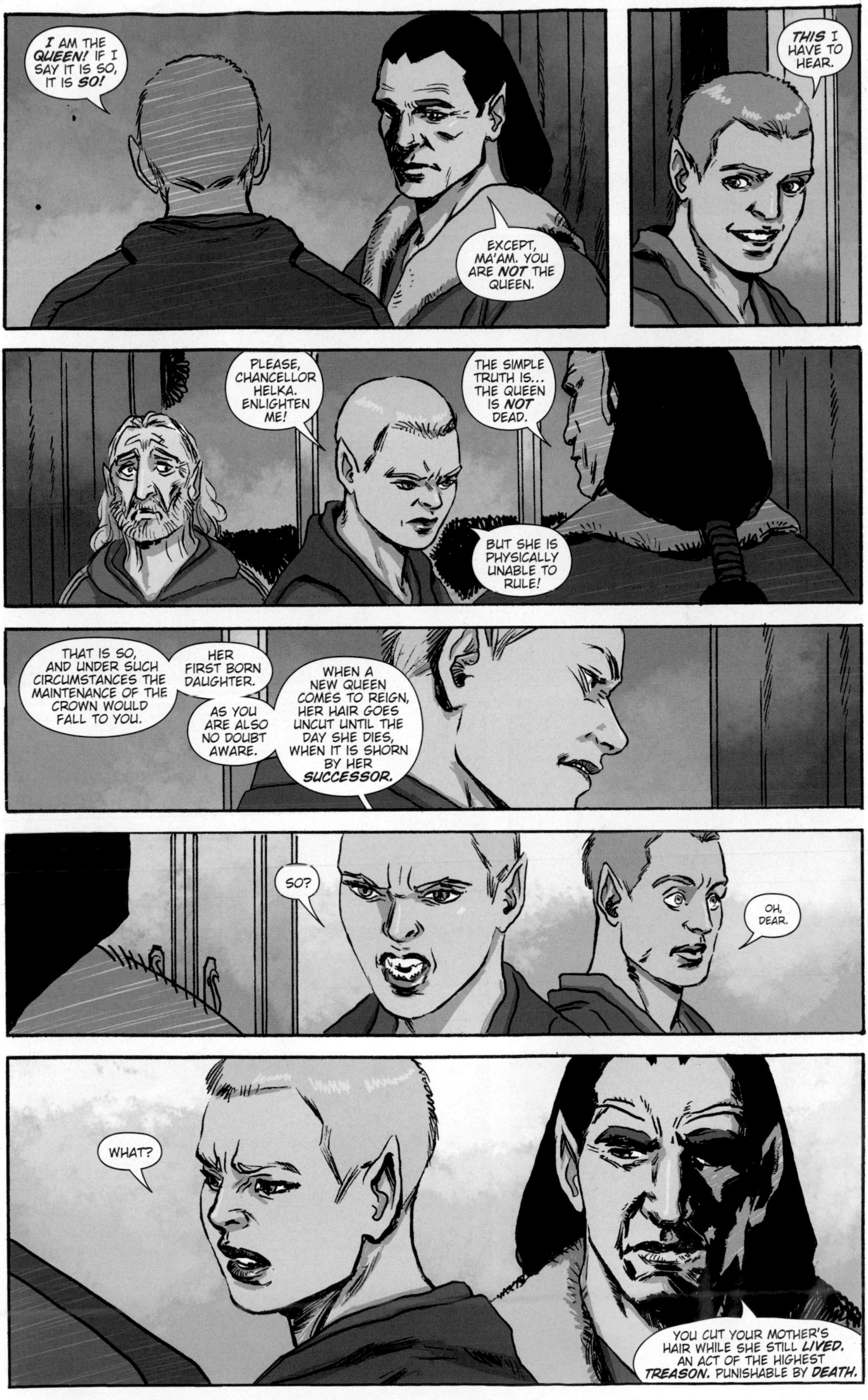

I AM THE QUEEN! IF I SAY IT IS SO, IT IS SO!
EXCEPT, MA'AM. YOU ARE NOT THE QUEEN.
THIS I HAVE TO HEAR.
PLEASE, CHANCELLOR HELKA. ENLIGHTEN ME!
THE SIMPLE TRUTH IS... THE QUEEN IS NOT DEAD.
BUT SHE IS PHYSICALLY UNABLE TO RULE!
THAT IS SO, AND UNDER SUCH CIRCUMSTANCES THE MAINTENANCE OF THE CROWN WOULD FALL TO YOU.
HER FIRST BORN DAUGHTER.
AS YOU ARE ALSO NO DOUBT AWARE.
WHEN A NEW QUEEN COMES TO REIGN, HER HAIR GOES UNCUT UNTIL THE DAY SHE DIES, WHEN IT IS SHORN BY HER SUCCESSOR.
SO?
OH, DEAR.
WHAT?
YOU CUT YOUR MOTHER'S HAIR WHILE SHE STILL LIVED. AN ACT OF THE HIGHEST TREASON. PUNISHABLE BY DEATH.

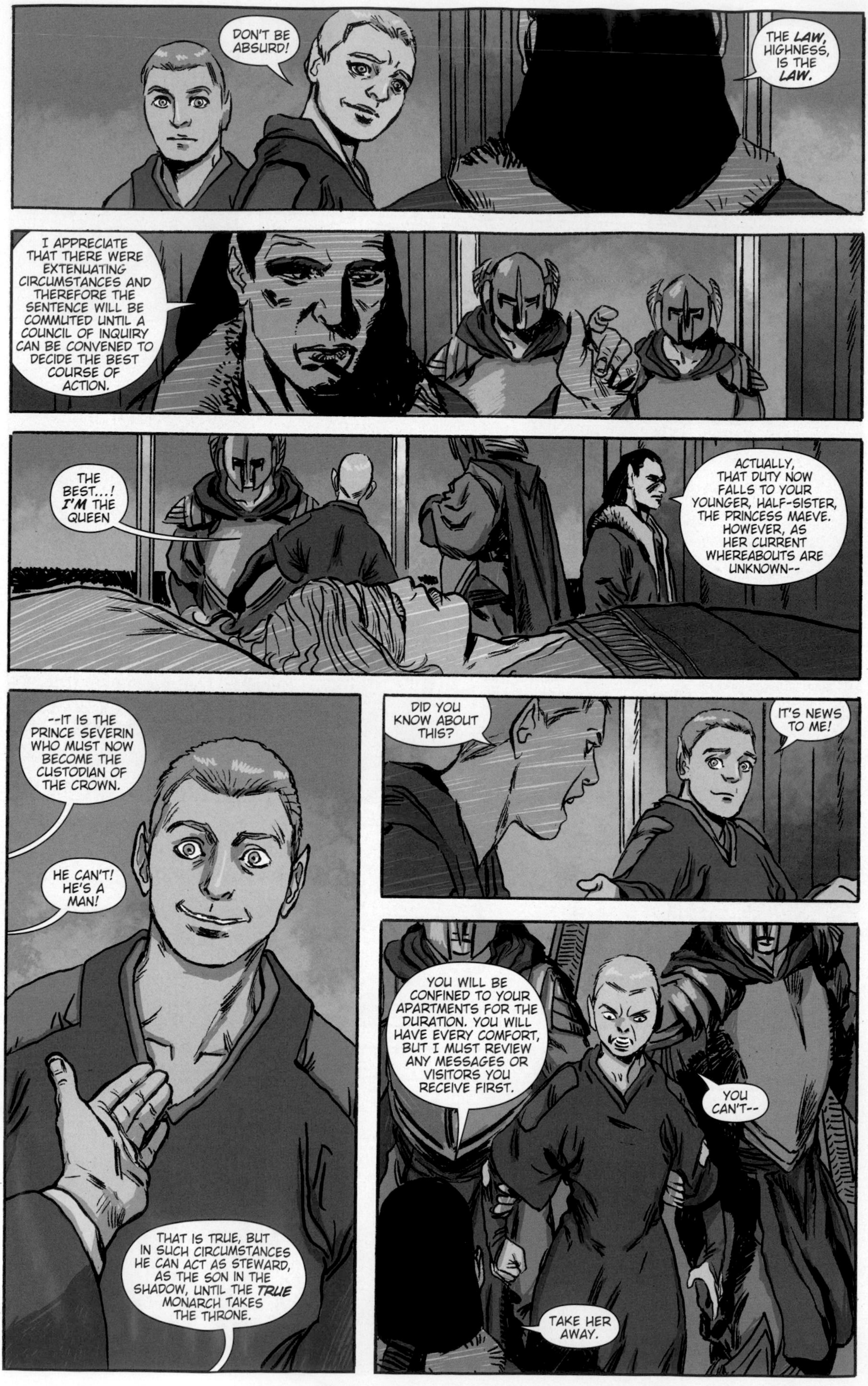
DON'T BE ABSURD!
THE LAW, HIGHNESS, IS THE LAW.
I APPRECIATE THAT THERE WERE EXTENUATING CIRCUMSTANCES AND THEREFORE THE SENTENCE WILL BE COMMUTED UNTIL A COUNCIL OF INQUIRY CAN BE CONVENED TO DECIDE THE BEST COURSE OF ACTION.
THE BEST...! I'M THE QUEEN
ACTUALLY, THAT DUTY NOW FALLS TO YOUR YOUNGER, HALF-SISTER, THE PRINCESS MAEVE. HOWEVER, AS HER CURRENT WHEREABOUTS ARE UNKNOWN--
--IT IS THE PRINCE SEVERIN WHO MUST NOW BECOME THE CUSTODIAN OF THE CROWN.
HE CAN'T! HE'S A MAN!
THAT IS TRUE, BUT IN SUCH CIRCUMSTANCES HE CAN ACT AS STEWARD, AS THE SON IN THE SHADOW, UNTIL THE TRUE MONARCH TAKES THE THRONE.
DID YOU KNOW ABOUT THIS?
IT'S NEWS TO ME!
YOU WILL BE CONFINED TO YOUR APARTMENTS FOR THE DURATION. YOU WILL HAVE EVERY COMFORT, BUT I MUST REVIEW ANY MESSAGES OR VISITORS YOU RECEIVE FIRST.
YOU CAN'T--
TAKE HER AWAY.

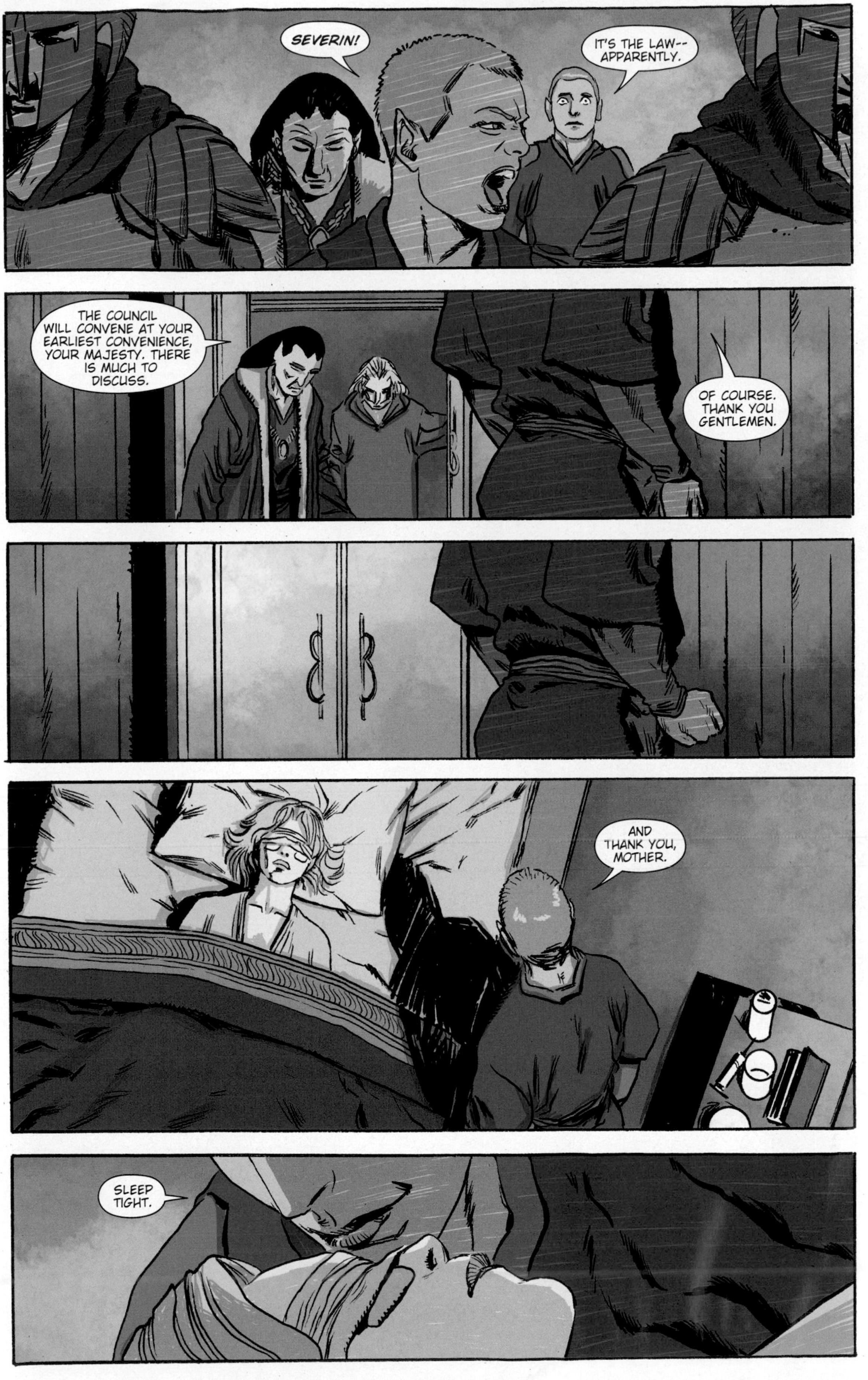
SEVERIN!
IT'S THE LAW-- APPARENTLY.
THE COUNCIL WILL CONVENE AT YOUR EARLIEST CONVENIENCE, YOUR MAJESTY. THERE IS MUCH TO DISCUSS.
OF COURSE. THANK YOU GENTLEMEN.
AND THANK YOU, MOTHER.
SLEEP TIGHT.

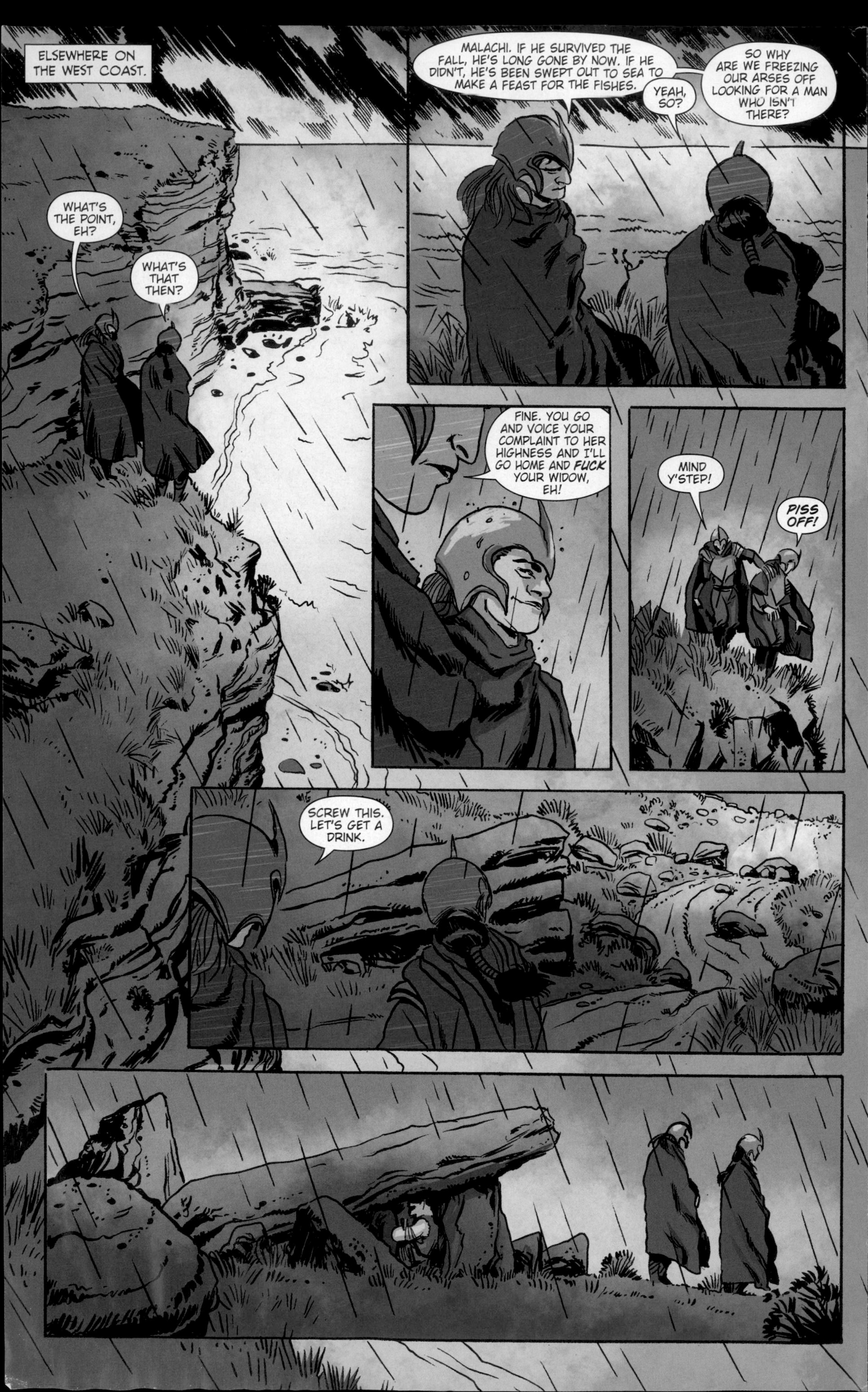

ELSEWHERE ON THE WEST COAST.
WHAT'S THE POINT, EH?
WHAT'S THAT THEN?
MALACHI. IF HE SURVIVED THE FALL, HE'S LONG GONE BY NOW. IF HE DIDN'T, HE'S BEEN SWEPT OUT TO SEA TO MAKE A FEAST FOR THE FISHES.
YEAH, SO?
SO WHY ARE WE FREEZING OUR ARSES OFF LOOKING FOR A MAN WHO ISN'T THERE?
FINE. YOU GO AND VOICE YOUR COMPLAINT TO HER HIGHNESS AND I'LL GO HOME AND FUCK YOUR WIDOW, EH!
MIND Y'STEP!
PISS OFF!
SCREW THIS. LET'S GET A DRINK.

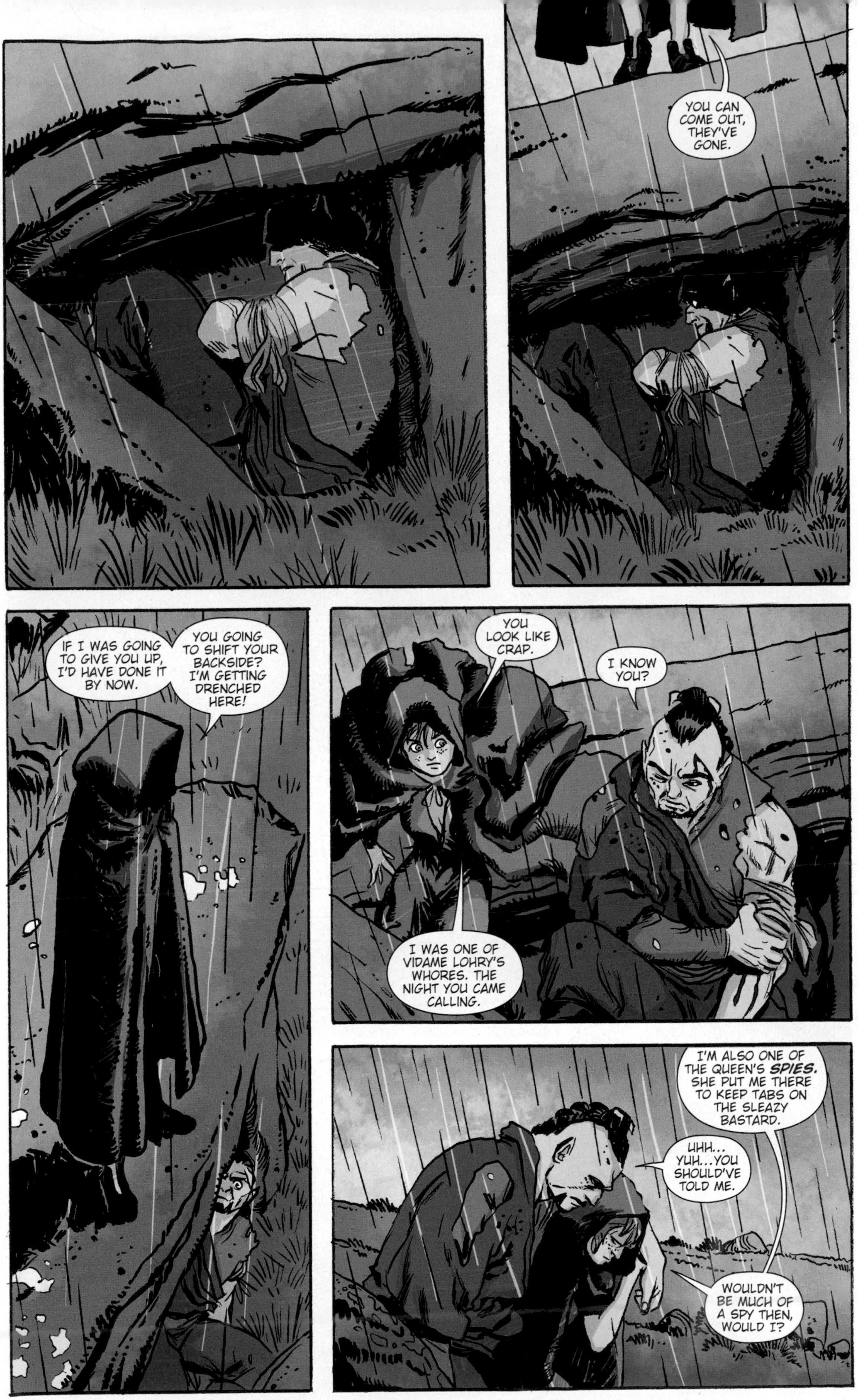
YOU CAN COME OUT, THEY'VE GONE.
IF I WAS GOING TO GIVE YOU UP, I'D HAVE DONE IT BY NOW.
YOU GOING TO SHIFT YOUR BACKSIDE? I'M GETTING DRENCHED HERE!
YOU LOOK LIKE CRAP.
I KNOW YOU?
I WAS ONE OF VIDAME LOHRY'S WHORES. THE NIGHT YOU CAME CALLING.
I'M ALSO ONE OF THE QUEEN'S SPIES. SHE PUT ME THERE TO KEEP TABS ON THE SLEAZY BASTARD.
UHH... YUH...YOU SHOULD'VE TOLD ME.
WOULDN'T BE MUCH OF A SPY THEN, WOULD I?

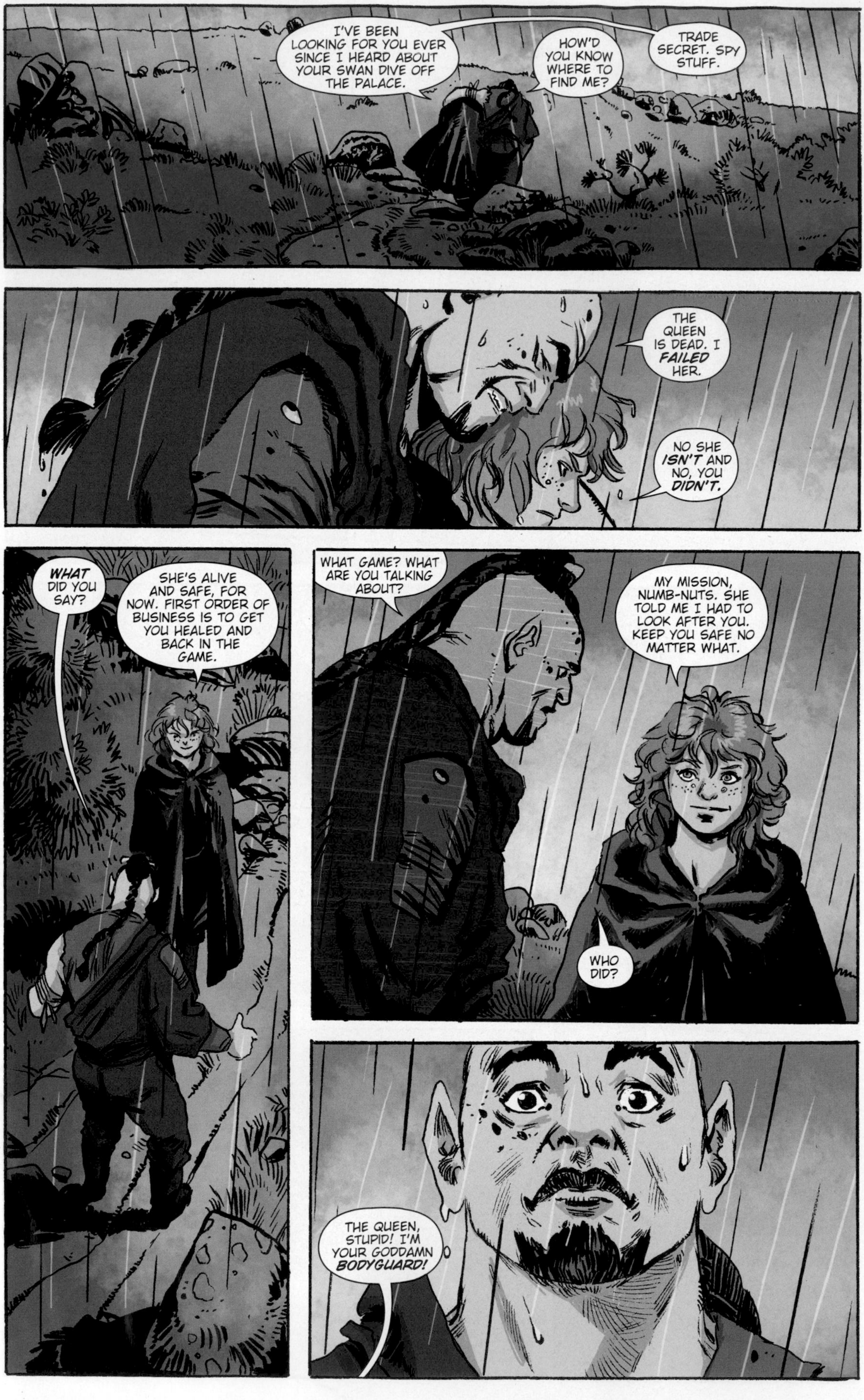
I'VE BEEN LOOKING FOR YOU EVER SINCE I HEARD ABOUT YOUR SWAN DIVE OFF THE PALACE.
HOW'D YOU KNOW WHERE TO FIND ME?
TRADE SECRET. SPY STUFF.
THE QUEEN IS DEAD. I FAILED HER.
NO SHE ISN'T AND NO, YOU DIDN'T.
WHAT DID YOU SAY?
SHE'S ALIVE AND SAFE, FOR NOW. FIRST ORDER OF BUSINESS IS TO GET YOU HEALED AND BACK IN THE GAME.
WHAT GAME? WHAT ARE YOU TALKING ABOUT?
MY MISSION, NUMB-NUTS. SHE TOLD ME I HAD TO LOOK AFTER YOU. KEEP YOU SAFE NO MATTER WHAT.
WHO DID?
THE QUEEN, STUPID! I'M YOUR GODDAMN BODYGUARD!

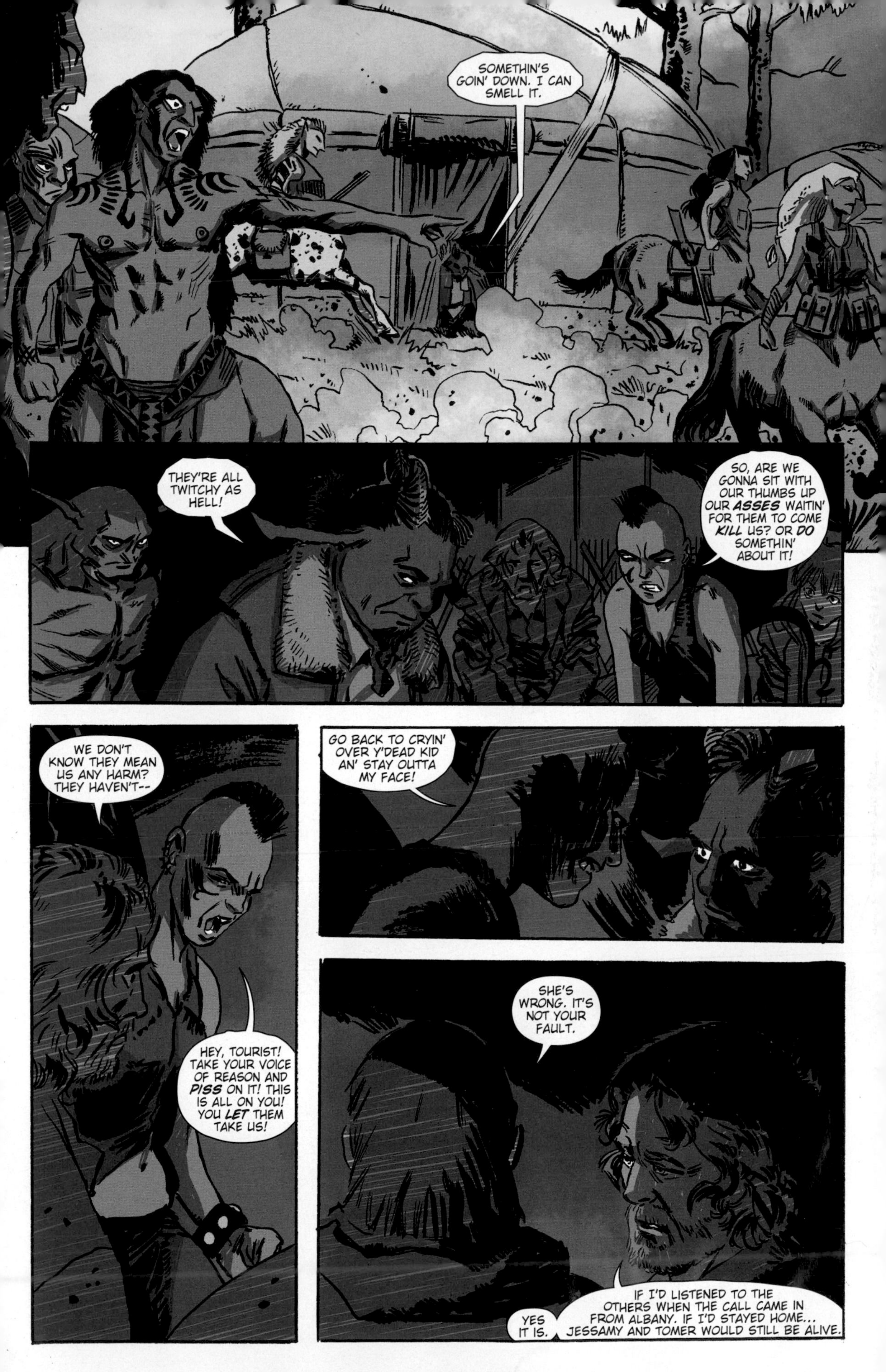
SOMETHIN'S GOIN' DOWN. I CAN SMELL IT.
THEY'RE ALL TWITCHY AS HELL!
SO, ARE WE GONNA SIT WITH OUR THUMBS UP OUR ASSES WAITIN' FOR THEM TO COME KILL US? OR DO SOMETHIN' ABOUT IT!
WE DON'T KNOW THEY MEAN US ANY HARM? THEY HAVEN'T--
HEY, TOURIST! TAKE YOUR VOICE OF REASON AND PISS ON IT! THIS IS ALL ON YOU! YOU LET THEM TAKE US!
GO BACK TO CRYIN' OVER Y'DEAD KID AN' STAY OUTTA MY FACE!
SHE'S WRONG. IT'S NOT YOUR FAULT.
YES IT IS.
IF I'D LISTENED TO THE OTHERS WHEN THE CALL CAME IN FROM ALBANY. IF I'D STAYED HOME... JESSAMY AND TOMER WOULD STILL BE ALIVE.

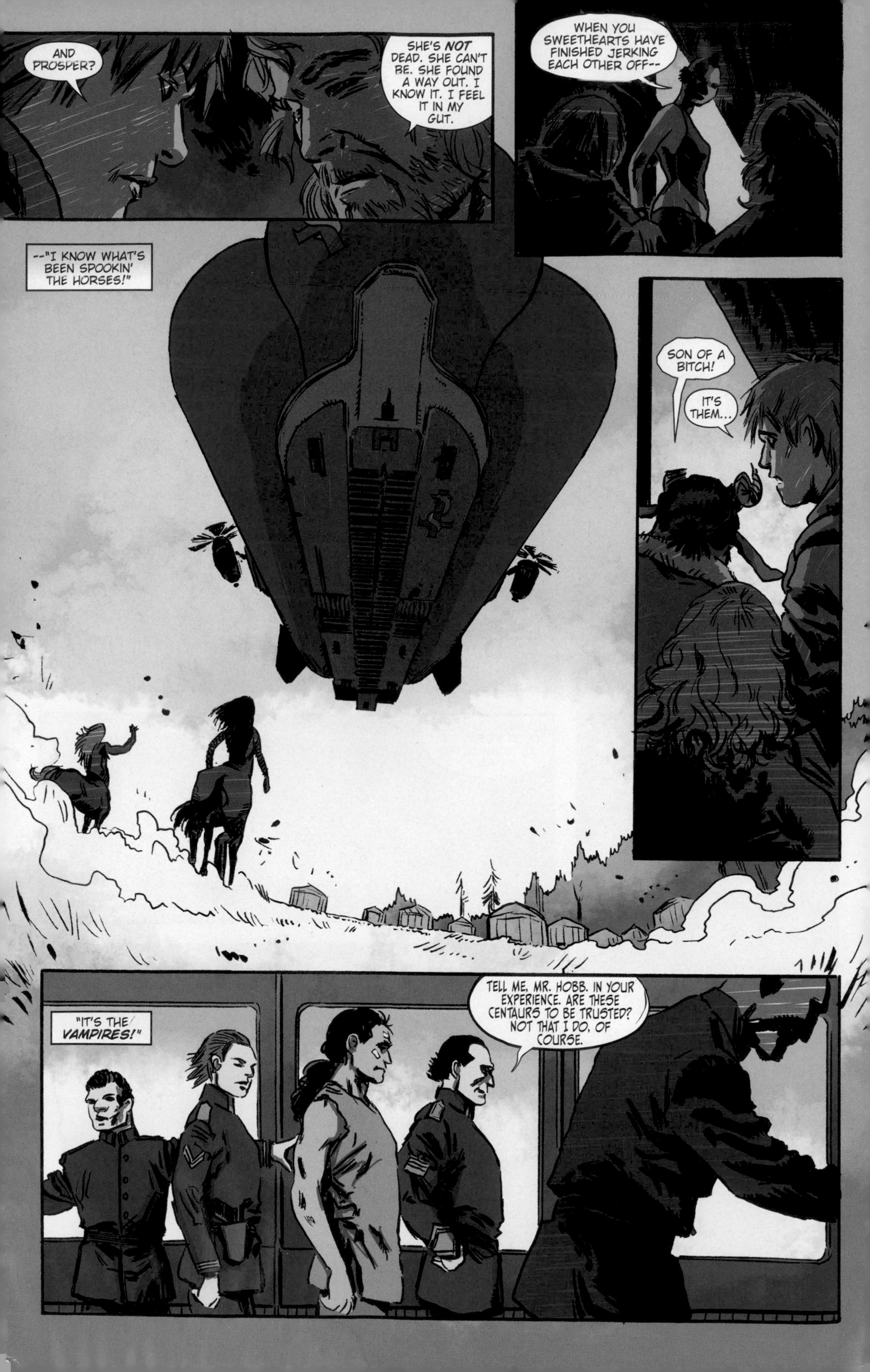
AND PROSPER?
SHE'S NOT DEAD. SHE CAN'T BE. SHE FOUND A WAY OUT. I KNOW IT. I FEEL IT IN MY GUT.
WHEN YOU SWEETHEARTS HAVE FINISHED JERKING EACH OTHER OFF--
--"I KNOW WHAT'S BEEN SPOOKIN' THE HORSES!"
SON OF A BITCH!
IT'S THEM...
"IT'S THE VAMPIRES!"
TELL ME, MR. HOBB. IN YOUR EXPERIENCE. ARE THESE CENTAURS TO BE TRUSTED? NOT THAT I DO, OF COURSE.

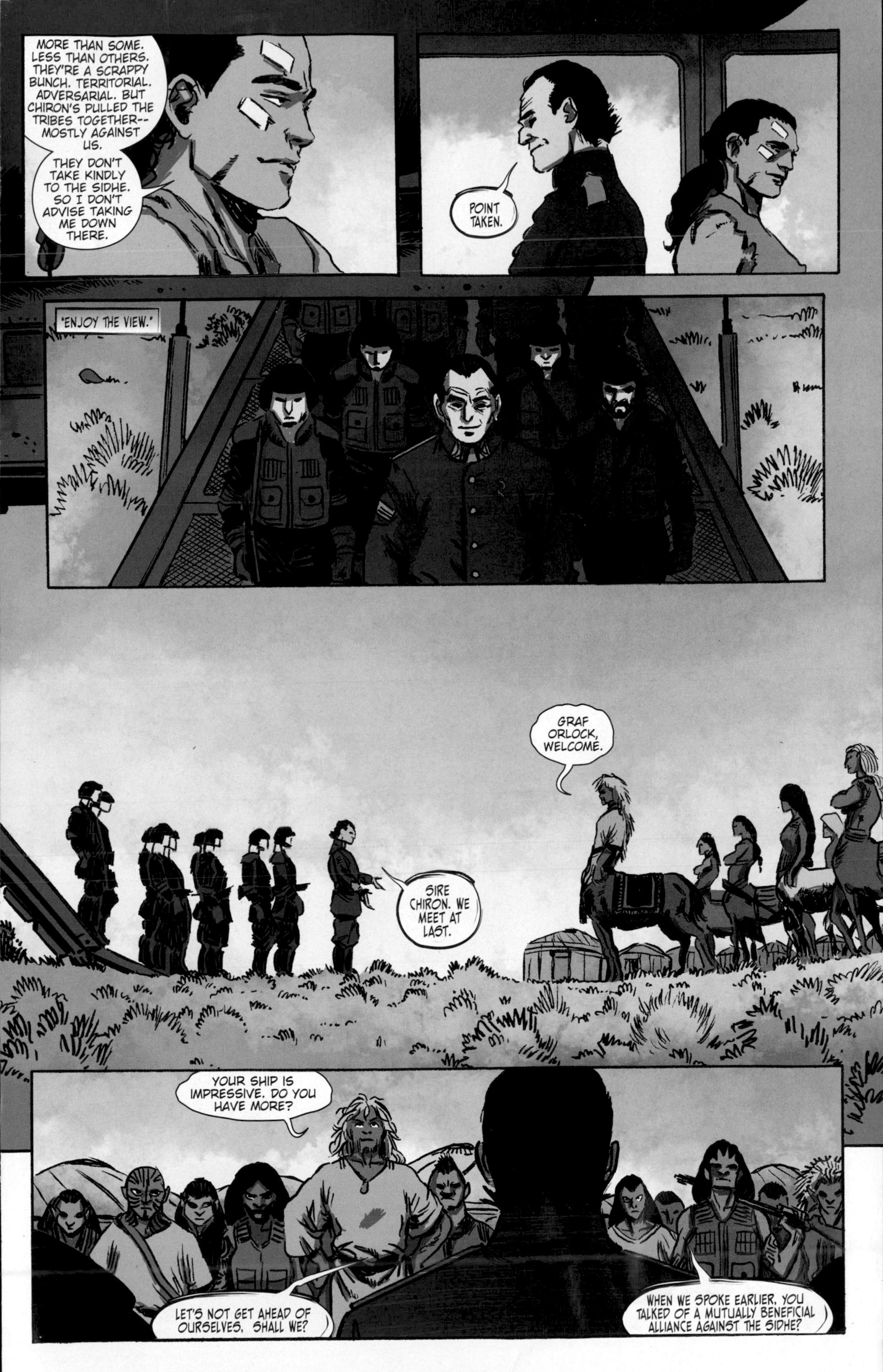
MORE THAN SOME. LESS THAN OTHERS. THEY'RE A SCRAPPY BUNCH. TERRITORIAL. ADVERSARIAL. BUT CHIRON'S PULLED THE TRIBES TOGETHER-- MOSTLY AGAINST US.
THEY DON'T TAKE KINDLY TO THE SIDHE. SO I DON'T ADVISE TAKING ME DOWN THERE.
POINT TAKEN.
"ENJOY THE VIEW."
GRAF ORLOCK, WELCOME.
SIRE CHIRON. WE MEET AT LAST.
YOUR SHIP IS IMPRESSIVE. DO YOU HAVE MORE?
LET'S NOT GET AHEAD OF OURSELVES, SHALL WE?
WHEN WE SPOKE EARLIER, YOU TALKED OF A MUTUALLY BENEFICIAL ALLIANCE AGAINST THE SIDHE?

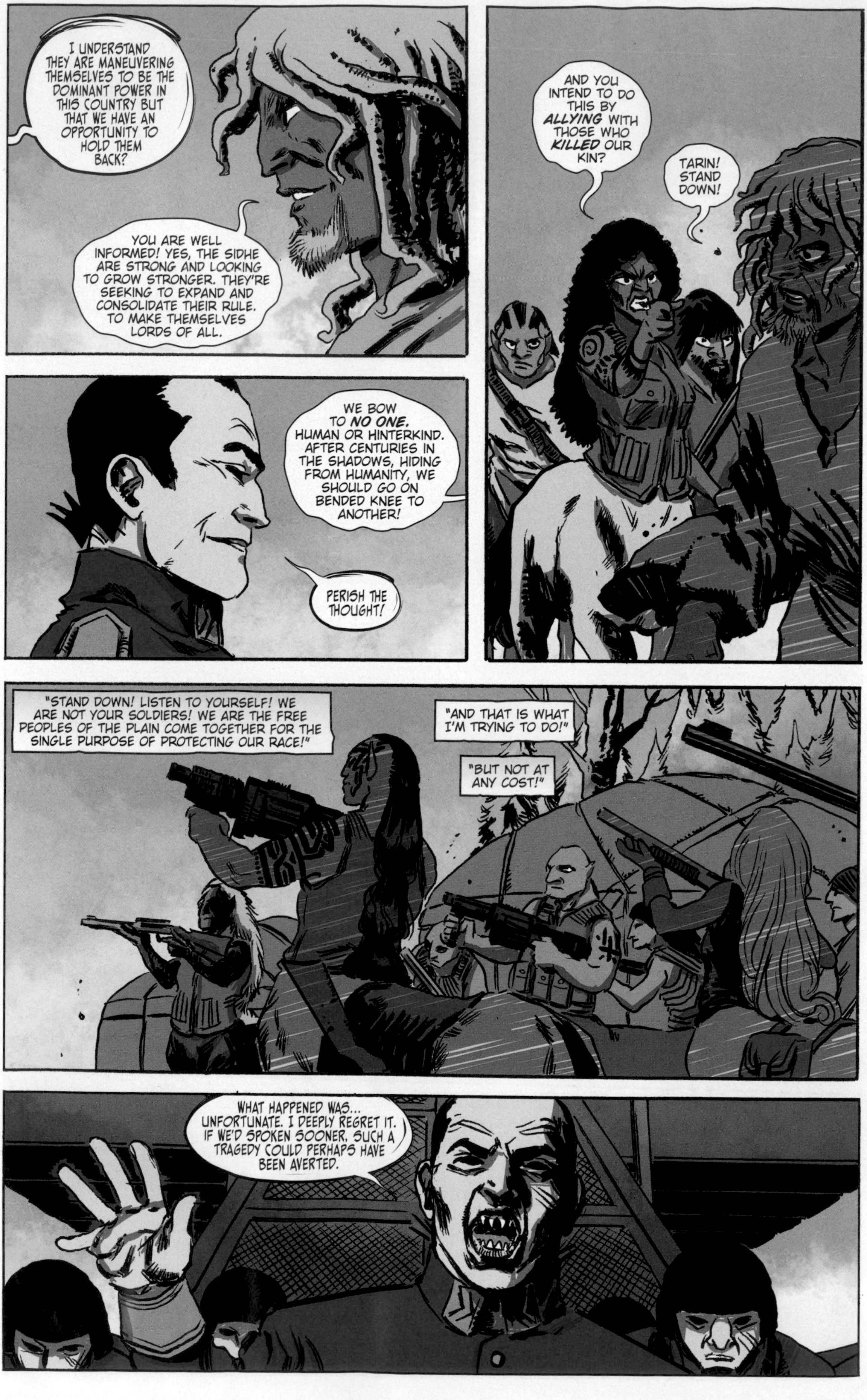
I UNDERSTAND THEY ARE MANEUVERING THEMSELVES TO BE THE DOMINANT POWER IN THIS COUNTRY BUT THAT WE HAVE AN OPPORTUNITY TO HOLD THEM BACK?
YOU ARE WELL INFORMED! YES, THE SIDHE ARE STRONG AND LOOKING TO GROW STRONGER. THEY'RE SEEKING TO EXPAND AND CONSOLIDATE THEIR RULE. TO MAKE THEMSELVES LORDS OF ALL.
WE BOW TO NO ONE. HUMAN OR HINTERKIND. AFTER CENTURIES IN THE SHADOWS, HIDING FROM HUMANITY, WE SHOULD GO ON BENDED KNEE TO ANOTHER!
PERISH THE THOUGHT!
AND YOU INTEND TO DO THIS BY ALLYING WITH THOSE WHO KILLED OUR KIN?
TARIN! STAND DOWN!
"STAND DOWN! LISTEN TO YOURSELF! WE ARE NOT YOUR SOLDIERS! WE ARE THE FREE PEOPLES OF THE PLAIN COME TOGETHER FOR THE SINGLE PURPOSE OF PROTECTING OUR RACE!"
"AND THAT IS WHAT I'M TRYING TO DO!"
"BUT NOT AT ANY COST!"
WHAT HAPPENED WAS... UNFORTUNATE. I DEEPLY REGRET IT. IF WE'D SPOKEN SOONER, SUCH A TRAGEDY COULD PERHAPS HAVE BEEN AVERTED.

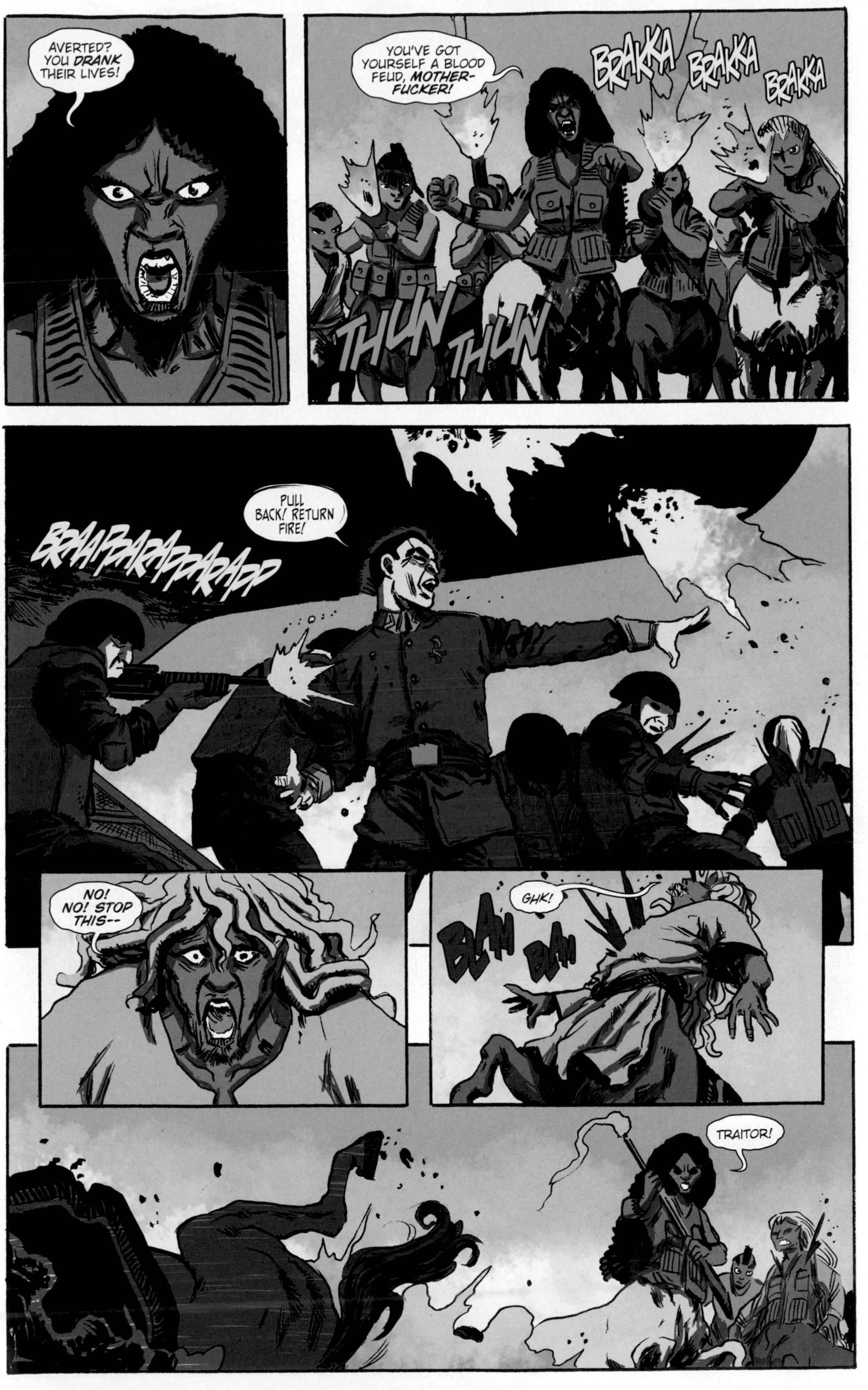
AVERTED? YOU DRANK THEIR LIVES!
YOU'VE GOT YOURSELF A BLOOD FEUD, MOTHER-FUCKER!
BRAKKA BRAKKA BRAKKA
THUN THUN
PULL BACK! RETURN FIRE!
BRAAPBARAPPARAPP
NO! NO! STOP THIS--
GHK!
BLAM BLAM
TRAITOR!

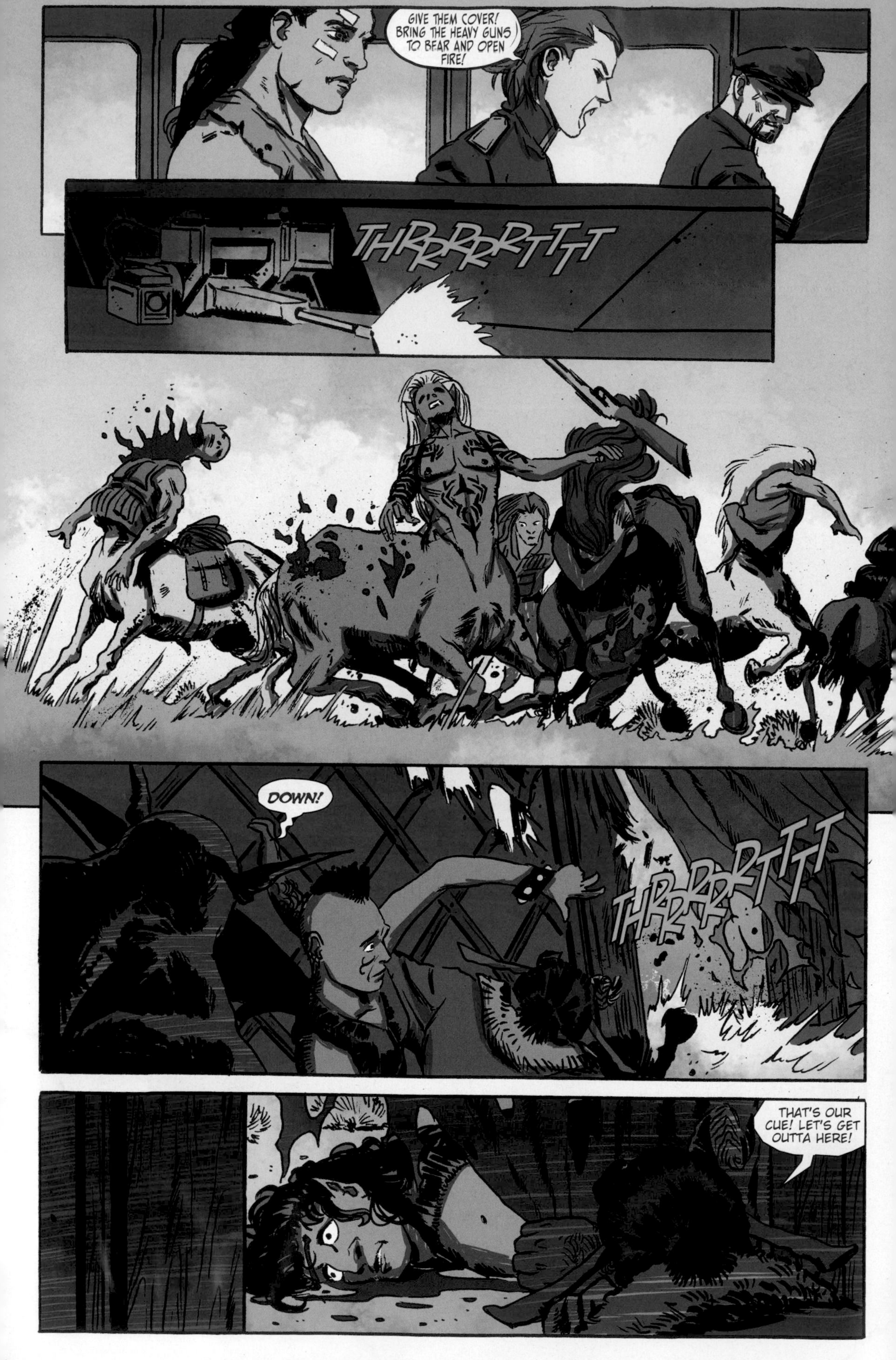
GIVE THEM COVER! BRING THE HEAVY GUNS TO BEAR AND OPEN FIRE!
THRRRRRRTTTT
DOWN!
THRRRRRRTTTT
THAT'S OUR CUE! LET'S GET OUTTA HERE!

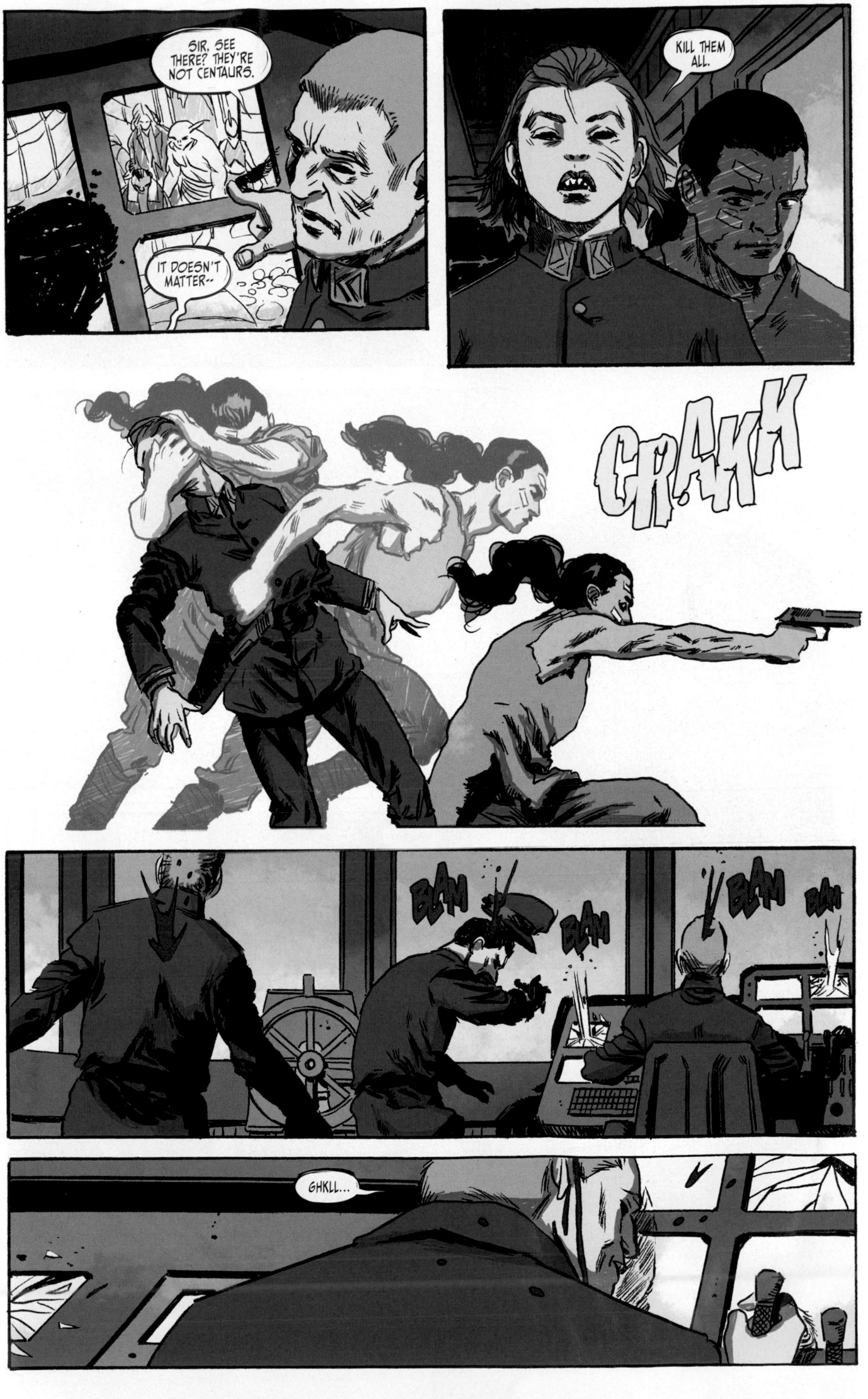
SIR, SEE THERE? THEY'RE NOT CENTAURS.
IT DOESN'T MATTER--
KILL THEM ALL.
CRAKK
BLAM
BLAM
BLAM
BLAM
GHKLL...

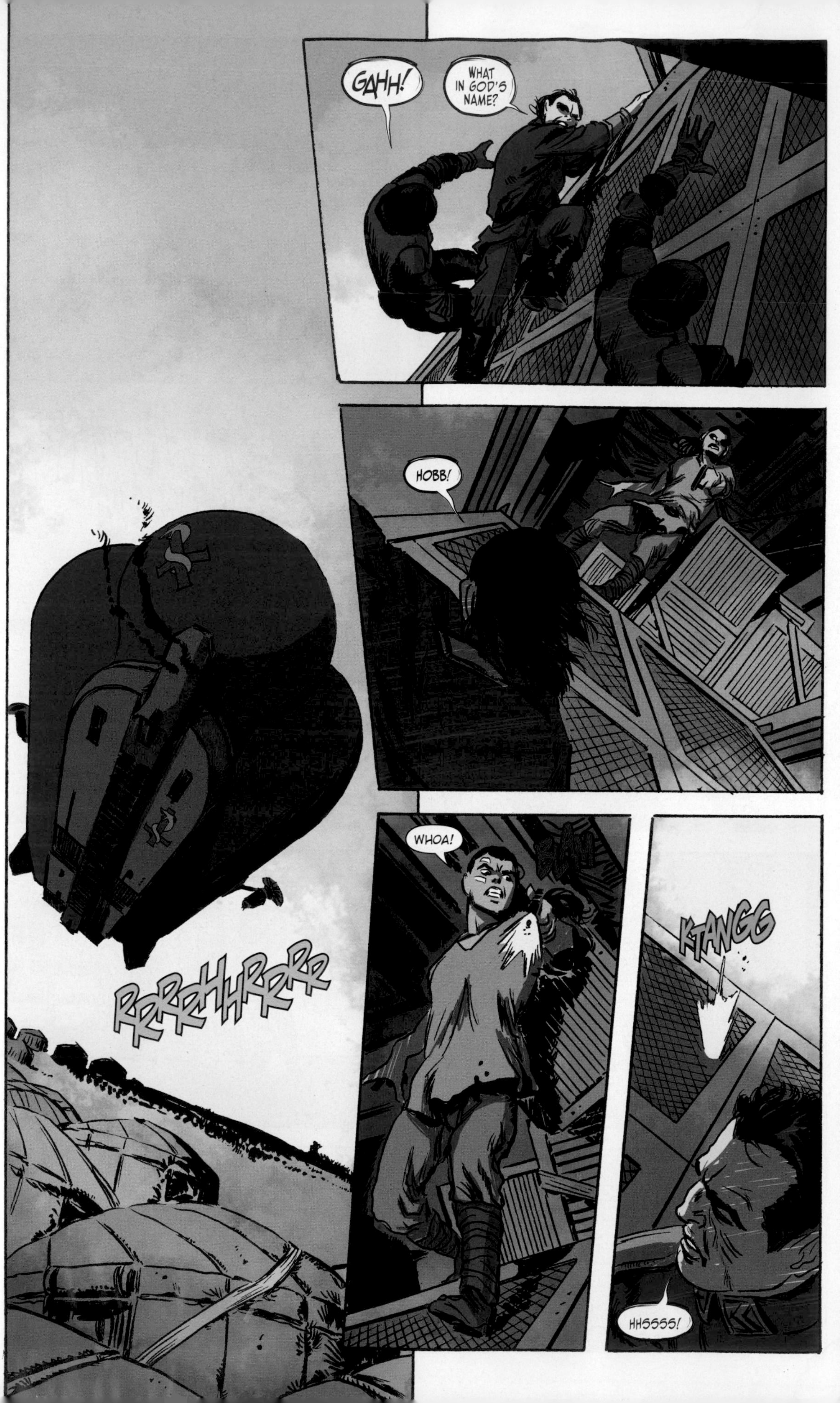
GAHH!
WHAT IN GOD'S NAME?
HOBB!
RRRRHRRRR
WHOA!
KTANGG
HHSSSS!

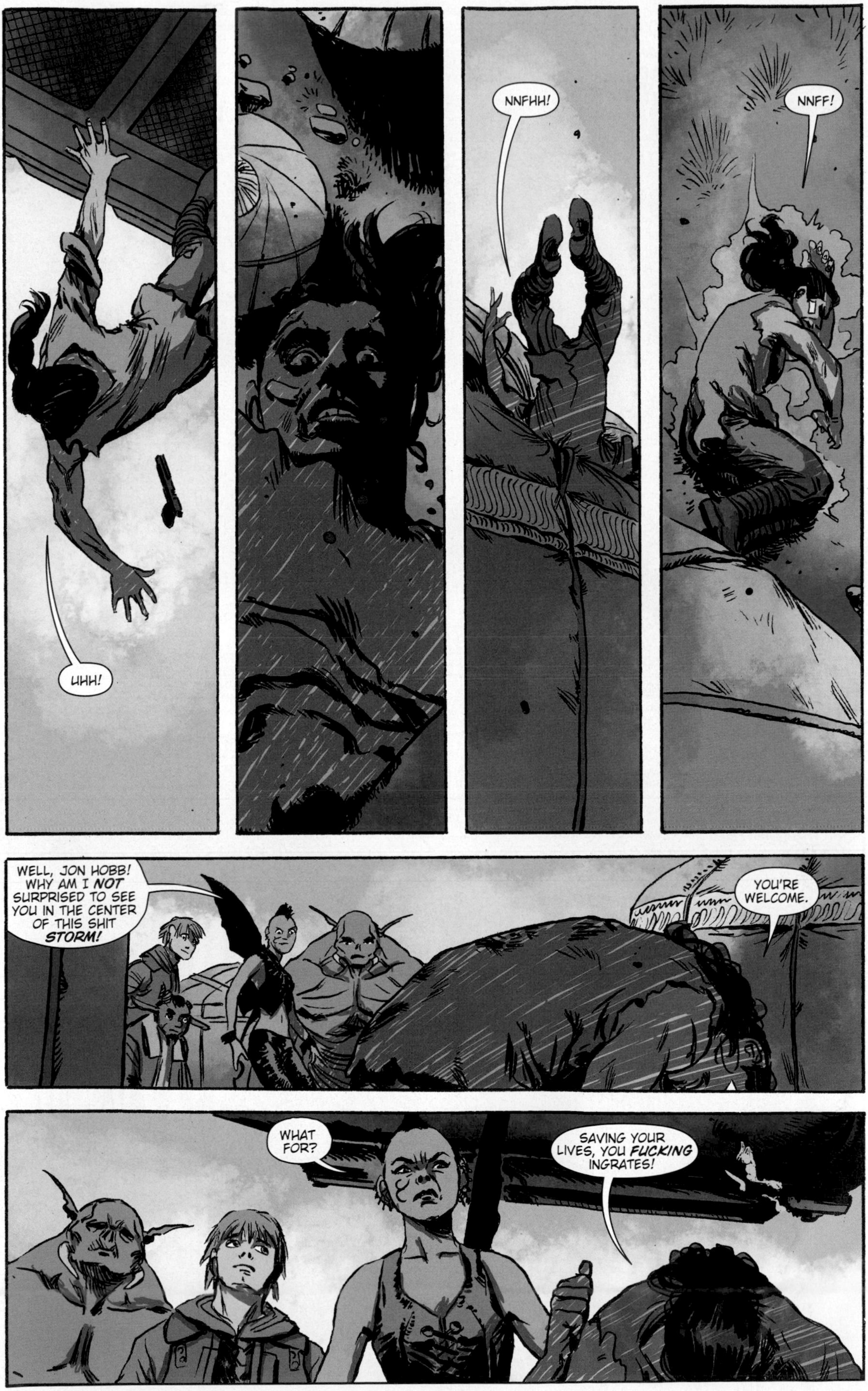
UHH!
NNFHH!
NNFF!
WELL, JON HOBB! WHY AM I NOT SURPRISED TO SEE YOU IN THE CENTER OF THIS SHIT STORM!
YOU'RE WELCOME.
WHAT FOR?
SAVING YOUR LIVES, YOU FUCKING INGRATES!

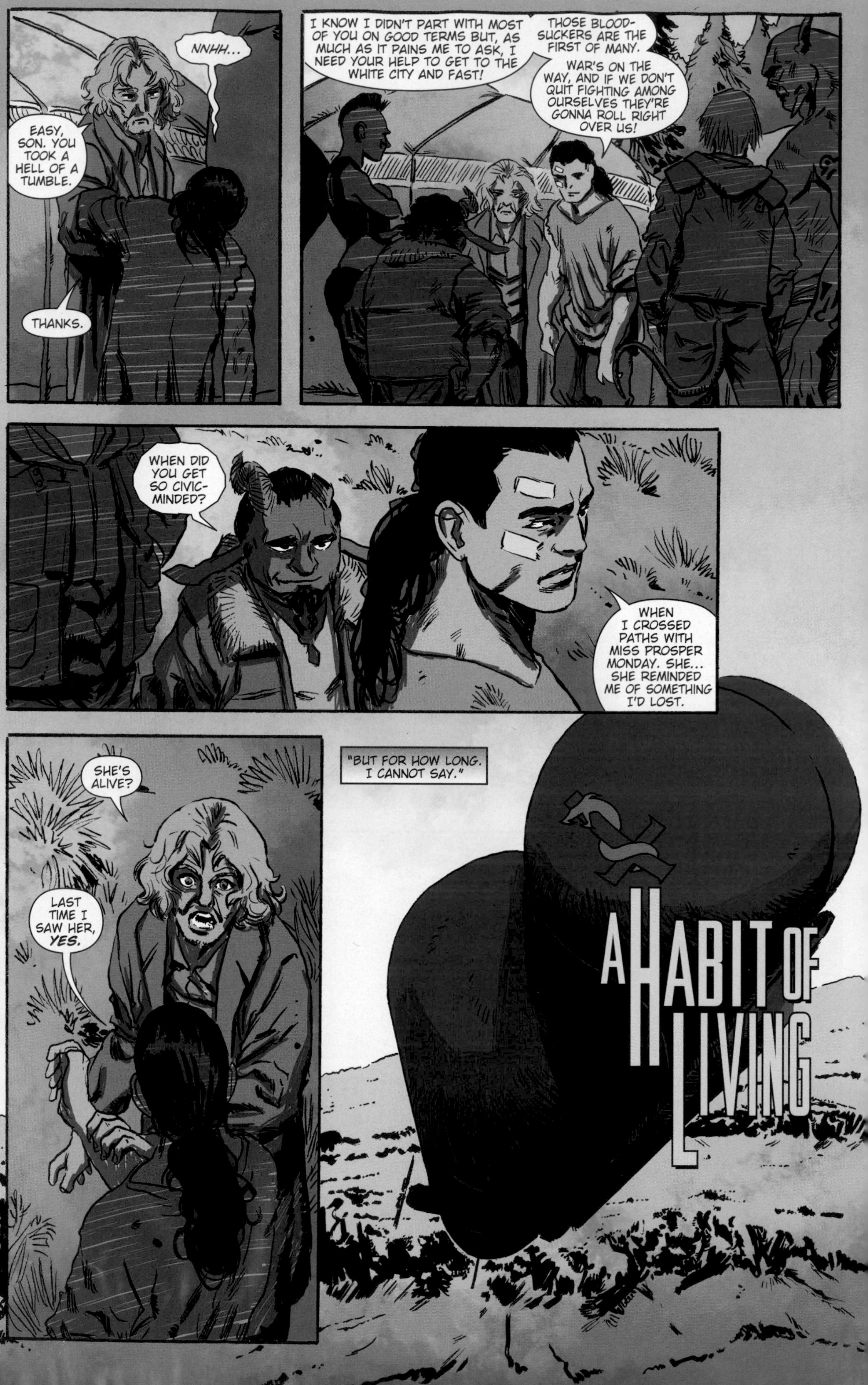
NNHH...
EASY, SON. YOU TOOK A HELL OF A TUMBLE.
THANKS.
I KNOW I DIDN'T PART WITH MOST OF YOU ON GOOD TERMS BUT, AS MUCH AS IT PAINS ME TO ASK, I NEED YOUR HELP TO GET TO THE WHITE CITY AND FAST!
THOSE BLOOD-SUCKERS ARE THE FIRST OF MANY.
WAR'S ON THE WAY, AND IF WE DON'T QUIT FIGHTING AMONG OURSELVES THEY'RE GONNA ROLL RIGHT OVER US!
WHEN DID YOU GET SO CIVIC-MINDED?
WHEN I CROSSED PATHS WITH MISS PROSPER MONDAY. SHE... SHE REMINDED ME OF SOMETHING I'D LOST.
SHE'S ALIVE?
LAST TIME I SAW HER, *YES.*
"BUT FOR HOW LONG. I CANNOT SAY."
A HABIT OF LIVING

WRITTEN IN GRAPHITE

THUMBNAIL LAYOUTS BY
FRANCESCO TRIFOGLI

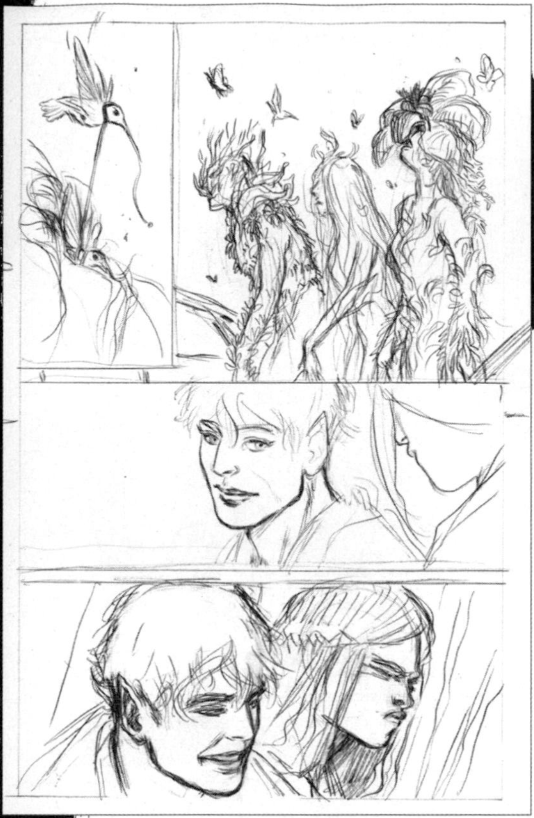

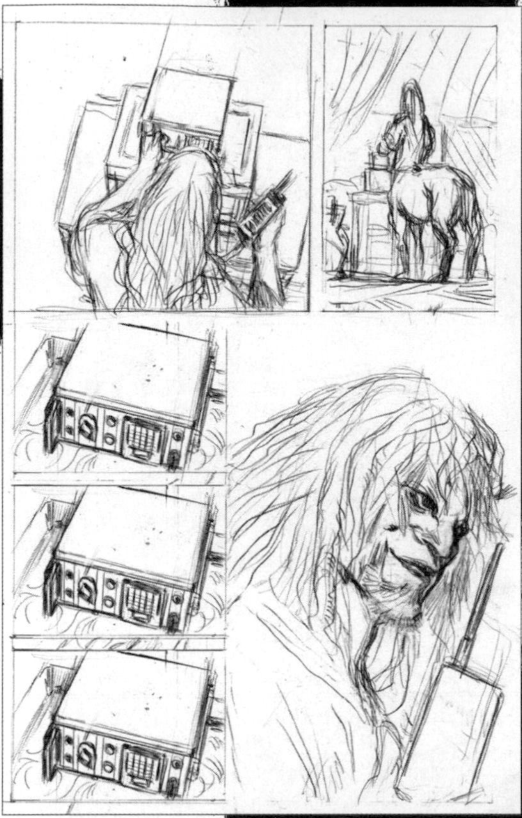

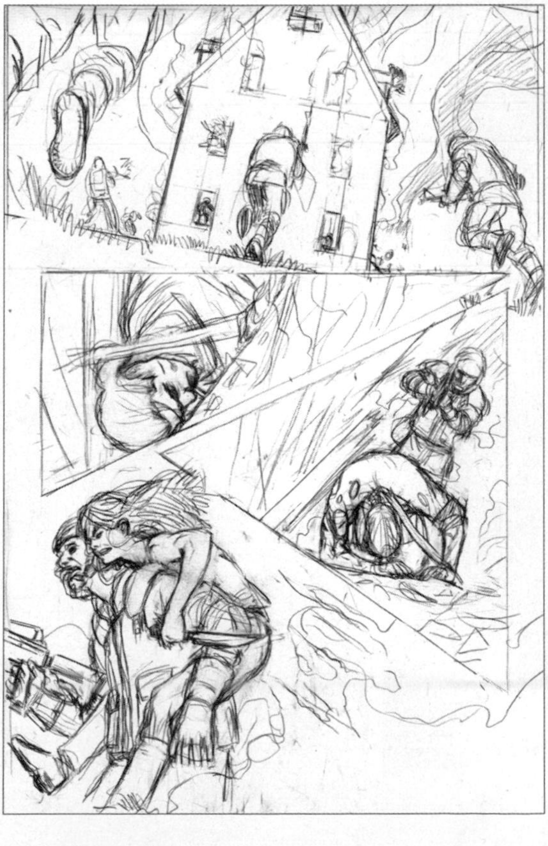

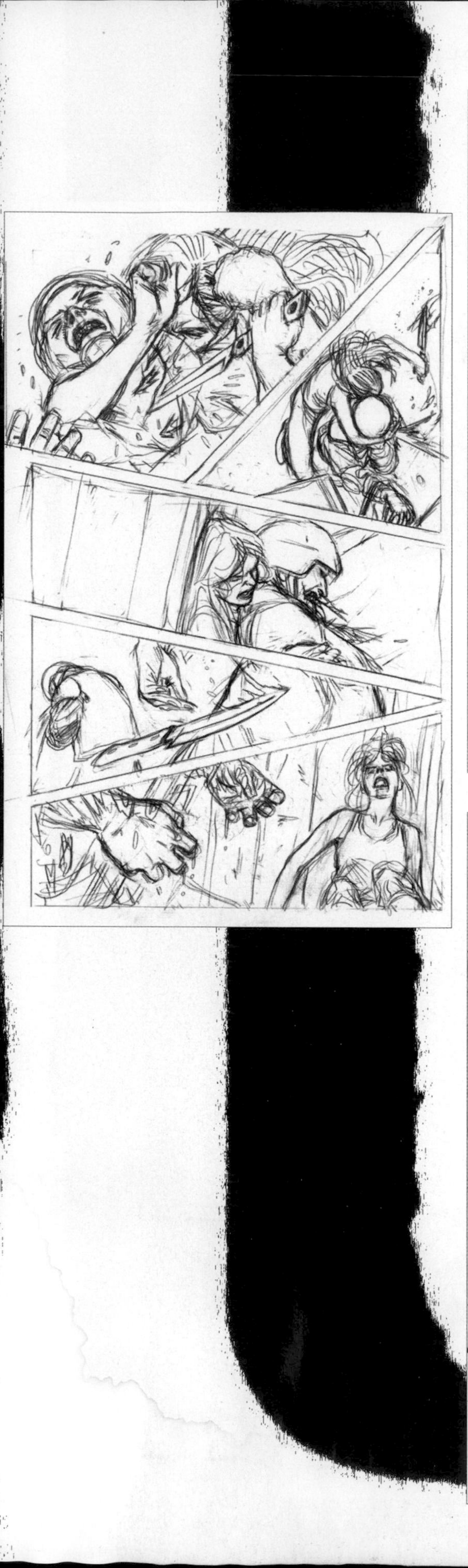

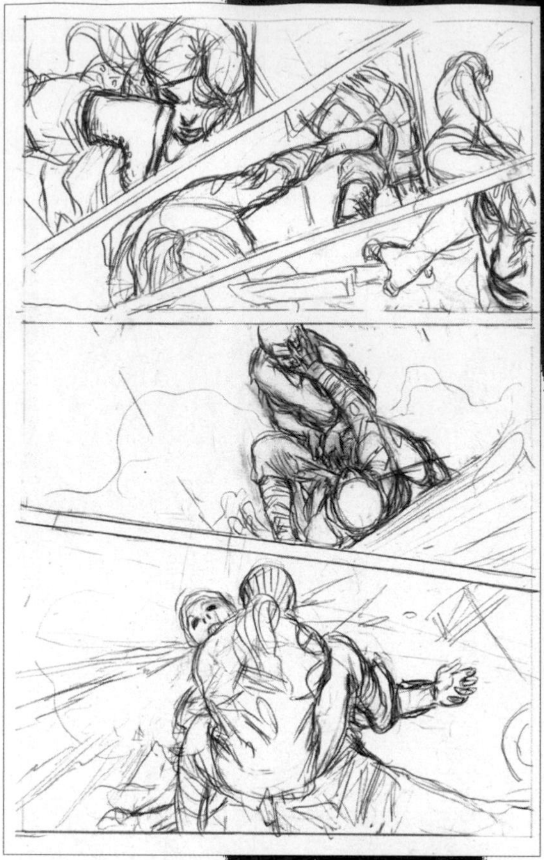

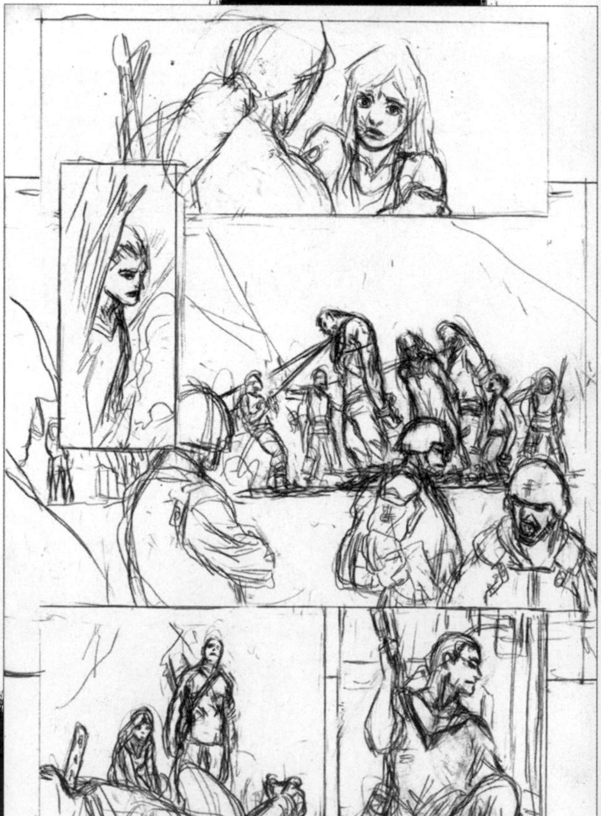

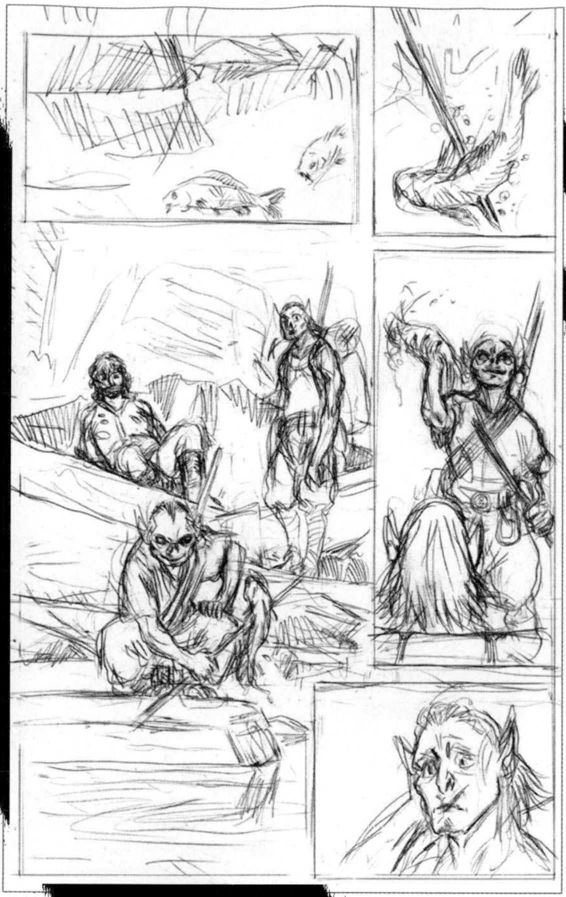

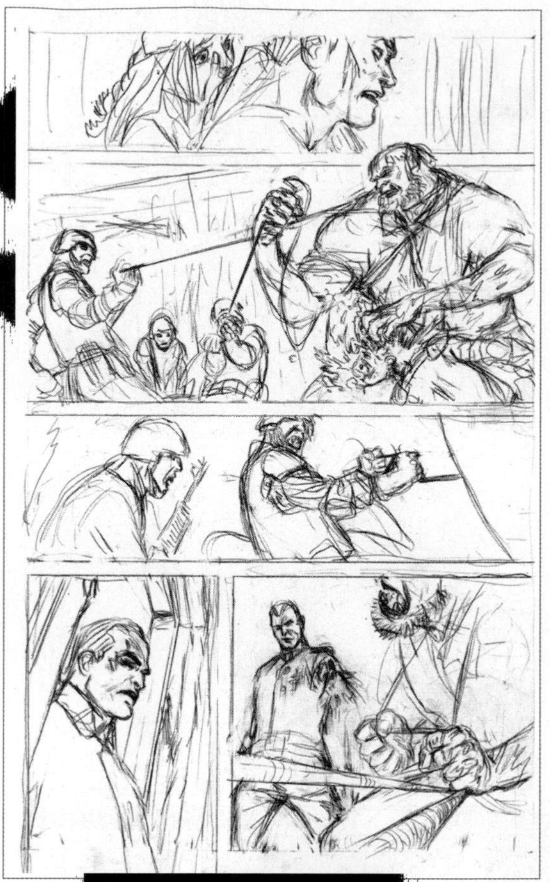

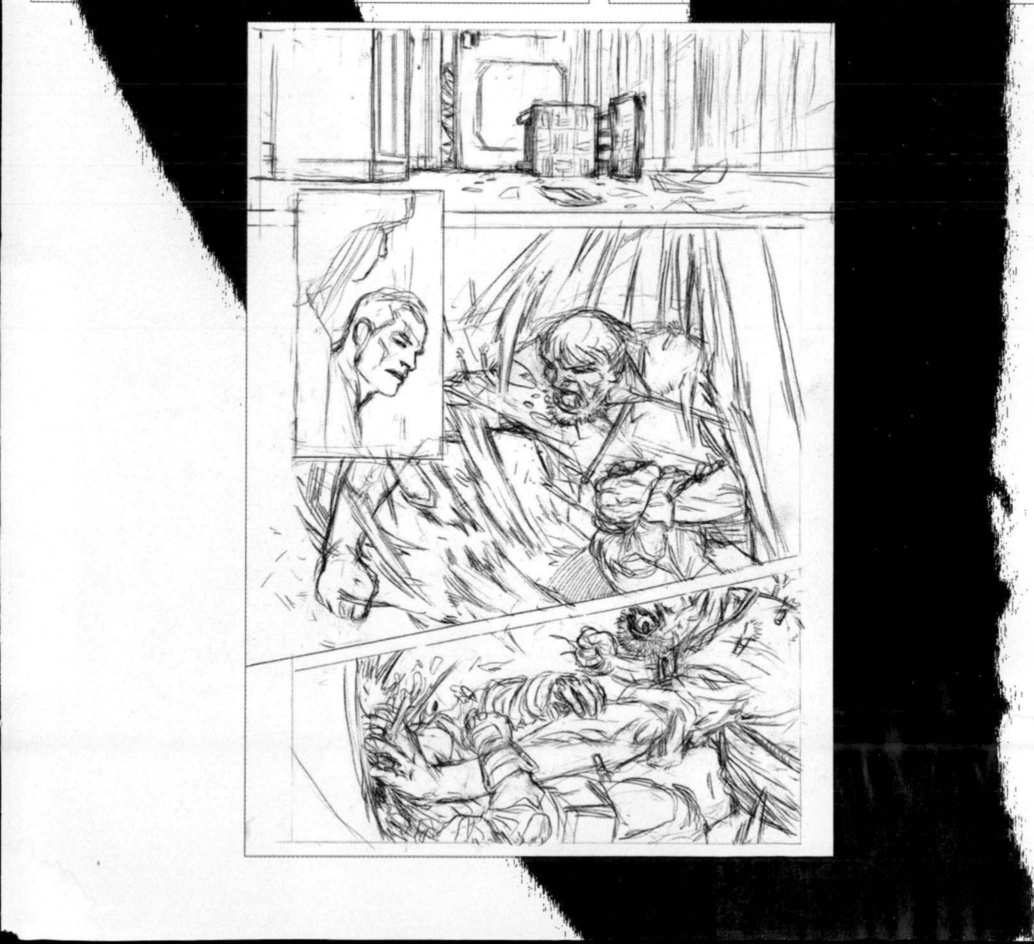

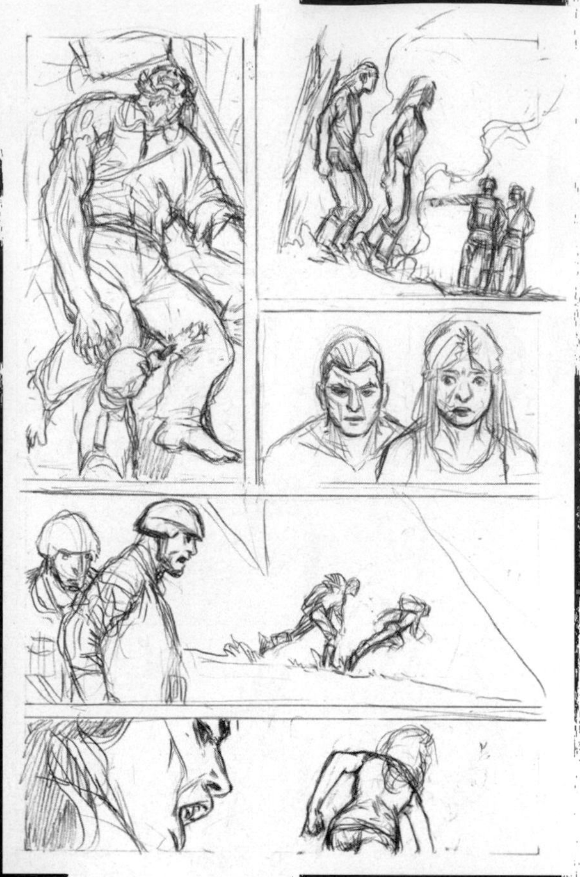

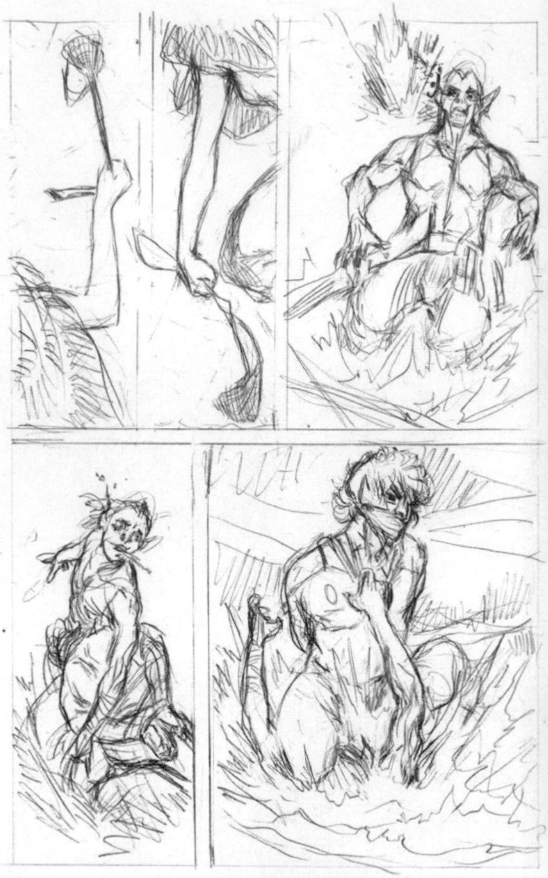

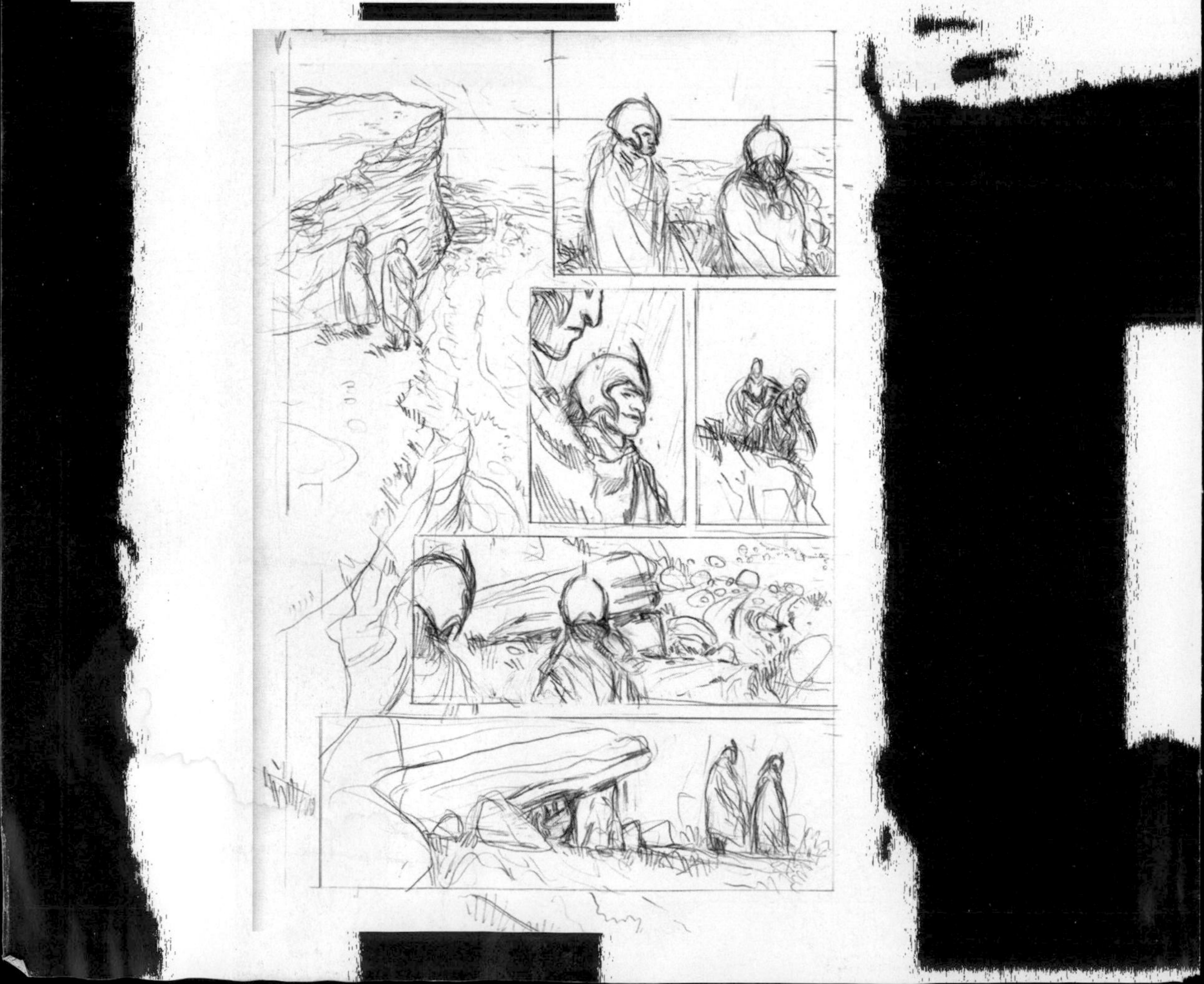

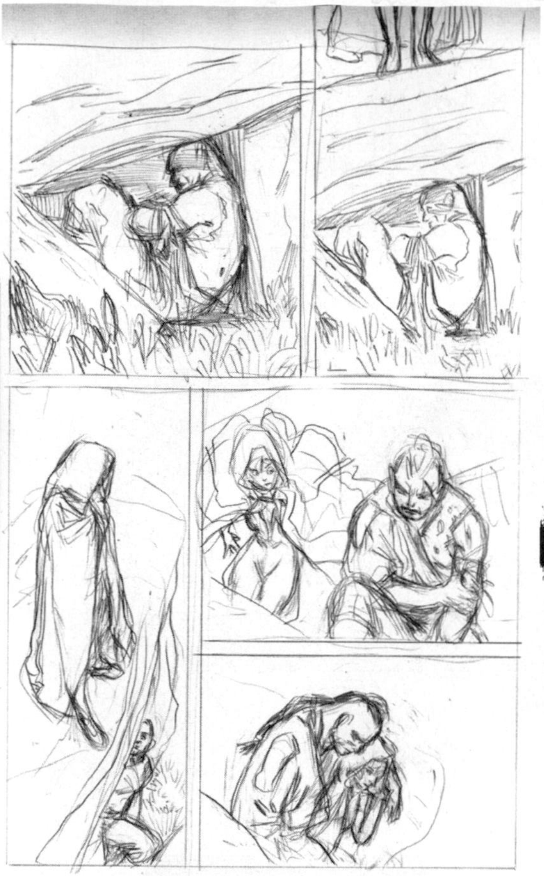

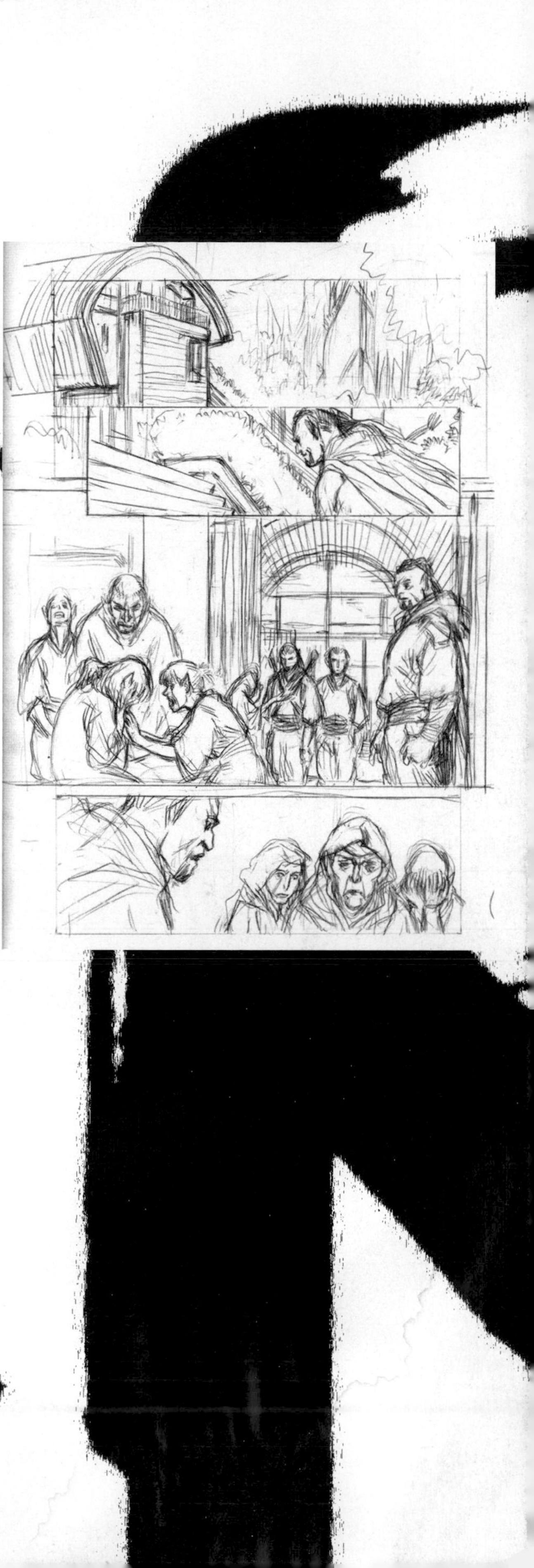

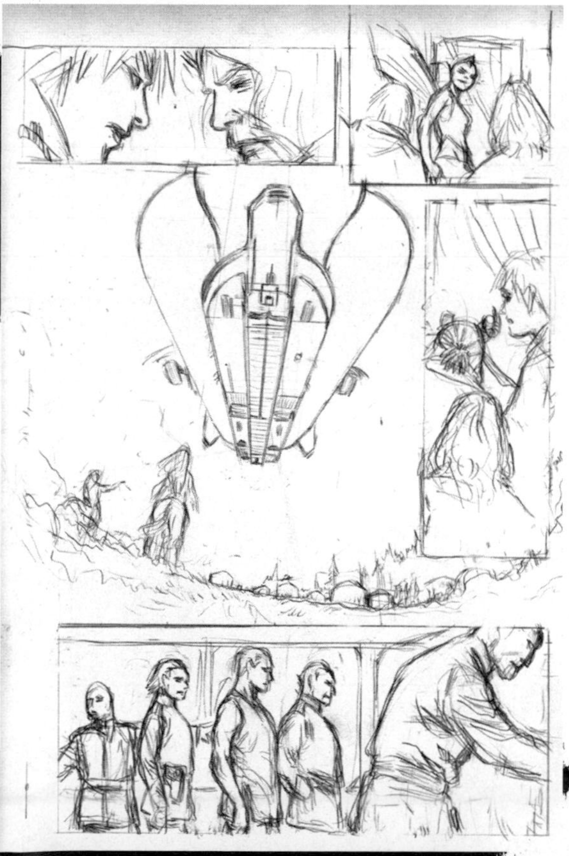

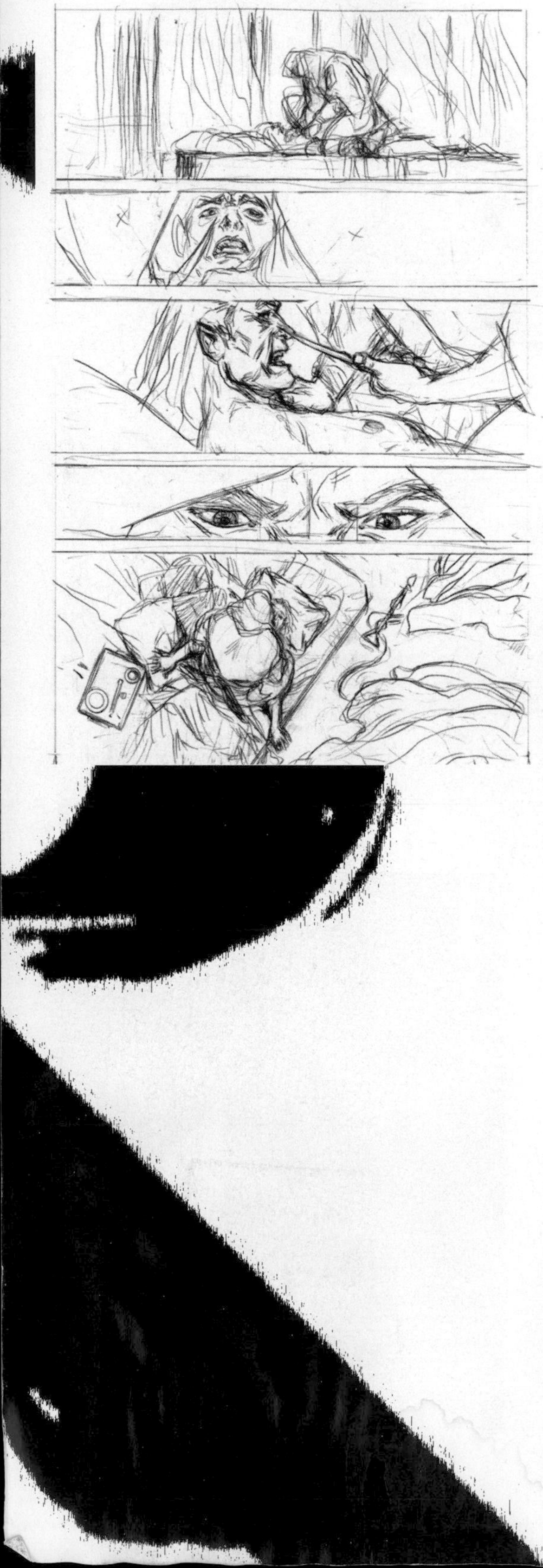

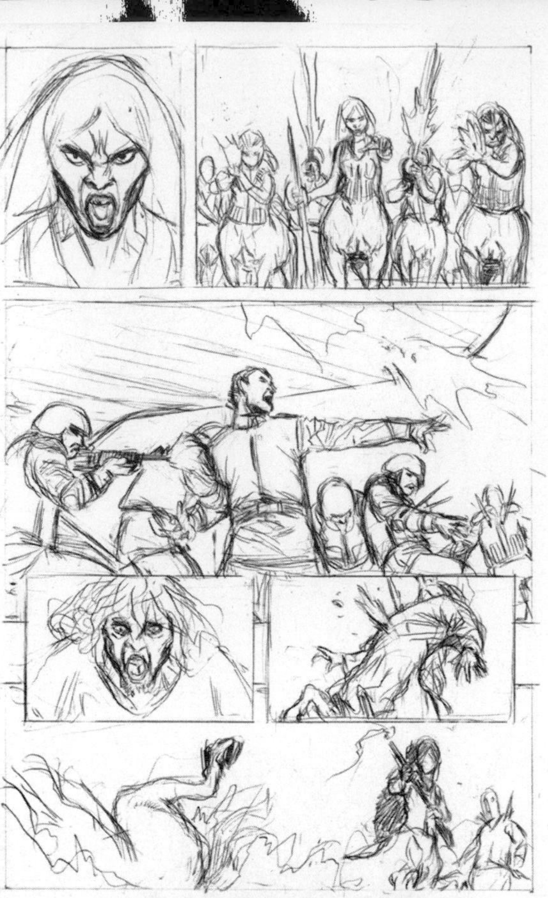

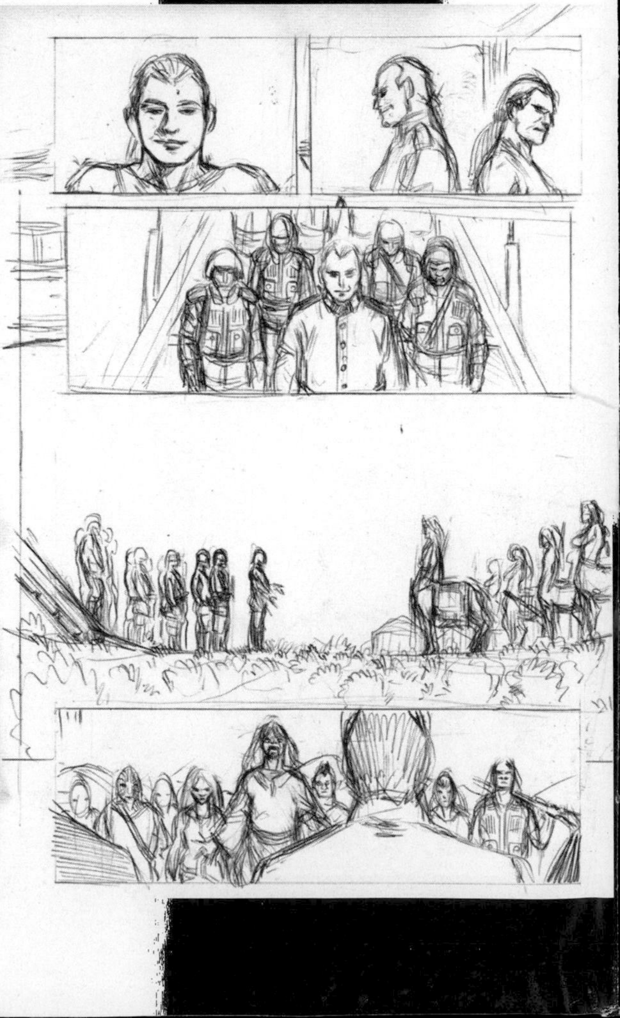

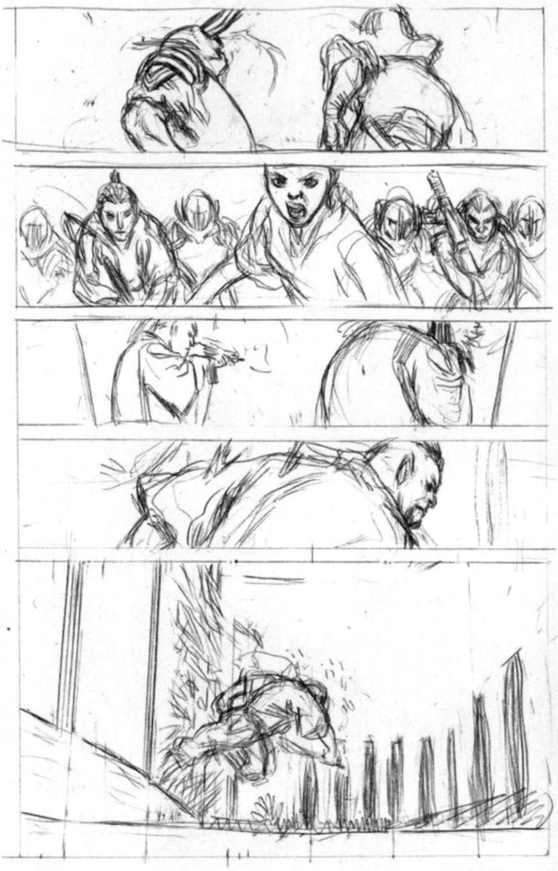

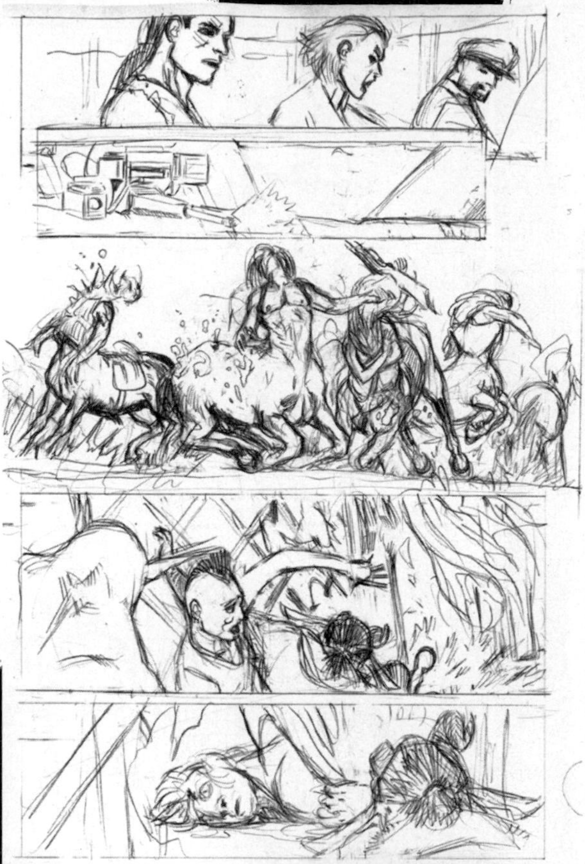

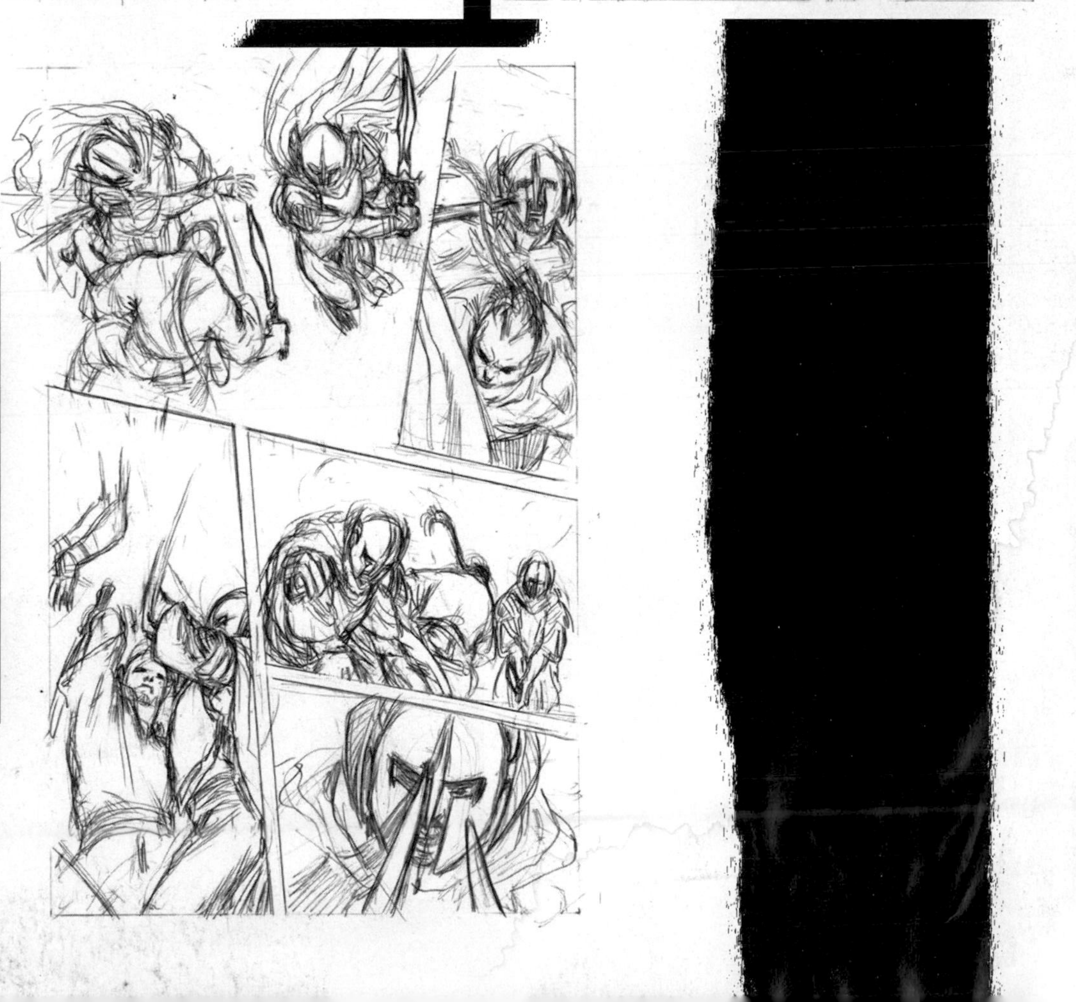

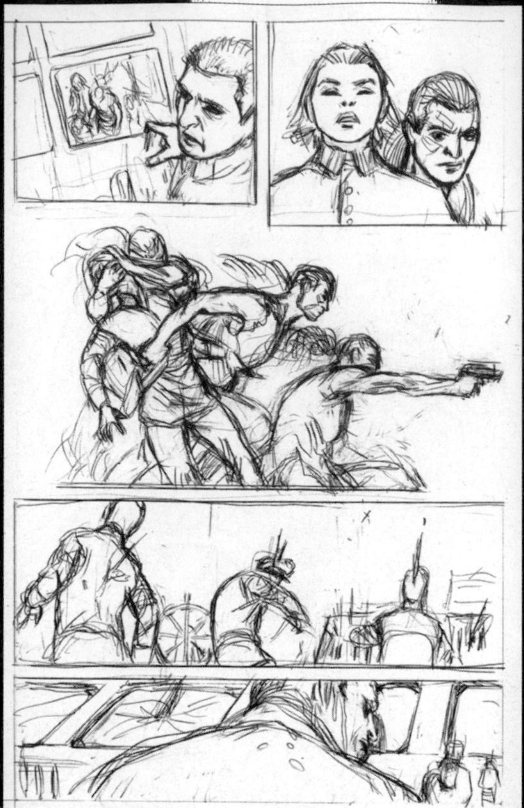

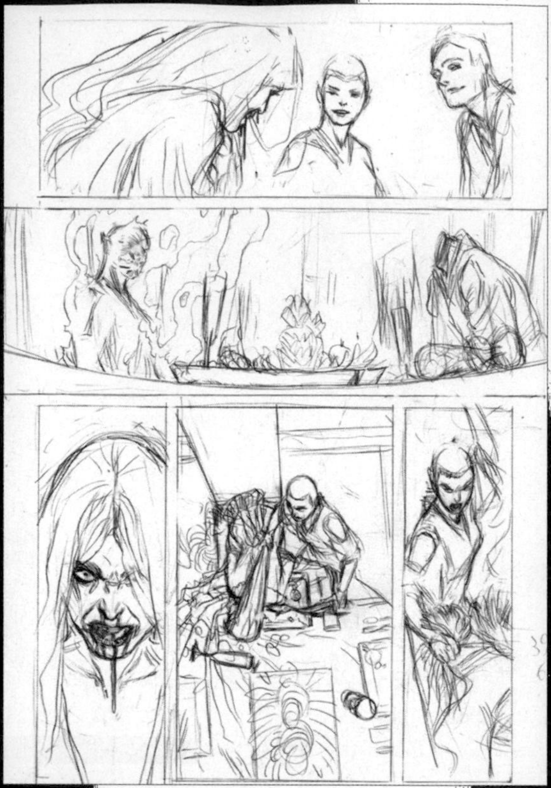

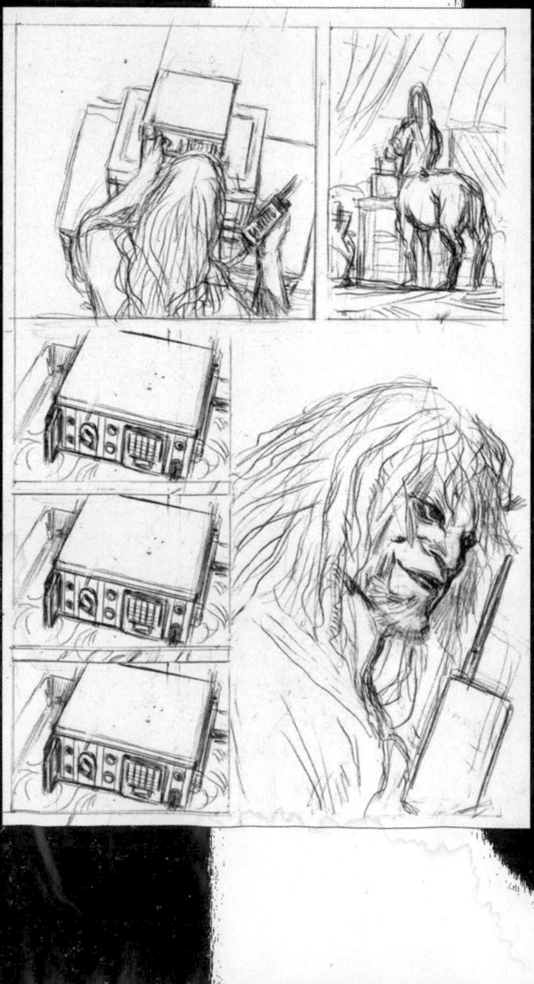

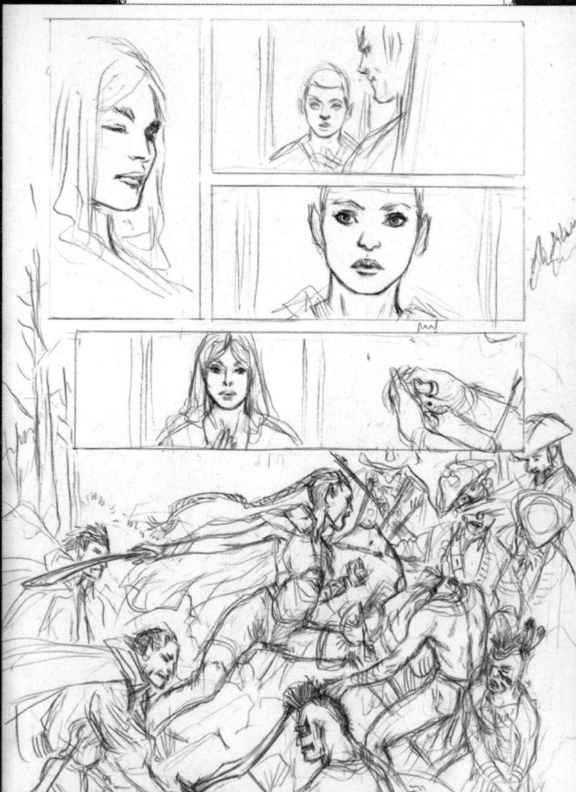

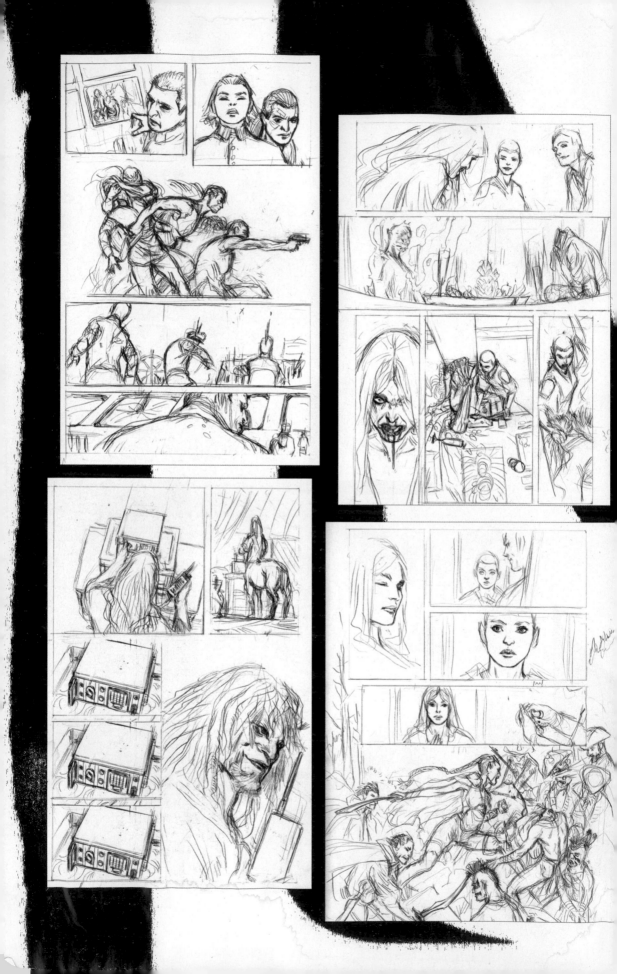